The Healthy 5-Ingredient
Air Fryer Cookbook

1000 | Affordable, Quick & Healthy Recipes for Beginners and Advanced Users to Eat Healthily

Katherine R. Majeski

CONTENT

Introduction 1
Tips For Air Fryer Success 2
Breakfast & Brunch Recipes 5

1. Sausage Quiche 5
2. Easy & Tasty Salsa Chicken 5
3. Black's Bangin' Casserole 5
4. Eggplant Spread 5
5. Parsley Omelet 5
6. Egg Muffins 5
7. Breakfast Chimichangas 5
8. Scotch Eggs 6
9. Lemon Butter Artichokes 6
10. Strawberry Rhubarb Parfait 6
11. Herb Carrots 6
12. Strawberry Pastry 6
13. Buttered Eggs In Hole 6
14. Chives Spinach Frittata 6
15. Soppressata Pizza 6
16. Eggs & Tomatoes Scramble 6
17. Strawberry Toast 7
18. Breakfast Tea 7
19. Peppers Cups 7
20. Parmesan Breakfast Casserole 7
21. Air Fryer Bacon 7
22. Garlic-cheese Biscuits 7
23. Tuna And Arugula Salad 7
24. Simple Egg Soufflé 7
25. Cheesy Sausage Sticks 7
26. Hash Brown 8
27. Cinnamon Flavored Grilled Pineapples 8
28. Air Fryer Sausage 8
29. Mozzarella Rolls 8
30. Ham And Egg Toast Cups 8
31. Bacon & Hot Dogs Omelet 8
32. Chocolate-hazelnut Bear Claws 8
33. Maple-bacon Doughnuts 8
34. Smoked Fried Tofu 9
35. Grilled Tofu Sandwich 9
36. Paprika Cauliflower Bake 9
37. Paprika Zucchini Spread 9
38. Mushroom Leek Frittata 9
39. Lemon Dill Scallops 9
40. Chi Spacca's Bistecca 9
41. Crust-less Quiche 9
42. Bread Cups Omelette 9
43. Breakfast Sausage Casserole 10
44. Rice Paper Bacon 10
45. Almond Pesto Salmon 10
46. Egg Porridge 10
47. Spanish Omelet 10
48. Medium Rare Simple Salt And Pepper Steak 10
49. Mushroom Frittata 10
50. Sausage Solo 10
51. Bacon And Hot Dogs Omelet 11
52. Taj Tofu 11
53. Breakfast Sandwich 11
54. Coconut Berries Bowls 11
55. Easy Egg Bites 11
56. Yummy Ham Rolls 11
57. Green Beans Salad 11
58. All-in-one Breakfast Toast 11
59. Eggs Salad 12
60. Spinach Spread 12
61. Mediterranean Egg Sandwich 12
62. Baked Eggs 12
63. Sweet And Spicy Breakfast Sausage 12
64. Mozzarella Cups 12
65. Puffed Egg Tarts 12
66. Hash Browns 12
67. Eggs, Mushrooms And Tomatoes Scramble 13
68. Avocado Eggs 13
69. Pineapple Cornbread 13
70. Egg Baked Omelet 13
71. Olives Eggs 13
72. Chicken Bites 13
73. Pancakes 13
74. Egg & Mushroom Scramble 13
75. Cheesy Sandwich 14
76. Bacon Cups 14
77. Egg Muffin Sandwich 14
78. Spicy Egg And Bacon Wraps 14
79. Zucchini Squash Mix 14
80. Mini Tomato Quiche 14

#	Recipe	Page
81.	Avocado And Cabbage Salad	14
82.	Oregano And Coconut Scramble	14
83.	Artichokes And Parsley Frittata	14
84.	Almond Oatmeal	15
85.	Scrambled Mug Eggs	15
86.	Buttery Scallops	15
87.	Strawberry Oatmeal	15
88.	Hashbrown Potatoes Lyonnaise	15
89.	Green Beans Bowls	15
90.	Broccoli Casserole	15
91.	Roasted Asparagus With Serrano & Parmesan	15
92.	Italian Chicken	15
93.	Flaxseed Porridge	16
94.	Mushrooms Spread	16
95.	Peppers Bowls	16
96.	Milky Scrambled Eggs	16
97.	Banana Chia Seed Pudding	16
98.	Spinach Egg Breakfast	16
99.	Crispy Bacon	16
100.	Sweet Potato-cinnamon Toast	16
101.	Exquisite German Pancake	16
102.	Vanilla Toast	17
103.	Bacon & Eggs	17
104.	Creamy Parsley Soufflé	17
105.	Sausage Bacon Fandango	17
106.	French Toast Sticks	17
107.	Eggs Ramekins	17
108.	Onion And Cheese Omelet	17
109.	Green Scramble	17
110.	Okra Hash	17
111.	Hole In One	17
112.	Craving Cinnamon Toast	18
113.	Roasted Golden Mini Potatoes	18
114.	Hard-boiled Eggs	18
115.	Spinach Eggs And Cheese	18
116.	Bacon & Egg Muffins	18
117.	Not-so-english Muffins	18
118.	Peppered Maple Bacon Knots	18
119.	Cheesy Omelet	18
120.	Green Beans And Eggs	19
121.	Seasoned Herbed Sourdough Croutons	19
122.	Banana-nut Muffins	19
123.	Sausage Egg Muffins	19
124.	Almond Crust Chicken	19
125.	Breakfast Muffins	19

Snacks & Appetizers Recipes 20

#	Recipe	Page
126.	Sweet Potato Tots	20
127.	Cheesy Polenta Sticks	20
128.	Amazing Blooming Onion	20
129.	Roasted Peppers	20
130.	Okra Chips	20
131.	Fried Green Tomatoes	20
132.	Chili Pepper Kale Chips	20
133.	Lemon Green Beans	20
134.	Mini Pepper Poppers	21
135.	Country Style Chard	21
136.	Eggplant Fries	21
137.	Parmesan & Garlic Cauliflower	21
138.	Cashew Bowls	21
139.	Sweet Apple Fries	21
140.	Roasted Spicy Hot Dogs	21
141.	Fried Goat Cheese	22
142.	Bbq Lil Smokies	22
143.	Croutons	22
144.	Hillbilly Cheese Surprise	22
145.	Flax Cheese Chips	22
146.	Bacon Avocado Wraps	22
147.	Healthy Vegetable Kabobs	22
148.	Buffalo Bites	22
149.	Fried Olives	23
150.	Skinny Fries	23
151.	Cinnamon Apple Crisps	23
152.	Brussels Sprouts	23
153.	Avocado Sticks	23
154.	Friday's Fries	23
155.	Fried Mushrooms	24
156.	Cheesy Bacon Bread	24
157.	Zucchini And Tomato Salsa	24
158.	Bacon Jalapeno Poppers	24
159.	Corn Dog Bites	24
160.	Sweet And Spicy Carrot Sticks	24
161.	Cheddar Cheese Lumpia Rolls	24
162.	Roasted Carrots	25
163.	Homemade Mayonnaise	25
164.	Pickled Bacon Bowls	25
165.	Green Beans & S	25
166.	Crunchy Bacon Bites	25
167.	Crispy Kale Chips	25
168.	Bow Tie Pasta Chips	25
169.	Cajun Kale Chips	25
170.	Blistered Shishito Peppers	25
171.	The Best Party Mix Ever	26
172.	Tomatoes & Herbs	26
173.	Air Fry Bacon	26

#	Recipe	Page
174.	Warm And Salty Edamame	26
175.	Radish Chips	26
176.	Cheese Wafers	26
177.	Fried Mozzarella Sticks	26
178.	Peppers Dip	27
179.	Greek Turkey Meatballs	27
180.	Broccoli Cheese Nuggets	27
181.	Pork Rinds	27
182.	Creamy Cheddar Eggs	27
183.	Broccoli Florets	27
184.	Leeks Dip	27
185.	Parmesan Zucchini Chips	27
186.	Curly's Cauliflower	28
187.	Apple Rollups	28
188.	Bacon-wrapped Sausage Skewers	28
189.	Cheese Crackers	28
190.	Tofu	28
191.	Parmesan Green Beans Sticks	28
192.	Easy Carrot Dip	28
193.	Pickled Fries	28
194.	Spicy Dip	28
195.	Cauliflower Poppers	29
196.	Korean-style Wings	29
197.	Pork Egg Rolls	29
198.	Cabbage Chips	29
199.	Green Olive And Mushroom Tapenade	29
200.	Sausage And Cheese Rolls	29
201.	Ham & Cheese Rolls	30
202.	Cheese Dip	30
203.	Crispy Shrimps	30
204.	Onion Dip	30
205.	Sesame Tortilla Chips	30
206.	Fried Pickles	30
207.	Baked Tortillas	30
208.	Curried Sweet Potato Fries	30
209.	Fruit Pastries	31
210.	Potato Chips	31
211.	Puerto Rican Tostones	31
212.	Grilled Cheese Sandwich Deluxe	31
213.	Roasted Almonds	31
214.	Easy Crispy Prawns	31
215.	Za'atar Garbanzo Beans	31
216.	Greek Street Tacos	31
217.	Grilled Cheese Sandwich	32
218.	Grilled Cheese Sandwiches	32
219.	Cheese Sandwich	32
220.	Sweet Potato Chips	32
221.	Coconut Cheese Sticks	32
222.	Chili Calamari Rings	32
223.	Paprika Chips	32
224.	Mozzarella Sticks	32
225.	Crust-less Meaty Pizza	32
226.	Squash Fries	33
227.	Barbecue Little Smokies	33
228.	Asparagus	33
229.	Chocolate Cookie Dough Balls	33
230.	Chipotle Jicama Hash	33
231.	Air Fryer Plantains	33
232.	Rutabaga Fries	33
233.	Hot Cheesy Dip	33
234.	Turkey Bacon Dates	34
235.	Garlic Eggplant Chips	34
236.	Onion Rings	34
237.	Chocolate Bacon Bites	34
238.	Fried Kale Chips	34
239.	Kohlrabi Chips	34
240.	Italian-style Tomato-parmesan Crisps	34
241.	Roasted Peanuts	34
242.	Jalapeño Guacamole	35
243.	Spinach Dip	35
244.	Quick And Easy Popcorn	35
245.	Brussels Sprout Crisps	35
246.	Simple Banana Chips	35
247.	Tortilla Chips	35
248.	Rumaki	35
249.	Cocktail Flanks	36
250.	Classic Deviled Eggs	36

Beef, pork & Lamb Recipes 37

#	Recipe	Page
251.	Crispy Pierogi With Kielbasa And Onions	37
252.	Pork Tenderloin With Bacon & Veggies	37
253.	Salted Porterhouse With Sage 'n Thyme Medley	37
254.	Charred Onions 'n Steak Cube Bbq	37
255.	Buttery Pork Chops	37
256.	Bacon Wrapped Filets Mignons	37
257.	Herbed Beef Roast	38
258.	Beef With Tomato Sauce And Fennel	38
259.	Orange And Brown Sugar–glazed Ham	38
260.	Za'atar Lamb Loin Chops	38
261.	Corned Beef	38
262.	Empanadas	38
263.	Mustard Lamb Loin Chops	38
264.	Adobo Oregano Beef	38
265.	Glazed Ham	39
266.	Salted Steak Pan Fried Steak	39

267. Bacon Blue Cheese Burger 39
268. Paprika Beef And Spinach 39
269. Simple Lamb Chops 39
270. Pork Chops On The Grill Simple Recipe 39
271. Glazed Pork Shoulder 39
272. Bacon Wrapped Filet Mignon 40
273. Ground Beef 40
274. Jumbo Italian Meatballs 40
275. Steak Bites And Spicy Dipping Sauce 40
276. Steak Fingers 40
277. Air Fried Grilled Steak 40
278. Crispy Five-spice Pork Belly 40
279. Pesto-rubbed Veal Chops 41
280. Cajun Sweet-sour Grilled Pork 41
281. Hot Dogs 41
282. Balsamic Pork Chops 41
283. Lamb Burgers 41
284. Honey-sriracha Pork Ribs 41
285. Honey Mesquite Pork Chops 42
286. Barbecue-style Beef Cube Steak 42
287. Strawberry Pork Ribs 42
288. Lamb Chops And Lemon Yogurt Sauce 42
289. Another Easy Teriyaki Bbq Recipe 42
290. Garlic Butter Pork Chops 42
291. Beef Bulgogi 42
292. Italian Meatballs 43
293. Garlicky Lamb Chops 43
294. Coconut Pork And Green Beans 43
295. Chili-espresso Marinated Steak 43
296. Pork Belly Marinated In Onion-coconut Cream 43
297. Simple Garlic 'n Herb Meatballs 43
298. Meatloaf 43
299. Cheeseburgers 44
300. Caramelized Pork 44
301. Mustard Pork 44
302. Smoked Brisket With Dill Pickles 44
303. Marinated Beef 44
304. Sweet Pork Belly 44
305. Wasabi-coated Pork Loin Chops 44
306. Italian Pork 44
307. Lemon-butter Veal Cutlets 45
308. Lamb With Paprika Cilantro Sauce 45
309. Mustard'n Italian Dressing On Flank Steak 45
310. Garlic-rosemary Lamb Bbq 45
311. Salty Lamb Chops 45
312. Fat Burger Bombs 45
313. Mustard Beef Mix 45
314. Tomato Salsa Topped Grilled Flank Steak 45
315. Easy & The Traditional Beef Roast Recipe 46
316. Roasted Lamb 46
317. Crunchy Fried Pork Loin Chops 46
318. Smoked Chili Lamb Chops 46
319. Smoked Sausage And Bacon Shashlik 46
320. Pork And Garlic Sauce 46
321. Marinated Flank Steak 46
322. Garlic Dill Leg Of Lamb 46
323. Cheddar Bacon Ranch Pinwheels 47
324. Simple Lamb Bbq With Herbed Salt 47
325. Char-grilled Skirt Steak With Fresh Herbs 47
326. Garlic Fillets 47
327. Grilled Prosciutto Wrapped Fig 47
328. Veggie Stuffed Beef Rolls 47
329. Garlic Pork And Ginger Sauce 47
330. Pepper Pork Chops 47
331. Easy Corn Dog Bites 48
332. Steak Total 48
333. Maple'n Soy Marinated Bee f48
334. Ribs And Chimichuri Mix 48
335. Pork Chops 48
336. Crouton-breaded Pork Chops 48
337. Buttered Striploin Steak 48
338. Bacon Wrapped Pork Tenderloin 48
339. Champagne-vinegar Marinated Skirt Steak 48
340. Simple Herbs De Provence Pork Loin Roast 49
341. Simple New York Strip Steak 49
342. Kielbasa Chunks With Pineapple & Peppers 49
343. Bjorn's Beef Steak 49
344. Cumin Pork Steak 49
345. Lamb Loin Chops With Lemon 49
346. Cream Cheese Pork 49
347. Roasted Ribeye Steak With Rum 49
348. Ham Pinwheels 50
349. Pork Chops Marinate In Honey-mustard 50
350. Sausage Meatballs 50
351. Easy Rib Eye Steak 50
352. Steak Kebabs 50
353. Fantastic Leg Of Lamb 50
354. Chili Loin Medallions 50
355. Bourbon-bbq Sauce Marinated Beef Bbq 50
356. Baby Back Ribs 51
357. Butter Beef 51
358. Basil Pork 51
359. Super Simple Steaks 51
360. Rib Eye Steak Seasoned With Italian Herb 51
361. Garlic Lamb Roast 51
362. Veal Rolls 51
363. Pesto Coated Rack Of Lamb 52
364. Beef And Tomato Sauce 52
365. Beef Short Ribs 52
366. Pretzel-coated Pork Tenderloin 52

367. Beef & Mushrooms ... 52	372. Grilled Sausages With Bbq Sauce ... 53
368. Extra Crispy Country-style Pork Riblets ... 52	373. Tonkatsu ... 53
369. Top Loin Beef Strips With Blue Cheese ... 52	374. Bacon With Shallot And Greens ... 53
370. Pork Tenderloin With Bacon And Veggies ... 53	375. Japanese Miso Steak ... 53
371. Rosemary Lamb Steak ... 53	

Poultry Recipes 54

376. Mozzarella Turkey Rolls ... 54	418. Strawberry Turkey ... 59
377. Texas Bbq Chicken Thighs ... 54	419. Baked Chicken Nachos ... 59
378. Poppin' Pop Corn Chicken ... 54	420. Cinnamon Balsamic Duck ... 59
379. Naked Cheese, Chicken Stuffing 'n Green Beans ... 54	421. Parmesan Chicken Tenders ... 59
380. Oregano Duck Spread ... 54	422. Quick' n Easy Brekky Eggs 'n Cream ... 59
381. Buffalo Chicken Strips ... 54	423. Chicken Gruyere ... 60
382. Almond Coconut Chicken Tenders ... 54	424. Goulash ... 60
383. Quick And Crispy Chicken ... 55	425. Bacon Chicken Mix ... 60
384. Chili Chicken Cutlets ... 55	426. Southern Fried Chicken ... 60
385. Quick Chicken For Filling ... 55	427. Sausage Stuffed Chicken ... 60
386. Herbed Duck Legs ... 55	428. Spicy Chicken ... 60
387. Chicken & Jalapeño Pepper Quesadilla ... 55	429. Crispy Cajun Fried Chicken ... 60
388. Paprika Chicken Legs With Turnip ... 55	430. Honey & Garlic Chicken Wings ... 60
389. Pepper Turkey Bacon ... 55	431. Cheese Herb Chicken Wings ... 61
390. Marjoram Chicken ... 55	432. Sweet-mustardy Thighs ... 61
391. Spicy Chicken Wings ... 56	433. Teriyaki Chicken Kebabs ... 61
392. Jalapeno Chicken Breasts ... 56	434. Garlicky Meatballs ... 61
393. Buttered Duck Breasts ... 56	435. Lemon Pepper Chicken Legs ... 61
394. Fried Chicken Legs ... 56	436. Bbq Chicken Wings ... 61
395. Surprisingly Tasty Chicken ... 56	437. Flavorful Cornish Hen ... 62
396. Thyme Butter Turkey Breast ... 56	438. Pretzel-crusted Chicken ... 62
397. Honey & Garlic Chicken Breasts ... 56	439. Chicken With Mushrooms ... 62
398. Creamy Onion Chicken ... 56	440. Turkey Scotch Eggs ... 62
399. Honey Chicken Drumsticks ... 57	441. Greek Chicken Meatballs ... 62
400. Stuffed Chicken ... 57	442. Creamy Chicken Breasts With Crumbled Bacon ... 62
401. Chicken Chunks ... 57	443. Fried Chicken Halves ... 62
402. Chicken Breasts With Sweet Chili Adobo ... 57	444. Simple Chicken Wings ... 62
403. Juicy Turkey Breast Tenderloin ... 57	445. Lemon Grilled Chicken Breasts ... 63
404. Zesty Ranch Chicken Drumsticks ... 57	446. Turkey Wings ... 63
405. Ricotta And Thyme Chicken ... 57	447. Lime And Thyme Duck ... 63
406. Chicken Cordon Bleu ... 57	448. Yummy Shredded Chicken ... 63
407. Tarragon & Garlic Roasted Chicken ... 58	449. Buttered Spinach-egg Omelet ... 63
408. Roasted Chicken ... 58	450. Whole Chicken ... 63
409. Chicken Enchiladas ... 58	451. Creamy Duck Strips ... 63
410. Chicken Nuggets ... 58	452. Buttermilk-fried Chicken Thighs ... 63
411. Chicken Breast With Prosciutto And Brie ... 58	453. Popcorn Chicken ... 64
412. Almond Flour Battered Chicken Cordon Bleu ... 58	454. Juicy & Spicy Chicken Wings ... 64
413. Paprika Duck ... 58	455. Roasted Chicken With Potatoes ... 64
414. Breaded Chicken Tenderloins ... 58	456. Garlic Chicken Wings ... 64
415. Cilantro Drumsticks ... 59	457. Parsley Duck ... 64
416. Vinegar Chicken ... 59	458. Lime And Mustard Marinated Chicken ... 64
417. Paprika Liver Spread ... 59	459. Simple Turkey Breast ... 64

460. Breadcrumb Turkey Breasts ... 64
461. Sage And Chicken Escallops ... 65
462. Crispy Chicken Thighs ... 65
463. Mesmerizing Honey Chicken Drumsticks ... 65
464. Blackened Chicken Tenders ... 65
465. Sweet Chicken Breasts ... 65
466. Simple Paprika Duck ... 65
467. Teriyaki Chicken Legs ... 65
468. Chicken Sausage In Dijon Sauce ... 65
469. Chinese Chicken Wings ... 66
470. Chicken & Prawn Paste ... 66
471. Spinach 'n Bacon Egg Cups ... 66
472. Almond Flour Coco-milk Battered Chicken ... 66
473. Shaking Tarragon Chicken Tenders ... 66
474. Family Farm's Chicken Wings ... 66
475. Easy & Crispy Chicken Wings ... 66
476. Fajita Style Chicken Breast ... 66
477. Lemon & Garlic Chicken ... 67
478. Cheese Stuffed Turkey Breasts ... 67
479. Chili And Paprika Chicken Wings ... 67
480. Tomato Chicken Mix ... 67
481. Chicken Quarters With Broccoli And Rice ... 67
482. Grilled Chicken Wings With Curry-yogurt Sauce ... 67
483. Tangy Chicken With Parsley And Lime ... 67
484. Rosemary Partridge ... 67
485. Italian Chicken Thighs ... 68
486. One-tray Parmesan Wings ... 68
487. Crumbed Sage Chicken Scallopini4 ... 68
488. Betty's Baked Chicken ... 68
489. Herb Seasoned Turkey Breast ... 68
490. Caprese Chicken With Balsamic Sauce ... 68
491. Marinated Chicken ... 68
492. Bacon-wrapped Turkey With Cheese ... 68
493. Grilled Chicken Recipe From Jamaica ... 69
494. Fried Chicken Thighs ... 69
495. Five Spice Duck Legs ... 69
496. Grilled Chicken Pesto ... 69
497. Cajun Seasoned Chicken ... 69
498. Turkey-hummus Wraps ... 69
499. Thyme Turkey Nuggets ... 69
500. Sesame Chicken Wings ... 69

Fish & Seafood Recipes ... 70

501. Mango Shrimp Skewers ... 70
502. Herbed Garlic Lobster ... 70
503. Better Fish Sticks ... 70
504. Potato-wrapped Salmon Fillets ... 70
505. Quick 'n Easy Tuna-mac Casserole ... 70
506. Coconut Jerk Shrimp ... 70
507. Celery Leaves 'n Garlic-oil Grilled Turbot ... 71
508. Cod And Sauce ... 71
509. Char-grilled Drunken Halibut ... 71
510. Tilapia Teriyaki ... 71
511. Smoked Halibut And Eggs In Brioche ... 71
512. Grilled Scallops With Pesto ... 71
513. Miso Fish ... 71
514. Crusty Pesto Salmon ... 71
515. Lime 'n Chat Masala Rubbed Snapper ... 72
516. Egg Frittata With Smoked Trout ... 72
517. Rosemary-infused Butter Scallops ... 72
518. Marinated Scallops With Butter And Beer ... 72
519. Quick And Easy Shrimp ... 72
520. Beer Battered Cod Filet ... 72
521. Zesty Mahi Mahi ... 72
522. Fish Sticks For Kids ... 72
523. Crab Rangoon ... 72
524. Lemon Shrimp And Zucchinis ... 73
525. Basil And Paprika Cod ... 73
526. Cajun Salmon With Lemon ... 73
527. Buttered Scallops ... 73
528. Sweet & Sour Glazed Salmon ... 73
529. Curried Sweet-and-spicy Scallops ... 73
530. Spicy Mackerel ... 73
531. Basil Scallops ... 74
532. Salmon Patties ... 74
533. Air Fried Cod With Basil Vinaigrette ... 74
534. Simple Salmon Patties ... 74
535. Almond Flour Coated Crispy Shrimps ... 74
536. Fish Fillets ... 74
537. Fish Taco Bowl ... 74
538. Fish Fillet Sandwich ... 74
539. Lemon Garlic Shrimp ... 75
540. Nutritious Salmon ... 75
541. Sesame Seeds Coated Tuna ... 75
542. Outrageous Crispy Fried Salmon Skin ... 75
543. Lime, Oil 'n Leeks On Grilled Swordfish ... 75
544. Coconut Calamari ... 75
545. Juicy Salmon And Asparagus Parcels ... 75
546. Salmon And Blackberry Sauce ... 75
547. Restaurant-style Flounder Cutlets ... 76
548. Butter Lobster ... 76
549. Ahi Tuna Steaks ... 76
550. Teriyaki Salmon ... 76
551. Rice Flour Coated Shrimp ... 76
552. Super-simple Scallops ... 76

553. Salmon Topped With Creamy Avocado-cashew Sauce 76
554. Sesame Tuna Steak 76
555. Cilantro Cod Mix 77
556. Crispy Calamari 77
557. Fish-in-chips 77
558. Beer-battered Cod 77
559. Parmesan Walnut Salmon 77
560. Bacon-wrapped Cajun Scallops 77
561. Buttery Cod 78
562. Fish Sticks 78
563. Breaded Hake 78
564. Crispy Fish Fingers 78
565. Honey-glazed Salmon 78
566. Chili Squid Rings 78
567. Chili-lime Shrimp 78
568. Easy Grilled Pesto Scallops 78
569. Japanese Citrus Soy Squid 79
570. Breaded Scallops 79
571. Quick & Easy Air Fried Salmon 79
572. Butter Flounder Fillets 79
573. Air Fried Dilly Trout 79
574. Lemon-roasted Salmon Fillets 79
575. Shrimp And Parsley Olives 79
576. Cajun Seasoned Salmon Filet 79
577. Fried Catfish Fillets 79
578. Cajun Flounder Fillets 80
579. Swordfish With Capers And Tomatoes 80
580. Horseradish-crusted Salmon Fillets 80
581. Crispy Prawn In Bacon Wraps 80
582. Lime Cod 80
583. French Clams 80
584. Air Fried Catfish 80
585. Foil Packet Lobster Tail 80
586. Mahi-mahi "burrito" Fillets 81
587. Lemon Butter Scallops 81
588. Fried Shrimps With Sweet Chili Sauce 81
589. Miso-rubbed Salmon Fillets 81
590. Fried Tilapia Bites 81
591. Air Fried Calamari 81
592. Hot Prawns 82
593. Cajun Lemon Salmon 82
594. Maple Glazed Salmon 82
595. Citrusy Branzini On The Grill 82
596. Healthy And Easy To Make Salmon 82
597. Bacon Wrapped Shrimp 82
598. Tilapia Fish Fillets 82
599. Prawns 82
600. Crispy Smelts 83
601. Bacon Wrapped Scallops 83
602. Ghee Shrimp And Green Beans 83
603. Sweet And Sour Glazed Cod 83
604. Salmon Cakes 83
605. Authentic Alaskan Crab Legs 83
606. Greek-style Grilled Scallops 83
607. Coriander Cod And Green Beans 83
608. Ham Tilapia 84
609. Cajun Spiced Veggie-shrimp Bake 84
610. Nacho Chips Crusted Prawns 84
611. Breaded Flounder 84
612. Broiled Tilapia 84
613. Amazing Salmon Fillets 84
614. Snow Crab Legs 84
615. Thyme Scallops 84
616. Crab Legs 85
617. Creamy Salmon 85
618. Salmon Croquettes 85
619. Rosemary Garlic Prawns 85
620. Salmon And Olives 85
621. Shrimp Skewers 85
622. Butter Paprika Swordfish 85
623. Perfect Soft-shelled Crabs 85
624. Clams And Sauce 86
625. Italian Mackerel 86

Vegetable & Side Dishes 87

626. Artichokes Sauté 87
627. Cumin Artichokes 87
628. Carrot Crisps 87
629. Bacon-wrapped Avocados 87
630. Homemade Potato Puffs 87
631. Asian Green Beans 87
632. Steak Fries 87
633. Herbed Garlic Radishes 87
634. Chicken Wings With Alfredo Sauce 88
635. Cheesy Cauliflower Tots 88
636. Yellow Squash And Zucchinis Dish 88
637. Zucchinis And Arugula Mix 88
638. Collard Greens Sauté 88
639. Air-fried Brussels Sprouts 88
640. Mozzarella Green Beans 88
641. Simple Stuffed Bell Peppers 88
642. Mustard Greens Mix 89
643. Roasted Potatoes & Cheese 89
644. Maple Glazed Corn 89
645. Lemon Tempeh 89

646. Roasted Brussels Sprouts With Bacon 89
647. Coconut Mushrooms Mix 89
648. Jicama Fries 89
649. Mozzarella Asparagus Mix 89
650. Air-fried Crispy Chicken Thighs 89
651. Cheesy Onion Rings 90
652. Paprika Jicama 90
653. Spanish Chorizo With Brussels Sprouts 90
654. Tasty Herb Tomatoes 90
655. Turmeric Cauliflower Rice 90
656. Beet Fries 90
657. Green Bean Crisps 90
658. Corn Muffins 90
659. Elegant Carrot Cookies 91
660. Perfect Crispy Tofu 91
661. Garlic Radishes 91
662. Balsamic Radishes 91
663. Cheesy Texas Toast 91
664. Easy Celery Root Mix 91
665. Lemon Kale 91
666. Beet Wedges Dish 91
667. Butter Broccoli 91
668. Perfect Broccolini 92
669. Roasted Acorn Squash 92
670. Ghee Savoy Cabbage 92
671. Garlic-parmesan French Fries 92
672. Garlic Tomatoes Recipe 92
673. Cheesy Sticks With Sweet Thai Sauce 92
674. Duck Fat Roasted Red Potatoes 92
675. Parsley Savoy Cabbage Mix 92
676. Air-frier Baked Potatoes 93
677. Roasted Mushrooms 93
678. Cheesy Ranch Broccoli 93
679. Fried Agnolotti 93
680. Paprika Green Beans 93
681. Herbed Croutons With Brie Cheese 93
682. Cheddar Asparagus 93
683. Sriracha Chili Chicken Wings 93
684. Roasted Broccoli 93
685. Mushrooms, Sautéed 93
686. Lemon And Butter Artichokes 94
687. Pop Corn Broccoli 94
688. Tomato Candy 94
689. Skinny Pumpkin Chips 94
690. Hot Chicken Wingettes 94
691. Simple Cheese Sandwich 94
692. Yeast Rolls 94
693. Cheesy Bacon Fries 94
694. Curry Cabbage Sauté 95
695. Garlic Asparagus 95
696. Perfect French Fries 95
697. Sweet Butternut Squash 95
698. Mediterranean Bruschetta 95
699. Crispy Bacon With Butterbean Dip 95
700. Crispy Chicken Nuggets 95
701. Mustard Endives 96
702. Spicy Cheese Lings 96
703. Taco Okra 96
704. Dill Tomato 96
705. Simple Taro Fries 96
706. Low-carb Pita Chips 96
707. Classic French Fries 96
708. Paprika Asparagus 96
709. Fried Mashed Potato Balls 96
710. Delicious Chicken Taquitos 97
711. Roasted Coconut Carrots 97
712. Balsamic Greens Sauté 97
713. Parmesan Veggie Mix 97
714. Bacon & Asparagus Spears 97
715. Corn-crusted Chicken Tenders 97
716. Avocado And Green Beans 97
717. Crispy Cauliflower Bites 97
718. Tandoori Cauliflower 97
719. Coconut Chives Sprouts 98
720. Macaroni And Cheese 98
721. Garlic Mushrooms 98
722. Cheese Zucchini Rolls 98
723. Baked Potato For One 98
724. Green Beans 98
725. Parmesan Artichoke Hearts 98
726. Balsamic Garlic Kale 98
727. Garlicky Chips With Herbs 98
728. Turmeric Kale Mix 99
729. Collard Greens And Bacon Recipe 99
730. Parmesan Crusted Pickles 99
731. Mouth-watering Salami Sticks 99
732. Rosemary Roasted Potatoes With Lemon 99
733. Ghee Lemony Endives 99
734. Balsamic And Garlic Cabbage Mix 99
735. Tender Eggplant Fries 99
736. Air-fried Cheesy Broccoli With Garlic 99
737. Roasted Belgian Endive With Pistachios And Lemon 100
738. Roasted Almond Delight 100
739. Calamari With Olives 100
740. Zesty Salmon Jerky 100
741. Flatbread 100
742. Super Cabbage Canapes 100
743. Cauliflower Tots 100
744. Basic Pepper French Fries 101
745. Cabbage Slaw 101

746. Basil Squash 101
747. Cheddar-garlic Drop Biscuits 101
748. Green Peas With Mint 101
749. Green Beans And Tomatoes Recipe 101
750. Super-crispy Asparagus Fries 101

Vegan & Vegetarian Recipes 102

751. Hearty Carrots 102
752. Garlic-roasted Brussels Sprouts With Mustard 102
753. Curried Cauliflower Florets 102
754. Potato, Eggplant, And Zucchini Chips 102
755. Traditional Jacket Potatoes 102
756. Sweet And Spicy Barbecue Tofu 102
757. Cinnamon Sugar Tortilla Chips 102
758. Roasted Cauliflower 103
759. Cottage Cheese And Potatoes 103
760. Pineapple Appetizer Ribs 103
761. Easy Roast Winter Vegetable Delight 103
762. Parsley-loaded Mushrooms 103
763. Brussels Sprouts With Balsamic Oil 103
764. Breadcrumbs Stuffed Mushrooms 103
765. Air Fried Halloumi With Veggies 103
766. Spinach And Feta Pinwheels 104
767. Easy Crispy Shawarma Chickpeas 104
768. Spicy Celery Sticks 104
769. Caprese Eggplant Stacks 104
770. Baked Green Beans 104
771. Bell Peppers Cups 104
772. Spinach & Feta Crescent Triangles 104
773. Classic Baked Banana 104
774. Family Favorite Potatoes 105
775. Cool Mini Zucchini's 105
776. Layered Ravioli Bake 105
777. Zucchini Gratin 105
778. Swiss Cheese And Eggplant Crisps 105
779. Salted Beet Chips 105
780. Healthy Avocado Fries 105
781. Corn Cakes 105
782. Broccoli Salad 106
783. Caribbean-style Fried Plantains 106
784. Rosemary Olive-oil Over Shrooms N Asparagus 106
785. Stuffed Mushrooms With Bacon & Cheese 106
786. Spiced Up Potato Wedges 106
787. Radish And Mozzarella Salad With Balsamic Vinaigrette 106
788. Croissant Rolls 106
789. Crispy Marinated Tofu 106
790. Cottage And Mayonnaise Stuffed Peppers 107
791. Sweet And Spicy Parsnips 107
792. Cheesy Bbq Tater Tot 107
793. Turmeric Crispy Chickpeas 107
794. Cheesy Cauliflower Crust Pizza 107
795. Scrumptiously Healthy Chips 107
796. Delightful Mushrooms 107
797. Feta Cheese Triangles 108
798. Caramelized Brussels Sprout 108
799. Sesame Seeds Bok Choy(1) 108
800. Herbed Potatoes 108
801. Red Wine Infused Mushrooms 108
802. Tender Butternut Squash Fry 108
803. Easy Fried Tomatoes 108
804. Broccoli With Olives 108
805. Cauliflower Steaks Gratin 109
806. Twice-baked Broccoli-cheddar Potatoes 109
807. Eggplant Caviar 109
808. Easy Fry Portobello Mushroom 109
809. Curried Eggplant 109
810. Chipotle Chickpea Tacos 109
811. Roasted Brussels Sprouts & Pine Nuts 109
812. Spicy Corn Fritters 110
813. Zucchini Topped With Coconut Cream 'n Bacon 110
814. Zucchini Garlic-sour Cream Bake 110
815. Cheese Stuffed Tomatoes 110
816. Lemony Green Beans 110
817. Portobello Mini Pizzas 110
818. Hasselback Potatoes 110
819. Gourmet Wasabi Popcorn 111
820. Okra With Green Beans 111
821. Crispy Brussels Sprout Chips 111
822. Roasted Brussels Sprouts 111
823. Healthy Apple-licious Chips 111
824. Italian Seasoned Easy Pasta Chips 111
825. Kurkuri Bhindi (indian Fried Okra) 111
826. Sweet And Sour Brussel Sprouts 111
827. Easy Glazed Carrots 111
828. Sweet Potato French Fries 112
829. Baked Polenta With Chili-cheese 112
830. Poblano & Tomato Stuffed Squash 112
831. Tacos 112
832. Sautéed Spinach 112
833. Air-fried Sweet Potato 112
834. Almond Asparagus 112
835. Roasted Mushrooms In Herb-garlic Oil 112
836. Cheesy Vegetarian Lasagna 113
837. Pesto Vegetable Kebabs 113
838. Air-fried Cauliflower 113

839. Indian Plantain Chips 113
840. Crispy 'n Healthy Avocado Fingers 113
841. Cheesy Broccoli With Eggs 113
842. Crispy Air-fried Tofu 113
843. Chewy Glazed Parsnips 114
844. Jalapeno Stuffed With Bacon 'n Cheeses 114
845. Feisty Baby Carrots 114
846. Toasted Ravioli 114
847. Mushroom 'n Bell Pepper Pizza 114
848. Green Bean Casserole 114
849. Spaghetti Squash 114
850. Crispy Ham Rolls 114
851. Sautéed Green Beans 115
852. Cinnamon Pear Chips 115
853. Crispy Shawarma Broccoli 115
854. Cheesy Kale 115
855. Basil Tomatoes 115
856. Grilled 'n Glazed Strawberries 115
857. Crispy Wings With Lemony Old Bay Spice .. 115
858. Roasted Vegetable Grilled Cheese 115
859. Cheese And Bean Enchiladas 116
860. Rice Flour Crusted Tofu 116
861. Black Bean And Rice Burrito Filling 116
862. Hearty Apple Chips 116
863. Crunchy Parmesan Zucchini 116
864. Vegetable Nuggets 116
865. Extreme Zucchini Fries 116
866. Perfectly Roasted Mushrooms 117
867. Avocado Rolls 117
868. Herbed Eggplant 117
869. Salted Garlic Zucchini Fries 117
870. Melted Cheese 'n Almonds On Tomato 117
871. Parmesan Asparagus 117
872. Spicy Potatoes 117
873. Tangy Asparagus And Broccoli 118
874. Chili Fried Okra 118
875. Garden Fresh Green Beans 118

Desserts Recipes 119

876. Hot Coconut 'n Cocoa Buns 119
877. Grilled Banana Boats 119
878. Dark Chocolate Peanut Butter S'mores 119
879. Chocolate Molten Lava Cake 119
880. Apple Tart 119
881. Nutella And Banana Pastries 119
882. Lemon Cookies 120
883. Apple Fritters 120
884. Apple Crumble 120
885. Strawberry Frozen Dessert 120
886. Blueberry Cookies 120
887. Bacon Cookies 120
888. Cauliflower Rice Pudding 120
889. Keto Butter Balls 121
890. Cinnamon Fried Plums 121
891. Moon Pie 121
892. Cocoa Spread 121
893. Swedish Chocolate Mug Cake 121
894. Delicious Apple Pie 121
895. Apple Jam 121
896. Currant Cream Ramekins 121
897. Sage Cream 121
898. Butter Custard 121
899. Chocolate Banana Pastries 122
900. Cream Cheese Muffins 122
901. Molten Lava Cakes 122
902. Chocolate Peanut Butter Cups 122
903. Cinnamon Apple Chips 122
904. Cream Cups 122
905. Fried Twinkies 122
906. Chocolate Raspberry Wontons 123
907. Lemon Mousse 123
908. Crème Brulee 123
909. Sugar Pork Rinds 123
910. Coconut Sunflower Cookies 123
911. Fruity Tacos 123
912. Creamy Pudding 123
913. Chocolate Soufflé 123
914. Cherry Pie 124
915. Sweet Potato Pie Rolls 124
916. Lemon Bars Recipe 124
917. Lemon Curd 124
918. Lemon Berries Stew 124
919. Caramel Baked Apples 124
920. White Chocolate Chip Cookies 124
921. Apple Pie Crumble 125
922. Coconut Cupcakes 125
923. Shortbread Fingers 125
924. Grape Stew 125
925. Apple Pastry Pouch 125
926. Roasted Pumpkin Seeds & Cinnamon 125
927. Butter Plums 125
928. Baked Plum Cream 126
929. Peanut Cookies 126
930. Chocolate Candies 126
931. Peanut Butter Cookies 126

#	Recipe	Page
932.	Macaroon Bites	126
933.	Oreo-coated Peanut Butter Cups	126
934.	Banana Fritters	126
935.	Berry Layer Cake	127
936.	Midnight Nutella® Banana Sandwich	127
937.	Cranberry Cream Surprise	127
938.	Chocolate And Avocado Cream	127
939.	Coconut Pillow	127
940.	Crispy Fruit Tacos	127
941.	Chocolate Brownie	127
942.	Marshmallow Pastries	127
943.	Air Fried Snickerdoodle Poppers	128
944.	Raspberry Pudding Surprise	128
945.	Ricotta Lemon Cake	128
946.	Cheesecake Cups	128
947.	Chocolate Mug Cake	128
948.	Pineapple Sticks	128
949.	Chocolate Banana Sandwiches	128
950.	Baked Apple	128
951.	Brownies Muffins	128
952.	Fried Banana S'mores	129
953.	Crusty	129
954.	Monkey Bread	129
955.	Almond Meringue Cookies	129
956.	Blackberry Cream	129
957.	Almond Shortbread Cookies	129
958.	Orange Marmalade	129
959.	Apple Dumplings	130
960.	Yummy Banana Cookies	130
961.	Delicious Vanilla Custard	130
962.	Choco-coconut Puddin	130
963.	Coconut Berry Pudding	130
964.	Chocolate Cheesecake	130
965.	Chocolate-covered Maple Bacon	130
966.	Cream Cheese Pound Cake	131
967.	No Flour Lime Muffins	131
968.	Nutty Fudge Muffins	131
969.	Avocado Pudding	131
970.	Choco-berry Fudge Sauce	131
971.	Chocolate Apple Chips	131
972.	Cranberry Jam	131
973.	Dark Chocolate Cake	131
974.	Bananas & Ice Cream	132
975.	Chia Chocolate Cookies	132
976.	Chocolate Chip Cookies	132
977.	Ricotta And Lemon Cake Recipe	132
978.	Molten Lava Cake	132
979.	Chocolate Pudding	132
980.	Strawberry Cups	132
981.	Baked Apples	132
982.	Tortilla Fried Pies	132
983.	Air Fried Doughnuts	133
984.	Lemon Bars	133
985.	White Chocolate Berry Cheesecake	133
986.	Hearty Banana Pastry	133
987.	Black & White Brownies	133
988.	S'mores Pockets	133
989.	Banana Oatmeal Cookies	134
990.	Berry Pudding	134
991.	Basic Butter Cookies	134
992.	Chocolate Mayonnaise Cake	134
993.	Delicious Spiced Apples	134
994.	Fiesta Pastries	134
995.	Glazed Chocolate Doughnut Holes	134
996.	Vanilla Bean Dream	135
997.	English Lemon Tarts	135
998.	Lemon Berry Jam	135
999.	Chocolate Macaroons	135
1000.	Pumpkin Pie	135

RECIPE INDEX 136

Introduction

This cookbook is written for all those people who have busy lives and who wish to maintain their health by eating less oily food items. If you find it hard to prepare a meal that is easy and healthy then this kitchen appliance can perform magic for you. Geared toward air fryer newbies, this essential guide will take you through all facets of the air fryer and have you transforming basic ingredients into dynamic dishes in no time.

Now you can stop worrying about the oil and fat content in your food as the Air Fryer helps you keep the fat content low while keeping the nutrients intact. In this book, we are covering more than 1000 recipes with only 5 ingredients or less that break down into a wide variety of categories.

I know that the guide that comes with your air fryer is well intended, but not especially useful, leaving you to trial and error experimentation. While here comes my cookbook, which will solve all those problem, nicely.
All the recipes in this book are simple, easy and easy to follow. For any food lovers like me and those fond of cooking, air fryer is super cool and minimizes many of your manual efforts.
Let's enjoy these delicious meals and master your Air Fryer!

Tips For Air Fryer Success

Know Your Appliance

First, and most important, read your appliance manual. All air fryers are not created equal. Features differ among models. Even timers work differently. Parts of some air fryers may be dishwasher safe, but you may have to hand-wash others. Any misuse of your air fryer or its parts could void the warranty. Read all safety information, and never use the machine in any way that violates the manufacturer's instructions for safe use. In addition to keeping you safe, your manual should provide details about your model's features and functions. Most of us hate reading instructions or manuals, but it's worth taking the time to understand how to use it. Sometimes that can make all the difference between frustration and success.

Cooking Time

Many factors can affect cooking times, including size, volume, and temperature of food, thickness of breading, and so on. Even your local humidity levels can affect required cooking times. Wattage is another factor. All recipes in this cookbook were tested in 1,425-watt air fryers. A unit with a higher or lower wattage may cook somewhat faster or slower. For most recipes, total cooking time shouldn't vary by more than a minute or two, but to avoid overcooking, check food early and often. Always start with the shortest cooking time listed in a recipe. Check for doneness at that point and continue cooking if necessary. When you try a recipe for the first time and the minimum cooking time is, say, 20 minutes or longer, check the dish at about 15 minutes just to be safe. If you're new to air frying, don't be afraid to pause your air fryer often to open the drawer and check foods. That's the best way to save dinner before it overcooks or burns.

Minimum Temperatures for Food Safety

Consuming raw or undercooked eggs, fish, game, meats, poultry, seafood, or shellfish may increase your risk of foodborne illness. To ensure that foods are safe to eat, ground beef, lamb, pork, and veal should be cooked to a minimum of 160°F. Other cuts of these meats such as beef steaks should be cooked to at least 145°F. All turkey and chicken should be cooked to a minimum of 165°F. Minimum safe temperatures

for fish and seafood can vary, and you can find complete information about these foods and more at https://www.foodsafety.gov/keep/charts/mintemp.html.

Cooking in Batches

For best results, always cut foods into uniform pieces so they cook more evenly. Follow recipes to know whether foods can be stacked or must cook in a single layer. Directions will indicate whether you need to turn or shake the basket to redistribute foods during cooking. All recipes developed for this cookbook were tested in air fryers with an interior capacity of approximately 3 quarts. Using these "standard"-size air fryers often requires cooking in two batches, but many foods cook so quickly that this additional cooking time doesn't matter.

For foods that require lengthy cooking time, the first batch may cool too much while the second batch is cooking, but the solution is simple. Air fryers do an excellent job of reheating foods. Right before your second batch finishes cooking, place your first batch on top so it reheats for serving. If there's not enough room in your air fryer basket, wait until the second batch is done, remove it, and reheat the first batch for a minute or two. Keep this strategy in mind any time you need to heat up leftovers. They come out hot and crispy—unlike microwave-reheated foods, which can feel soggy, rubbery, or tough.

You can also buy a larger air fryer. Some models have a capacity of approximately 5 quarts. If you have an air fryer of this size, you may be able to cook many of our recipes in a single batch. Follow recipe instructions as to whether a particular food can be crowded or stacked, and fill the basket accordingly. You may need to adjust recipe times slightly, but after cooking a few recipes, you'll know how to judge that.

Smoking

Select a suitable location for your unit. If possible, place it near your range so you can use the vent hood if needed. Follow the manufacturer's instructions to protect your countertop and to allow the required amount of open space around the back, sides, and top of your air fryer. Smoking isn't a frequent problem but does occur when cooking meats or other foods with a high fat content. Adding water to the air fryer drawer can help sometimes but not always. Coconut, for example, tends to smoke no matter what. An accumulation of grease in the bottom of your air fryer can also cause smoking. Prevent this problem by keeping the drawer clean and free of food or fat buildup.

Excessive smoking, especially black smoke, is not normal. This could result from an electrical malfunction, in which case unplug your appliance immediately and contact the manufacturer.

Terms & Techniques

Using an air fryer isn't complicated, but for most people it's a completely new method of cooking. The information below will help clarify the commonly used terms and techniques in our recipes.

Baking Pan

All baked goods in this cookbook were tested using a 6 x 6 x 3-inch baking pan. You can use any ovenproof dish that fits in your air fryer, but plan ahead. When the food is done, how are you going to remove the dish from the air fryer basket without burning yourself? You can fashion one from folded aluminum foil, but it's easier and safer to buy a pan with a handle. Some pans are rather pricey but well worth the investment so you can enjoy air fryer cooking to the fullest.

Cooking Spray

In addition to Oil for Misting (see page xiii), this is another option for adding a light coating of oil to foods. Cooking sprays are convenient, they nicely prevent food from sticking in your air fryer basket or baking pan, and they're a good choice for misting delicate foods when even extra-light olive oil would add unwanted flavor.

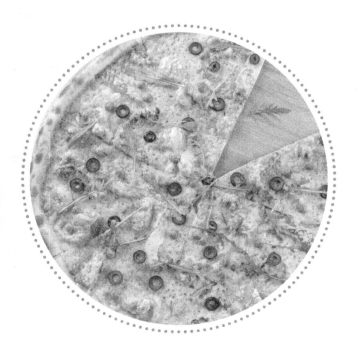

Dredging Station

This assembly line setup makes quick work of breading foods for air fryer cooking. Depending on the recipe, you'll need two or three shallow containers lined up on the counter in the order in which you plan to dip foods. For example, you may have flour in one dish, a beaten egg in a second dish, and breadcrumbs in a third. Proper organization speeds up the coating process. Dredging stations appear in recipes throughout this cookbook, but for convenience we include specific instructions in each recipe.

Food-Grade Gloves

Occasionally our recipes instruct you to mix by hand because that's the best—and sometimes only—way to accomplish certain tasks. You can buy disposable food-grade gloves from restaurant supply stores and numerous vendors online. Poly gloves aren't great because they fit loosely and are less flexible. We prefer powder-free, food-grade vinyl or latex with a snug fit. Gloves are a necessity for handling hot peppers because the oils can cause chemical burns when transferred from bare fingers to eyes.

Muffin Cups

Each recipe indicates which kind of muffin papers to use. With very liquid batters, foil muffin cups hold up better. You may even need to double or triple them. In that case, remove the paper liners, stack two or three foil cups together, and then mist with oil if the recipe requires it. You also can use oven-safe silicone muffin cups, which are sturdy enough to hold most fillings without losing shape while cooking.

Oil for Misting

Most of the time we use a pump-style oil sprayer. It's easy to use and works well whether you need a heavy coating or just a light mist. Refillable oil misters also help reduce the number of cans that end up in landfills. In our misters, we use extra-light olive oil. It has a higher smoke point than extra-virgin olive oil, and it has a very mild taste that won't interfere with other seasonings or overpower the flavor of your foods (except some sweets or very mildly flavored dishes). You can use a pastry brush in a pinch, but we don't recommend it because you'll end up using far more oil than necessary.

Breakfast & Brunch Recipes

Sausage Quiche
Servings: 4 | Cooking Time: 35 Minutes
- 12 large eggs
- 1 cup heavy cream
- 1 tsp black pepper
- 12 oz sugar-free breakfast sausage
- 2 cups shredded cheddar cheese

1. Preheat your fryer to 375°F/190°C.
2. In a large bowl, whisk the eggs, heavy cream, salad and pepper together.
3. Add the breakfast sausage and cheddar cheese.
4. Pour the mixture into a greased casserole dish.
5. Bake for 25 minutes.
6. Cut into 12 squares and serve hot.

Easy & Tasty Salsa Chicken
Servings: 4 | Cooking Time: 30 Minutes
- 1 lb chicken thighs, boneless and skinless
- 1 cup salsa
- Pepper
- Salt

1. Preheat the air fryer to 350 F.
2. Place chicken thighs into the air fryer baking dish and season with pepper and salt. Top with salsa.
3. Place in the air fryer and cook for 30 minutes.
4. Serve and enjoy.

Black's Bangin' Casserole
Servings: 4 | Cooking Time: 40 Minutes
- 5 eggs
- 3 tbsp chunky tomato sauce
- 2 tbsp heavy cream
- 2 tbsp grated parmesan cheese

1. Preheat your fryer to 350°F/175°C.
2. Combine the eggs and cream in a bowl.
3. Mix in the tomato sauce and add the cheese.
4. Spread into a glass baking dish and bake for 25-35 minutes.
5. Top with extra cheese.
6. Enjoy!

Eggplant Spread
Servings: 4 | Cooking Time: 20 Minutes
- 3 eggplants
- Salt and black pepper to the taste
- 2 tablespoons chives, chopped
- 2 tablespoons olive oil
- 2 teaspoons sweet paprika

1. Put the eggplants in your air fryer's basket and cook them for 20 minutes at 380 degrees F. Peel the eggplants, put them in a blender, add the rest of the ingredients, pulse well, divide into bowls and serve for breakfast.

Parsley Omelet
Servings: 4 | Cooking Time: 15 Minutes
- 4 eggs, whisked
- 1 tablespoon parsley, chopped
- ½ teaspoons cheddar cheese, shredded
- 1 avocado, peeled, pitted and cubed
- Cooking spray

1. In a bowl, mix all the ingredients except the cooking spray and whisk well. Grease a baking pan that fits the Air Fryer with the cooking spray, pour the omelet mix, spread, introduce the pan in the machine and cook at 370 degrees F for 15 minutes. Serve for breakfast.

Egg Muffins
Servings: 4 | Cooking Time: 11 Minutes
- 4 eggs
- salt and pepper
- olive oil
- 4 English muffins, split
- 1 cup shredded Colby Jack cheese
- 4 slices ham or Canadian bacon

1. Preheat air fryer to 390°F.
2. Beat together eggs and add salt and pepper to taste. Spray air fryer baking pan lightly with oil and add eggs. Cook for 2minutes, stir, and continue cooking for 4minutes, stirring every minute, until eggs are scrambled to your preference. Remove pan from air fryer.
3. Place bottom halves of English muffins in air fryer basket. Take half of the shredded cheese and divide it among the muffins. Top each with a slice of ham and one-quarter of the eggs. Sprinkle remaining cheese on top of the eggs. Use a fork to press the cheese into the egg a little so it doesn't slip off before it melts.
4. Cook at 360°F for 1 minute. Add English muffin tops and cook for 4minutes to heat through and toast the muffins.

Breakfast Chimichangas
Servings: 4 | Cooking Time: 8 Minutes
- Four 8-inch flour tortillas
- ½ cup canned refried beans
- 1 cup scrambled eggs
- ½ cup grated cheddar or Monterey jack cheese
- 1 tablespoon vegetable oil
- 1 cup salsa

1. Lay the flour tortillas out flat on a cutting board. In the center of each tortilla, spread 2 tablespoons refried beans. Next, add ¼ cup eggs and 2 tablespoons cheese to each tortilla.
2. To fold the tortillas, begin on the left side and fold to the center. Then fold the right side into the center. Next fold the bottom and top down and roll over to completely seal the chimichanga. Using a pastry brush or oil mister, brush the tops of the tortilla packages with oil.
3. Preheat the air fryer to 400°F for 4 minutes. Place the chimichangas into the air fryer basket, seam side down, and air fry for 4 minutes. Using tongs, turn over the chimichangas and cook for an additional 2 to 3 minutes or until light golden brown.

Scotch Eggs
Servings: 6 | Cooking Time: 15 Minutes
- 1 pound ground pork breakfast sausage
- 6 large hard-boiled eggs, peeled
- 1 cup all-purpose flour
- 2 large eggs, beaten
- 2 cups plain bread crumbs

1. Preheat the air fryer to 375°F.
2. Separate sausage into six equal amounts and flatten into patties.
3. Form sausage patties around hard-boiled eggs, completely enclosing them.
4. In three separate small bowls, place flour, eggs, and bread crumbs.
5. Roll each sausage-covered egg first in flour, then egg, and finally bread crumbs. Place rolled eggs in the air fryer basket and spritz them with cooking spray.
6. Cook 15 minutes, turning halfway through cooking time and spraying any dry spots with additional cooking spray. Serve warm.

Lemon Butter Artichokes
Servings: 4 | Cooking Time: 15 Minutes
- 2 medium artichokes, trimmed and halved
- 2 tbsp fresh lemon juice
- 1 tbsp butter, melted
- Pepper
- Salt

1. Place artichokes into the air fryer basket. Drizzle with butter and lemon juice and season with pepper and salt.
2. Cook at 380 F for 15 minutes.
3. Serve and enjoy.

Strawberry Rhubarb Parfait
Servings: 1 | Cooking Time: 1-2 Days
- 1 package crème fraîche or plain full-fat yogurt (8.5 oz)
- 2 tbsp toasted flakes
- 2 tbsp toasted coconut flakes
- 6 tbsp homemade strawberry and rhubarb jam (4.25 oz)

1. Add the jam into a dessert bowl (3 tbsp per serving).
2. Add the crème fraîche and garnish with the toasted and coconut flakes.
3. Serve!

Herb Carrots
Servings: 4 | Cooking Time: 20 Minutes
- 1 lb baby carrots, trimmed
- 1 tsp herb de Provence
- Pepper
- 2 tbsp fresh lime juice
- 2 tsp olive oil
- Salt

1. Add carrots into the bowl and toss with remaining ingredients.
2. Transfer carrots into the air fryer basket and cook at 320 F for 20 minutes.
3. Serve and enjoy.

Strawberry Pastry
Servings: 8 | Cooking Time: 15 Minutes Per Batch
- 1 package refrigerated piecrust
- 1 large egg, whisked
- 2 tablespoons whole milk
- 1 cup strawberry jam
- ½ cup confectioners' sugar
- ½ teaspoon vanilla extract

Directions:
1. Preheat the air fryer to 320°F. Cut parchment paper to fit the air fryer basket.
2. On a lightly floured surface, lay piecrusts out flat. Cut each piecrust round into six 4" × 3" rectangles, reserving excess dough.
3. Form remaining dough into a ball, then roll out and cut four additional 4" × 3" rectangles, bringing the total to sixteen.
4. For each pastry, spread 2 tablespoons jam on a pastry rectangle, leaving a 1" border around the edges. Top with a second pastry rectangle and use a fork to gently press all four edges together. Repeat with remaining jam and pastry.
5. Brush tops of each pastry with egg and cut an X in the center of each to prevent excess steam from building up.
6. Place pastries on parchment in the air fryer basket, working in batches as necessary. Cook 12 minutes, then carefully flip and cook an additional 3 minutes until each side is golden brown. Let cool 10 minutes.
7. In a small bowl, whisk confectioners' sugar, milk, and vanilla. Brush each pastry with glaze, then place in the refrigerator 5 minutes to set before serving.

Buttered Eggs In Hole
Servings: 2 | Cooking Time: 11 Minutes
- 2 eggs
- Salt and pepper to taste
- 2 tbsp butter

1. Place a heatproof bowl in the fryer's basket and brush with butter. Make a hole in the middle of the bread slices with a bread knife and place in the heatproof bowl in 2 batches. Break an egg into the center of each hole. Season with salt and pepper. Close the air fryer and cook for 4 minutes at 330 F. Turn the bread with a spatula and cook for another 4 minutes. Serve as a breakfast accompaniment.

Chives Spinach Frittata
Servings: 4 | Cooking Time: 20 Minutes
- 1 tablespoon chives, chopped
- 8 ounces spinach, torn
- 6 eggs, whisked
- 1 eggplant, cubed
- Cooking spray
- Salt and black pepper to the taste

1. In a bowl, mix the eggs with the rest of the ingredients except the cooking spray and whisk well. Grease a pan that fits your air fryer with the cooking spray, pour the frittata mix, spread and put the pan in the machine. Cook at 380 degrees F for 20 minutes, divide between plates and serve for breakfast.

Soppressata Pizza
Servings: 2 | Cooking Time: 15 Minutes
- 1 tbsp dried oregano
- 1/3 cup mozzarella cheese
- 4 basil leaves
- ½ cup passata
- 4 oz soppressata, chopped

1. Preheat the Air fryer to 380 F. Grease the air fryer basket with cooking spray.
2. Spread the passata over the pizza crust, sprinkle with oregano, mozzarella cheese and finish with soppressata. Transfer to the air fryer basket and cook for 10 minutes. Top with basil leaves to serve.

Eggs & Tomatoes Scramble
Servings: 4 | Cooking Time: 9 Minutes
- ¾ cup milk
- 4 eggs
- Salt and freshly ground black pepper
- 8 grape tomatoes, halved
- ½ cup Parmesan cheese, grated

1. Set the temperature of Air Fryer to 355 degrees F. Grease an Air Fryer pan with cooking spray.
2. In a bowl, mix together the milk, eggs, salt, and black pepper.
3. Transfer the egg mixture into the prepared pan.
4. Air Fry for about 6 minutes until the edges begin to set.
5. With a wooden spatula, stir the egg mixture.
6. Top with the tomatoes and Air Fry for about 3 minutes or until the eggs are done.
7. Serve warm with the topping of cheese.

Strawberry Toast
Servings: 4 | Cooking Time: 8 Minutes
- 4 slices bread, ½-inch thick
- 1 cup sliced strawberries
- butter-flavored cooking spray
- 1 teaspoon sugar

1. Spray one side of each bread slice with butter-flavored cooking spray. Lay slices sprayed side down.
2. Divide the strawberries among the bread slices.
3. Sprinkle evenly with the sugar and place in the air fryer basket in a single layer.
4. Cook at 390°F for 8 minutes. The bottom should look brown and crisp and the top should look glazed.

Breakfast Tea
Servings: 1 | Cooking Time: 5 Minutes
- 16 oz water
- 1 tbsp ghee
- ½ tsp vanilla extract
- 2 tea bags
- 1 tbsp coconut oil

1. Make the tea and put it to one aside.
2. In a bowl, melt the ghee.
3. Add the coconut oil and vanilla to the melted ghee.
4. Pour the tea from a cup into a Nutribullet cup.
5. Screw on the lid and blend thoroughly.

Peppers Cups
Servings: 12 | Cooking Time: 12 Minutes
- 6 green bell peppers
- ½ teaspoon ground black pepper
- 12 egg
- ½ teaspoon chili flakes

1. Cut the green bell peppers into halves and remove the seeds. Then crack the eggs in every bell pepper half and sprinkle with ground black pepper and chili flakes. After this, preheat the air fryer to 395F. Put the green bell pepper halves in the air fryer (cook for 2-3 halves per one time of cooking). Cook the egg peppers for 4 minutes. Repeat the same steps with remaining egg peppers.

Parmesan Breakfast Casserole
Servings: 3 | Cooking Time: 20 Minutes
- 5 eggs
- 2 tbsp heavy cream
- 3 tbsp chunky tomato sauce
- 2 tbsp parmesan cheese, grated

1. Preheat the air fryer to 325 F.
2. In mixing bowl, combine together cream and eggs.
3. Add cheese and tomato sauce and mix well.
4. Spray air fryer baking dish with cooking spray.
5. Pour mixture into baking dish and place in the air fryer basket.
6. Cook for 20 minutes.
7. Serve and enjoy.

Air Fryer Bacon
Servings: 6 | Cooking Time: 9 Minutes
- 6 bacon strips
- ½ tablespoon olive oil

1. Preheat the Air fryer to 350 o F and grease an Air fryer basket with olive oil.
2. Cook for about 9 minutes and flip the bacon.
3. Cook for 3 more minutes until crispy and serve warm.

Garlic-cheese Biscuits
Servings: 8 | Cooking Time: 8 Minutes
- 1 cup self-rising flour
- 1 teaspoon garlic powder
- 2 tablespoons butter, diced
- 2 ounces sharp Cheddar cheese, grated
- ½ cup milk
- cooking spray

1. Preheat air fryer to 330°F.
2. Combine flour and garlic in a medium bowl and stir together.
3. Using a pastry blender or knives, cut butter into dry ingredients.
4. Stir in cheese.
5. Add milk and stir until stiff dough forms.
6. If dough is too sticky to handle, stir in 1 or 2 more tablespoons of self-rising flour before shaping. Biscuits should be firm enough to hold their shape. Otherwise, they'll stick to the air fryer basket.
7. Divide dough into 8 portions and shape into 2-inch biscuits about ¾-inch thick.
8. Spray air fryer basket with nonstick cooking spray.
9. Place all 8 biscuits in basket and cook at 330°F for 8 minutes.

Tuna And Arugula Salad
Servings: 4 | Cooking Time: 15 Minutes
- ½ pound smoked tuna, flaked
- 2 spring onions, chopped
- A pinch of salt and black pepper
- 1 cup arugula
- 1 tablespoon olive oil

1. In a bowl, all the ingredients except the oil and the arugula and whisk. Preheat the Air Fryer over 360 degrees F, add the oil and grease it. Pour the tuna mix, stir well, and cook for 15 minutes. In a salad bowl, combine the arugula with the tuna mix, toss and serve for breakfast.

Simple Egg Soufflé
Servings: 2 | Cooking Time: 8 Minutes
- 2 eggs
- 2 tbsp heavy cream
- 1 tbsp parsley, chopped
- 1/4 tsp chili pepper
- 1/4 tsp pepper
- Salt

1. In a bowl, whisk eggs with remaining gradients.
2. Spray two ramekins with cooking spray.
3. Pour egg mixture into the prepared ramekins and place into the air fryer basket.
4. Cook soufflé at 390 F for 8 minutes.
5. Serve and enjoy.

Cheesy Sausage Sticks
Servings: 3 | Cooking Time: 8 Minutes
- 6 small pork sausages
- ½ cup Mozzarella cheese, shredded
- 1 tablespoon mascarpone
- ½ cup almond flour
- 2 eggs, beaten
- Cooking spray

1. Pierce the hot dogs with wooden coffee sticks to get the sausages on the sticks". Then in the bowl mix up almond flour, Mozzarella cheese, and mascarpone. Microwave the mixture for 15 seconds or until you get a melted mixture. Then stir the egg in the cheese mixture and whisk it until smooth. Coat every sausage stick in the cheese mixture. Then preheat the air fryer to 375F. Spray the air fryer basket with cooking spray. Place the sausage stock in the air fryer and cook them for 4 minutes from each side or until they are light brown.

Hash Brown

Servings: 2 | Cooking Time: 20 Minutes
- 12 oz grated fresh cauliflower (about ½ a medium-sized head)
- 4 slices bacon, chopped
- 3 oz onion, chopped
- 1 tbsp butter, softened

1. In a skillet, sauté the bacon and onion until brown.
2. Add in the cauliflower and stir until tender and browned.
3. Add the butter steadily as it cooks.
4. Season to taste with salt and pepper.
5. Enjoy!

Cinnamon Flavored Grilled Pineapples

Servings: 2 | Cooking Time: 15 Minutes
- 5 pineapple slices
- ½ cup brown sugar
- 1 tbsp basil, chopped for garnish
- 1 tbsp honey, for garnish

1. Preheat your air fryer to 340 F. In a small bowl, mix brown sugar and cinnamon. Drizzle the sugar mixture over your pineapple slices and set aside for 20 minutes. Place the pineapple rings in the air fryer cooking basket and cook for 10 minutes. Flip the pineapples and cook for 10 minutes more. Serve with basil and a drizzle of honey.

Air Fryer Sausage

Servings: 5 | Cooking Time: 20 Minutes
- 5 raw and uncooked sausage links
- 1 tablespoon olive oil

1. Preheat the Air fryer to 360 o F and grease an Air fryer basket with olive oil.
2. Cook for about 15 minutes and flip the sausages.
3. Cook for 5 more minutes and serve warm.

Mozzarella Rolls

Servings: 6 | Cooking Time: 6 Minutes
- 6 wonton wrappers
- 1 tablespoon keto tomato sauce
- ½ cup Mozzarella, shredded
- 1 oz pepperoni, chopped
- 1 egg, beaten
- Cooking spray

1. In the big bowl mix up together shredded Mozzarella, pepperoni, and tomato sauce. When the mixture is homogenous transfer it on the wonton wraps. Wrap the wonton wraps in the shape of sticks. Then brush them with beaten eggs. Preheat the air fryer to 400F. Spray the air fryer basket with cooking spray. Put the pizza sticks in the air fryer and cook them for 3 minutes from each side.

Ham And Egg Toast Cups

Servings: 2 | Cooking Time: 5 Minutes
- 2 eggs
- 2 slices of ham
- 2 tablespoons butter
- Cheddar cheese, for topping
- Salt, to taste
- Black pepper, to taste

1. Preheat the Air fryer to 400 o F and grease both ramekins with melted butter.
2. Place each ham slice in the greased ramekins and crack each egg over ham slices.
3. Sprinkle with salt, black pepper and cheddar cheese and transfer into the Air fryer basket.
4. Cook for about 5 minutes and remove the ramekins from the basket.
5. Serve warm.

Bacon & Hot Dogs Omelet

Servings: 2 | Cooking Time: 10 Minutes
- 4 eggs
- 1 bacon slice, chopped
- 2 hot dogs, chopped
- 2 small onions, chopped

1. Set the temperature of Air Fryer to 320 degrees F.
2. In an Air Fryer baking pan, crack the eggs and beat them well.
3. Now, add in the remaining ingredients and gently, stir to combine.
4. Air Fry for about 10 minutes.
5. Serve hot.

Chocolate-hazelnut Bear Claws

Servings: 4 | Cooking Time: 10 Minutes
- 1 sheet frozen puff pastry dough, thawed
- 1 large egg, beaten
- ½ cup chocolate-hazelnut spread
- 1 tablespoon confectioners' sugar
- 1 tablespoon sliced almonds

1. Preheat the air fryer to 320°F.
2. Unfold puff pastry and cut into four equal squares.
3. Brush egg evenly over puff pastry.
4. To make each bear claw, spread 2 tablespoons chocolate-hazelnut spread over a pastry square. Fold square horizontally to form a triangle and cut four evenly spaced slits about halfway through the top of folded square. Repeat with remaining spread and pastry squares.
5. Sprinkle confectioners' sugar and almonds over bear claws and place directly in the air fryer basket. Cook 10 minutes until puffy and golden brown. Serve warm.

Maple-bacon Doughnuts

Servings: 8 | Cooking Time: 5 Minutes
- 1 can refrigerated biscuit dough, separated
- 1 cup confectioners' sugar
- ¼ cup heavy cream
- 1 teaspoon maple extract
- 6 slices bacon, cooked and crumbled

1. Preheat the air fryer to 350°F.
2. Place biscuits in the air fryer basket and cook 5 minutes, turning halfway through cooking time, until golden brown. Let cool 5 minutes.
3. In a medium bowl, whisk together confectioners' sugar, cream, and maple extract until smooth.
4. Dip top of each doughnut into glaze and set aside to set for 5 minutes. Top with crumbled bacon and serve immediately.

Smoked Fried Tofu
Servings: 2 | Cooking Time: 22 Minutes
- 1 tofu block; pressed and cubed
- 1 tbsp. smoked paprika
- 1/4 cup cornstarch
- Salt and black pepper to the taste
- Cooking spray

1. Grease your air fryer's basket with cooking spray and heat the fryer at 370 degrees F.
2. In a bowl; mix tofu with salt, pepper, smoked paprika and cornstarch and toss well.
3. Add tofu to you air fryer's basket and cook for 12 minutes shaking the fryer every 4 minutes. Divide into bowls and serve for breakfast.

Grilled Tofu Sandwich
Servings: 1 | Cooking Time: 20 Minutes
- 1 1-inch thick Tofu slice
- 2 tsp olive oil divided
- Salt and pepper, to taste
- ¼ cup red cabbage, shredded
- ¼ tsp vinegar

1. Preheat the air fryer to 350 F, add in the bread slices and toast for 3 minutes; set aside. Brush the tofu with 1 tsp oil and place in the air fryer; grill for 5 minutes on each side. Combine the cabbage, remaining oil, and vinegar, and season with salt and pepper. Place the tofu on top of one bread slice, place the cabbage over, and top with the other bread slice. Serve and enjoy.

Paprika Cauliflower Bake
Servings: 4 | Cooking Time: 20 Minutes
- 2 cups cauliflower florets, separated
- 4 eggs, whisked
- 1 teaspoon sweet paprika
- 2 tablespoons butter, melted
- A pinch of salt and black pepper

1. Heat up your air fryer at 320 degrees F, grease with the butter, add cauliflower florets on the bottom, then add eggs whisked with paprika, salt and pepper, toss and cook for 20 minutes. Divide between plates and serve for breakfast.

Paprika Zucchini Spread
Servings: 4 | Cooking Time: 15 Minutes
- 4 zucchinis, roughly chopped
- 1 tablespoon sweet paprika
- Salt and black pepper to the taste
- 1 tablespoon butter, melted

1. Grease a baking pan that fits the Air Fryer with the butter, add all the ingredients, toss, and cook at 360 degrees F for 15 minutes. Transfer to a blender, pulse well, divide into bowls and serve for breakfast.

Mushroom Leek Frittata
Servings: 4 | Cooking Time: 32 Minutes
- 6 eggs
- 1 cup leeks, sliced
- 6 oz mushrooms, sliced
- Salt

1. Preheat the air fryer to 325 F.
2. Spray air fryer baking dish with cooking spray and set aside.
3. Heat another pan over medium heat. Spray pan with cooking spray.
4. Add mushrooms, leeks, and salt in a pan sauté for 6 minutes.
5. Break eggs in a bowl and whisk well.
6. Transfer sautéed mushroom and leek mixture into the prepared baking dish.
7. Pour egg over mushroom mixture.
8. Place dish in the air fryer and cook for 32 minutes.
9. Serve and enjoy.

Lemon Dill Scallops
Servings: 4 | Cooking Time: 5 Minutes
- 1 lb scallops
- 1 tsp dill, chopped
- Pepper
- 2 tsp olive oil
- 1 tbsp fresh lemon juice
- Salt

1. Add scallops into the bowl and toss with oil, dill, lemon juice, pepper, and salt.
2. Add scallops into the air fryer basket and cook at 360 F for 5 minutes.
3. Serve and enjoy.

Chi Spacca's Bistecca
Servings: 4 | Cooking Time: 45 Minutes
- 2 pounds bone-in rib eye steak
- 1 packet Italian herb mix
- Salt and pepper to taste
- 1 tablespoon olive oil

1. Preheat the air fryer at 3900F.
2. Place the grill pan accessory in the air fryer.
3. Season the steak with salt, pepper, Italian herb mix, and olive oil. Cover top with foil.
4. Grill for 45 minutes and flip the steak halfway through the cooking time.

Crust-less Quiche
Servings: 2 | Cooking Time: 30 Minutes
- 4 eggs
- ½ cup tomatoes, chopped
- 1 cup Gouda cheese, shredded
- ¼ cup onion, chopped
- ½ cup milk
- Salt, to taste

1. Preheat the Air fryer to 340 oF and grease 2 ramekins lightly.
2. Mix together all the ingredients in a ramekin until well combined.
3. Place in the Air fryer and cook for about 30 minutes.
4. Dish out and serve.

Bread Cups Omelette
Servings: 4 | Cooking Time: 25 Minutes
- 5 eggs, beaten
- A pinch of salt
- ½ tsp thyme, dried
- 3 strips precooked bacon, chopped
- 2 tbsp heavy cream
- 4 Gouda cheese mini wedges, thin slices

1. Preheat your air fryer 330 F. Cut the tops off the rolls and remove the inside with your fingers. Line the rolls with a slice of cheese and press down, so the cheese conforms to the inside of the roll. In a bowl, mix eggs with heavy cream, bacon, thyme, salt and pepper.
2. Stuff the rolls with the egg mixture. Lay the rolls in your air fryer's cooking basket and bake for 8 to 12 minutes or until the eggs become puffy and the roll shows a golden brown texture.

Breakfast Sausage Casserole
Servings: 4 | Cooking Time: 50 Minutes
- 8 eggs, beaten
- 1 head chopped cauliflower
- 1 lb sausage, cooked and crumbled
- 2 cups heavy whipping cream
- 1 cup sharp cheddar cheese, grated

1. Cook the sausage as usual.
2. In a large bowl, mix the sausage, heavy whipping cream, chopped cauliflower, cheese and eggs.
3. Pour into a greased casserole dish.
4. Cook for 45 minutes at 350°F/175°C, or until firm.
5. Top with cheese and serve.

Rice Paper Bacon
Servings: 4 | Cooking Time: 30 Minutes
- 3 tbsp. soy sauce or tamari
- 2 tbsp. cashew butter
- 2 tbsp. liquid smoke
- 2 tbsp. water
- 4 pc white rice paper, cut into 1-inch thick strips

1. Pre-heat your Air Fryer at 350°F.
2. Mix together the soy sauce/tamari, liquid smoke, water, and cashew butter in a large bowl.
3. Take the strips of rice paper and soak them for 5 minutes. Arrange in one layer in the bottom of your fryer.
4. Cook for 15 minutes, ensuring they become crispy, before serving with some vegetables.

Almond Pesto Salmon
Servings: 2 | Cooking Time: 12 Minutes
- 2 salmon fillets
- 2 tbsp butter, melted
- ¼ cup pesto
- ¼ cup almond, ground

1. Mix together pesto and almond.
2. Brush salmon fillets with melted butter and place into the air fryer baking dish.
3. Top salmon fillets with pesto and almond mixture.
4. Place dish in the air fryer and cook at 390 F for 12 minutes.
5. Serve and enjoy.

Egg Porridge
Servings: 1 | Cooking Time: 15 Minutes
- 2 organic free-range eggs
- 1/3 cup organic heavy cream without food additives
- 2 packages of your preferred sweetener
- 2 tbsp grass-fed butter ground organic cinnamon to taste

1. In a bowl add the eggs, cream and sweetener, and mix together.
2. Melt the butter in a saucepan over a medium heat. Lower the heat once the butter is melted.
3. Combine together with the egg and cream mixture.
4. While Cooking, mix until it thickens and curdles.
5. When you see the first signs of curdling, remove the saucepan immediately from the heat.
6. Pour the porridge into a bowl. Sprinkle cinnamon on top and serve immediately.

Spanish Omelet
Servings: 2 | Cooking Time: 15 Minutes
- 3 eggs
- Cayenne or black pepper
- ½ cup finely chopped vegetables of your choosing.

1. In a pan on high heat, stir-fry the vegetables in extra virgin olive oil until lightly crispy.
2. Cook the eggs with one tablespoon of water and a pinch of pepper.
3. When almost cooked, top with the vegetables and flip to cook briefly.
4. Serve

Medium Rare Simple Salt And Pepper Steak
Servings: 3 | Cooking Time: 30 Minutes
- 1 ½ pounds skirt steak
- Salt and pepper to taste

1. Preheat the air fryer at 3900F.
2. Place the grill pan accessory in the air fryer.
3. Season the skirt steak with salt and pepper.
4. Place on the grill pan and cook for 15 minutes per batch.
5. Flip the meat halfway through the cooking time.

Mushroom Frittata
Servings: 1 | Cooking Time: 13 Minutes
- 1 cup egg whites
- 1 cup spinach, chopped
- 2 mushrooms, sliced
- 2 tbsp parmesan cheese, grated
- Salt

1. Spray pan with cooking spray and heat over medium heat.
2. Add mushrooms and sauté for 2-3 minutes. Add spinach and cook for 1-2 minutes or until wilted.
3. Transfer mushroom spinach mixture into the air fryer pan.
4. Whisk egg whites in a mixing bowl until frothy. Season with a pinch of salt.
5. Pour egg white mixture into the spinach and mushroom mixture and sprinkle with parmesan cheese.
6. Place pan in air fryer basket and cook frittata at 350 F for 8 minutes.
7. Slice and serve.

Sausage Solo
Servings: 4 | Cooking Time: 22 Minutes
- 6 eggs
- 4 cooked sausages, sliced
- 2 bread slices, cut into sticks
- ½ cup mozzarella cheese, grated
- ½ cup cream

1. Preheat the Air fryer to 355 o F and grease 4 ramekins lightly.
2. Whisk together eggs and cream in a bowl and beat well.
3. Transfer the egg mixture into ramekins and arrange the bread sticks and sausage slices around the edges.
4. Top with mozzarella cheese evenly and place the ramekins in Air fryer basket.
5. Cook for about 22 minutes and dish out to serve warm.

Bacon And Hot Dogs Omelet

Servings: 2 | Cooking Time: 10 Minutes

- 4 eggs
- 1 bacon slice, chopped
- 2 hot dogs, chopped
- 2 small onions, chopped
- 2 tablespoons milk
- Salt and black pepper, to taste

1. Preheat the Air fryer to 325 o F and grease an Air Fryer pan.
2. Whisk together eggs and stir in the remaining ingredients.
3. Stir well to combine and place in the Air fryer.
4. Cook for about 10 minutes and serve hot.

Taj Tofu

Servings: 4 | Cooking Time: 40 Minutes

- 1 block firm tofu, pressed and cut into 1-inch thick cubes
- 2 tbsp. soy sauce
- 2 tsp. sesame seeds, toasted
- 1 tsp. rice vinegar
- 1 tbsp. cornstarch

1. Set your Air Fryer at 400°F to warm.
2. Add the tofu, soy sauce, sesame seeds and rice vinegar in a bowl together and mix well to coat the tofu cubes. Then cover the tofu in cornstarch and put it in the basket of your fryer.
3. Cook for 25 minutes, giving the basket a shake at five-minute intervals to ensure the tofu cooks evenly.

Breakfast Sandwich

Servings: 1 | Cooking Time: 10 Minutes

- 1 English muffin
- 2 slices of bacon
- Salt and pepper, to taste

1. Preheat air fryer to 395 F. Crack the egg into a ramekin. Place the muffin, egg and bacon in air fryer. Cook for 6 minutes. Let cool slightly. Cut the muffin in half. Place the egg on one half and season with salt and pepper. Arrange the bacon on top. Top with the other muffin half.

Coconut Berries Bowls

Servings: 4 | Cooking Time: 15 Minutes

- 1 and ½ cups coconut milk
- ½ cup blackberries
- 2 teaspoon stevia
- ½ cup coconut, shredded

1. In your air fryer's pan, mix all the ingredients, stir, cover and cook at 360 degrees F for 15 minutes. Divide into bowls and serve for breakfast.

Easy Egg Bites

Servings: 2 | Cooking Time: 9 Minutes

- 2 large eggs
- ¼ cup full-fat cottage cheese
- ¼ cup shredded sharp Cheddar cheese
- ¼ teaspoon salt
- ⅛ teaspoon ground black pepper
- 6 tablespoons diced cooked ham

1. Preheat the air fryer to 300°F. Spray six silicone muffin cups with cooking spray.
2. In a blender, place eggs, cottage cheese, Cheddar, salt, and pepper. Pulse five times until smooth and frothy.
3. Place 1 tablespoon ham in the bottom of each prepared baking cup, then divide egg mixture among cups.
4. Place in the air fryer basket and cook 9 minutes until egg bites are firm in the center. Carefully remove cups from air fryer basket and cool 3 minutes before serving. Serve warm.

Yummy Ham Rolls

Servings: 4 | Cooking Time: 20 Minutes

- 1 sheet puff pastry
- 4 handful gruyere cheese; grated
- 8 ham slices; chopped
- 4 tsp. mustard

1. Roll out puff pastry on a working surface, divide cheese, ham and mustard, roll tight and cut into medium rounds.
2. Place all rolls in air fryer and cook for 10 minutes at 370 degrees F. Divide rolls on plates and serve for breakfast.

Green Beans Salad

Servings: 4 | Cooking Time: 20 Minutes

- 2 cups green beans, cut into medium pieces
- 2 cups tomatoes, cubed
- Salt and black pepper to the taste
- 1 teaspoon hot paprika
- 1 tablespoons cilantro, chopped
- Cooking spray

1. In a bowl, mix all the ingredients except the cooking spray and the cilantro and whisk them well. Grease a pan that fits the air fryer with the cooking spray, pour the green beans and tomatoes mix into the pan, sprinkle the cilantro on top, put the pan into the machine and cook at 360 degrees F for 20 minutes. Serve right away.

All-in-one Breakfast Toast

Servings: 1 | Cooking Time: 10 Minutes

- 1 strip of bacon, diced
- 1 slice of 1-inch thick bread (such as Texas Toast or hand-sliced bread)
- 1 tablespoon softened butter (optional)
- 1 egg
- salt and freshly ground black pepper
- ¼ cup grated Colby or Jack cheese

1. Preheat the air fryer to 400°F.
2. Air-fry the bacon for 3 minutes, shaking the basket once or twice while it cooks. Remove the bacon to a paper towel lined plate and set aside.
3. Use a sharp paring knife to score a large circle in the middle of the slice of bread, cutting halfway through, but not all the way through to the cutting board. Press down on the circle in the center of the bread slice to create an indentation. If using, spread the softened butter on the edges and in the hole of the bread.
4. Transfer the slice of bread, hole side up, to the air fryer basket. Crack the egg into the center of the bread, and season with salt and pepper.
5. Air-fry at 380°F for 5 minutes. Sprinkle the grated cheese around the edges of the bread leaving the center of the yolk uncovered, and top with the cooked bacon. Press the cheese and bacon into the bread lightly to help anchor it to the bread and prevent it from blowing around in the air fryer.
6. Air-fry for one or two more minutes (depending on how you like your egg cooked), just to melt the cheese and finish cooking the egg. Serve immediately.

Eggs Salad
Servings: 4 | Cooking Time: 10 Minutes
- 1 tablespoon lime juice
- 4 eggs, hard boiled, peeled and sliced
- 2 cups baby spinach
- Salt and black pepper to the taste
- 3 tablespoons heavy cream
- 2 tablespoons olive oil

1. In your Air Fryer, mix the spinach with cream, eggs, salt and pepper, cover and cook at 360 degrees F for 6 minutes. Transfer this to a bowl, add the lime juice and oil, toss and serve for breakfast.

Spinach Spread
Servings: 4 | Cooking Time: 10 Minutes
- 2 tablespoons coconut cream
- 3 cups spinach leaves
- 2 tablespoons cilantro
- 2 tablespoons bacon, cooked and crumbled
- Salt and black pepper to the taste

1. In a pan that fits the air fryer, combine all the ingredients except the bacon, put the pan in the machine and cook at 360 degrees F for 10 minutes. Transfer to a blender, pulse well, divide into bowls and serve with bacon sprinkled on top.

Mediterranean Egg Sandwich
Servings: 1 | Cooking Time: 8 Minutes
- 1 large egg
- 5 baby spinach leaves, chopped
- 1 tablespoon roasted bell pepper, chopped
- 1 English muffin
- 1 thin slice prosciutto or Canadian bacon

1. Spray a ramekin with cooking spray or brush the inside with extra-virgin olive oil.
2. In a small bowl, whisk together the egg, baby spinach, and bell pepper.
3. Split the English muffin in half and spray the inside lightly with cooking spray or brush with extra-virgin olive oil.
4. Preheat the air fryer to 350°F for 2 minutes. Place the egg ramekin and open English muffin into the air fryer basket, and cook at 350°F for 5 minutes. Open the air fryer drawer and add the prosciutto or bacon; cook for an additional 1 minute.
5. To assemble the sandwich, place the egg on one half of the English muffin, top with prosciutto or bacon, and place the remaining piece of English muffin on top.

Baked Eggs
Servings: 4 | Cooking Time: 6 Minutes
- 4 large eggs
- 1/8 teaspoon black pepper
- 1/8 teaspoon salt

1. Preheat the air fryer to 330°F. Place 4 silicone muffin liners into the air fryer basket.
2. Crack 1 egg at a time into each silicone muffin liner. Sprinkle with black pepper and salt.
3. Bake for 6 minutes. Remove and let cool 2 minutes prior to serving.

Sweet And Spicy Breakfast Sausage
Servings: 6 | Cooking Time: 10 Minutes
- 1 pound 84% lean ground pork
- 2 tablespoons brown sugar
- 1 teaspoon salt
- ½ teaspoon ground black pepper
- ½ teaspoon garlic powder
- ½ teaspoon dried fennel
- ½ teaspoon crushed red pepper flakes

1. Preheat the air fryer to 400°F.
2. In a large bowl, mix all ingredients until well combined. Divide mixture into eight portions and form into patties.
3. Spritz patties with cooking spray and place in the air fryer basket. Cook 10 minutes until patties are brown and internal temperature reaches at least 145°F. Serve warm.

Mozzarella Cups
Servings: 2 | Cooking Time: 6 Minutes
- 2 eggs
- 2 oz Mozzarella, grated
- 1 oz Parmesan, grated
- 1 teaspoon coconut oil, melted
- ¼ teaspoon chili powder

1. Crack the eggs and separate egg yolks and egg whites. Then whisk the egg whites till the soft peaks. Separately whisk the egg yolks until smooth and add chili powder. Then carefully add egg whites, Parmesan, and Mozzarella. Stir the ingredients. Brush the silicone egg molds with coconut oil. Then put the cheese-egg mixture in the molds with the help of the spoon. Transfer the molds in the air fryer and cook at 385F for 6 minutes.

Puffed Egg Tarts
Servings: 4 | Cooking Time: 42 Minutes
- 1 sheet frozen puff pastry half, thawed and cut into 4 squares
- ¾ cup Monterey Jack cheese, shredded and divided
- 4 large eggs
- 1 tablespoon fresh parsley, minced
- 1 tablespoon olive oil

1. Preheat the Air fryer to 390 o F
2. Place 2 pastry squares in the air fryer basket and cook for about 10 minutes.
3. Remove Air fryer basket from the Air fryer and press each square gently with a metal tablespoon to form an indentation.
4. Place 3 tablespoons of cheese in each hole and top with 1 egg each.
5. Return Air fryer basket to Air fryer and cook for about 11 minutes.
6. Remove tarts from the Air fryer basket and sprinkle with half the parsley.
7. Repeat with remaining pastry squares, cheese and eggs.
8. Dish out and serve warm.

Hash Browns
Servings: 2 | Cooking Time: 30 Minutes
- 2 large russet potatoes, peeled
- 1 tablespoon olive oil
- 2 cups cold water
- ½ teaspoon salt

1. Grate potatoes into a bowl filled with cold water. Let soak 10 minutes. Drain into a colander, then press into paper towels to remove excess moisture.

2. Dry the bowl and return potatoes to it. Toss with oil and salt.
3. Preheat the air fryer to 375°F. Spray a 6" round cake pan with cooking spray.
4. Pour potatoes into prepared pan, pressing them down.
5. Cook 20 minutes until brown and crispy. Serve warm.

Eggs, Mushrooms And Tomatoes Scramble

Servings: 4 | Cooking Time: 11 Minutes

- ¾ cup milk
- 4 eggs
- 8 grape tomatoes, halved
- ½ cup mushrooms, sliced
- 1 tablespoon chives, chopped
- Salt and black pepper, to taste

1. Preheat the Air fryer to 360 o F and grease an Air Fryer pan.
2. Whisk eggs with milk, salt, and black pepper in a bowl.
3. Transfer the egg mixture into the Air Fryer pan and cook for about 6 minutes.
4. Add mushrooms, grape tomatoes and chives and cook for about 5 minutes.
5. Dish out and serve warm.

Avocado Eggs

Servings: 4 | Cooking Time: 15 Minutes

- 2 large avocados, sliced
- 1 cup breadcrumbs
- ½ cup flour 2 eggs, beaten
- ¼ tsp. paprika
- Salt and pepper to taste

1. Pre-heat your Air Fryer at 400°F for 5 minutes.
2. Sprinkle some salt and pepper on the slices of avocado. Optionally, you can enhance the flavor with a half-tsp. of dried oregano.
3. Lightly coat the avocados with flour. Dredge them in the eggs, before covering with breadcrumbs. Transfer to the fryer and cook for 6 minutes.

Pineapple Cornbread

Servings: 5 | Cooking Time: 15 Minutes

- 1 (8½-ounces) package Jiffy corn muffin
- 7 ounces canned crushed pineapple
- 1/3 cup canned pineapple juice
- 1 egg

1. In a bowl, mix together all the ingredients.
2. Set the temperature of Air Fryer to 330 degrees F. Grease a round cake pan. (6"x 3")
3. Place the mixture evenly into the prepared pan.
4. Arrange the cake pan into an Air Fryer basket.
5. Air Fry for about 15 minutes or until a toothpick inserted in the center comes out clean.
6. Remove from Air Fryer and place the pan onto a wire rack for about 10-15 minutes.
7. Carefully, take out the bread from pan and put onto a wire rack until it is completely cool before slicing.
8. Cut the bread into desired size slices and serve.

Egg Baked Omelet

Servings: 1 | Cooking Time: 15 Minutes

- tbsp. ricotta cheese
- 1 tbsp. chopped parsley
- 1 tsp. olive oil
- 3 eggs
- ¼ cup chopped spinach
- Salt and pepper to taste

1. Set your Air Fryer at 330°F and allow to warm with the olive oil inside.
2. In a bowl, beat the eggs with a fork and sprinkle some salt and pepper as desired.
3. Add in the ricotta, spinach, and parsley and then transfer to the Air Fryer. Cook for 10 minutes before serving.

Olives Eggs

Servings: 4 | Cooking Time: 15 Minutes

- 1 cup kalamata olives, pitted and sliced
- 1 cup cherry tomatoes, cubed
- 4 eggs, whisked
- A pinch of salt and black pepper
- Cooking spray

1. Grease the air fryer with cooking spray, add all the ingredients, toss, cover and cook at 365 degrees F for 10 minutes. Divide between plates and serve for breakfast.

Chicken Bites

Servings: 4 | Cooking Time: 8 Minutes

- 1 cup ground chicken, cooked
- ½ cup Cheddar cheese, shredded
- 1 egg, beaten
- ½ teaspoon salt
- Cooking spray

1. Put ground chicken and Cheddar cheese in the bowl. Add egg and salt and mix up the ingredients until you get a homogenous mixture. Preheat the air fryer to 390F. Spray the air fryer basket with the cooking spray from inside. Then make the small bites with the help of the scooper and place them in the air fryer basket. Cook the chicken and cheese bites for 4 minutes and then flip them on another side. Cook the bites for 4 minutes more.

Pancakes

Servings: 2 | Cooking Time: 15 Minutes

- 2 tbsp coconut oil
- 1 tsp maple extract
- 2 tbsp cashew milk
- 2 eggs
- 2/3 oz/20g pork rinds

1. Grind up the pork rinds until fine and mix with the rest of the ingredients, except the oil.
2. Add the oil to a skillet. Add a quarter-cup of the batter and fry until golden on each side. Continue adding the remaining batter.

Egg & Mushroom Scramble

Servings: 2 | Cooking Time: 10 Minutes

- 4 eggs
- Salt and freshly ground black pepper, as needed
- 2 tablespoons unsalted butter
- ½ cup fresh mushrooms, finely chopped
- 2 tablespoons Parmesan cheese, shredded

1. Set the temperature of Air Fryer to 285 degrees F.
2. In a bowl, mix together the eggs, salt, and black pepper.
3. In a baking pan, melt the butter and tilt the pan to spread the butter in the bottom.
4. Add the beaten eggs and Air Fry for about 4-5 minutes
5. Add in the mushrooms and cheese and cook for 5 minutes, stirring occasionally.
6. Serve hot.

Cheesy Sandwich
Servings: 1 | Cooking Time:18 Minutes
- 2 bread slices
- 2 cheddar cheese slices
- 2 tsp. butter
- A pinch of sweet paprika

1. Spread butter on bread slices, add cheddar cheese on one, sprinkle paprika, top with the other bread slices, cut into 2 halves; arrange them in your air fryer and cook at 370 °F, for 8 minutes; flipping them once, arrange on a plate and serve.

Bacon Cups
Servings: 2 | Cooking Time: 40 Minutes
- 2 eggs
- 1 slice tomato
- 3 slices bacon
- 2 slices ham
- 2 tsp grated parmesan cheese

1. Preheat your fryer to 375°F/190°C.
2. Cook the bacon for half of the directed time.
3. Slice the bacon strips in half and line 2 greased muffin tins with 3 half-strips of bacon
4. Put one slice of ham and half slice of tomato in each muffin tin on top of the bacon
5. Crack one egg on top of the tomato in each muffin tin and sprinkle each with half a teaspoon of grated parmesan cheese.
6. Bake for 20 minutes.
7. Remove and let cool.
8. Serve!

Egg Muffin Sandwich
Servings: 1 | Cooking Time: 15 Minutes
- 1 egg
- 2 slices bacon
- 1 English muffin

1. Pre-heat your Air Fryer at 395°F
2. Take a ramekin and spritz it with cooking spray. Break an egg into the ramekin before transferring it to the basket of your fryer, along with the English muffin and bacon slices, keeping each component separate.
3. Allow to cook for 6 minutes. After removing from the fryer, allow to cool for around two minutes. Halve the muffin.
4. Create your sandwich by arranging the egg and bacon slices on the base and topping with the other half of the muffin.

Spicy Egg And Bacon Wraps
Servings:3 | Cooking Time: 15 Minutes
- 2 previously scrambled eggs
- 3 slices bacon, cut into strips
- 3 tbsp salsa
- 3 tbsp cream cheese, divided
- 1 cup grated pepper Jack cheese

1. Preheat air fryer to 390 F. Spread cream cheese onto tortillas. Divide the eggs and bacon between the tortillas. Top with salsa. Sprinkle some grated cheese over. Roll up the tortillas. Cook for 10 minutes.

Zucchini Squash Mix
Servings: 4 | Cooking Time: 35 Minutes
- 1 lb zucchini, sliced
- 1 tbsp parsley, chopped
- 1 yellow squash, halved, deseeded, and chopped
- 1 tbsp olive oil
- Pepper
- Salt

1. Add all ingredients into the large bowl and mix well.
2. Transfer bowl mixture into the air fryer basket and cook at 400 F for 35 minutes.
3. Serve and enjoy.

Mini Tomato Quiche
Servings:2 | Cooking Time:30 Minutes
- 4 eggs
- ½ cup tomatoes, chopped
- 1 cup Gouda cheese, shredded
- ¼ cup onion, chopped
- ½ cup milk
- Salt, to taste

1. Preheat the Air fryer to 340 o F and grease a large ramekin with cooking spray.
2. Mix together all the ingredients in a ramekin and transfer into the air fryer basket.
3. Cook for about 30 minutes and dish out to serve hot.

Avocado And Cabbage Salad
Servings: 4 | Cooking Time: 15 Minutes
- 2 cups red cabbage, shredded
- A drizzle of olive oil
- 1 red bell pepper, sliced
- 1 small avocado, peeled, pitted and sliced
- Salt and black pepper to the taste

1. Grease your air fryer with the oil, add all the ingredients, toss, cover and cook at 400 degrees F for 15 minutes. Divide into bowls and serve cold for breakfast.

Oregano And Coconut Scramble
Servings: 4 | Cooking Time: 20 Minutes
- 8 eggs, whisked
- 2 tablespoons oregano, chopped
- Salt and black pepper to the taste
- 2 tablespoons parmesan, grated
- ¼ cup coconut cream

1. In a bowl, mix the eggs with all the ingredients and whisk. Pour this into a pan that fits your air fryer, introduce it in the preheated fryer and cook at 350 degrees F for 20 minutes, stirring often. Divide the scramble between plates and serve for breakfast.

Artichokes And Parsley Frittata
Servings: 4 | Cooking Time: 12 Minutes
- 1 pound artichoke hearts, steamed and chopped
- Salt and black pepper to the taste
- 4 eggs, whisked
- 1 green onion, chopped
- 2 tablespoons parsley, chopped
- Cooking spray

1. Grease a pan that fits your air fryer with cooking spray. In a bowl, mix all the other ingredients, whisk well and pour evenly into the

pan. Introduce the pan in the air fryer, cook at 390 degrees F for 12 minutes, divide between plates and serve for breakfast.

Almond Oatmeal
Servings: 4 | Cooking Time: 15 Minutes
- 2 cups almond milk
- 2 teaspoons stevia
- 1 cup coconut, shredded
- 2 teaspoons vanilla extract

1. In a pan that fits your air fryer, mix all the ingredients, stir well, introduce the pan in the machine and cook at 360 degrees F for 15 minutes. Divide into bowls and serve for breakfast.

Scrambled Mug Eggs
Servings: 1 | Cooking Time: 5 Minutes
- 1 mug
- Salt and pepper
- Your favorite buffalo wing sauce
- 2 eggs
- Shredded cheese

1. Crack the eggs into a mug and whisk until blended.
2. Put the mug into your microwave and cook for 1.5 – 2 minutes, depending on the power of your microwave.
3. Leave for a few minutes and remove from the microwave.
4. Sprinkle with salt and pepper. Add your desired amount of cheese on top.
5. Using a fork, mix everything together.
6. Then add your favorite buffalo or hot sauce and mix again.
7. Serve!

Buttery Scallops
Servings: 2 | Cooking Time: 8 Minutes
- 1 lb jumbo scallops
- 1 tbsp fresh lemon juice
- 2 tbsp butter, melted

1. Preheat the air fryer to 400 F.
2. In a small bowl, mix together lemon juice and butter.
3. Brush scallops with lemon juice and butter mixture and place into the air fryer basket.
4. Cook scallops for 4 minutes. Turn halfway through.
5. Again brush scallops with lemon butter mixture and cook for 4 minutes more. Turn halfway through.
6. Serve and enjoy.

Strawberry Oatmeal
Servings: 4 | Cooking Time: 10 Minutes
- 1 cup strawberries, chopped
- 1 cup almond milk
- ½ teaspoon vanilla extract
- 1 cup steel cut oats
- 2 tablespoons sugar
- Cooking spray

1. Spray your air fryer with cooking spray and then add all ingredients; toss and cover.
2. Cook at 365 degrees F for 10 minutes.
3. Divide into bowls and serve.

Hashbrown Potatoes Lyonnaise
Servings: 4 | Cooking Time: 33 Minutes
- 1 Vidalia (or other sweet) onion, sliced
- 1 teaspoon butter, melted
- 1 teaspoon brown sugar
- 2 large russet potatoes (about 1 pound), sliced ½-inch thick
- 1 tablespoon vegetable oil
- salt and freshly ground black pepper

1. Preheat the air fryer to 370°F.
2. Toss the sliced onions, melted butter and brown sugar together in the air fryer basket. Air-fry for 8 minutes, shaking the basket occasionally to help the onions cook evenly.
3. While the onions are cooking, bring a 3-quart saucepan of salted water to a boil on the stovetop. Par-cook the potatoes in boiling water for 3 minutes. Drain the potatoes and pat them dry with a clean kitchen towel.
4. Add the potatoes to the onions in the air fryer basket and drizzle with vegetable oil. Toss to coat the potatoes with the oil and season with salt and freshly ground black pepper.
5. Increase the air fryer temperature to 400°F and air-fry for 22 minutes tossing the vegetables a few times during the cooking time to help the potatoes brown evenly. Season to taste again with salt and freshly ground black pepper and serve warm.

Green Beans Bowls
Servings: 2 | Cooking Time: 20 Minutes
- 1 cup green beans, halved
- 2 spring onions, chopped
- 4 eggs, whisked
- Salt and black pepper to the taste
- ¼ teaspoon cumin, ground

1. Preheat the air fryer at 360 degrees F, add all the ingredients, toss, cover, cook for 20 minutes, divide into bowls and serve for breakfast.

Broccoli Casserole
Servings: 4 | Cooking Time: 25 Minutes
- 1 broccoli head, florets separated and roughly chopped
- 2 ounces cheddar cheese, grated
- 4 eggs, whisked
- 1 cup almond milk
- 2 teaspoons cilantro, chopped
- Salt and black pepper to the taste

1. In a bowl, mix the eggs with the milk, cilantro, salt and pepper and whisk. Put the broccoli in your air fryer, add the eggs mix over it, spread, sprinkle the cheese on top, cook at 350 degrees F for 25 minutes, divide between plates and serve for breakfast.

Roasted Asparagus With Serrano & Parmesan
Servings: 4 | Cooking Time: 15 Minutes
- 2 tbsp polive oil
- 12 slices Serrano ham
- ¼ cup Parmesan cheese, grated
- Salt and black pepper to taste

1. Preheat your Air Fryer to 350 F. Spray the air fryer basket with cooking spray.
2. Season asparagus with salt and black pepper. Wrap each ham slice around each asparagus spear one end to the other end.
3. Drizzle with olive oil and arrange on the air fryer basket. Cook for 10 minutes, shaking once halfway through. When ready, scatter with Parmesan cheese to serve.

Italian Chicken
Servings: 4 | Cooking Time: 20 Minutes
- 4 chicken thighs
- ¼ tsp onion powder
- ½ tsp garlic powder
- 2 ½ tsp dried Italian herbs

- 2 tbsp butter, melted

1. Brush chicken with melted butter.
2. Mix together Italian herbs, onion powder, and garlic powder and rub over chicken.
3. Place chicken into the air fryer basket and cook at 380 F for 20 minutes.
4. Serve and enjoy.

Flaxseed Porridge

Servings: 4 | Cooking Time: 5 Minutes

- 1 cup flax seeds
- 1 tbsp butter
- 4 tbsp honey
- 1 tbsp peanut butter
- 4 cups milk

1. Preheat the air fryer to 390 F. Combine all of the ingredients in an ovenproof bowl. Place in the air fryer and cook for 5 minutes. Stir and serve.

Mushrooms Spread

Servings: 4 | Cooking Time: 20 Minutes

- 1 cup white mushrooms
- ¼ cup mozzarella, shredded
- ½ cup coconut cream
- A pinch of salt and black pepper
- Cooking spray

1. Put the mushrooms in your air fryer's basket, grease with cooking spray and cook at 370 degrees F for 20 minutes. Transfer to a blender, add the remaining ingredients, pulse well, divide into bowls and serve as a spread.

Peppers Bowls

Servings: 4 | Cooking Time: 20 Minutes

- ½ cup cheddar cheese, shredded
- 2 tablespoons chives, chopped
- A pinch of salt and black pepper
- ¼ cup coconut cream
- 1 cup red bell peppers, chopped
- Cooking spray

1. In a bowl, mix all the ingredients except the cooking spray and whisk well. Pour the mix in a baking pan that fits the air fryer greased with cooking spray and place the pan in the machine. Cook at 360 degrees F for 20 minutes, divide between plates and serve for breakfast.

Milky Scrambled Eggs

Servings: 2 | Cooking Time: 9 Minutes

- ¾ cup milk
- 8 grape tomatoes, halved
- 1 tablespoon butter
- 4 eggs
- ½ cup Parmesan cheese, grated
- Salt and black pepper, to taste

1. Preheat the Air fryer to 360 o F and grease an Air fryer pan with butter.
2. Whisk together eggs with milk, salt and black pepper in a bowl.
3. Transfer the egg mixture into the prepared pan and place in the Air fryer.
4. Cook for about 6 minutes and stir in the grape tomatoes and cheese.
5. Cook for about 3 minutes and serve warm.

Banana Chia Seed Pudding

Servings: 1 | Cooking Time: 1-2 Days

- 1 can full-fat coconut milk
- 1 medium- or small-sized banana, ripe
- ½ tsp cinnamon
- 1 tsp vanilla extract
- ¼ cup chia seeds

1. In a bowl, mash the banana until soft.
2. Add the remaining ingredients and mix until incorporated.
3. Cover and place in your refrigerator overnight.
4. Serve!

Spinach Egg Breakfast

Servings: 4 | Cooking Time: 20 Minutes

- 3 eggs
- 1/4 cup parmesan cheese, grated
- 3 oz cottage cheese
- 1/4 cup coconut milk
- 4 oz spinach, chopped

1. Preheat the air fryer to 350 F.
2. Add eggs, milk, half parmesan cheese, and cottage cheese in a bowl and whisk well. Add spinach and stir well.
3. Pour mixture into the air fryer baking dish.
4. Sprinkle remaining half parmesan cheese on top.
5. Place dish in the air fryer and cook for 20 minutes.
6. Serve and enjoy.

Crispy Bacon

Servings: 6 | Cooking Time: 20 Minutes

- 12 ounces bacon

1. Preheat the air fryer to 350°F for 3 minutes.
2. Lay out the bacon in a single layer, slightly overlapping the strips of bacon.
3. Air fry for 10 minutes or until desired crispness.
4. Repeat until all the bacon has been cooked.

Sweet Potato-cinnamon Toast

Servings: 6 | Cooking Time: 8 Minutes

- 1 small sweet potato, cut into ⅜-inch slices
- oil for misting
- ground cinnamon

1. Preheat air fryer to 390°F.
2. Spray both sides of sweet potato slices with oil. Sprinkle both sides with cinnamon to taste.
3. Place potato slices in air fryer basket in a single layer.
4. Cook for 4 minutes, turn, and cook for 4 more minutes or until potato slices are barely fork tender.

Exquisite German Pancake

Servings: 4 | Cooking Time: 30 Minutes

- 2 tbsp unsalted butter
- ½ cup flour
- 2 tbsp sugar, powdered
- ½ cup milk
- 1½ cups fresh strawberries, sliced

1. Preheat your air fryer to 330 F. Add butter to a pan and melt over low heat. In a bowl, mix flour, milk, eggs and vanilla until fully incorporated. Add the mixture to the pan with melted butter.

2. Place the pan in your air fryer's cooking basket and cook for 12-16 minutes until the pancake is fluffy and golden brown. Drizzle powdered sugar and toss sliced strawberries on top.

Vanilla Toast

Servings: 6 | Cooking Time: 10 Minutes
- ½ cup sugar
- 1 ½ tsp cinnamon
- 1 stick of butter, softened
- 1 tsp vanilla extract

1. Preheat the air fryer to 400 F. Combine all ingredients, except the bread, in a bowl. Spread the buttery cinnamon mixture onto the bread slices. Place the bread slices in the air fryer. Cook for 5 minutes.

Bacon & Eggs

Servings: 1 | Cooking Time: 5 Minutes
- Parsley
- Cherry tomatoes
- 1/3 oz/150g bacon
- eggs

1. Fry up the bacon and put it to the side.
2. Scramble the eggs in the bacon grease, with some pepper and salt. If you want, scramble in some cherry tomatoes. Sprinkle with some parsley and enjoy.

Creamy Parsley Soufflé

Servings: 2 | Cooking Time: 10 Minutes
- 2 eggs
- 1 tablespoon fresh parsley, chopped
- 1 fresh red chili pepper, chopped
- 2 tablespoons light cream
- Salt, to taste

1. Preheat the Air fryer to 390 o F and grease 2 soufflé dishes.
2. Mix together all the ingredients in a bowl until well combined.
3. Transfer the mixture into prepared soufflé dishes and place in the Air fryer.
4. Cook for about 10 minutes and dish out to serve warm.

Sausage Bacon Fandango

Servings: 4 | Cooking Time: 20 Minutes
- 8 bacon slices
- 8 chicken sausages
- 4 eggs
- Salt and black pepper, to taste

1. Preheat the Air fryer to 320 o F and grease 4 ramekins lightly.
2. Place bacon slices and sausages in the Air fryer basket.
3. Cook for about 10 minutes and crack 1 egg in each prepared ramekin.
4. Season with salt and black pepper and cook for about 10 more minutes.
5. Divide bacon slices and sausages in serving plates.
6. Place 1 egg in each plate and serve warm.

French Toast Sticks

Servings: 4 | Cooking Time: 8 Minutes
- 4 slices Texas toast, or other thick-sliced bread
- 2 large eggs
- ¼ cup heavy cream
- 4 tablespoons salted butter, melted
- ½ cup granulated sugar
- 1 ½ tablespoons ground cinnamon

1. Preheat the air fryer to 350°F. Cut parchment paper to fit the air fryer basket.
2. Slice each piece of bread into four even sticks.
3. In a medium bowl, whisk together eggs and cream. Dip each bread stick into mixture and place on parchment in the air fryer basket.
4. Cook 5 minutes, then carefully turn over and cook an additional 3 minutes until golden brown on both sides.
5. Drizzle sticks with butter and toss to ensure they're covered on all sides.
6. In a medium bowl, mix sugar and cinnamon. Dip both sides of each stick into the mixture and shake off excess. Serve warm.

Eggs Ramekins

Servings: 5 | Cooking Time: 6 Minutes
- 5 eggs
- 1 teaspoon coconut oil, melted
- ¼ teaspoon ground black pepper

1. Brush the ramekins with coconut oil and crack the eggs inside. Then sprinkle the eggs with ground black pepper and transfer in the air fryer. Cook the baked eggs for 6 minutes at 355F.

Onion And Cheese Omelet

Servings: 1 | Cooking Time: 15 Minutes
- 2 tbsp grated cheddar cheese
- 1 tsp soy sauce
- ½ onion, sliced
- ¼ tsp pepper
- 1 tbsp olive oil

1. Whisk the eggs along with the pepper and soy sauce. Preheat the air fryer to 350 F. Heat the olive oil and add the egg mixture and the onion. Cook for 8 to 10 minutes. Top with the grated cheddar cheese.

Green Scramble

Servings: 4 | Cooking Time: 20 Minutes
- 1 tablespoon olive oil
- ½ teaspoon smoked paprika
- 12 eggs, whisked
- 3 cups baby spinach
- Salt and black pepper to the taste

1. In a bowl, mix all the ingredients except the oil and whisk them well. Heat up your air fryer at 360 degrees F, add the oil, heat it up, add the eggs and spinach mix, cover, cook for 20 minutes, divide between plates and serve.

Okra Hash

Servings: 4 | Cooking Time: 20 Minutes
- 2 cups okra
- 1 tablespoon butter, melted
- 4 eggs, whisked
- A pinch of salt and black pepper

1. Grease a pan that fits the air fryer with the butter. In a bowl, combine the okra with eggs, salt and pepper, whisk and pour into the pan. Introduce the pan in the air fryer and cook at 350 degrees F for 20 minutes. Divide the mix between plates and serve.

Hole In One

Servings: 1 | Cooking Time: 7 Minutes
- 1 slice bread
- 1 teaspoon soft butter
- 1 egg
- salt and pepper
- 1 tablespoon shredded Cheddar cheese
- 2 teaspoons diced ham

1. Place a 6 x 6-inch baking dish inside air fryer basket and preheat fryer to 330°F.

2. Using a 2½-inch-diameter biscuit cutter, cut a hole in center of bread slice.
3. Spread softened butter on both sides of bread.
4. Lay bread slice in baking dish and crack egg into the hole. Sprinkle egg with salt and pepper to taste.
5. Cook for 5minutes.
6. Turn toast over and top it with shredded cheese and diced ham.
7. Cook for 2 more minutes or until yolk is done to your liking.

Craving Cinnamon Toast
Servings:6 | Cooking Time: 15 Minutes
- Pepper to taste
- 1 stick butter
- 1½ tbsp cinnamon
- ½ cup sugar
- 1½ tbsp vanilla extract

1. In a microwave-proof bowl, mix butter, pepper, sugar and vanilla extract. Warm and stir the mixture for 30 seconds until everything melts. Pour the mixture over bread slices. Lay the bread slices in your air fryer's cooking basket and cook for 5 minutes at 400 F. Serve with fresh banana and berry sauce.

Roasted Golden Mini Potatoes
Servings:4 | Cooking Time: 22 Minutes
- 6 cups water
- 1 pound baby Dutch yellow potatoes, quartered
- 2 tablespoons olive oil
- ¾ teaspoon seasoned salt
- ½ teaspoon ground black pepper
- ½ teaspoon garlic powder
- ¼ teaspoon salt

1. In a medium saucepan over medium-high heat bring water to a boil. Add potatoes and boil 10 minutes until fork-tender, then drain and gently pat dry.
2. Preheat the air fryer to 400°F.
3. Drizzle oil over potatoes, then sprinkle with garlic powder, seasoned salt, salt, and pepper.
4. Place potatoes in the air fryer basket and cook 12 minutes, shaking the basket three times during cooking. Potatoes will be done when golden brown and edges are crisp. Serve warm.

Hard-boiled Eggs
Servings: 2 | Cooking Time: 16 Minutes
- 4 eggs
- ¼ teaspoon salt

1. Place the eggs in the air fryer and cook them for 16 minutes at 250F. When the eggs are cooked, cool them in the ice water. After this, peel the eggs and cut into halves. Sprinkle the eggs with salt.

Spinach Eggs And Cheese
Servings: 2 | Cooking Time: 40 Minutes
- 3 whole eggs
- 3-4 oz chopped spinach
- ¼ cup of milk
- 3 oz cottage cheese
- ¼ cup parmesan cheese

1. Preheat your fryer to 375°F/190°C.
2. In a large bowl, whisk the eggs, cottage cheese, the parmesan and the milk.
3. Mix in the spinach.
4. Transfer to a small, greased, fryer dish.
5. Sprinkle the cheese on top.
6. Bake for 25-30 minutes.
7. Let cool for 5 minutes and serve.

Bacon & Egg Muffins
Servings:10 | Cooking Time: 30 Minutes
- 10 bacon rashers, cut into small pieces
- ½ cup chopped chives
- 1 cup grated cheddar cheese
- Cooking spray
- 1 brown onion, chopped
- Salt and black pepper to taste

1. Spray a muffin pan with cooking spray. In a bowl, add eggs, bacon, chives, onion, cheese, salt, and pepper, and stir to combine. Pour into muffin pan and place in the fryer. Cook for 12 minutes at 330 F, until nice and set.

Not-so-english Muffins
Servings: 4 | Cooking Time: 10 Minutes
- 2 strips turkey bacon, cut in half crosswise
- 2 whole-grain English muffins, split
- 1 cup fresh baby spinach, long stems removed
- ¼ ripe pear, peeled and thinly sliced
- 4 slices Provolone cheese

1. Place bacon strips in air fryer basket and cook for 2minutes. Check and separate strips if necessary so they cook evenly. Cook for 4 more minutes, until crispy. Remove and drain on paper towels.
2. Place split muffin halves in air fryer basket and cook at 390°F for 2minutes, just until lightly browned.
3. Open air fryer and top each muffin with a quarter of the baby spinach, several pear slices, a strip of bacon, and a slice of cheese.
4. Cook at 360°F for 2minutes, until cheese completely melts.

Peppered Maple Bacon Knots
Servings: 6 | Cooking Time: 8 Minutes
- 1 pound maple smoked center-cut bacon
- ¼ cup maple syrup
- ¼ cup brown sugar
- coarsely cracked black peppercorns

1. Tie each bacon strip in a loose knot and place them on a baking sheet.
2. Combine the maple syrup and brown sugar in a bowl. Brush each knot generously with this mixture and sprinkle with coarsely cracked black pepper.
3. Preheat the air fryer to 390°F.
4. Air-fry the bacon knots in batches. Place one layer of knots in the air fryer basket and air-fry for 5 minutes. Turn the bacon knots over and air-fry for an additional 3 minutes.
5. Serve warm.

Cheesy Omelet
Servings:1 | Cooking Time: 15 Minutes
- Black pepper to taste
- 1 cup cheddar cheese, shredded
- 1 whole onion, chopped
- 2 tbsp soy sauce

1. Preheat your air fryer to 340 F. Drizzle soy sauce over the chopped onions. Place the onions in your air fryer's cooking basket and cook for 8 minutes. In a bowl, mix the beaten eggs with salt and pepper.
2. Pour the egg mixture over onions (in the cooking basket) and cook for 3 minutes. Add cheddar cheese over eggs and bake for 2 more minutes. Serve with fresh basil and enjoy!

Green Beans And Eggs

Servings: 4 | Cooking Time: 20 Minutes

- 1 pound green beans, roughly chopped
- Cooking spray
- 2 eggs, whisked
- Salt and black pepper to the taste
- 1 tablespoon sweet paprika
- 4 ounces sour cream

1. Grease a pan that fits your air fryer with the cooking spray and mix all the ingredients inside. Put the pan in the Air Fryer and cook at 360 degrees F for 20 minutes. Divide between plates and serve.

Seasoned Herbed Sourdough Croutons

Servings: 4 | Cooking Time: 7 Minutes

- 4 cups cubed sourdough bread, 1-inch cubes (about 8 ounces)
- 1 tablespoon olive oil
- 1 teaspoon fresh thyme leaves
- ¼ – ½ teaspoon salt
- freshly ground black pepper

1. Combine all ingredients in a bowl and taste to make sure it is seasoned to your liking.
2. Preheat the air fryer to 400°F.
3. Toss the bread cubes into the air fryer and air-fry for 7 minutes, shaking the basket once or twice while they cook.
4. Serve warm or store in an airtight container.

Banana-nut Muffins

Servings: 12 | Cooking Time: 15 Minutes Per Batch

- 1 ½ cups all-purpose flour
- ½ cup granulated sugar
- 1 teaspoon baking powder
- ½ cup salted butter, melted
- 1 large egg
- 2 medium bananas, peeled and mashed
- ½ cup chopped pecans

1. Preheat the air fryer to 300°F.
2. In a large bowl, whisk together flour, sugar, and baking powder.
3. Add butter, egg, and bananas to dry mixture. Stir until well combined. Batter will be thick.
4. Gently fold in pecans. Divide batter evenly among twelve silicone or aluminum muffin cups, filling cups about halfway full.
5. Place cups in the air fryer basket, working in batches as necessary. Cook 15 minutes until muffin edges are brown and a toothpick inserted into the center comes out clean. Let cool 5 minutes before serving.

Sausage Egg Muffins

Servings: 4 | Cooking Time: 30 Minutes

- 6 oz Italian sausage
- 6 eggs
- 1/8 cup heavy cream
- 3 oz cheese

1. Preheat the fryer to 350°F/175°C.
2. Grease a muffin pan.
3. Slice the sausage links and place them two to a tin.
4. Beat the eggs with the cream and season with salt and pepper.
5. Pour over the sausages in the tin.
6. Sprinkle with cheese and the remaining egg mixture.
7. Cook for 20 minutes or until the eggs are done and serve!

Almond Crust Chicken

Servings: 2 | Cooking Time: 25 Minutes

- 2 chicken breasts, skinless and boneless
- 1 tbsp Dijon mustard
- 2 tbsp mayonnaise
- ¼ cup almonds
- Pepper
- Salt

1. Add almond into the food processor and process until finely ground. Transfer almonds on a plate and set aside.
2. Mix together mustard and mayonnaise and spread over chicken.
3. Coat chicken with almond and place into the air fryer basket and cook at 350 F for 25 minutes.
4. Serve and enjoy.

Breakfast Muffins

Servings: 1 | Cooking Time: 30 Minutes

- 1 medium egg
- ¼ cup heavy cream
- 1 slice cooked bacon (cured, pan-fried, cooked)
- 1 oz cheddar cheese
- Salt and black pepper (to taste)

1. Preheat your fryer to 350°F/175°C.
2. In a bowl, mix the eggs with the cream, salt and pepper.
3. Spread into muffin tins and fill the cups half full.
4. Place 1 slice of bacon into each muffin hole and half ounce of cheese on top of each muffin.
5. Bake for around 15-20 minutes or until slightly browned.
6. Add another ½ oz of cheese onto each muffin and broil until the cheese is slightly browned. Serve!

Snacks & Appetizers Recipes

Sweet Potato Tots

Servings: 24 | Cooking Time: 31 Minutes

- 2 sweet potatoes, peeled
- 1/2 tsp cajun seasoning
- Salt

1. Add water in large pot and bring to boil. Add sweet potatoes in pot and boil for 15 minutes. Drain well.
2. Grated boil sweet potatoes into a large bowl using a grated.
3. Add cajun seasoning and salt in grated sweet potatoes and mix until well combined.
4. Spray air fryer basket with cooking spray.
5. Make small tot of sweet potato mixture and place in air fryer basket.
6. Cook at 400 F for 8 minutes. Turn tots to another side and cook for 8 minutes more.
7. Serve and enjoy.

Cheesy Polenta Sticks

Servings: 4 | Cooking Time: 6 Minutes

- 2½ cups cooked polenta
- 1 tablespoon olive oil
- ¼ cup Parmesan cheese
- Salt, to taste

1. Preheat the Air fryer to 350 o F and grease a baking dish with olive oil.
2. Place polenta in the baking dish and refrigerate, covered for about 1 hour.
3. Remove from the refrigerator and cut into desired sized slices.
4. Place polenta sticks into the Air fryer and season with salt.
5. Top with Parmesan cheese and cook for about 6 minutes.
6. Dish out and serve warm.

Amazing Blooming Onion

Servings: 4 | Cooking Time: 40 Minutes

- 4 medium/small onions
- 1 tbsp. olive oil
- 4 dollops of butter

1.1 Peel the onion. Cut off the top and bottom.
2.2 To make it bloom, cut as deeply as possible without slicing through it completely. 4 cuts [i.e. 8 segments] should do it.
3.3 Place the onions in a bowl of salted water and allow to absorb for 4 hours to help eliminate the sharp taste and induce the blooming process.
4.4 Pre-heat your Air Fryer to 355°F.
5.5 Transfer the onions to the Air Fryer. Pour over a light drizzle of olive oil and place a dollop of butter on top of each onion.
6.6 Cook or roast for 30 minutes. Remove the outer layer before serving if it is too brown.

Roasted Peppers

Servings: 4 | Cooking Time: 40 Minutes

- 12 medium bell peppers
- 1 tbsp. Maggi sauce
- 1 sweet onion, small
- 1 tbsp. extra virgin olive oil

1.1 Warm up the olive oil and Maggi sauce in Air Fryer at 320°F.
2.2 Peel the onion, slice it into 1-inch pieces, and add it to the Air Fryer.
3.3 Wash and de-stem the peppers. Slice them into 1-inch pieces and remove all the seeds, with water if necessary [ensuring to dry the peppers afterwards].
4.4 Place the peppers in the Air Fryer.
5.5 Cook for about 25 minutes, or longer if desired. Serve hot.

Okra Chips

Servings: 4 | Cooking Time: 16 Minutes

- 1¼ pounds Thin fresh okra pods, cut into 1-inch pieces
- 1½ tablespoons Vegetable or canola oil
- ¾ teaspoon Coarse sea salt or kosher salt

1. Preheat the air fryer to 400°F.
2. Toss the okra, oil, and salt in a large bowl until the pieces are well and evenly coated.
3. When the machine is at temperature, pour the contents of the bowl into the basket. Air-fry, tossing several times, for 16 minutes, or until crisp and quite brown (maybe even a little blackened on the thin bits).
4. Pour the contents of the basket onto a wire rack. Cool for a couple of minutes before serving.

Fried Green Tomatoes

Servings: 2 | Cooking Time: 10 Minutes

- 2 medium green tomatoes
- 1 egg
- ¼ cup blanched finely ground flour
- 1/3 cup parmesan cheese, grated

1. Slice the tomatoes about a half-inch thick.
2. Crack the egg into a bowl and beat it with a whisk. In a separate bowl, mix together the flour and parmesan cheese.
3. Dredge the tomato slices in egg, then dip them into the flour-cheese mixture to coat. Place each slice into the fryer basket. They may need to be cooked in multiple batches.
4. Cook at 400°F for seven minutes, turning them halfway through the cooking time, and then serve warm.

Chili Pepper Kale Chips

Servings: 14 | Cooking Time: 8 Minutes

- 1 lb kale, wash, dry and cut into pieces
- 2 tsp olive oil
- 1 tsp chili pepper
- 1 tsp salt

1. Preheat the air fryer to 370 F.
2. Add kale pieces into the air fryer basket. Drizzle kale with oil.
3. Sprinkle chili pepper and salt over the kale and toss well.
4. Cook kale for 5 minutes. Shake well and cook for 3 minutes more.
5. Serve and enjoy.

Lemon Green Beans

Servings: 4 | Cooking Time: 20 Minutes

- 1 lemon, juiced
- 1 lb. green beans, washed and destemmed
- ¼ tsp. extra virgin olive oil
- Sea salt to taste
- Black pepper to taste

1. Pre-heat the Air Fryer to 400°F.

2. Put the green beans in your Air Fryer basket and drizzle the lemon juice over them.
3. Sprinkle on the pepper and salt. Pour in the oil, and toss to coat the green beans well.
4. Cook for 10 – 12 minutes and serve warm.

Mini Pepper Poppers
Servings: 4 | Cooking Time: 10 Minutes
- 8 mini sweet peppers
- ¼ cup pepper jack cheese, shredded
- 4 slices sugar-free bacon, cooked and crumbled
- 4 oz. full-fat cream cheese, softened

1. Prepare the peppers by cutting off the tops and halving them lengthwise. Then take out the membrane and the seeds.
2. In a small bowl, combine the pepper jack cheese, bacon, and cream cheese, making sure to incorporate everything well
3. Spoon equal-sized portions of the cheese-bacon mixture into each of the pepper halves.
4. Place the peppers inside your fryer and cook for eight minutes at 400°F. Take care when removing them from the fryer and enjoy warm.

Country Style Chard
Servings: 2 | Cooking Time: 5 Minutes
- 4 slices bacon, chopped
- 2 tbsp butter
- 2 tbsp fresh lemon juice
- ½ tsp garlic paste
- 1 bunch Swiss chard, stems removed, leaves cut into 1-inch pieces

1. On a medium heat, cook the bacon in a skillet until the fat begins to brown.
2. Melt the butter in the skillet and add the lemon juice and garlic paste.
3. Add the chard leaves and cook until they begin to wilt.
4. Cover and turn up the heat to high.
5. Cook for 3 minutes.
6. Mix well, sprinkle with salt and serve.

Eggplant Fries
Servings: 18 | Cooking Time: 10 Minutes
- ¾ cup All-purpose flour or tapioca flour
- 1 Large egg(s), well beaten
- 1 cup Seasoned Italian-style dried bread crumbs (gluten-free, if a concern)
- 3 tablespoons (about ½ ounce) Finely grated Asiago or Parmesan cheese
- 3 Peeled ½-inch-thick eggplant slices (each about 3 inches in diameter)
- Olive oil spray

1. Preheat the air fryer to 375°F (or 380°F or 390°F, if one of these is the closest setting).
2. Set up and fill three shallow soup plates or small pie plates on your counter: one for the flour, one for the egg(s), and one for the bread crumbs mixed with the cheese until well combined.
3. Cut each eggplant slice into six ½-inch-wide strips or sticks. Dip one strip in the flour, coating it well on all sides. Gently shake off the excess flour, then dip the strip in the beaten egg(s) to coat it without losing the flour. Let any excess egg slip back into the rest, then roll the strip in the bread-crumb mixture to coat evenly on all sides, even the ends. Set the strips aside on a cutting board and continue dipping and coating the remaining strips as you did the first one.
4. Generously coat the strips with olive oil spray on all sides. Set them in the basket in one layer and air-fry undisturbed for 10 minutes, or until golden brown and crisp. If the machine is at 390°F, the strips may be done in 8 minutes.
5. Remove the basket from the machine and cool for a couple of minutes. Then use kitchen tongs to transfer the eggplant fries to a wire rack to cool for only a minute or two more before serving.

Parmesan & Garlic Cauliflower
Servings: 4 | Cooking Time: 40 Minutes
- 3/4 cup cauliflower florets
- 2 tbsp butter
- 1 clove garlic, sliced thinly
- 2 tbsp shredded parmesan
- 1 pinch of salt

1. Preheat your fryer to 350°F/175°C.
2. On a low heat, melt the butter with the garlic for 5-10 minutes.
3. Strain the garlic in a sieve.
4. Add the cauliflower, parmesan and salt.
5. Bake for 20 minutes or until golden.

Cashew Bowls
Servings: 4 | Cooking Time: 5 Minutes
- 4 oz cashew
- 1 teaspoon ranch seasoning
- 1 teaspoon sesame oil

1. Preheat the air fryer to 375F. Mix up cashew with ranch seasoning and sesame oil and put in the preheated air fryer. Cook the cashew for 4 minutes. Then shake well and cook for 1 minute more.

Sweet Apple Fries
Servings: 3 | Cooking Time: 8 Minutes
- 2 Medium-size sweet apple(s), such as Gala or Fuji
- 1 Large egg white(s)
- 2 tablespoons Water
- 1½ cups Finely ground gingersnap crumbs (gluten-free, if a concern)
- Vegetable oil spray

1. Preheat the air fryer to 375°F.
2. Peel and core an apple, then cut it into 12 slices (see the headnote for more information). Repeat with more apples as necessary.
3. Whisk the egg white(s) and water in a medium bowl until foamy. Add the apple slices and toss well to coat.
4. Spread the gingersnap crumbs across a dinner plate. Using clean hands, pick up an apple slice, let any excess egg white mixture slip back into the rest, and dredge the slice in the crumbs, coating it lightly but evenly on all sides. Set it aside and continue coating the remaining apple slices.
5. Lightly coat the slices on all sides with vegetable oil spray, then set them curved side down in the basket in one layer. Air-fry undisturbed for 6 minutes, or until browned and crisp. You may need to air-fry the slices for 2 minutes longer if the temperature is at 360°F.
6. Use kitchen tongs to transfer the slices to a wire rack. Cool for 2 to 3 minutes before serving.

Roasted Spicy Hot Dogs
Servings: 6 | Cooking Time: 20 Minutes
- 6 hot dogs
- 1 tablespoon mustard
- 6 tablespoons ketchup, no sugar added

1. Place the hot dogs in the lightly greased Air Fryer basket.
2. Bake at 380 degrees F for 15 minutes, turning them over halfway through the cooking time to promote even cooking.
3. Serve on cocktail sticks with the mustard and ketchup. Enjoy!

Fried Goat Cheese

Servings: 3 | Cooking Time: 4 Minutes

- 7 ounces 1- to 1½-inch-diameter goat cheese log
- 2 Large egg(s)
- 1¾ cups Plain dried bread crumbs (gluten-free, if a concern)
- Vegetable oil spray

1. Slice the goat cheese log into ½-inch-thick rounds. Set these flat on a small cutting board, a small baking sheet, or a large plate. Freeze uncovered for 30 minutes.
2. Preheat the air fryer to 400°F.
3. Set up and fill two shallow soup plates or small pie plates on your counter: one in which you whisk the egg(s) until uniform and the other for the bread crumbs.
4. Take the goat cheese rounds out of the freezer. With clean, dry hands, dip one round in the egg(s) to coat it on all sides. Let the excess egg slip back into the rest, then dredge the round in the bread crumbs, turning it to coat all sides, even the edges. Repeat this process—egg, then bread crumbs—for a second coating. Coat both sides of the round and its edges with vegetable oil spray, then set it aside. Continue double-dipping, double-dredging, and spraying the remaining rounds.
5. Place the rounds in one layer in the basket. Air-fry undisturbed for 4 minutes, or until lightly browned and crunchy. Do not overcook. Some of the goat cheese may break through the crust. A few little breaks are fine but stop the cooking before the coating reaches structural failure.
6. Remove the basket from the machine and set aside for 3 minutes. Use a nonstick-safe spatula, and maybe a flatware fork for balance, to transfer the rounds to a wire rack. Cool for 5 minutes more before serving.

Bbq Lil Smokies

Servings: 6 | Cooking Time: 20 Minutes

- 1 pound beef cocktail wieners
- 10 ounces barbecue sauce, no sugar added

1. Start by preheating your Air Fryer to 380 degrees F.
2. Prick holes into your sausages using a fork and transfer them to the baking pan.
3. Cook for 13 minutes. Spoon the barbecue sauce into the pan and cook an additional 2 minutes.
4. Serve with toothpicks. Bon appétit!

Croutons

Servings: 4 | Cooking Time: 5 Minutes

- 4 slices sourdough bread, diced into small cubes
- 2 tablespoons salted butter, melted
- 1 teaspoon chopped fresh parsley
- 2 tablespoons grated Parmesan cheese

1. Preheat the air fryer to 400°F.
2. Place bread cubes in a large bowl.
3. Pour butter over bread cubes. Add parsley and Parmesan. Toss bread cubes until evenly coated.
4. Place bread cubes in the air fryer basket in a single layer. Cook 5 minutes until well toasted. Serve cooled for maximum crunch.

Hillbilly Cheese Surprise

Servings: 6 | Cooking Time: 40 Minutes

- 4 cups broccoli florets
- ¼ cup ranch dressing
- ½ cup sharp cheddar cheese, shredded
- ¼ cup heavy whipping cream
- Kosher salt and pepper to taste

1. Preheat your fryer to 375°F/190°C.
2. In a bowl, combine all of the ingredients until the broccoli is well-covered.
3. In a casserole dish, spread out the broccoli mixture.
4. Bake for 30 minutes.
5. Take out of your fryer and mix.
6. If the florets are not tender, bake for another 5 minutes until tender.
7. Serve!

Flax Cheese Chips

Servings: 2 | Cooking Time: 20 Minutes

- 1 ½ cup cheddar cheese
- 4 tbsp ground flaxseed meal
- Seasonings of your choice

1. Preheat your fryer to 425°F/220°C.
2. Spoon 2 tablespoons of cheddar cheese into a mound, onto a non-stick pad.
3. Spread out a pinch of flax seed on each chip.
4. Season and bake for 10-15 minutes.

Bacon Avocado Wraps

Servings: 4 | Cooking Time: 15 Minutes

- 2 avocados, peeled, pitted and cut into 12 wedges
- 12 bacon strips
- 1 tablespoon ghee, melted

1. Wrap each avocado wedge in a bacon strip, brush them with the ghee, put them in your air fryer's basket and cook at 360 degrees F for 15 minutes. Serve as an appetizer.

Healthy Vegetable Kabobs

Servings: 4 | Cooking Time: 10 Minutes

- 1/2 onion
- 1 eggplant
- Pepper
- 1 zucchini
- 2 bell peppers
- Salt

1. Cut all vegetables into 1-inch pieces.
2. Thread vegetables onto the soaked wooden skewers and season with pepper and salt.
3. Place skewers into the air fryer basket and cook for 10 minutes at 390 F. Turn halfway through.
4. Serve and enjoy.

Buffalo Bites

Servings: 16 | Cooking Time: 12 Minutes

- 1 pound ground chicken
- 8 tablespoons buffalo wing sauce
- 2 ounces Gruyère cheese, cut into 16 cubes
- 1 tablespoon maple syrup

1. Mix 4 tablespoons buffalo wing sauce into all the ground chicken.
2. Shape chicken into a log and divide into 16 equal portions.
3. With slightly damp hands, mold each chicken portion around a

cube of cheese and shape into a firm ball. When you have shaped 8 meatballs, place them in air fryer basket.
4. Cook at 390°F for approximately 5minutes. Shake basket, reduce temperature to 360°F, and cook for 5 minutes longer.
5. While the first batch is cooking, shape remaining chicken and cheese into 8 more meatballs.
6. Repeat step 4 to cook second batch of meatballs.
7. In a medium bowl, mix the remaining 4 tablespoons of buffalo wing sauce with the maple syrup. Add all the cooked meatballs and toss to coat.
8. Place meatballs back into air fryer basket and cook at 390°F for 2 minutes to set the glaze. Skewer each with a toothpick and serve.

Fried Olives

Servings: 5 | Cooking Time: 10 Minutes

- ⅓ cup All-purpose flour or tapioca flour
- 1 Large egg white(s)
- 1 tablespoon Brine from the olive jar
- ⅔ cup Plain dried bread crumbs (gluten-free, if a concern)
- 15 Large pimiento-stuffed green olives
- Olive oil spray

1. Preheat the air fryer to 400°F.
2. Pour the flour in a medium-size zip-closed plastic bag. Whisk the egg white and pickle brine in a medium bowl until foamy. Spread out the bread crumbs on a dinner plate.
3. Pour all the olives into the bag with the flour, seal, and shake to coat the olives. Remove a couple of olives, shake off any excess flour, and drop them into the egg white mixture. Toss gently but well to coat. Pick them up one at a time and roll each in the bread crumbs until well coated on all sides, even the ends. Set them aside on a cutting board as you finish the rest. When done, coat the olives with olive oil spray on all sides.
4. Place the olives in the basket in one layer. Air-fry for 8 minutes, gently shaking the basket once halfway through the cooking process to rearrange the olives, until lightly browned.
5. Gently pour the olives onto a wire rack and cool for at least 10 minutes before serving. Once cooled, the olives may be stored in a sealed container in the fridge for up to 2 days. To rewarm them, set them in the basket of a heated 400°F air fryer undisturbed for 2 minutes.

Skinny Fries

Servings: 2 | Cooking Time: 15 Minutes

- 2 to 3 russet potatoes, peeled and cut into ¼-inch sticks
- 2 to 3 teaspoons olive or vegetable oil
- salt

1. Cut the potatoes into ¼-inch strips. (A mandolin with a julienne blade is really helpful here.) Rinse the potatoes with cold water several times and let them soak in cold water for at least 10 minutes or as long as overnight.
2. Preheat the air fryer to 380°F.
3. Drain and dry the potato sticks really well, using a clean kitchen towel. Toss the fries with the oil in a bowl and then air-fry the fries in two batches at 380°F for 15 minutes, shaking the basket a couple of times while they cook.
4. Add the first batch of French fries back into the air fryer basket with the finishing batch and let everything warm through for a few minutes. As soon as the fries are done, season them with salt and transfer to a plate or basket. Serve them warm with ketchup or your favorite dip.

Cinnamon Apple Crisps

Servings: 1 | Cooking Time: 22 Minutes

- 1 large apple
- ½ teaspoon ground cinnamon
- 2 teaspoons avocado oil or coconut oil

1. Preheat the air fryer to 300°F.
2. Using a mandolin or knife, slice the apples to ¼-inch thickness. Pat the apples dry with a paper towel or kitchen cloth. Sprinkle the apple slices with ground cinnamon. Spray or drizzle the oil over the top of the apple slices and toss to coat.
3. Place the apple slices in the air fryer basket. To allow for even cooking, don't overlap the slices; cook in batches if necessary.
4. Cook for 20 minutes, shaking the basket every 5 minutes. After 20 minutes, increase the air fryer temperature to 330°F and cook another 2 minutes, shaking the basket every 30 seconds. Remove the apples from the basket before they get too dark.
5. Spread the chips out onto paper towels to cool completely, at least 5 minutes. Repeat with the remaining apple slices until they're all cooked.

Brussels Sprouts

Servings: 2 | Cooking Time: 15 Minutes

- 2 cups Brussels sprouts, sliced in half
- 1 tbsp. balsamic vinegar
- 1 tbsp. olive oil
- ¼ tsp. salt

1. Toss all of the ingredients together in a bowl, coating the Brussels sprouts well.
2. Place the sprouts in the Air Fryer basket and air fry at 400°F for 10 minutes, shaking the basket at the halfway point.

Avocado Sticks

Servings: 2 | Cooking Time: 10 Minutes

- 2 avocados
- 1 ½ tbsp. water
- 1 cup flour
- 4 egg yolks
- Salt and pepper
- 1 cup herbed butter

1. Halve the avocados, twist to open, and take out the pits. Cut each half into three equal slices.
2. In a bowl, combine the egg yolks and water. Season with salt and pepper to taste and whisk together.
3. Pour the flour into a shallow bowl.
4. Coat each slice of avocado in the flour, then in the egg, before dipping it in the flour again. Ensure the flour coats the avocado well and firmly.
5. Pre-heat the fryer at 400°F. When it is warm, put the avocados inside and cook for eight minutes.
6. Take care when removing the avocados from the fryer and enjoy with a side of the herbed butter.

Friday's Fries

Servings: 2 | Cooking Time: 25 Minutes

- 1 large eggplant, cut into 3-inch slices
- ¼ cup water
- 1 tbsp. olive oil
- ¼ cup cornstarch
- ¼ tsp. salt

1. Pre-heat the Air Fryer to 400°F.
2. In a bowl, combine the water, olive oil, cornstarch, and salt.

3. Coat the sliced eggplant with the mixture.
4. Put the coated eggplant slices in the Air Fryer basket and cook for 20 minutes.

Fried Mushrooms

Servings: 4 | Cooking Time: 40 Minutes

- 2 lb. button mushrooms
- 3 tbsp. white or French vermouth [optional]
- 1 tbsp. coconut oil
- 2 tsp. herbs of your choice
- ½ tsp. garlic powder

1.1 Wash and dry the mushrooms. Slice them into quarters.
2.2 Pre-heat your Air Fryer at 320°F and add the coconut oil, garlic powder, and herbs to the basket.
3.3 Briefly cook the ingredients for 2 minutes and give them a stir. Put the mushrooms in the air fryer and cook for 25 minutes, stirring occasionally throughout.
4.4 Pour in the white vermouth and mix. Cook for an additional 5 minutes.
5.5 Serve hot.

Cheesy Bacon Bread

Servings: 2 | Cooking Time: 25 Minutes

- 4 slices sugar-free bacon, cooked and chopped
- 2 eggs
- ¼ cup pickled jalapenos, chopped
- ¼ cup parmesan cheese, grated
- 2 cups mozzarella cheese, shredded

1. Add all of the ingredients together in a bowl and mix together.
2. Cut out a piece of parchment paper that will fit the base of your fryer's basket. Place it inside the fryer
3. With slightly wet hands, roll the mixture into a circle. You may have to form two circles to cook in separate batches, depending on the size of your fryer.
4. Place the circle on top of the parchment paper inside your fryer. Cook at 320°F for ten minutes.
5. Turn the bread over and cook for another five minutes.
6. The bread is ready when it is golden and cooked all the way through. Slice and serve warm.

Zucchini And Tomato Salsa

Servings: 6 | Cooking Time: 15 Minutes

- 1 and ½ pounds zucchinis, roughly cubed
- 2 spring onions, chopped
- 2 tomatoes, cubed
- Salt and black pepper to the taste
- 1 tablespoon balsamic vinegar

1. In a pan that fits your air fryer, mix all the ingredients, toss, introduce the pan in the fryer and cook at 360 degrees F for 15 minutes. Divide the salsa into cups and serve cold.

Bacon Jalapeno Poppers

Servings: 10 | Cooking Time: 8 Minutes

- 10 jalapeno peppers, cut in half and remove seeds
- 1/3 cup cream cheese, softened
- 5 bacon strips, cut in half

1. Preheat the air fryer to 370 F.
2. Stuff cream cheese into each jalapeno half.
3. Wrap each jalapeno half with half bacon strip and place in the air fryer basket.
4. Cook for 6-8 minutes.
5. Serve and enjoy.

Corn Dog Bites

Servings: 3 | Cooking Time: 12 Minutes

- 3 cups Purchased cornbread stuffing mix
- ⅓ cup All-purpose flour
- 2 Large egg(s), well beaten
- 3 Hot dogs, cut into 2-inch pieces (vegetarian hot dogs, if preferred)
- Vegetable oil spray

1. Preheat the air fryer to 375°F.
2. Put the cornbread stuffing mix in a food processor. Cover and pulse to grind into a mixture like fine bread crumbs.
3. Set up and fill three shallow soup plates or small pie plates on your counter: one for the flour, one for the egg(s), and one for the stuffing mix crumbs.
4. Dip a hot dog piece in the flour to coat it completely, then gently shake off any excess. Dip the hot dog piece into the egg(s) and gently roll it around to coat all surfaces, then pick it up and allow any excess egg to slip back into the rest. Set the hot dog piece in the stuffing mix crumbs and roll it gently to coat it evenly and well on all sides, even the ends. Set it aside on a cutting board and continue dipping and coating the remaining hot dog pieces.
5. Give the coated hot dog pieces a generous coating of vegetable oil spray on all sides, then set them in the basket in one layer with some space between them. Air-fry undisturbed for 10 minutes, or until golden brown and crunchy. (You'll need to add 2 minutes in the air fryer if the temperature is at 360°F.)
6. Use a nonstick-safe spatula, and perhaps a flatware fork for balance, to transfer the corn dog bites to a wire rack. Cool for 5 minutes before serving.

Sweet And Spicy Carrot Sticks

Servings: 2 | Cooking Time: 12 Minutes

- 1 large carrot, peeled and cut into sticks
- 1 tablespoon fresh rosemary, chopped finely
- 1 tablespoon olive oil
- 2 teaspoons sugar
- ¼ teaspoon cayenne pepper
- Salt and black pepper, to taste

1. Preheat the Air fryer to 390 o F and grease an Air fryer basket
2. Mix carrot with all other ingredients in a bowl until well combined.
3. Arrange the carrot sticks in the Air fryer basket and cook for about 12 minutes.
4. Dish out and serve warm.

Cheddar Cheese Lumpia Rolls

Servings: 5 | Cooking Time: 20 Minutes

- 5 ounces mature cheddar cheese, cut into 15 sticks
- 15 pieces spring roll lumpia wrappers
- 2 tablespoons sesame oil

1. Wrap the cheese sticks in the lumpia wrappers. Transfer to the Air Fryer basket. Brush with sesame oil.
2. Bake in the preheated Air Fryer at 395 degrees for 10 minutes or until the lumpia wrappers turn golden brown. Work in batches.
3. Shake the Air Fryer basket occasionally to ensure even cooking. Bon appétit!

Roasted Carrots
Servings: 2 | Cooking Time: 20 Minutes
- 1 tbsp. olive oil
- 3 cups baby carrots or carrots, cut into large chunks
- 1 tbsp. honey
- Salt and pepper to taste

1. In a bowl, coat the carrots with the honey and olive oil before sprinkling on some salt and pepper.
2. Place into the Air Fryer and cook at 390°F for 12 minutes. Serve hot.

Homemade Mayonnaise
Servings: 4 | Cooking Time: 30 Minutes
- 1 large egg
- Juice from 1 lemon.
- 1 tsp dry mustard
- ½ tsp black pepper
- 1 cup avocado oil

1. Combine the egg and lemon juice in a container and let sit for 20 minutes.
2. Add the dry mustard, pepper, and avocado oil.
3. Insert an electric whisk into the container.
4. Blend for 30 seconds.
5. Transfer to a sealed container and store in your refrigerator.

Pickled Bacon Bowls
Servings: 4 | Cooking Time: 20 Minutes
- 4 dill pickle spears, sliced in half and quartered
- 8 bacon slices, halved
- 1 cup avocado mayonnaise

1. Wrap each pickle spear in a bacon slice, put them in your air fryer's basket and cook at 400 degrees F for 20 minutes. Divide into bowls and serve as a snack with the mayonnaise.

Green Beans & S
Servings: 4 | Cooking Time: 15 Minutes
- 1 lb fresh green beans, trimmed
- 2 tbsp butter
- ¼ cup sliced s
- 2 tsp lemon pepper

1. Steam the green beans for 8 minutes, until tender, then drain.
2. On a medium heat, melt the butter in a skillet.
3. Sauté the s until browned.
4. Sprinkle with salt and pepper.
5. Mix in the green beans.

Crunchy Bacon Bites
Servings: 4 | Cooking Time: 10 Minutes
- 4 bacon strips, cut into small pieces
- 1/2 cup pork rinds, crushed
- 1/4 cup hot sauce

1. Add bacon pieces in a bowl.
2. Add hot sauce and toss well.
3. Add crushed pork rinds and toss until bacon pieces are well coated.
4. Transfer bacon pieces in air fryer basket and cook at 350 F for 10 minutes.
5. Serve and enjoy.

Crispy Kale Chips
Servings: 4 | Cooking Time: 3 Minutes
- 1 head fresh kale, stems and ribs removed and cut into 1½ inch pieces
- 1 tablespoon olive oil
- 1 teaspoon soy sauce

1. Preheat the Air fryer to 380 o F and grease an Air fryer basket.
2. Mix together all the ingredients in a bowl until well combined.
3. Arrange the kale in the Air fryer basket and cook for about 3 minutes, flipping in between.
4. Dish out and serve warm.

Bow Tie Pasta Chips
Servings: 6 | Cooking Time: 10 Minutes
- 2 cups white bow tie pasta
- 1 tablespoon olive oil
- 1 tablespoon nutritional yeast
- 1½ teaspoons Italian seasoning blend
- ½ teaspoon salt

1. Cook the pasta for 1/2 the time called for on the package. Toss the drained pasta
2. with the olive oil or aquafaba, nutritional yeast, Italian seasoning, and salt.
3. Place about half of the mixture in your air fryer basket if yours is small; larger ones may be able to do cook in one batch.
4. Cook on 390°F (200°C) for 5 minutes. Shake the basket and cook 3 to 5 minutes more or until crunchy.

Cajun Kale Chips
Servings: 4 | Cooking Time: 4 Minutes
- 3 kale heads, cut into pieces
- 2 tbsp Worcestershire sauce
- 2 tbsp sesame oil
- 1 1/2 tsp Cajun spice mix
- Pepper
- Salt

1. Add all ingredients into the large bowl and toss well.
2. Transfer kale into the air fryer basket and cook at 195 F for 4-5 minutes.
3. Serve and enjoy.

Blistered Shishito Peppers
Servings: 3 | Cooking Time: 5 Minutes
- 6 ounces (about 18) Shishito peppers
- Vegetable oil spray
- For garnishing Coarse sea or kosher salt and lemon wedges

1. Preheat the air fryer to 400°F.
2. Put the peppers in a bowl and lightly coat them with vegetable oil spray. Toss gently, spray again, and toss until the peppers are glistening but not drenched.
3. Pour the peppers into the basket, spread them into as close to one layer as you can, and air-fry for 5 minutes, tossing and rearranging the peppers at the 2- and 4-minute marks, until the peppers are blistered and even blackened in spots.
4. Pour the peppers into a bowl, add salt to taste, and toss gently. Serve the peppers with lemon wedges to squeeze over them.

The Best Party Mix Ever

Servings: 10 | Cooking Time: 15 Minutes
- 2 cups mini pretzels
- 1 cup mini crackers
- 1 cup peanuts
- 1 tablespoon Creole seasoning
- 2 tablespoons butter, melted

1. Toss all ingredients in the Air Fryer basket.
2. Cook in the preheated Air Fryer at 360 degrees F approximately 9 minutes until lightly toasted. Shake the basket periodically. Enjoy!

Tomatoes & Herbs

Servings: 2 | Cooking Time: 30 Minutes
- 2 large tomatoes, washed and cut into halves
- Herbs, such as oregano, basil, thyme, rosemary, sage to taste
- Cooking spray
- Pepper to taste
- Parmesan, grated [optional]
- Parsley, minced [optional]

1. Spritz both sides of each tomato half with a small amount of cooking spray.
2. Coat the tomatoes with a light sprinkling of pepper and the herbs of your choice.
3. Place the tomatoes in the basket, cut-side-up. Cook at 320°F for 20 minutes, or longer if necessary.
4. Serve hot, at room temperature, or chilled as a refreshing summer snack. Optionally, you can garnish them with grated Parmesan and minced parsley before serving.

Air Fry Bacon

Servings: 11 | Cooking Time: 10 Minutes
- 11 bacon slices

1. Place half bacon slices in air fryer basket.
2. Cook at 400 F for 10 minutes.
3. Cook remaining half bacon slices using same steps.
4. Serve and enjoy.

Warm And Salty Edamame

Servings: 4 | Cooking Time: 10 Minutes
- 1 pound Unshelled edamame
- Vegetable oil spray
- ¾ teaspoon Coarse sea salt or kosher salt

1. Preheat the air fryer to 400°F.
2. Place the edamame in a large bowl and lightly coat them with vegetable oil spray. Toss well, spray again, and toss until they are evenly coated.
3. When the machine is at temperature, pour the edamame into the basket and air-fry, tossing the basket quite often to rearrange the edamame, for 7 minutes, or until warm and aromatic. (Air-fry for 10 minutes if the edamame were frozen and not thawed.)
4. Pour the edamame into a bowl and sprinkle the salt on top. Toss well, then set aside for a couple of minutes before serving with an empty bowl on the side for the pods.

Radish Chips

Servings: 1 | Cooking Time: 15 Minutes
- 2 cups water
- 1 lb. radishes
- ½ tsp. garlic powder
- ¼ tsp. onion powder
- 2 tbsp. coconut oil, melted

1. Boil the water over the stove.
2. In the meantime, prepare the radish chips. Slice off the tops and bottoms and, using a mandolin, shave into thin slices of equal size. Alternatively, this step can be completed using your food processor if it has a slicing blade.
3. Put the radish chips in the pot of boiling water and allow to cook for five minutes, ensuring they become translucent. Take care when removing from the water and place them on a paper towel to dry.
4. Add the radish chips, garlic powder, onion powder, and melted coconut oil into a bowl and toss to coat. Transfer the chips to your fryer.
5. Cook at 320°F for five minutes, occasionally giving the basket a good shake to ensure even cooking. The chips are done when cooked through and crispy. Serve immediately.

Cheese Wafers

Servings: 4 | Cooking Time: 6 Minutes Per Batch
- 4 ounces sharp Cheddar cheese, grated
- ¼ cup butter
- ½ cup flour
- ¼ teaspoon salt
- ½ cup crisp rice cereal
- oil for misting or cooking spray

1. Cream the butter and grated cheese together. You can do it by hand, but using a stand mixer is faster and easier.
2. Sift flour and salt together. Add it to the cheese mixture and mix until well blended.
3. Stir in cereal.
4. Place dough on wax paper and shape into a long roll about 1 inch in diameter. Wrap well with the wax paper and chill for at least 4 hours.
5. When ready to cook, preheat air fryer to 360°F.
6. Cut cheese roll into ¼-inch slices.
7. Spray air fryer basket with oil or cooking spray and place slices in a single layer, close but not touching.
8. Cook for 6 minutes or until golden brown. When done, place them on paper towels to cool.
9. Repeat previous step to cook remaining cheese bites.

Fried Mozzarella Sticks

Servings: 7 | Cooking Time: 5 Minutes
- 7 1-ounce string cheese sticks, unwrapped
- ½ cup All-purpose flour or tapioca flour
- 2 Large egg(s), well beaten
- 2¼ cups Seasoned Italian-style dried bread crumbs (gluten-free, if a concern)
- Olive oil spray

1. Unwrap the string cheese and place the pieces in the freezer for 20 minutes (but not longer, or they will be too frozen to soften in the time given in the air fryer).
2. Preheat the air fryer to 400°F.
3. Set up and fill three shallow soup plates or small pie plates on your counter: one for the flour, one for the egg(s), and one for the bread crumbs.
4. Dip a piece of cold string cheese in the flour until well coated (keep the others in the freezer). Gently tap off any excess flour, then set the stick in the egg(s). Roll it around to coat, let any excess egg mixture slip back into the rest, and set the stick in the bread crumbs. Gently roll it around to coat it evenly, even the ends. Now dip it back in the egg(s), then again in the bread crumbs, rolling it to coat well and evenly. Set the stick aside on a cutting board and coat the remaining pieces of string cheese in the same way.
5. Lightly coat the sticks all over with olive oil spray. Place them in

the basket in one layer and air-fry undisturbed for 5 minutes, or until golden brown and crisp.
6. Remove the basket from the machine and cool for 5 minutes. Use a nonstick-safe spatula to transfer the mozzarella sticks to a serving platter. Serve hot.

Peppers Dip

Servings: 6 | Cooking Time: 20 Minutes

- 8 ounces cream cheese, soft
- 4 ounces mozzarella, grated
- 2 bacon slices, cooked and crumbled
- A pinch of salt and black pepper
- 4 ounces parmesan, grated
- 2 roasted red peppers, chopped

1. In a pan that fits your air fryer, mix all the ingredients and whisk really well. Introduce the pan in the fryer and cook at 400 degrees F for 20 minutes. Divide into bowls and serve cold.

Greek Turkey Meatballs

Servings: 5 | Cooking Time: 15 Minutes Per Batch

- 1 pound 85/15 ground turkey
- ½ cup diced red onion
- ½ cup bread crumbs
- ¼ teaspoon ground black pepper
- 1 cup chopped fresh spinach
- ½ cup crumbled feta cheese
- ½ teaspoon salt

1. Preheat the air fryer to 350°F.
2. In a large bowl, mix all ingredients until well combined.
3. Roll mixture into balls, about 1 heaping tablespoon for each, to make twenty meatballs.
4. Spritz with cooking spray and place in the air fryer basket, working in batches as necessary. Cook 15 minutes, shaking the basket three times during cooking time, until golden brown and internal temperature reaches at least 165°F. Serve warm.

Broccoli Cheese Nuggets

Servings: 4 | Cooking Time: 15 Minutes

- 1/4 cup almond flour
- 2 cups broccoli florets, cooked until soft
- 1 cup cheddar cheese, shredded
- 2 egg whites
- 1/8 tsp salt

1. Preheat the air fryer to 325 F.
2. Spray air fryer basket with cooking spray.
3. Add cooked broccoli into the bowl and using masher mash broccoli into the small pieces.
4. Add remaining ingredients to the bowl and mix well to combine.
5. Make small nuggets from broccoli mixture and place into the air fryer basket.
6. Cook broccoli nuggets for 15 minutes. Turn halfway through.
7. Serve and enjoy.

Pork Rinds

Servings: 3 | Cooking Time: 10 Minutes

- 6 oz pork skin
- 1 tablespoon keto tomato sauce
- 1 teaspoon olive oil

1. Chop the pork skin into the rinds and sprinkle with the sauce and olive oil. Mix up well. Then preheat the air fryer to 400F. Place the pork skin rinds in the air fryer basket in one layer and cook for 10 minutes. Flip the rinds on another side after 5 minutes of cooking.

Creamy Cheddar Eggs

Servings: 8 | Cooking Time: 16 Minutes

- 4 eggs
- 2 oz pork rinds
- ¼ cup Cheddar cheese, shredded
- 1 tablespoon heavy cream
- 1 teaspoon fresh dill, chopped

1. Place the eggs in the air fryer and cook them at 255F for 16 minutes. Then cool the eggs in the cold water and peel. Cut every egg into the halves and remove the egg yolks. Transfer the egg yolks in the mixing bowl. Add shredded cheese, heavy cream, and fresh dill. Stir the mixture with the help of the fork until smooth and add pork rinds. Mix it up. Fill the egg whites with the egg yolk mixture.

Broccoli Florets

Servings: 4 | Cooking Time: 20 Minutes

- 1 lb. broccoli, cut into floretsq
- 1 tbsp. lemon juice
- 1 tbsp. olive oil
- 1 tbsp. sesame seeds
- 3 garlic cloves, minced

1. In a bowl, combine all of the ingredients, coating the broccoli well.
2. Transfer to the Air Fryer basket and air fry at 400°F for 13 minutes.

Leeks Dip

Servings: 6 | Cooking Time: 12 Minutes

- 2 spring onions, minced
- 2 tablespoons butter, melted
- 3 tablespoons coconut milk
- 4 leeks, sliced
- ¼ cup coconut cream
- Salt and white pepper to the taste

1. In a pan that fits your air fryer, mix all the ingredients and whisk them well. Introduce the pan in the fryer and cook at 390 degrees F for 12 minutes. Divide into bowls and serve.

Parmesan Zucchini Chips

Servings: 1 | Cooking Time: 10 Minutes

- 2 medium zucchini
- 1 oz. pork rinds, finely ground
- ½ cup parmesan cheese, grated
- 1 egg

1. Cut the zucchini into slices about a quarter-inch thick. Lay on a paper towel to dry.
2. In a bowl, combine the ground pork rinds and the grated parmesan.
3. In a separate bowl, beat the egg with a fork.
4. Take a zucchini slice and dip it into the egg, then into the pork rind-parmesan mixture, making sure to coat it evenly. Repeat with the rest of the slices. Lay them in the basket of your fryer, taking care not to overlap. This step may need to be completed in more than one batch.
5. Cook at 320°F for five minutes. Turn the chips over and allow to cook for another five minutes.
6. Allow to cool to achieve a crispier texture or serve warm. Enjoy!

Curly's Cauliflower
Servings: 4 | Cooking Time: 30 Minutes
- 4 cups bite-sized cauliflower florets
- 1 cup friendly bread crumbs, mixed with 1 tsp. salt
- ¼ cup melted butter [vegan/other]
- ¼ cup buffalo sauce [vegan/other]
- Mayo [vegan/other] or creamy dressing for dipping

1.1 In a bowl, combine the butter and buffalo sauce to create a creamy paste.
2.2 Completely cover each floret with the sauce.
3.3 Coat the florets with the bread crumb mixture. Cook the florets in the Air Fryer for approximately 15 minutes at 350°F, shaking the basket occasionally.
4.4 Serve with a raw vegetable salad, mayo or creamy dressing.

Apple Rollups
Servings: 8 | Cooking Time: 5 Minutes
- 8 slices whole wheat sandwich bread
- 4 ounces Colby Jack cheese, grated
- ½ small apple, chopped
- 2 tablespoons butter, melted

1. Remove crusts from bread and flatten the slices with rolling pin. Don't be gentle. Press hard so that bread will be very thin.
2. Top bread slices with cheese and chopped apple, dividing the ingredients evenly.
3. Roll up each slice tightly and secure each with one or two toothpicks.
4. Brush outside of rolls with melted butter.
5. Place in air fryer basket and cook at 390°F for 5minutes, until outside is crisp and nicely browned.

Bacon-wrapped Sausage Skewers
Servings: 2 | Cooking Time: 8 Minutes
- 5 Italian chicken sausages
- 10 slices bacon

1. Preheat your air fryer to 370°F/190°C.
2. Cut the sausage into four pieces.
3. Slice the bacon in half.
4. Wrap the bacon over the sausage.
5. Skewer the sausage.
6. Fry for 4-5 minutes until browned.

Cheese Crackers
Servings:4 | Cooking Time: 10 Minutes Per Batch
- 4 ounces sharp Cheddar cheese, shredded
- ½ cup all-purpose flour
- 2 tablespoons salted butter, cubed
- ½ teaspoon salt
- 2 tablespoons cold water

1. In a large bowl, using an electric hand mixer, mix all ingredients until dough forms. Pack dough together into a ball and wrap tightly in plastic wrap. Chill in the freezer 15 minutes.
2. Preheat the air fryer to 375°F. Cut parchment paper to fit the air fryer basket.
3. Spread a separate large sheet of parchment paper on a work surface. Remove dough from the freezer and roll out ¼" thick on parchment paper. Use a pizza cutter to cut dough into 1" squares.
4. Place crackers on precut parchment in the air fryer basket and cook 10 minutes, working in batches as necessary.
5. Allow crackers to cool at least 10 minutes before serving.

Tofu
Servings: 4 | Cooking Time: 20 Minutes
- 15 oz. extra firm tofu, drained and cut into cubes
- 1 tsp. chili flakes
- ¾ cup cornstarch
- ¼ cup cornmeal
- Pepper to taste
- Salt to taste

1. In a bowl, combine the cornmeal, cornstarch, chili flakes, pepper, and salt.
2. Coat the tofu cubes completely with the mixture.
3. Pre-heat your Air Fryer at 350°F.
4. Spritz the basket with cooking spray.
5. Transfer the coated tofu to the basket and air fry for 8 minutes, shaking the basket at the 4-minute mark.

Parmesan Green Beans Sticks
Servings: 4 | Cooking Time: 12 Minutes
- 12 ounces green beans, trimmed
- 1 cup parmesan, grated
- 1 egg, whisked
- A pinch of salt and black pepper
- ¼ teaspoon sweet paprika

1. In a bowl, mix the parmesan with salt, pepper and the paprika and stir. Put the egg in a separate bowl, Dredge the green beans in egg and then in the parmesan mix. Arrange the green beans in your air fryer's basket and cook at 380 degrees F for 12 minutes. Serve as a snack.

Easy Carrot Dip
Servings: 6 | Cooking Time: 15 Minutes
- 2 cups carrots, grated
- 1/4 tsp cayenne pepper
- 4 tbsp butter, melted
- 1 tbsp chives, chopped
- Pepper
- Salt

1. Add all ingredients into the air fryer baking dish and stir until well combined.
2. Place dish in the air fryer and cook at 380 F for 15 minutes.
3. Transfer cook carrot mixture into the blender and blend until smooth.
4. Serve and enjoy.

Pickled Fries
Servings:4 | Cooking Time: 8 Minutes
- 2 pickles, sliced
- 1 tablespoon dried dill
- 1 egg, beaten
- 2 tablespoons flax meal

1. Dip the sliced pickles in the egg and then sprinkle with dried ill and flax meal. Place them in the air fryer basket in one layer and cook at 400F for 8 minutes.

Spicy Dip
Servings: 6 | Cooking Time: 5 Minutes
- 12 oz hot peppers, chopped
- Salt
- 1 1/2 cups apple cider vinegar
- Pepper

1. Add all ingredients into the air fryer baking dish and stir well.
2. Place dish in the air fryer and cook at 380 F for 5 minutes.
3. Transfer pepper mixture into the blender and blend until smooth.
4. Serve and enjoy.

Cauliflower Poppers
Servings: 6 | Cooking Time: 16 Minutes
- 1 large head cauliflower, cut into bite-sized florets
- 2 tablespoons olive oil
- Salt and freshly ground black pepper, as needed

1. Drizzle the cauliflower florets with oil.
2. Sprinkle with salt and black pepper.
3. Set the temperature of Air Fryer to 390 degrees F.
4. Place the cauliflower florets in a greased Air Fryer basket in a single layer in 2 batches.
5. Air Fry for about 8 minutes, shaking once halfway through.
6. Serve hot.

Korean-style Wings
Servings: 4 | Cooking Time: 20 Minutes
- 1 pound chicken wings, drums and flats separated
- ½ teaspoon salt
- ¼ teaspoon ground black pepper
- ¼ cup gochujang sauce
- 2 tablespoons soy sauce
- 1 teaspoon ground ginger
- ¼ cup mayonnaise

1. Preheat the air fryer to 350°F.
2. Sprinkle wings with salt and pepper. Place wings in the air fryer basket and cook 15 minutes, turning halfway through cooking time.
3. In a medium bowl, mix gochujang sauce, soy sauce, ginger, and mayonnaise.
4. Toss wings in sauce mixture and adjust the air fryer temperature to 400°F.
5. Place wings back in the air fryer basket and cook an additional 5 minutes until the internal temperature reaches at least 165°F. Serve warm.

Pork Egg Rolls
Servings: 4 | Cooking Time: 17 Minutes
- ½ pound 84% lean ground pork
- 3 tablespoons low-sodium soy sauce, divided
- ½ teaspoon salt
- 2 cups broccoli slaw
- ½ teaspoon ground ginger
- 8 egg roll wrappers

1. In a medium skillet over medium heat, crumble ground pork and cook about 10 minutes until fully cooked and no pink remains. Drain fat and return meat to skillet.
2. Pour 2 tablespoons soy sauce over pork, then sprinkle with salt and stir. Reduce heat to low and cook 2 minutes.
3. Add broccoli slaw. Pour remaining soy sauce over broccoli slaw and sprinkle with ginger. Stir and continue cooking 5 minutes until slaw is tender.
4. Preheat the air fryer to 350°F.
5. For each egg roll, position a wrapper so that one corner is pointed toward you. Spoon 3 tablespoons pork mixture across the wrapper near the corner closest to you.
6. Roll the point closest to you over the filling. Fold the left and right corners toward the center, then roll the wrapper closed toward the far corner. Repeat with remaining wrappers and filling.
7. Place in the air fryer basket seam side down and cook 10 minutes, turning halfway through cooking time. Serve warm.

Cabbage Chips
Servings: 6 | Cooking Time: 30 Minutes
- 1 large cabbage head, tear cabbage leaves into pieces
- 2 tbsp olive oil
- 1/4 cup parmesan cheese, grated
- Pepper
- Salt

1. Preheat the air fryer to 250 F.
2. Add all ingredients into the large mixing bowl and toss well.
3. Spray air fryer basket with cooking spray.
4. Divide cabbage in batches.
5. Add one cabbage chips batch in air fryer basket and cook for 25-30 minutes at 250 F or until chips are crispy and lightly golden brown.
6. Serve and enjoy.

Green Olive And Mushroom Tapenade
Servings: 1 | Cooking Time: 10 Minutes
- ¾ pound Brown or Baby Bella mushrooms, sliced
- 1½ cups (about ½ pound) Pitted green olives
- 3 tablespoons Olive oil
- 1½ tablespoons Fresh oregano leaves, loosely packed
- ¼ teaspoon Ground black pepper

1. Preheat the air fryer to 400°F.
2. When the machine is at temperature, arrange the mushroom slices in as close to an even layer as possible in the basket. They will overlap and even stack on top of each other.
3. Air-fry for 10 minutes, tossing the basket and rearranging the mushrooms every 2 minutes, until shriveled but with still-noticeable moisture.
4. Pour the mushrooms into a food processor. Add the olives, olive oil, oregano leaves, and pepper. Cover and process until grainy, not too much, just not fully smooth for better texture, stopping the machine at least once to scrape down the inside of the canister. Scrape the tapenade into a bowl and serve warm, or cover and refrigerate for up to 4 days. (The tapenade will taste better if it comes back to room temperature before serving.)

Sausage And Cheese Rolls
Servings: 3 | Cooking Time: 18 Minutes
- 3 3- to 3½-ounce sweet or hot Italian sausage links
- 2 1-ounce string cheese stick(s), unwrapped and cut in half lengthwise
- Three quarters from one thawed sheet (cut the sheet into four quarters; wrap and refreeze one of them) A 17.25-ounce box frozen puff pastry

1. Preheat the air fryer to 400°F.
2. When the machine is at temperature, set the sausage links in the basket and air-fry undisturbed for 12 minutes, or until cooked through.
3. Use kitchen tongs to transfer the links to a wire rack. Cool for 15 minutes. (If necessary, pour out any rendered fat that has collected below the basket in the machine.)
4. Cut the sausage links in half lengthwise. Sandwich half a string cheese stick between two sausage halves, trimming the ends so the cheese doesn't stick out beyond the meat.
5. Roll each piece of puff pastry into a 6 x 6-inch square on a clean, dry work surface. Set the sausage-cheese sandwich at one edge and roll it up in the dough. The ends will be open like a pig-in-a-blanket. Repeat with the remaining puff pastry, sausage, and cheese.

6. Set the rolls seam side down in the basket. Air-fry undisturbed for 6 minutes, or until puffed and golden brown.
7. Use a nonstick-safe spatula, and perhaps a flatware fork for balance, to transfer the rolls to a wire rack. Cool for at least 5 minutes before serving.

Ham & Cheese Rolls
Servings: 4 | Cooking Time: 5 Minutes
- 16 slices ham
- 1 package chive and onion cream cheese (8 oz)
- 16 slices thin Swiss cheese

1. Place the ham on a chopping board.
2. Dry the slices with a paper towel.
3. Thinly spread 2 teaspoons of Swiss cheese over each slice of ham.
4. On the clean section of ham, add a half inch slice of cheese.
5. On the cheese side, fold the ham over the cheese and roll it up.
6. Leave it as is, or slice into smaller rolls.

Cheese Dip
Servings: 10 | Cooking Time: 10 Minutes
- 1 pound mozzarella, shredded
- 1 tablespoon thyme, chopped
- 6 garlic cloves, minced
- 3 tablespoons olive oil
- 1 teaspoon rosemary, chopped
- A pinch of salt and black pepper

1. In a pan that fits your air fryer, mix all the ingredients, whisk really well, introduce in the air fryer and cook at 370 degrees F for 10 minutes. Divide into bowls and serve right away.

Crispy Shrimps
Servings: 2 | Cooking Time: 8 Minutes
- 1 egg
- ¼ pound nacho chips, crushed
- 10 shrimps, peeled and deveined
- 1 tablespoon olive oil
- Salt and black pepper, to taste

1. Preheat the Air fryer to 365 o F and grease an Air fryer basket.
2. Crack egg in a shallow dish and beat well.
3. Place the nacho chips in another shallow dish.
4. Season the shrimps with salt and black pepper, coat into egg and then roll into nacho chips.
5. Place the coated shrimps into the Air fryer basket and cook for about 8 minutes.
6. Dish out and serve warm.

Onion Dip
Servings: 8 | Cooking Time: 25 Minutes
- 2 lbs onion, chopped
- 1/2 tsp baking soda
- 6 tbsp butter, softened
- Pepper
- Salt

1. Melt butter in a pan over medium heat.
2. Add onion and baking soda and sauté for 5 minutes.
3. Transfer onion mixture into the air fryer baking dish.
4. Place in the air fryer and cook at 370 F for 25 minutes.
5. Serve and enjoy.

Sesame Tortilla Chips
Servings: 4 | Cooking Time: 4 Minutes
- 4 low carb tortillas
- ½ teaspoon salt
- 1 teaspoon sesame oil

1. Cut the tortillas into the strips. Preheat the air fryer to 365F. Place the tortilla strips in the air fryer basket and sprinkle with sesame oil. Cook them for 3 minutes. Then give a shake to the chips and sprinkle with salt. Cook the chips for 1 minute more.

Fried Pickles
Servings: 2 | Cooking Time: 15 Minutes
- 1 egg
- 1 tablespoon milk
- ¼ teaspoon hot sauce
- 2 cups sliced dill pickles, well drained
- ¾ cup breadcrumbs
- oil for misting or cooking spray

1. Preheat air fryer to 390°F.
2. Beat together egg, milk, and hot sauce in a bowl large enough to hold all the pickles.
3. Add pickles to the egg wash and stir well to coat.
4. Place breadcrumbs in a large plastic bag or container with lid.
5. Drain egg wash from pickles and place them in bag with breadcrumbs. Shake to coat.
6. Pile pickles into air fryer basket and spray with oil.
7. Cook for 5 minutes. Shake basket and spray with oil.
8. Cook 5 more minutes. Shake and spray again. Separate any pickles that have stuck together and mist any spots you've missed.
9. Cook for 5 minutes longer or until dark golden brown and crispy.

Baked Tortillas
Servings: 4 | Cooking Time: 30 Minutes
- 1 large head of cauliflower divided into florets.
- 4 large eggs
- 2 garlic cloves (minced)
- 1 ½ tsp herbs (whatever your favorite is - basil, oregano, thyme)
- ½ tsp salt

1. Preheat your fryer to 375°F/190°C.
2. Put parchment paper on two baking sheets.
3. In a food processor, break down the cauliflower into rice.
4. Add ¼ cup water and the riced cauliflower to a saucepan.
5. Cook on a medium high heat until tender for 10 minutes. Drain.
6. Dry with a clean kitchen towel.
7. Mix the cauliflower, eggs, garlic, herbs and salt.
8. Make 4 thin circles on the parchment paper.
9. Bake for 20 minutes, until dry.

Curried Sweet Potato Fries
Servings: 3 | Cooking Time: 20 Minutes
- 2 small sweet potatoes, peel and cut into fries shape
- 1/4 tsp coriander
- 1/2 tsp curry powder
- 2 tbsp olive oil
- 1/4 tsp sea salt

1. Add all ingredients into the large mixing bowl and toss well.
2. Spray air fryer basket with cooking spray.
3. Transfer sweet potato fries in the air fryer basket.
4. Cook for 20 minutes at 370 F. Shake halfway through.
5. Serve and enjoy.

Fruit Pastries

Servings: 8 | Cooking Time: 20 Minutes

- ½ of apple, peeled, cored and chopped
- 1 teaspoon fresh orange zest, finely grated
- ½ tablespoon white sugar
- ½ teaspoon ground cinnamon
- 7.05 ounces prepared frozen puff pastry

1. In a bowl, mix together all the ingredients except puff pastry.
2. Cut the pastry in 16 squares.
3. Using a teaspoon, place apple mixture in the center of each square.
4. Fold each square into a triangle and slightly press the edges with your wet fingers.
5. Then, using a fork, firmly press the edges.
6. Set the temperature of Air Fryer to 390 degrees F.
7. Add the pastries into an Air Fryer basket in a single layer in 2 batches.
8. Air Fry for about 10 minutes.
9. Enjoy!

Potato Chips

Servings: 2 | Cooking Time: 15 Minutes

- 2 medium potatoes
- 2 teaspoons extra-light olive oil
- oil for misting or cooking spray
- salt and pepper

1. Peel the potatoes.
2. Using a mandoline or paring knife, shave potatoes into thin slices, dropping them into a bowl of water as you cut them.
3. Dry potatoes as thoroughly as possible with paper towels or a clean dish towel. Toss potato slices with the oil to coat completely.
4. Spray air fryer basket with cooking spray and add potato slices.
5. Stir and separate with a fork.
6. Cook 390°F for 5minutes. Stir and separate potato slices. Cook 5 more minutes. Stir and separate potatoes again. Cook another 5minutes.
7. Season to taste.

Puerto Rican Tostones

Servings: 2 | Cooking Time: 15 Minutes

- 1 ripe plantain, sliced
- 1 tablespoon sunflower oil
- A pinch of grated nutmeg
- A pinch of kosher salt

Directions:
1. Toss the plantains with the oil, nutmeg, and salt in a bowl.
2. Cook in the preheated Air Fryer at 400 degrees F for 10 minutes, shaking the cooking basket halfway through the cooking time.
3. Adjust the seasonings to taste and serve immediately.

Grilled Cheese Sandwich Deluxe

Servings: 4 | Cooking Time: 6 Minutes

- 8 ounces Brie
- 8 slices oat nut bread
- 1 large ripe pear, cored and cut into ½-inch-thick slices
- 2 tablespoons butter, melted

1. Spread a quarter of the Brie on each of four slices of bread.
2. Top Brie with thick slices of pear, then the remaining 4 slices of bread.
3. Lightly brush both sides of each sandwich with melted butter.
4. Cooking 2 at a time, place sandwiches in air fryer basket and cook at 360°F for 6minutes or until cheese melts and outside looks golden brown.

Roasted Almonds

Servings: 8 | Cooking Time: 8 Minutes

- 2 cups almonds
- 1/4 tsp pepper
- 1 tsp paprika
- 1 tbsp garlic powder
- 1 tbsp soy sauce

1. Add pepper, paprika, garlic powder, and soy sauce in a bowl and stir well.
2. Add almonds and stir to coat.
3. Spray air fryer basket with cooking spray.
4. Add almonds in air fryer basket and cook for 6-8 minutes at 320 F. Shake basket after every 2 minutes.
5. Serve and enjoy.

Easy Crispy Prawns

Servings: 4 | Cooking Time: 10 Minutes

- 1 egg
- ½ pound nacho chips, crushed
- 18 prawns, peeled and deveined
- Salt and black pepper, to taste

1. Preheat the Air fryer to 355 o F and grease an Air fryer basket.
2. Crack egg in a shallow dish and beat well.
3. Place the crushed nacho chips in another shallow dish.
4. Coat prawns into egg and then roll into nacho chips.
5. Place the coated prawns into the Air fryer basket and cook for about 10 minutes.
6. Dish out and serve warm.

Za'atar Garbanzo Beans

Servings: 6 | Cooking Time: 12 Minutes

- One 14.5-ounce can garbanzo beans, drained and rinsed
- 1 tablespoon extra-virgin olive oil
- 6 teaspoons za'atar seasoning mix
- 2 tablespoons chopped parsley
- Salt and pepper, to taste

1. Preheat the air fryer to 390°F.
2. In a medium bowl, toss the garbanzo beans with olive oil and za'atar seasoning.
3. Pour the beans into the air fryer basket and cook for 12 minutes, or until toasted as you like. Stir every 3 minutes while roasting.
4. Remove the beans from the air fryer basket into a serving bowl, top with fresh chopped parsley, and season with salt and pepper.

Greek Street Tacos

Servings: 8 | Cooking Time: 3 Minutes

- 8 small flour tortillas (4-inch diameter)
- 8 tablespoons hummus
- 4 tablespoons crumbled feta cheese
- 4 tablespoons chopped kalamata or other olives (optional)
- olive oil for misting

1. Place 1 tablespoon of hummus or tapenade in the center of each tortilla. Top with 1 teaspoon of feta crumbles and 1 teaspoon of chopped olives, if using.
2. Using your finger or a small spoon, moisten the edges of the tortilla all around with water.
3. Fold tortilla over to make a half-moon shape. Press center gently.

Then press the edges firmly to seal in the filling.
4. Mist both sides with olive oil.
5. Place in air fryer basket very close but try not to overlap.
6. Cook at 390°F for 3minutes, just until lightly browned and crispy.

Grilled Cheese Sandwich
Servings: 2 | Cooking Time: 5 Minutes
- 4 slices bread
- 4 ounces Cheddar cheese slices
- 2 teaspoons butter or oil

1. Lay the four cheese slices on two of the bread slices and top with the remaining two slices of bread.
2. Brush both sides with butter or oil and cut the sandwiches in rectangular halves.
3. Place in air fryer basket and cook at 390°F for 5minutes until the outside is crisp and the cheese melts.

Grilled Cheese Sandwiches
Servings: 2 | Cooking Time:5 Minutes
- 4 white bread slices
- ½ cup melted butter, softened
- ½ cup sharp cheddar cheese, grated
- 1 tablespoon mayonnaise

1. Preheat the Air fryer to 355 o F and grease an Air fryer basket.
2. Spread the mayonnaise and melted butter over one side of each bread slice.
3. Sprinkle the cheddar cheese over the buttered side of the 2 slices.
4. Cover with the remaining slices of bread and transfer into the Air fryer basket.
5. Cook for about 5 minutes and dish out to serve warm.

Cheese Sandwich
Servings: 2 | Cooking Time: 5 Minutes
- 4 white bread slices
- ½ cup butter, softened
- ½ cup sharp cheddar cheese, grated

1. Set the temperature of Air Fryer to 355 degrees F.
2. Spread the butter evenly over one side of each bread slice.
3. Sprinkle the cheese over buttered side of 2 slices.
4. Top with the remaining slices of bread.
5. Place the sandwiches in an Air Fryer basket in a single layer.
6. Air Fry for about 4-5 minutes.
7. Serve.

Sweet Potato Chips
Servings: 4 | Cooking Time: 10 Minutes
- 2 medium sweet potatoes, washed
- 1 tablespoon avocado oil
- ½ teaspoon salt
- 2 cups filtered water
- 2 teaspoons brown sugar

1. Using a mandolin, slice the potatoes into ⅛-inch pieces.
2. Add the water to a large bowl. Place the potatoes in the bowl, and soak for at least 30 minutes.
3. Preheat the air fryer to 350°F.
4. Drain the water and pat the chips dry with a paper towel or kitchen cloth. Toss the chips with the avocado oil, brown sugar, and salt. Liberally spray the air fryer basket with olive oil mist.
5. Set the chips inside the air fryer, separating them so they're not on top of each other. Cook for 5 minutes, shake the basket, and cook another 5 minutes, or until browned.
6. Remove and let cool a few minutes prior to serving. Repeat until all the chips are cooked.

Coconut Cheese Sticks
Servings:4 | Cooking Time: 4 Minutes
- 1 egg, beaten
- 1 teaspoon ground paprika
- Cooking spray
- 4 tablespoons coconut flakes
- 6 oz Provolone cheese

1. Cut the cheese into sticks. Then dip every cheese stick in the beaten egg. After this, mix up coconut flakes and ground paprika. Coat the cheese sticks in the coconut mixture. Preheat the air fryer to 400F. Put the cheese sticks in the air fryer and spray them with cooking spray. Cook the meal for 2 minutes from each side. Cool them well before serving.

Chili Calamari Rings
Servings:2 | Cooking Time: 15 Minutes
- 1 pound calamari rings
- ½ teaspoon avocado oil
- 1 teaspoon black pepper
- ¼ teaspoon chili powder

1. In the air fryer, mix the calamari with black pepper and the other ingredients and toss. Cook the onion rings at 400F for 10 minutes.

Paprika Chips
Servings: 4 | Cooking Time: 5 Minutes
- 8 ounces cheddar cheese, shredded
- 1 teaspoon sweet paprika

1. Divide the cheese in small heaps in a pan that fits the air fryer, sprinkle the paprika on top, introduce the pan in the machine and cook at 400 degrees F for 5 minutes. Cool the chips down and serve them.

Mozzarella Sticks
Servings: 4 | Cooking Time: 5 Minutes
- 1 egg
- 1 tablespoon water
- 8 eggroll wraps
- 8 mozzarella string cheese "sticks"
- sauce for dipping

1. Beat together egg and water in a small bowl.
2. Lay out egg roll wraps and moisten edges with egg wash.
3. Place one piece of string cheese on each wrap near one end.
4. Fold in sides of egg roll wrap over ends of cheese, and then roll up.
5. Brush outside of wrap with egg wash and press gently to seal well.
6. Place in air fryer basket in single layer and cook 390°F for 5 minutes. Cook an additional 1 or 2minutes, if necessary, until they are golden brown and crispy.
7. Serve with your favorite dipping sauce.

Crust-less Meaty Pizza
Servings: 1 | Cooking Time: 15 Minutes
- ½ cup mozzarella cheese, shredded
- 2 slices sugar-free bacon, cooked and crumbled
- ¼ cup ground sausage, cooked
- 7 slices pepperoni
- 1 tbsp. parmesan cheese, grated

1. Spread the mozzarella across the bottom of a six-inch cake pan. Throw on the bacon, sausage, and pepperoni, then add a sprinkle of the parmesan cheese on top. Place the pan inside your air fryer.
2. Cook at 400°F for five minutes. The cheese is ready once brown in color and bubbly. Take care when removing the pan from the fryer and serve.

Squash Fries

Servings: 2 | Cooking Time: 35 Minutes

- 14 ounces butternut squash, peeled, seeded and cut into strips
- 2 teaspoons olive oil
- ½ teaspoon ground cinnamon
- ½ teaspoon red chili powder
- ¼ teaspoon garlic salt
- Salt and freshly ground black pepper, as needed

1. Set the temperature of Air Fryer to 440 degrees F. Line a baking sheet with parchment paper.
2. Take a bowl, add all the listed ingredients and toss to coat well.
3. Place the butternut squash strips onto the prepared baking sheet in a single layer.
4. Arrange the baking sheet in an Air Fryer basket.
5. Air Fry for about 35 minutes.
6. Serve.

Barbecue Little Smokies

Servings: 6 | Cooking Time: 20 Minutes

- 1 pound beef cocktail wieners
- 10 ounces barbecue sauce

1. Start by preheating your Air Fryer to 380 degrees F.
2. Prick holes into your sausages using a fork and transfer them to the baking pan.
3. Cook for 13 minutes. Spoon the barbecue sauce into the pan and cook an additional 2 minutes.
4. Serve with toothpicks. Bon appétit!

Asparagus

Servings: 4 | Cooking Time: 15 Minutes

- 10 asparagus spears, woody end cut off
- 1 clove garlic, minced
- 4 tbsp. olive oil
- Pepper to taste
- Salt to taste

1. Set the Air Fryer to 400°F and allow to heat for 5 minutes.
2. In a bowl, combine the garlic and oil.
3. Cover the asparagus with this mixture and put it in the fryer basket. Sprinkle over some pepper and salt.
4. Cook for 10 minutes and serve hot.

Chocolate Cookie Dough Balls

Servings: 6 | Cooking Time: 20 Minutes

- 16½ ounces store-bought chilled chocolate chip cookie dough
- ¼ cup butter, melted
- ½ cup chocolate cookie crumbs
- 2 tablespoons sugar

1. Cut the cookie dough into 12 equal-sized pieces and then, shape each into a ball.
2. Add the melted butter in a shallow dish.
3. In another dish, mix together the cookie crumbs, and sugar.
4. Dip each cookie ball in the melted butter and then evenly coat with the cookie crumbs.

5. In the bottom of a baking sheet, place the coated cookie balls and freeze for at least 2 hours.
6. Preheat the air fryer to 350 degrees F.
7. Line the air fryer basket with a piece of foil.
8. Place the cookies balls in an Air Fryer basket in a single layer in 2 batches.
9. Air Fry for about 10 minutes.
10. Enjoy!

Chipotle Jicama Hash

Servings: 2 | Cooking Time: 15 Minutes

- 4 slices bacon, chopped
- 12 oz jicama, peeled and diced
- 4 oz purple onion, chopped
- 1 oz green bell pepper (or poblano), seeded and chopped
- 4 tbsp Chipotle mayonnaise

1. Using a skillet, brown the bacon on a high heat.
2. Remove and place on a towel to drain the grease.
3. Use the remaining grease to fry the onions and jicama until brown.
4. When ready, add the bell pepper and cook the hash until tender.
5. Transfer the hash onto two plates and serve each plate with 4 tablespoons of Chipotle mayonnaise.

Air Fryer Plantains

Servings: 4 | Cooking Time: 10 Minutes

- 2 ripe plantains
- 2 teaspoons avocado oil
- 1/8 teaspoon salt

1. Preheat the Air fryer to 400 o F and grease an Air fryer basket.
2. Mix the plantains with avocado oil and salt in a bowl.
3. Arrange the coated plantains in the Air fryer basket and cook for about 10 minutes.
4. Dish out in a bowl and serve immediately.

Rutabaga Fries

Servings: 8 | Cooking Time: 18 Minutes

- 1 lb rutabaga, cut into fries shape
- 2 tsp olive oil
- 1 tsp garlic powder
- 1/2 tsp chili pepper
- 1/2 tsp salt

1. Add all ingredients into the large mixing bowl and toss to coat.
2. Preheat the air fryer to 365 F.
3. Transfer rutabaga fries into the air fryer basket and cook for 18 minutes. Shake 2-3 times.
4. Serve and enjoy.

Hot Cheesy Dip

Servings: 6 | Cooking Time: 12 Minutes

- 12 ounces coconut cream
- 2 teaspoons keto hot sauce
- 8 ounces cheddar cheese, grated

1. In ramekin, mix the cream with hot sauce and cheese and whisk. Put the ramekin in the fryer and cook at 390 degrees F for 12 minutes. Whisk, divide into bowls and serve as a dip.

Turkey Bacon Dates
Servings: 16 | Cooking Time: 7 Minutes
- 16 whole, pitted dates
- 16 whole almonds
- 6 to 8 strips turkey bacon

1. Stuff each date with a whole almond.
2. Depending on the size of your stuffed dates, cut bacon strips into halves or thirds. Each strip should be long enough to wrap completely around a date.
3. Wrap each date in a strip of bacon with ends overlapping and secure with toothpicks.
4. Place in air fryer basket and cook at 390°F for 7 minutes, until bacon is as crispy as you like.
5. Drain on paper towels or wire rack. Serve hot or at room temperature.

Garlic Eggplant Chips
Servings: 4 | Cooking Time: 25 Minutes
- 1 eggplant, sliced
- 1 teaspoon garlic powder
- 1 tablespoon olive oil

1. Mix up olive oil and garlic powder. Then brush every eggplant slice with a garlic powder mixture. Preheat the air fryer to 400F. Place the eggplant slices in the air fryer basket in one layer and cook them for 15 minutes. Then flip the eggplant slices on another side and cook for 10 minutes.

Onion Rings
Servings: 4 | Cooking Time: 12 Minutes
- 1 cup all-purpose flour
- 1 tablespoon seasoned salt
- 1 cup whole milk
- 1 large egg
- 1 cup panko bread crumbs
- 1 large Vidalia onion, peeled and sliced into ¼"-thick rings

1. Preheat the air fryer to 350°F.
2. In a large bowl, whisk together flour and seasoned salt.
3. In a medium bowl, whisk together milk and egg. Place bread crumbs in a separate large bowl.
4. Dip onion rings into flour mixture to coat and set them aside. Pour milk mixture into the bowl of flour and stir to combine.
5. Dip onion rings into wet mixture and then press into bread crumbs to coat.
6. Place onion rings in the air fryer basket and spritz with cooking spray. Cook 12 minutes until the edges are crispy and golden. Serve warm.

Chocolate Bacon Bites
Servings: 4 | Cooking Time: 10 Minutes
- 4 bacon slices, halved
- 1 cup dark chocolate, melted
- A pinch of pink salt

1. Dip each bacon slice in some chocolate, sprinkle pink salt over them, put them in your air fryer's basket and cook at 350 degrees F for 10 minutes. Serve as a snack.

Fried Kale Chips
Servings: 2 | Cooking Time: 10 Minutes
- 1 head kale, torn into 1 ½-inch pieces
- 1 tbsp. olive oil
- 1 tsp. soy sauce

1. Wash and dry the kale pieces.
2. Transfer the kale to a bowl and coat with the soy sauce and oil.
3. Place it in the Air Fryer and cook at 400°F for 3 minutes, tossing it halfway through the cooking process.

Kohlrabi Chips
Servings: 10 | Cooking Time: 20 Minutes
- 1 lb kohlrabi, peel and slice thinly
- 1 tsp paprika
- 1 tbsp olive oil
- 1 tsp salt

1. Preheat the air fryer to 320 F.
2. Add all ingredients into the bowl and toss to coat.
3. Transfer kohlrabi into the air fryer basket and cook for 20 minutes. Toss halfway through.
4. Serve and enjoy.

Italian-style Tomato-parmesan Crisps
Servings: 4 | Cooking Time: 20 Minutes
- 4 Roma tomatoes, sliced
- 2 tablespoons olive oil
- Sea salt and white pepper, to taste
- 1 teaspoon Italian seasoning mix
- 4 tablespoons Parmesan cheese, grated

1. Start by preheating your Air Fryer to 350 degrees F. Generously grease the Air Fryer basket with nonstick cooking oil.
2. Toss the sliced tomatoes with the remaining ingredients. Transfer them to the cooking basket without overlapping.
3. Cook in the preheated Air Fryer for 5 minutes. Shake the cooking basket and cook an additional 5 minutes. Work in batches.
4. Serve with Mediterranean aioli for dipping, if desired. Bon appétit!

Roasted Peanuts
Servings: 10 | Cooking Time: 14 Minutes
- 2½ cups raw peanuts
- 1 tablespoon olive oil
- Salt, as required

1. Set the temperature of Air Fryer to 320 degrees F.
2. Add the peanuts in an Air Fryer basket in a single layer.
3. Air Fry for about 9 minutes, tossing twice.
4. Remove the peanuts from Air Fryer basket and transfer into a bowl.
5. Add the oil, and salt and toss to coat well.
6. Return the nuts mixture into Air Fryer basket.
7. Air Fry for about 5 minutes.
8. Once done, transfer the hot nuts in a glass or steel bowl and serve.

Jalapeño Guacamole
Servings: 4 | Cooking Time: 30 Minutes
- 2 Hass avocados, ripe
- ¼ red onion
- 1 jalapeño
- 1 tbsp fresh lime juice
- Sea salt

1. Spoon the avocado innings into a bowl.
2. Dice the jalapeño and onion.
3. Mash the avocado to the desired consistency.
4. Add in the onion, jalapeño and lime juice.
5. Sprinkle with salt.

Spinach Dip
Servings: 2 | Cooking Time: 15 Minutes
- 8 ounces full-fat cream cheese, softened
- ½ cup mayonnaise
- 2 teaspoons minced garlic
- 1 cup grated Parmesan cheese
- 1 package frozen chopped spinach, thawed and drained

1. Preheat the air fryer to 320°F.
2. In a large bowl, mix cream cheese, mayonnaise, garlic, and Parmesan.
3. Fold in spinach. Scrape mixture into a 6" round baking dish and place in the air fryer basket.
4. Cook 15 minutes until mixture is bubbling and top begins to turn brown. Serve warm.

Quick And Easy Popcorn
Servings: 4 | Cooking Time: 20 Minutes
- 2 tablespoons dried corn kernels
- 1 teaspoon safflower oil
- Kosher salt, to taste
- 1 teaspoon red pepper flakes, crushed

1. Add the dried corn kernels to the Air Fryer basket; brush with safflower oil.
2. Cook at 395 degrees F for 15 minutes, shaking the basket every 5 minutes.
3. Sprinkle with salt and red pepper flakes. Bon appétit!

Brussels Sprout Crisps
Servings: 4 | Cooking Time: 20 Minutes
- 1 pound Brussels sprouts, ends and yellow leaves removed and halved lengthwise
- Salt and black pepper, to taste
- 1 tablespoon toasted sesame oil
- 1 teaspoon fennel seeds
- Chopped fresh parsley, for garnish

1. Place the Brussels sprouts, salt, pepper, sesame oil, and fennel seeds in a resealable plastic bag. Seal the bag and shake to coat.
2. Air-fry at 380 degrees F for 15 minutes or until tender. Make sure to flip them over halfway through the cooking time.
3. Serve sprinkled with fresh parsley. Bon appétit!

Simple Banana Chips
Servings: 8 | Cooking Time: 10 Minutes
- 2 raw bananas, peeled and sliced
- 2 tablespoons olive oil
- Salt and black pepper, to taste

1. Preheat the Air fryer to 355 o F and grease an Air fryer basket.
2. Drizzle banana slices evenly with olive oil and arrange in the Air fryer basket.
3. Cook for about 10 minutes and season with salt and black pepper.
4. Dish out and serve warm.

Tortilla Chips
Servings: 4 | Cooking Time: 5 Minutes Per Batch
- 8 white corn tortillas
- ¼ cup olive oil
- 2 tablespoons lime juice
- ½ teaspoon salt

1. Preheat the air fryer to 350°F.
2. Cut each tortilla into fourths and brush lightly with oil.
3. Place chips in a single layer in the air fryer basket, working in batches as necessary. Cook 5 minutes, shaking the basket halfway through cooking time.
4. Sprinkle with lime juice and salt. Serve warm.

Rumaki
Servings: 24 | Cooking Time: 12 Minutes
- 10 ounces raw chicken livers
- 1 can sliced water chestnuts, drained
- ¼ cup low-sodium teriyaki sauce
- 12 slices turkey bacon
- toothpicks

1. Cut livers into 1½-inch pieces, trimming out tough veins as you slice.
2. Place livers, water chestnuts, and teriyaki sauce in small container with lid. If needed, add another tablespoon of teriyaki sauce to make sure livers are covered. Refrigerate for 1 hour.
3. When ready to cook, cut bacon slices in half crosswise.
4. Wrap 1 piece of liver and 1 slice of water chestnut in each bacon strip. Secure with toothpick.
5. When you have wrapped half of the livers, place them in the air fryer basket in a single layer.
6. Cook at 390°F for 12 minutes, until liver is done and bacon is crispy.
7. While first batch cooks, wrap the remaining livers. Repeat step 6 to cook your second batch.

Cocktail Flanks

Servings: 4 | Cooking Time: 45 Minutes

- 1x 12-oz. package cocktail franks
- 1x 8-oz. can crescent rolls

1.1 Drain the cocktail franks and dry with paper towels.
2.2 Unroll the crescent rolls and slice the dough into rectangular strips, roughly 1" by 1.5".
3.3 Wrap the franks in the strips with the ends poking out. Leave in the freezer for 5 minutes.
4.4 Pre-heat the Air Fryer to 330°F.
5.5 Take the franks out of the freezer and put them in the cooking basket. Cook for 6 – 8 minutes.
6.6 Reduce the heat to 390°F and cook for another 3 minutes or until a golden-brown color is achieved.

Classic Deviled Eggs

Servings: 3 | Cooking Time: 20 Minutes

- 5 eggs
- 2 tablespoons mayonnaise
- 2 tablespoons sweet pickle relish
- Sea salt, to taste
- 1/2 teaspoon mixed peppercorns, crushed

1. Place the wire rack in the Air Fryer basket; lower the eggs onto the wire rack.
2. Cook at 270 degrees F for 15 minutes.
3. Transfer them to an ice-cold water bath to stop the cooking. Peel the eggs under cold running water; slice them into halves.
4. Mash the egg yolks with the mayo, sweet pickle relish, and salt; spoon yolk mixture into egg whites. Arrange on a nice serving platter and garnish with the mixed peppercorns. Bon appétit!

Beef, pork & Lamb Recipes

Crispy Pierogi With Kielbasa And Onions
Servings: 3 | Cooking Time: 20 Minutes
- 6 Frozen potato and cheese pierogi, thawed (about 12 pierogi to 1 pound)
- ½ pound Smoked kielbasa, sliced into ½-inch-thick rounds
- ¾ cup Very roughly chopped sweet onion, preferably Vidalia
- Vegetable oil spray

1. Preheat the air fryer to 375°F.
2. Put the pierogi, kielbasa rounds, and onion in a large bowl. Coat them with vegetable oil spray, toss well, spray again, and toss until everything is glistening.
3. When the machine is at temperature, dump the contents of the bowl it into the basket. (Items may be leaning against each other and even on top of each other.) Air-fry, tossing and rearranging everything twice so that all covered surfaces get exposed, for 20 minutes, or until the sausages have begun to brown and the pierogi are crisp.
4. Pour the contents of the basket onto a serving platter. Wait a minute or two just to take make sure nothing's searing hot before serving.

Pork Tenderloin With Bacon & Veggies
Servings: 3 | Cooking Time: 28 Minutes
- 3 potatoes
- ¾ pound frozen green beans
- 6 bacon slices
- 3 (6-ounces) pork tenderloins
- 2 tablespoons olive oil

1. Set the temperature of air fryer to 390 degrees F. Grease an air fryer basket.
2. With a fork, pierce the potatoes.
3. Place potatoes into the prepared air fryer basket and air fry for about 15 minutes.
4. Wrap one bacon slice around 4-6 green beans.
5. Coat the pork tenderloins with oil
6. After 15 minutes, add the pork tenderloins into air fryer basket with potatoes and air fry for about 5-6 minutes.
7. Remove the pork tenderloins from basket.
8. Place bean rolls into the basket and top with the pork tenderloins.
9. Air fry for another 7 minutes.
10. Remove from air fryer and transfer the pork tenderloins onto a platter.
11. Cut each tenderloin into desired size slices.
12. Serve alongside the potatoes and green beans rolls.

Salted Porterhouse With Sage 'n Thyme Medley
Servings: 2 | Cooking Time: 40 Minutes
- ¼ cup fish sauce
- 2 tablespoons marjoram
- 2 tablespoons thyme
- 2 porterhouse steaks
- 2 tablespoons sage
- Salt and pepper to taste

1. Place all ingredients in a Ziploc bag and allow to marinate in the fridge for at least 2 hours.
2. Preheat the air fryer to 3900F.
3. Place the grill pan accessory in the air fryer.
4. Grill for 20 minutes per batch.
5. Flip every 10 minutes for even grilling.

Charred Onions 'n Steak Cube Bbq
Servings: 3 | Cooking Time: 40 Minutes
- 1 cup red onions, cut into wedges
- 1 tablespoon dry mustard
- 1 tablespoon olive oil
- Salt and pepper to taste
- 1-pound boneless beef sirloin, cut into cubes

1. Preheat the air fryer to 3900F.
2. Place the grill pan accessory in the air fryer.
3. Toss all ingredients in a bowl and mix until everything is coated with the seasonings.
4. Place on the grill pan and cook for 40 minutes.
5. Halfway through the cooking time, give a stir to cook evenly.

Buttery Pork Chops
Servings: 4 | Cooking Time: 12 Minutes
- 4 boneless pork chops
- 1 teaspoon salt
- ½ teaspoon ground black pepper
- 4 tablespoons salted butter, sliced into 8 (½-tablespoon) pats, divided

1. Preheat the air fryer to 400°F.
2. Sprinkle pork chops with salt and pepper. Top each pork chop with a ½-tablespoon butter pat.
3. Place chops in the air fryer basket and cook 12 minutes, turning halfway through cooking time, until tops and edges are golden brown and internal temperature reaches at least 145°F.
4. Use remaining butter pats to top each pork chop while hot, then let cool 5 minutes before serving warm.

Bacon Wrapped Filets Mignons
Servings: 4 | Cooking Time: 18 Minutes
- 4 slices bacon (not thick cut)
- 4 (8-ounce) filets mignons
- 1 tablespoon fresh thyme leaves
- salt and freshly ground black pepper

1. Preheat the air fryer to 400°F.
2. Lay the bacon slices down on a cutting board and sprinkle the thyme leaves on the bacon slices. Remove any string tying the filets and place the steaks down on their sides on top of the bacon slices. Roll the bacon around the side of the filets and secure the bacon to the fillets with a toothpick or two.
3. Season the steaks generously with salt and freshly ground black pepper and transfer the steaks to the air fryer.
4. Air-fry for 18 minutes, turning the steaks over halfway through the cooking process. This should cook your steaks to about medium, depending on how thick they are. If you'd prefer your steaks medium-rare or medium-well, simply add or subtract two minutes from the cooking time. Remove the steaks from the air fryer and let them rest for 5 minutes before removing the toothpicks and serving. (Just enough time to quickly air-fry some vegetables to go with them!)

Herbed Beef Roast
Servings:5 | Cooking Time:45 Minutes
- 2 pounds beef roast
- 1 tablespoon olive oil
- 1 teaspoon dried rosemary, crushed
- 1 teaspoon dried thyme, crushed
- Salt, to taste

1. Preheat the Air fryer to 360 o F and grease an Air fryer basket.
2. Rub the roast generously with herb mixture and coat with olive oil.
3. Arrange the roast in the Air fryer basket and cook for about 45 minutes.
4. Dish out the roast and cover with foil for about 10 minutes.
5. Cut into desired size slices and serve.

Beef With Tomato Sauce And Fennel
Servings: 4 | Cooking Time: 20 Minutes
- 2 tablespoons olive oil
- 1 pound beef, cut into strips
- 1 fennel bulb, sliced
- Salt and black pepper to the taste
- 1 teaspoon sweet paprika
- ¼ cup keto tomato sauce

1. Heat up a pan that fits the air fryer with the oil over medium-high heat, add the beef and brown for 5 minutes. Add the rest of the ingredients, toss, put the pan in the machine and cook at 380 degrees F for 15 minutes. Divide the mix between plates and serve.

Orange And Brown Sugar–glazed Ham
Servings:8 | Cooking Time: 15 Minutes
- ½ cup brown sugar
- ¼ cup orange juice
- 2 tablespoons yellow mustard
- 1 fully cooked boneless ham
- 1 teaspoon salt
- ½ teaspoon ground black pepper

1. Preheat the air fryer to 375°F.
2. In a medium bowl, whisk together brown sugar, orange juice, and mustard until combined. Brush over ham until well coated. Sprinkle with salt and pepper.
3. Place in the air fryer basket and cook 15 minutes until heated through and edges are caramelized. Serve warm.

Za'atar Lamb Loin Chops
Servings:4 | Cooking Time:30 Minutes
- 8 (3½-ounces) bone-in lamb loin chops, trimmed
- 3 garlic cloves, crushed
- 1 tablespoon fresh lemon juice
- 1 teaspoon olive oil
- 1 tablespoon Za'ataro
- Salt and black pepper, to taste

1. Preheat the Air fryer to 400 o F and grease an Air fryer basket.
2. Mix the garlic, lemon juice, oil, Za'atar, salt, and black pepper in a large bowl.
3. Coat the chops generously with the herb mixture and arrange the chops in the Air fryer basket.
4. Cook for about 15 minutes, flipping twice in between and dish out the lamb chops to serve hot.

Corned Beef
Servings: 5 | Cooking Time: 4 Minutes
- 5 wonton wraps
- 8 oz corned beef, cooked
- 1 egg, beaten
- 3 oz Swiss cheese, shredded
- 1 teaspoon sunflower oil

1. Shred the corned beef with the help of the fork and mix it up with Swiss cheese. Then put the corned beef mixture on the wonton wraps and roll them into rolls. Dip every corned beef roll in the beaten egg. Preheat the air fryer to 400F. Put the wonton rolls in the air fryer in one layer and sprinkle with sunflower oil. Cook the meal for 2 minutes from each side or until the rolls are golden brown.

Empanadas
Servings:4 | Cooking Time: 28 Minutes
- 1 pound 80/20 ground beef
- ¼ cup taco seasoning
- ⅓ cup salsa
- 2 refrigerated piecrusts
- 1 cup shredded Colby-jack cheese

1. In a medium skillet over medium heat, brown beef about 10 minutes until cooked through. Drain fat, then add taco seasoning and salsa to the pan. Bring to a boil, then cook 30 seconds. Reduce heat and simmer 5 minutes. Remove from heat.
2. Preheat the air fryer to 370°F.
3. Cut three 5" circles from each piecrust, forming six total. Reroll scraps out to ½" thickness. Cut out two more 5" circles to make eight circles total.
4. For each empanada, place ¼ cup meat mixture onto the lower half of a pastry circle and top with 2 tablespoons cheese. Dab a little water along the edge of pastry and fold circle in half to fully cover meat and cheese, pressing the edges together. Use a fork to gently seal the edges. Repeat with remaining pastry, meat, and cheese.
5. Spritz empanadas with cooking spray. Place in the air fryer basket and cook 12 minutes, turning halfway through cooking time, until crust is golden. Serve warm.

Mustard Lamb Loin Chops
Servings:4 | Cooking Time:30 Minutes
- 8 (4-ounces) lamb loin chops
- 2 tablespoons Dijon mustard
- 1 tablespoon fresh lemon juice
- ½ teaspoon olive oil
- 1 teaspoon dried tarragon
- Salt and black pepper, to taste

1. Preheat the Air fryer to 390 o F and grease an Air fryer basket.
2. Mix the mustard, lemon juice, oil, tarragon, salt, and black pepper in a large bowl.
3. Coat the chops generously with the mustard mixture and arrange in the Air fryer basket.
4. Cook for about 15 minutes, flipping once in between and dish out to serve hot.

Adobo Oregano Beef
Servings: 4 | Cooking Time: 30 Minutes
- 1 pound beef roast, trimmed
- ½ teaspoon oregano, dried
- ¼ teaspoon garlic powder

- A pinch of salt and black pepper
- ½ teaspoon turmeric powder
- 1 tablespoon olive oil

1. In a bowl, mix the roast with the rest of the ingredients, and rub well. Put the roast in the air fryer's basket and cook at 390 degrees F for 30 minutes. Slice the roast, divide it between plates and serve with a side salad.

Glazed Ham

Servings:4 | Cooking Time:40 Minutes

- 1 pound (10½ ounce) ham joint
- ¾ cup whiskey
- 2 tablespoons French mustard
- 2 tablespoons honey

1. Preheat the Air fryer to 320 o F and grease an Air fryer pan.
2. Mix all the ingredients in a bowl except ham.
3. Keep ham joint for about 30 minutes at room temperature and place in the Air fryer pan.
4. Top with half of the whiskey mixture and transfer into the Air fryer.
5. Cook for about 15 minutes and flip the side.
6. Coat with the remaining whiskey mixture and cook for about 25 minutes.
7. Dish out in a platter and serve warm.

Salted Steak Pan Fried Steak

Servings:1 | Cooking Time: 15 Minutes

- 1-pound beef steak, bones removed
- 3 tablespoons coconut oil
- A dash of oregano
- Salt and pepper to taste

1. Place all ingredients in a Ziploc bag and allow to marinate in the fridge for at least 2 hours.
2. Preheat the air fryer.
3. Place the steak in the air fryer and cook for 15 minutes at 4000F.

Bacon Blue Cheese Burger

Servings:4 | Cooking Time: 15 Minutes

- 1 pound ground sirloin
- ½ cup crumbled blue cheese
- 8 slices bacon, cooked and crumbled
- 1 teaspoon Worcestershire sauce
- 1 teaspoon salt
- ½ teaspoon ground black pepper
- 4 pretzel buns

1. Preheat the air fryer to 370°F.
2. In a large bowl, mix sirloin, cheese, bacon, and Worcestershire until well combined.
3. Form into four patties and sprinkle each side with salt and pepper. Spritz with cooking spray and place in the air fryer basket.
4. Cook 15 minutes, turning halfway through cooking time, until internal temperature reaches at least 160°F for well-done. Place on pretzel buns to serve.

Paprika Beef And Spinach

Servings: 4 | Cooking Time: 25 Minutes

- 1 and ½ pounds beef meat, cubed
- Salt and black pepper to the taste
- 2 cup baby spinach
- 3 tablespoons olive oil
- 1 tablespoon sweet paprika
- ¼ cup beef stock

1. In a pan that fits your air fryer mix all the ingredients except the spinach, toss, introduce the pan the fryer and cook at 390 degrees F for 20 minutes. Add the spinach, cook for 5 minutes more, divide everything between plates and serve.

Simple Lamb Chops

Servings:2 | Cooking Time:6 Minutes

- 4 (4-ounces) lamb chops
- Salt and black pepper, to taste
- 1 tablespoon olive oil

1. Preheat the Air fryer to 390 o F and grease an Air fryer basket.
2. Mix the olive oil, salt, and black pepper in a large bowl and add chops.
3. Arrange the chops in the Air fryer basket and cook for about 6 minutes.
4. Dish out the lamb chops and serve hot.

Pork Chops On The Grill Simple Recipe

Servings:6 | Cooking Time: 50 Minutes

- 1 cup salt
- 1 cup sugar
- 6 pork chops
- 8 cups water

1. Place all ingredients in a deep bowl and allow to soak the pork chops in the brine solution for at least 2 days in the fridge.
2. Preheat the air fryer to 3900F.
3. Place the grill pan accessory in the air fryer.
4. Place the meat on the grill pan and cook for 50 minutes making sure to flip every 10 minutes for even grilling.

Glazed Pork Shoulder

Servings:5 | Cooking Time: 18 Minutes

- 1/3 cup soy sauce
- 2 tablespoons sugar
- 1 tablespoon honey
- 2 pounds pork shoulder, cut into 1½-inch thick slices

1. In a bowl, mix together all the soy sauce, sugar, and honey.
2. Add the pork and generously coat with marinade.
3. Cover and refrigerate to marinate for about 4-6 hours.
4. Set the temperature of air fryer to 335 degrees F. Grease an air fryer basket.
5. Place pork shoulder into the prepared air fryer basket.
6. Air fry for about 10 minutes and then, another 6-8 minutes at 390 degrees F.
7. Remove from air fryer and transfer the pork shoulder onto a platter.
8. With a piece of foil, cover the pork for about 10 minutes before serving.
9. Enjoy!

Bacon Wrapped Filet Mignon

Servings: 2 | Cooking Time: 15 Minutes

- 2 bacon slices
- 2 (6-ounces) filet mignon steaks
- Salt and black pepper, to taste
- 1 teaspoon avocado oil

1. Preheat the Air fryer to 375 o F and grease an Air fryer basket.
2. Wrap each mignon steak with 1 bacon slice and secure with a toothpick.
3. Season the steak generously with salt and black pepper and coat with avocado oil.
4. Arrange the steaks in the Air fryer basket and cook for about 15 minutes, flipping once in between.
5. Dish out the steaks and cut into desired size slices to serve.

Ground Beef

Servings: 4 | Cooking Time: 9 Minutes

- 1 pound 70/30 ground beef
- ¼ cup water
- 1 teaspoon salt
- ½ teaspoon ground black pepper
- 1 teaspoon garlic powder

1. Preheat the air fryer to 400°F.
2. In a medium bowl, mix beef with remaining ingredients. Place beef in a 6" round cake pan and press into an even layer.
3. Place in the air fryer basket and set the timer to 10 minutes. After 5 minutes, open the air fryer and stir ground beef with a spatula. Return to the air fryer.
4. After 2 more minutes, open the air fryer, remove the pan and drain any excess fat from the ground beef. Return to the air fryer for and cook 2 more minutes until beef is brown and no pink remains.

Jumbo Italian Meatballs

Servings: 6 | Cooking Time: 15 Minutes

- 1 pound 80/20 ground beef
- ⅓ cup Italian bread crumbs
- 1 large egg
- 2 teaspoons Italian seasoning
- ¼ cup grated Parmesan cheese
- 1 teaspoon salt
- ½ teaspoon ground black pepper

1. Preheat the air fryer to 400°F.
2. In a large bowl, mix all the ingredients. Roll mixture into balls, about 3" each, making twelve total.
3. Place meatballs in the air fryer basket and cook 15 minutes, shaking the basket twice during cooking, until meatballs are brown on the outside and internal temperature reaches at least 160°F. Serve warm.

Steak Bites And Spicy Dipping Sauce

Servings: 4 | Cooking Time: 8 Minutes

- 2 pounds sirloin steak, cut into 2" cubes
- 2 teaspoons salt
- 1 teaspoon ground black pepper
- 1 teaspoon garlic powder
- ½ cup mayonnaise
- 2 tablespoons sriracha

1. Preheat the air fryer to 400°F.
2. Sprinkle steak with salt, pepper, and garlic powder.
3. Place steak in the air fryer basket and cook 8 minutes, shaking the basket twice during cooking, until internal temperature reaches at least 160°F.
4. In a small bowl, combine mayonnaise and sriracha. Serve with steak bites for dipping.

Steak Fingers

Servings: 4 | Cooking Time: 8 Minutes

- 4 small beef cube steaks
- salt and pepper
- ½ cup flour
- oil for misting or cooking spray

1. Cut cube steaks into 1-inch-wide strips.
2. Sprinkle lightly with salt and pepper to taste.
3. Roll in flour to coat all sides.
4. Spray air fryer basket with cooking spray or oil.
5. Place steak strips in air fryer basket in single layer, very close together but not touching. Spray top of steak strips with oil or cooking spray.
6. Cook at 390°F for 4minutes, turn strips over, and spray with oil or cooking spray.
7. Cook 4 more minutes and test with fork for doneness. Steak fingers should be crispy outside with no red juices inside. If needed, cook an additional 4 minutes or until well done. (Don't eat beef cube steak rare.)
8. Repeat steps 5 through 7 to cook remaining strips.

Air Fried Grilled Steak

Servings: 2 | Cooking Time: 45 Minutes

- 2 top sirloin steaks
- 3 tablespoons butter, melted
- 3 tablespoons olive oil
- Salt and pepper to taste

1. Preheat the air fryer for 5 minutes.
2. Season the sirloin steaks with olive oil, salt and pepper.
3. Place the beef in the air fryer basket.
4. Cook for 45 minutes at 3500F.
5. Once cooked, serve with butter.

Crispy Five-spice Pork Belly

Servings: 6 | Cooking Time: 60-75 Minutes

- 1½ pounds Pork belly with skin
- 3 tablespoons Shaoxing (Chinese cooking rice wine), dry sherry, or white grape juice
- 1½ teaspoons Granulated white sugar
- ¾ teaspoon Five-spice powder (see the headnote)
- 1¼ cups Coarse sea salt or kosher salt

1. Preheat the air fryer to 350°F .
2. Set the pork belly skin side up on a cutting board. Use a meat fork to make dozens and dozens of tiny holes all across the surface of the skin. You can hardly make too many holes. These will allow the skin to bubble up and keep it from becoming hard as it roasts.
3. Turn the pork belly over so that one of its longer sides faces you. Make four evenly spaced vertical slits in the meat. The slits should go about halfway into the meat toward the fat.
4. Mix the Shaoxing or its substitute, sugar, and five-spice powder in a small bowl until the sugar dissolves. Massage this mixture across the meat and into the cuts.
5. Turn the pork belly over again. Blot dry any moisture on the skin. Make a double-thickness aluminum foil tray by setting two 10-inch-long pieces of foil on top of another. Set the pork belly skin side up in

the center of this tray. Fold the sides of the tray up toward the pork, crimping the foil as you work to make a high-sided case all around the pork belly. Seal the foil to the meat on all sides so that only the skin is exposed.

6. Pour the salt onto the skin and pat it down and in place to create a crust. Pick up the foil tray with the pork in it and set it in the basket.
7. Air-fry undisturbed for 35 minutes for a small batch, 45 minutes for a medium batch, or 50 minutes for a large batch.
8. Remove the foil tray with the pork belly still in it. Warning: The foil tray is full of scalding-hot fat. Discard the fat in the tray (not down the drain!), as well as the tray itself. Transfer the pork belly to a cutting board.
9. Raise the air fryer temperature to 375°F (or 380°F or 390°F, if one of these is the closest setting). Brush the salt crust off the pork, removing any visible salt from the sides of the meat, too.
10. When the machine is at temperature, return the pork belly skin side up to the basket. Air-fry undisturbed for 25 minutes, or until crisp and very well browned. If the machine is at 390°F, you may be able to shave 5 minutes off the cooking time so that the skin doesn't blacken.
11. Use a nonstick-safe spatula, and perhaps a silicone baking mitt, to transfer the pork belly to a wire rack. Cool for 10 minutes before serving.

Pesto-rubbed Veal Chops

Servings: 2 | Cooking Time: 12-15 Minutes
- ¼ cup Purchased pesto
- 2 10-ounce bone-in veal loin or rib chop(s)
- ½ teaspoon Ground black pepper

1. Preheat the air fryer to 400°F.
2. Rub the pesto onto both sides of the veal chop(s). Sprinkle one side of the chop(s) with the ground black pepper. Set aside at room temperature as the machine comes up to temperature.
3. Set the chop(s) in the basket. If you're cooking more than one chop, leave as much air space between them as possible. Air-fry undisturbed for 12 minutes for medium-rare, or until an instant-read meat thermometer inserted into the center of a chop (without touching bone) registers 135°F (not USDA-approved). Or air-fry undisturbed for 15 minutes for medium-well, or until an instant-read meat thermometer registers 145°F (USDA-approved).
4. Use kitchen tongs to transfer the chops to a cutting board or a wire rack. Cool for 5 minutes before serving.

Cajun Sweet-sour Grilled Pork

Servings: 3 | Cooking Time: 12 Minutes
- ¼ cup brown sugar
- 1/4 cup cider vinegar
- 1-lb pork loin, sliced into 1-inch cubes
- 2 tablespoons Cajun seasoning
- 3 tablespoons brown sugar

1. In a shallow dish, mix well pork loin, 3 tablespoons brown sugar, and Cajun seasoning. Toss well to coat. Marinate in the ref for 3 hours.
2. In a medium bowl mix well, brown sugar and vinegar for basting.
3. Thread pork pieces in skewers. Baste with sauce and place on skewer rack in air fryer.
4. For 12 minutes, cook on 360oF. Halfway through cooking time, turnover skewers and baste with sauce. If needed, cook in batches.
5. Serve and enjoy.

Hot Dogs

Servings: 8 | Cooking Time: 7 Minutes
- 8 beef hot dogs
- 8 hot dog buns

1. Preheat the air fryer to 400°F.
2. Place hot dogs in the air fryer basket and cook 7 minutes. Place each hot dog in a bun. Serve warm.

Balsamic Pork Chops

Servings: 4 | Cooking Time: 25 Minutes
- 4 pork chops
- 1 tablespoon smoked paprika
- 1 tablespoon olive oil
- 2 tablespoons balsamic vinegar
- ½ cup chicken stock
- A pinch of salt and black pepper

1. In a bowl, mix the pork chops with the rest of the ingredients and toss. Put the pork chops in your air fryer's basket and cook at 390 degrees F for 25 minutes. Divide between plates and serve.

Lamb Burgers

Servings: 2 | Cooking Time: 16 Minutes
- 8 oz lamb, minced
- ½ teaspoon salt
- ½ teaspoon ground black pepper
- ½ teaspoon dried cilantro
- 1 tablespoon water
- Cooking spray

1. In the mixing bowl mix up minced lamb, salt, ground black pepper, dried cilantro, and water.
2. Stir the meat mixture carefully with the help of the spoon and make 2 burgers.
3. Preheat the air fryer to 375F.
4. Spray the air fryer basket with cooking spray and put the burgers inside.
5. Cook them for 8 minutes from each side.

Honey-sriracha Pork Ribs

Servings: 4 | Cooking Time: 25 Minutes
- 3 pounds pork back ribs, white membrane removed
- 2 teaspoons salt
- 1 teaspoon ground black pepper
- ½ cup sriracha
- ⅓ cup honey
- 1 tablespoon lemon juice

1. Preheat the air fryer to 400°F.
2. Place ribs on a work surface and cut the rack into two pieces to fit in the air fryer basket.
3. Sprinkle ribs with salt and pepper and place in the air fryer basket meat side down. Cook 15 minutes.
4. In a small bowl, combine the sriracha, honey, and lemon juice to make a sauce.
5. Remove ribs from the air fryer basket and pour sauce over both sides. Return them to the air fryer basket meat side up and cook an additional 10 minutes until brown and the internal temperature reaches at least 190°F. Serve warm.

Honey Mesquite Pork Chops
Servings: 2 | Cooking Time: 10 Minutes
- 2 tablespoons mesquite seasoning
- ¼ cup honey
- 1 tablespoon olive oil
- 1 tablespoon water
- freshly ground black pepper
- 2 bone-in center cut pork chops (about 1 pound)

1. Whisk the mesquite seasoning, honey, olive oil, water and freshly ground black pepper together in a shallow glass dish. Pierce the chops all over and on both sides with a fork or meat tenderizer. Add the pork chops to the marinade and massage the marinade into the chops. Cover and marinate for 30 minutes.
2. Preheat the air fryer to 330°F.
3. Transfer the pork chops to the air fryer basket and pour half of the marinade over the chops, reserving the remaining marinade. Air-fry the pork chops for 6 minutes. Flip the pork chops over and pour the remaining marinade on top. Air-fry for an additional 3 minutes at 330°F. Then, increase the air fryer temperature to 400°F and air-fry the pork chops for an additional minute.
4. Transfer the pork chops to a serving plate, and let them rest for 5 minutes before serving. If you'd like a sauce for these chops, pour the cooked marinade from the bottom of the air fryer over the top.

Barbecue-style Beef Cube Steak
Servings: 2 | Cooking Time: 14 Minutes
- 2 4-ounce beef cube steak(s)
- 2 cups (about 8 ounces) Fritos (original flavor) or a generic corn chip equivalent, crushed to crumbs (see here)
- 6 tablespoons Purchased smooth barbecue sauce, any flavor (gluten-free, if a concern)

1. Preheat the air fryer to 375°F.
2. Spread the Fritos crumbs in a shallow soup plate or a small pie plate. Rub the barbecue sauce onto both sides of the steak(s). Dredge the steak(s) in the Fritos crumbs to coat well and thoroughly, turning several times and pressing down to get the little bits to adhere to the meat.
3. When the machine is at temperature, set the steak(s) in the basket. Leave as much air space between them as possible if you're working with more than one piece of beef. Air-fry undisturbed for 12 minutes, or until lightly brown and crunchy. If the machine is at 360°F, you may need to add 2 minutes to the cooking time.
4. Use kitchen tongs to transfer the steak(s) to a wire rack. Cool for 5 minutes before serving.

Strawberry Pork Ribs
Servings: 4 | Cooking Time: 35 Minutes
- 1-pound pork ribs, chopped
- 1 teaspoon Erythritol
- 1 tablespoon strawberries, pureed
- ½ teaspoon chili powder
- 1 teaspoon olive oil

1. In the shallow mix up Erythritol, strawberries, and chili powder. Sprinkle the pork ribs with the sweet mixture well. Then brush the meat with olive oil. Preheat the air fryer to 350F. Place the pork ribs in the air fryer and cook them for 35 minutes. Transfer the cooked ribs on the serving plate.

Lamb Chops And Lemon Yogurt Sauce
Servings: 4 | Cooking Time: 30 Minutes
- 4 lamb chops
- A pinch of salt and black pepper
- 1 cup Greek yogurt
- 2 tablespoons coconut oil, melted
- 1 teaspoon lemon zest, grated
- ½ teaspoon turmeric powder

1. In a bowl, mix the lamb chops with the rest of the ingredients and toss well. Put the chops in your air fryer's basket and cook at 380 degrees F for 15 minutes on each side. Divide between plates and serve.

Another Easy Teriyaki Bbq Recipe
Servings: 2 | Cooking Time: 15 Minutes
- 1 tbsp honey
- 1 tbsp mirin
- 1 tbsp soy sauce
- 1 thumb-sized piece of fresh ginger, grated
- 14 oz lean diced steak, with fat trimmed

1. Mix all Ingredients in a bowl and marinate for at least an hour. Turning over halfway through marinating time.
2. Thread mead into skewers. Place on skewer rack.
3. Cook for 5 minutes at 390oF or to desired doneness.
4. Serve and enjoy.

Garlic Butter Pork Chops
Servings: 4 | Cooking Time: 8 Minutes
- 4 pork chops
- 1 tablespoon coconut butter
- 2 teaspoons parsley
- 1 tablespoon coconut oil
- 2 teaspoons garlic, grated
- Salt and black pepper, to taste

1. Preheat the Air fryer to 350 o F and grease an Air fryer basket.
2. Mix all the seasonings, coconut oil, garlic, butter, and parsley in a bowl and coat the pork chops with it.
3. Cover the chops with foil and refrigerate to marinate for about 1 hour.
4. Remove the foil and arrange the chops in the Air fryer basket.
5. Cook for about 8 minutes and dish out in a bowl to serve warm.

Beef Bulgogi
Servings: 1 | Cooking Time: 15 Minutes
- ½ cup sliced mushrooms
- 2 tbsp bulgogi marinade
- 1 tbsp diced onion

1. Cut the beef into small pieces and place them in a bowl. Add the bulgogi and mix to coat the beef completely. Cover the bowl and place in the fridge for 3 hours. Preheat the air fryer to 350 F.
2. Transfer the beef to a baking dish; stir in the mushroom and onion. Cook for 10 minutes, until nice and tender. Serve with some roasted potatoes and a green salad.

Italian Meatballs
Servings: 8 | Cooking Time: 12 Minutes
- ¾ pound Lean ground beef
- 6 ounces Bulk mild or hot Italian sausage meat
- ½ cup Seasoned Italian-style dried bread crumbs
- 1 Large egg
- 3 tablespoons Whole or low-fat milk
- Olive oil spray

1. Preheat the air fryer to 375°F.
2. Mix the ground beef, Italian sausage meat, bread crumbs, egg, and milk in a bowl until well combined. Using clean hands, form this mixture into large meatballs, using a ¼ cup for each. Set the meatballs on a large cutting board and coat them on all sides with olive oil spray. Be gentle when you turn them. They're fragile.
3. When the machine is at temperature, set them in the basket with as much space between them as possible. The important thing is that they should not touch, even if there's only a fraction of an inch between them. Air-fry undisturbed for 12 minutes, or until an instant-read meat thermometer inserted into the center of a meatball registers 165°F.
4. Use kitchen tongs to gently pick up the meatballs one by one and transfer them to a cutting board or a serving platter. Cool for a few minutes before serving.

Garlicky Lamb Chops
Servings: 4 | Cooking Time: 22 Minutes
- 1 tablespoon fresh oregano, chopped
- 1 tablespoon fresh thyme, chopped
- 8 (4-ounce) lamb chops
- ¼ cup olive oil, divided
- 1 bulb garlic
- Salt and black pepper, to taste

1. Preheat the Air fryer to 390 o F and grease an Air fryer basket.
2. Rub the garlic bulb with about 2 tablespoons of the olive oil.
3. rrange the garlic bulb in the Air fryer basket and cook for about 12 minutes.
4. Mix remaining oil, herbs, salt and black pepper in a large bowl.
5. Coat the pork chops with about 1 tablespoon of the herb mixture.
6. Place half of the chops in the Air fryer basket with garlic bulb and cook for about 5 minutes.
7. Repeat with the remaining lamb chops and serve with herb mixture.

Coconut Pork And Green Beans
Servings: 4 | Cooking Time: 25 Minutes
- 4 pork chops
- 2 tablespoons coconut oil, melted
- 2 garlic cloves, minced
- A pinch of salt and black pepper
- ½ pound green beans, trimmed and halved
- 2 tablespoons keto tomato sauce

1. Heat up a pan that fits the air fryer with the oil over medium heat, add the pork chops and brown for 5 minutes. Add the rest of the ingredients, put the pan in the machine and cook at 390 degrees F for 20 minutes. Divide everything between plates and serve

Chili-espresso Marinated Steak
Servings: 3 | Cooking Time: 50 Minutes
- ½ teaspoon garlic powder
- 1 ½ pounds beef flank steak
- 1 teaspoon instant espresso powder
- 2 tablespoons olive oil
- 2 teaspoons chili powder
- Salt and pepper to taste

1. Preheat the air fryer to 3900F.
2. Place the grill pan accessory in the air fryer.
3. Make the dry rub by mixing the chili powder, salt, pepper, espresso powder, and garlic powder.
4. Rub all over the steak and brush with oil.
5. Place on the grill pan and cook for 40 minutes.
6. Halfway through the cooking time, flip the beef to cook evenly.

Pork Belly Marinated In Onion-coconut Cream
Servings: 3 | Cooking Time: 25 Minutes
- ½ pork belly, sliced to thin strips
- 1 onion, diced
- 1 tablespoon butter
- 4 tablespoons coconut cream
- Salt and pepper to taste

1. Place all ingredients in a mixing bowl and allow to marinate in the fridge for 2 hours.
2. Preheat the air fryer for 5 minutes.
3. Place the pork strips in the air fryer and bake for 25 minutes at 3500F.

Simple Garlic 'n Herb Meatballs
Servings: 4 | Cooking Time: 20 Minutes
- 1 clove of garlic, minced
- 1 egg, beaten
- 1 tablespoon breadcrumbs or flour
- 1 teaspoon dried mixed herbs
- 1-pound lean ground beef

1. Place all Ingredients in a mixing bowl and mix together using your hands.
2. Form small balls using your hands and set aside in the fridge to set.
3. Preheat the air fryer to 3900F.
4. Place the meatballs in the air fryer basket and cook for 20 minutes.
5. Halfway through the cooking time, give the meatballs a shake to cook evenly.

Meatloaf
Servings: 4 | Cooking Time: 40 Minutes
- 1 pound 80/20 lean ground beef
- 3 tablespoons Italian bread crumbs
- 2 tablespoons ketchup
- 1 large egg
- 1 teaspoon salt
- 2 tablespoons brown sugar

1. Preheat the air fryer to 350°F.
2. In a large bowl, combine beef, egg, bread crumbs, and salt.
3. In a small bowl, mix ketchup and brown sugar.
4. Form meat mixture into a 6" × 3" loaf and brush with ketchup mixture.
5. Place in the air fryer basket and cook 40 minutes until internal temperature reaches at least 160°F. Serve warm.

Cheeseburgers

Servings: 4 | Cooking Time: 10 Minutes

- 1 pound 70/30 ground beef
- ¼ teaspoon ground black pepper
- 4 hamburger buns
- ½ teaspoon salt
- 4 slices American cheese

1. Preheat the air fryer to 360°F.
2. Separate beef into four equal portions and form into patties.
3. Sprinkle both sides of patties with salt and pepper. Place in the air fryer basket and cook 10 minutes, turning halfway through cooking time, until internal temperature reaches at least 160°F.
4. For each burger, place a slice of cheese on a patty and place on a hamburger bun. Serve warm.

Caramelized Pork

Servings: 6 | Cooking Time: 17 Minutes

- 2 pounds pork shoulder, cut into 1½-inch thick slices
- 1/3 cup soy sauce
- 2 tablespoons sugar
- 1 tablespoon honey

1. Preheat the Air fryer to 335 o F and grease an Air fryer basket.
2. Mix all the ingredients in a large bowl and coat chops well.
3. Cover and refrigerate for about 8 hours.
4. Arrange the chops in the Air fryer basket and cook for about 10 minutes, flipping once in between.
5. Set the Air fryer to 390 o F and cook for 7 more minutes.
6. Dish out in a platter and serve hot.

Mustard Pork

Servings: 4 | Cooking Time: 30 Minutes

- 1 pound pork tenderloin, trimmed
- A pinch of salt and black pepper
- 2 tablespoons olive oil
- 3 tablespoons mustard
- 2 tablespoons balsamic vinegar

1. In a bowl, mix the pork tenderloin with the rest of the ingredients and rub well. Put the roast in your air fryer's basket and cook at 380 degrees F for 30 minutes. Slice the roast, divide between plates and serve.

Smoked Brisket With Dill Pickles

Servings: 6 | Cooking Time: 1 Hour

- ¼ teaspoon liquid smoke
- 1 cup dill pickles
- 3 pounds flat-cut brisket
- Salt and pepper to taste

1. Preheat the air fryer to 3900F.
2. Place the grill pan accessory in the air fryer.
3. Season the brisket with liquid smoke, salt, and pepper.
4. Place on the grill pan and cook for 30 minutes per batch.
5. Flip the meat halfway through cooking time for even grilling.
6. Serve with dill pickles.

Marinated Beef

Servings: 4 | Cooking Time: 35 Minutes

- 2 tablespoons olive oil
- Salt and black pepper to the taste
- 1 cup balsamic vinegar
- 3 garlic cloves, minced
- 4 medium beef steaks

1. In a bowl, mix steaks with the rest of the ingredients, and toss. Transfer the steaks to your air fryer's basket and cook at 390 degrees F for 35 minutes, flipping them halfway. Divide between plates and serve with a side salad.

Sweet Pork Belly

Servings: 6 | Cooking Time: 55 Minutes

- 1-pound pork belly
- 1 teaspoon salt
- 1 teaspoon butter, softened
- 1 teaspoon Splenda
- 1 teaspoon white pepper
- ½ teaspoon onion powder

1. Sprinkle the pork belly with salt, white pepper, and onion powder. Then preheat the air fryer to 385F. Put the pork belly in the air fryer and cook it for 45 minutes. Then turn the pork belly on another side and spread it with butter. After this, top the pork belly with Splenda and cook it at 400f for 10 minutes.

Wasabi-coated Pork Loin Chops

Servings: 3 | Cooking Time: 14 Minutes

- 1½ cups Wasabi peas
- ¼ cup Plain panko bread crumbs
- 1 Large egg white(s)
- 2 tablespoons Water
- 3 5- to 6-ounce boneless center-cut pork loin chops (about ½ inch thick)

1. Preheat the air fryer to 375°F .
2. Put the wasabi peas in a food processor. Cover and process until finely ground, about like panko bread crumbs. Add the bread crumbs and pulse a few times to blend.
3. Set up and fill two shallow soup plates or small pie plates on your counter: one for the egg white(s), whisked with the water until uniform; and one for the wasabi pea mixture.
4. Dip a pork chop in the egg white mixture, coating the chop on both sides as well as around the edge. Allow any excess egg white mixture to slip back into the rest, then set the chop in the wasabi pea mixture. Press gently and turn it several times to coat evenly on both sides and around the edge. Set aside, then dip and coat the remaining chop(s).
5. Set the chops in the basket with as much air space between them as possible. Air-fry, turning once at the 6-minute mark, for 12 minutes, or until the chops are crisp and browned and an instant-read meat thermometer inserted into the center of a chop registers 145°F. If the machine is at 360°F, you may need to add 2 minutes to the cooking time.
6. Use kitchen tongs to transfer the chops to a wire rack. Cool for a couple of minutes before serving.

Italian Pork

Servings: 2 | Cooking Time: 50 Minutes

- 8 oz pork loin
- ½ teaspoon salt
- 1 tablespoon sesame oil
- 1 teaspoon Italian herbs

1. In the shallow bowl mix up Italian herbs, salt, and sesame oil. Then brush the pork loin with the Italian herbs mixture and wrap in the foil. Preheat the air fryer to 350F. Put the wrapped pork loin in the air fryer and cook it for 50 minutes. When the time is over, remove the meat from the air fryer and discard the foil. Slice the pork loin into the servings.

Lemon-butter Veal Cutlets

Servings: 2 | Cooking Time: 4 Minutes

- 3 strips Butter (see step 2)
- 3 Thinly pounded 2-ounce veal leg cutlets (less than ¼ inch thick)
- ¼ teaspoon Lemon-pepper seasoning

1. Preheat the air fryer to 400°F.
2. Run a vegetable peeler lengthwise along a hard, cold stick of butter, making 2, 3, or 4 long strips as the recipe requires for the number of cutlets you're making.
3. Lay the veal cutlets on a clean, dry cutting board or work surface. Sprinkle about ⅛ teaspoon lemon-pepper seasoning over each. Set a strip of butter on top of each cutlet.
4. When the machine is at temperature, set the topped cutlets in the basket so that they don't overlap or even touch. Air-fry undisturbed for 4 minutes without turning.
5. Use a nonstick-safe spatula to transfer the cutlets to a serving plate or plates, taking care to keep as much of the butter on top as possible. Remove the basket from the drawer or from over the baking tray. Carefully pour the browned butter over the cutlets.

Lamb With Paprika Cilantro Sauce

Servings: 4 | Cooking Time: 30 Minutes

- 1 pound lamb, cubed
- 1 cup coconut cream
- 3 tablespoons sweet paprika
- 2 tablespoons olive oil
- 2 tablespoons cilantro, chopped
- Salt and black pepper to the taste

1. Heat up a pan that fits your air fryer with the oil over medium-high heat, add the meat and brown for 5 minutes. Add the rest of the ingredients, toss, put the pan in the air fryer and cook at 380 degrees F for 25 minutes. Divide everything into bowls and serve.

Mustard'n Italian Dressing On Flank Steak

Servings: 3 | Cooking Time: 45 Minutes

- ½ cup yellow mustard
- ½ teaspoon black pepper
- 1 ¼ pounds beef flank steak
- 1 cup Italian salad dressing
- Salt to taste

1. Place all ingredients in a Ziploc bag and allow to marinate in the fridge for at least 2 hours.
2. Preheat the air fryer to 390°F.
3. Place the grill pan accessory in the air fryer.
4. Grill for 15 minutes per batch making sure to flip the meat halfway through the cooking time.

Garlic-rosemary Lamb Bbq

Servings: 2 | Cooking Time: 12 Minutes

- 1-lb cubed lamb leg
- juice of 1 lemon
- fresh rosemary
- 3 smashed garlic cloves
- salt and pepper
- 1/2 cup olive oil

1. In a shallow dish, mix well all Ingredients and marinate for 3 hours.
2. Thread lamb pieces in skewers. Place on skewer rack in air fryer.
3. For 12 minutes, cook on 390oF. Halfway through cooking time, turnover skewers. If needed, cook in batches.
4. Serve and enjoy.

Salty Lamb Chops

Servings: 4 | Cooking Time: 8 Minutes

- 1-pound lamb chops
- 1 egg, beaten
- ½ teaspoon salt
- ½ cup coconut flour
- Cooking spray

1. Chop the lamb chops into small pieces (popcorn) and sprinkle with salt. Then add a beaten egg and stir the meat well. After this, add coconut flour and shake the lamb popcorn until all meat pieces are coated. Preheat the air fryer to 380F. Put the lamb popcorn in the air fryer and spray it with cooking spray. Cook the lamb popcorn for 4 minutes. Then shake the meat well and cook it for 4 minutes more.

Fat Burger Bombs

Servings: 6 | Cooking Time: 20 Minutes

- ½ pound ground beef
- 1 cup almond flour
- 12 slices uncured bacon, chopped
- 2 eggs, beaten
- 3 tablespoons olive oil
- Salt and pepper to taste

1. In a mixing bowl, combine all ingredients except for the olive oil.
2. Use your hands to form small balls with the mixture. Place in a baking sheet and allow to set in the fridge for at least 2 hours.
3. Preheat the air fryer for 5 minutes.
4. Brush the meat balls with olive oil on all sides.
5. Place in the air fryer basket.
6. Cook for 20 minutes at 3500F.
7. Halfway through the cooking time, shake the fryer basket for a more even cooking.

Mustard Beef Mix

Servings: 7 | Cooking Time: 30 Minutes

- 2-pound beef ribs, boneless
- 1 tablespoon Dijon mustard
- 1 tablespoon sunflower oil
- 1 teaspoon ground paprika
- 1 teaspoon cayenne pepper

1. In the shallow bowl mix up Dijon mustard and sunflower oil. Then sprinkle the beef ribs with ground paprika and cayenne pepper. After this, brush the meat with Dijon mustard mixture and leave for 10 minutes to marinate. Meanwhile, preheat the air fryer to 400F. Put the beef ribs in the air fryer to and cook them for 10 minutes. Then flip the ribs on another side and reduce the air fryer heat to 325F. Cook the ribs for 20 minutes more.

Tomato Salsa Topped Grilled Flank Steak

Servings: 4 | Cooking Time: 40 Minutes

- ¼ cup chopped cilantro
- 1 ½ pounds flank steak, pounded
- 1 red onion, chopped
- 1 teaspoon coriander powder
- 2 cups chopped tomatoes
- Salt and pepper to taste

1. Preheat the air fryer to 3900F.
2. Place the grill pan accessory in the air fryer.
3. Season the flank steak with salt and pepper.
4. Grill for 20 minutes per batch and make sure to flip the beef halfway through the cooking time.
5. Meanwhile, prepare the salsa by mixing in a bowl the tomatoes, cilantro, onions, and coriander. Season with more salt and pepper to taste.

Easy & The Traditional Beef Roast Recipe
Servings: 12 | Cooking Time: 2 Hours
- 1 cup organic beef broth
- 4 tablespoons olive oil
- 3 pounds beef round roast
- Salt and pepper to taste

1. Place in a Ziploc bag all the ingredients and allow to marinate in the fridge for 2 hours.
2. Preheat the air fryer for 5 minutes.
3. Transfer all ingredients in a baking dish that will fit in the air fryer.
4. Place in the air fryer and cook for 2 hours for 400°F.

Roasted Lamb
Servings: 4 | Cooking Time: 1 Hour 30 Minutes
- 2½ pounds half lamb leg roast, slits carved
- 2 garlic cloves, sliced into smaller slithers
- 1 tablespoon dried rosemary
- 1 tablespoon olive oil
- Cracked Himalayan rock salt and cracked peppercorns, to taste

1. Preheat the Air fryer to 400°F and grease an Air fryer basket.
2. Insert the garlic slithers in the slits and brush with rosemary, oil, salt, and black pepper.
3. Arrange the lamb in the Air fryer basket and cook for about 15 minutes.
4. Set the Air fryer to 350°F on the Roast mode and cook for 1 hour and 15 minutes.
5. Dish out the lamb chops and serve hot.

Crunchy Fried Pork Loin Chops
Servings: 3 | Cooking Time: 12 Minutes
- 1 cup All-purpose flour or tapioca flour
- 1 Large egg(s), well beaten
- 1½ cups Seasoned Italian-style dried bread crumbs (gluten-free, if a concern)
- 3 4- to 5-ounce boneless center-cut pork loin chops
- Vegetable oil spray

1. Preheat the air fryer to 350°F.
2. Set up and fill three shallow soup plates or small pie plates on your counter: one for the flour, one for the beaten egg(s), and one for the bread crumbs.
3. Dredge a pork chop in the flour, coating both sides as well as around the edge. Gently shake off any excess, then dip the chop in the egg(s), again coating both sides and the edge. Let any excess egg slip back into the rest, then set the chop in the bread crumbs, turning it and pressing gently to coat well on both sides and the edge. Coat the pork chop all over with vegetable oil spray and set aside so you can dredge, coat, and spray the additional chop(s).
4. Set the chops in the basket with as much air space between them as possible. Air-fry undisturbed for 12 minutes, or until brown and crunchy and an instant-read meat thermometer inserted into the center of a chop registers 145°F.
5. Use kitchen tongs to transfer the chops to a wire rack. Cool for 5 minutes before serving.

Smoked Chili Lamb Chops
Servings: 4 | Cooking Time: 20 Minutes
- 4 lamb chops
- ½ teaspoon chili powder
- 2 tablespoons olive oil
- A pinch of salt and black pepper
- 4 garlic cloves, minced
- ¼ teaspoon smoked paprika

1. In a bowl, mix the lamb with the rest of the ingredients and toss well. Transfer the chops to your air fryer's basket and cook at 390 degrees F for 10 minutes on each side. Serve with a side salad.

Smoked Sausage And Bacon Shashlik
Servings: 4 | Cooking Time: 20 Minutes
- 1 pound smoked Polish beef sausage, sliced
- 1 tablespoon mustard
- 1 tablespoon olive oil
- 2 tablespoons Worcestershire sauce
- 2 bell peppers, sliced
- Salt and ground black pepper, to taste

1. Toss the sausage with the mustard, olive, and Worcestershire sauce. Thread sausage and peppers onto skewers.
2. Sprinkle with salt and black pepper.
3. Cook in the preheated Air Fryer at 360 degrees F for 11 minutes. Brush the skewers with the reserved marinade. Bon appétit!

Pork And Garlic Sauce
Servings: 4 | Cooking Time: 25 Minutes
- 1 pound pork tenderloin, sliced
- A pinch of salt and black pepper
- 4 tablespoons butter, melted
- 2 teaspoons garlic, minced
- 1 teaspoon sweet paprika

1. Heat up a pan that fits the air fryer with the butter over medium heat, add all the ingredients except the pork medallions, whisk well and simmer for 4-5 minutes. Add the pork, toss, put the pan in your air fryer and cook at 380 degrees F for 20 minutes. Divide between plates and serve with a side salad.

Marinated Flank Steak
Servings: 4 | Cooking Time: 15 Minutes
- ¾ lb. flank steak
- 1 ½ tbsp. sake
- 1 tbsp. brown miso paste
- 1 tsp. honey
- 2 cloves garlic, pressed
- 1 tbsp. olive oil

1. Put all of the ingredients in a Ziploc bag. Shake to cover the steak well with the seasonings and refrigerate for at least 1 hour.
2. Coat all sides of the steak with cooking spray.
3. Put the steak in the Air Fryer baking pan.
4. Cook at 400°F for 12 minutes, turning the steak twice during the cooking time, then serve immediately.

Garlic Dill Leg Of Lamb
Servings: 2 | Cooking Time: 21 Minutes
- 9 oz leg of lamb, boneless
- 1 teaspoon minced garlic
- 2 tablespoons butter, softened
- ½ teaspoon dried dill
- ½ teaspoon salt

1. In the shallow bowl mix up minced garlic, butter, dried dill, and salt. Then rub the leg of lamb with butter mixture and place it in the air fryer. Cook it at 380F for 21 minutes.

Cheddar Bacon Ranch Pinwheels

Servings:5 | Cooking Time: 12 Minutes Per Batch

- 4 ounces full-fat cream cheese, softened
- 1 tablespoon dry ranch seasoning
- ½ cup shredded Cheddar cheese
- 1 sheet frozen puff pastry dough, thawed
- 6 slices bacon, cooked and crumbled

1. Preheat the air fryer to 320°F. Cut parchment paper to fit the air fryer basket.
2. In a medium bowl, mix cream cheese, ranch seasoning, and Cheddar. Unfold puff pastry and gently spread cheese mixture over pastry.
3. Sprinkle crumbled bacon on top. Starting from a long side, roll dough into a log, pressing in the edges to seal.
4. Cut log into ten pieces, then place on parchment in the air fryer basket, working in batches as necessary.
5. Cook 12 minutes, turning each piece after 7 minutes. Let cool 5 minutes before serving.

Simple Lamb Bbq With Herbed Salt

Servings:8 | Cooking Time: 1 Hour 20 Minutes

- 2 ½ tablespoons herb salt
- 2 tablespoons olive oil
- 4 pounds boneless leg of lamb, cut into 2-inch chunks

1. Preheat the air fryer to 3900F.
2. Place the grill pan accessory in the air fryer.
3. Season the meat with the herb salt and brush with olive oil.
4. Grill the meat for 20 minutes per batch.
5. Make sure to flip the meat every 10 minutes for even cooking.

Char-grilled Skirt Steak With Fresh Herbs

Servings:3 | Cooking Time: 30 Minutes

- 1 ½ pounds skirt steak, trimmed
- 1 tablespoon lemon zest
- 1 tablespoon olive oil
- 2 cups fresh herbs like tarragon, sage, and mint, chopped
- 4 cloves of garlic, minced
- Salt and pepper to taste

1. Preheat the air fryer to 3900F.
2. Place the grill pan accessory in the air fryer.
3. Season the steak with salt, pepper, lemon zest, herbs, and garlic.
4. Brush with oil.
5. Grill for 15 minutes and if needed cook in batches.

Garlic Fillets

Servings: 4 | Cooking Time: 15 Minutes

- 1-pound beef filet mignon
- 1 teaspoon minced garlic
- 1 tablespoon peanut oil
- ½ teaspoon salt
- 1 teaspoon dried oregano

1. Chop the beef into the medium size pieces and sprinkle with salt and dried oregano. Then add minced garlic and peanut oil and mix up the meat well. Place the bowl with meat in the fridge for 10 minutes to marinate. Meanwhile, preheat the air fryer to 400F. Put the marinated beef pieces in the air fryer and cook them for 10 minutes Then flip the beef on another side and cook for 5 minutes more.

Grilled Prosciutto Wrapped Fig

Servings:2 | Cooking Time: 8 Minutes

- 2 whole figs, sliced in quarters
- 8 prosciutto slices
- Pepper and salt to taste

1. Wrap a prosciutto slice around one slice of fid and then thread into skewer. Repeat process for remaining Ingredients. Place on skewer rack in air fryer.
2. For 8 minutes, cook on 390oF. Halfway through cooking time, turnover skewers.
3. Serve and enjoy.

Veggie Stuffed Beef Rolls

Servings:6 | Cooking Time:14 Minutes

- 2 pounds beef flank steak, pounded to 1/8-inch thickness
- 6 Provolone cheese slices
- 3-ounce roasted red bell peppers
- ¾ cup fresh baby spinach
- 3 tablespoons prepared pesto
- Salt and black pepper, to taste

1. Preheat the Air fryer to 400 o F and grease an Air fryer basket.
2. Place the steak onto a smooth surface and spread evenly with pesto.
3. Top with the cheese slices, red peppers and spinach.
4. Roll up the steak tightly around the filling and secure with the toothpicks.
5. Arrange the roll in the Air fryer basket and cook for about 14 minutes, flipping once in between.
6. Dish out in a platter and serve warm.

Garlic Pork And Ginger Sauce

Servings: 4 | Cooking Time: 35 Minutes

- 1 pound pork tenderloin, cut into strips
- 1 garlic clove, minced
- A pinch of salt and black pepper
- 1 tablespoon ginger, grated
- 3 tablespoons coconut aminos
- 2 tablespoons coconut oil, melted

1. Heat up a pan that fits the air fryer with the oil over medium-high heat, add the meat and brown for 3 minutes. Add the rest of the ingredients, cook for 2 minutes more, put the pan in the fryer and cook at 380 degrees F for 30 minutes Divide between plates and serve with a side salad.

Pepper Pork Chops

Servings:2 | Cooking Time:6 Minutes

- 2 pork chops
- 1 egg white
- ¾ cup xanthum gum
- ½ teaspoon sea salt
- ¼ teaspoon freshly ground black pepper
- 1 oil mister

1. Preheat the Air fryer to 400 o F and grease an Air fryer basket.
2. Whisk egg white with salt and black pepper in a bowl and dip the pork chops in it.
3. Cover the bowl and marinate for about 20 minutes.
4. Pour the xanthum gum over both sides of the chops and spray with oil mister.
5. Arrange the chops in the Air fryer basket and cook for about 6 minutes.
6. Dish out in a bowl and serve warm.

Easy Corn Dog Bites
Servings:2 | Cooking Time: 10 Minutes
- ½ cup all-purpose flour
- 1 ½ cup crushed cornflakes
- 2 large beef hot dogs, cut in half crosswise
- 2 large eggs, beaten
- Salt and pepper to taste

1. Preheat the air fryer to 3300F.
2. Skewer the hot dogs using the metal skewers included in the double layer rack accessory.
3. In a mixing bowl, combine the flour and eggs to form a batter. Season with salt and pepper to taste. Add water if too dry.
4. Dip the skewered hot dogs in the batter and dredge in cornflakes.
5. Place on the double layer rack accessory and cook for 10 minutes.

Steak Total
Servings: 4 | Cooking Time: 30 Minutes
- 2 lb. rib eye steak
- 1 tbsp. olive oil
- 1 tbsp. steak rub

1. Set the Air Fryer to 400°F and allow to warm for 4 minutes.
2. Massage the olive oil and steak rub into both sides of the steak.
3. Put the steak in the fryer's basket and cook for 14 minutes. Turn the steak over and cook on the other side for another 7 minutes.
4. Serve hot.

Maple'n Soy Marinated Beef
Servings:4 | Cooking Time: 45 Minutes
- 2 pounds sirloin flap steaks, pounded
- 3 tablespoons balsamic vinegar
- 3 tablespoons maple syrup
- 3 tablespoons soy sauce
- 4 cloves of garlic, minced

1. Preheat the air fryer to 3900F.
2. Place the grill pan accessory in the air fryer.
3. On a deep dish, place the flap steaks and season with soy sauce, balsamic vinegar, and maple syrup, and garlic.
4. Place on the grill pan and cook for 15 minutes in batches.

Ribs And Chimichuri Mix
Servings: 4 | Cooking Time: 35 Minutes
- 1-pound pork baby back ribs, boneless
- 2 tablespoons chimichuri sauce
- ½ teaspoon salt

1. Sprinkle the ribs with salt and brush with chimichuri sauce. Then preheat the air fryer to 365F. Put the pork ribs in the air fryer and cook for 35 minutes.

Pork Chops
Servings: 2 | Cooking Time: 16 Minutes
- 2 bone-in, centercut pork chops, 1-inch thick (10 ounces each)
- 2 teaspoons Worcestershire sauce
- salt and pepper
- cooking spray

1. Rub the Worcestershire sauce into both sides of pork chops.
2. Season with salt and pepper to taste.
3. Spray air fryer basket with cooking spray and place the chops in basket side by side.
4. Cook at 360°F for 16 minutes or until well done. Let rest for 5minutes before serving.

Crouton-breaded Pork Chops
Servings:4 | Cooking Time: 14 Minutes
- 4 boneless pork chops
- 1 teaspoon salt
- ½ teaspoon ground black pepper
- 2 cups croutons
- ½ teaspoon dried thyme
- ¼ teaspoon dried sage
- 1 large egg, whisked

1. Preheat the air fryer to 400°F.
2. Sprinkle pork chops with salt and pepper on both sides.
3. In a food processor, add croutons, thyme, and sage. Pulse five times until croutons are mostly broken down with a few medium-sized pieces remaining. Transfer to a medium bowl.
4. In a separate medium bowl, place egg. Dip each pork chop into egg, then press into crouton mixture to coat both sides. Spritz with cooking spray.
5. Place pork in the air fryer basket and cook 14 minutes, turning halfway through cooking time, until chops are golden brown and internal temperature reaches at least 145°F. Serve warm.

Buttered Striploin Steak
Servings:2 | Cooking Time:12 Minutes
- 2 (7-ounces) striploin steak
- 1½ tablespoons butter, softened
- Salt and black pepper, to taste

1. Preheat the Air fryer to 390 o F and grease an Air fryer basket.
2. Rub the steak generously with salt and black pepper and coat with butter.
3. Transfer the steak in the Air fryer basket and cook for about 12 minutes, flipping once in between.
4. Dish out the steak and cut into desired size slices to serve.

Bacon Wrapped Pork Tenderloin
Servings:4 | Cooking Time:30 Minutes
- 1 (1½ pound) pork tenderloins
- 4 bacon strips
- 2 tablespoons Dijon mustard

1. Preheat the Air fryer to 360 o F and grease an Air fryer basket.
2. Rub the tenderloin evenly with mustard and wrap the tenderloin with bacon strips.
3. Arrange the pork tenderloin in the Air fryer basket and cook for about 30 minutes, flipping once in between.
4. Dish out the steaks and cut into desired size slices to serve.

Champagne-vinegar Marinated Skirt Steak
Servings:2 | Cooking Time: 40 Minutes
- ¼ cup Dijon mustard
- 1 tablespoon rosemary leaves
- 1-pound skirt steak, trimmed
- 2 tablespoons champagne vinegar
- Salt and pepper to taste

1. Place all ingredients in a Ziploc bag and marinate in the fridge for 2 hours.
2. Preheat the air fryer to 3900F.
3. Place the grill pan accessory in the air fryer.
4. Grill the skirt steak for 20 minutes per batch.
5. Flip the beef halfway through the cooking time.

Simple Herbs De Provence Pork Loin Roast
Servings:4 | Cooking Time: 35 Minutes
- 4 pounds pork loin
- A pinch of garlic salt
- A pinch of herbs de Provence

1. Preheat the air fryer to 3300F.
2. Season pork with the garlic salt and herbs,
3. Place in the air fryer grill pan.
4. Cook for 30 to 35 minutes.

Simple New York Strip Steak
Servings:2 | Cooking Time:10 Minutes
- 1 (9½-ounces) New York strip steak
- 1 teaspoon olive oil
- Crushed red pepper flakes, to taste
- Salt and black pepper, to taste

1. Preheat the Air fryer to 400 o F and grease an Air fryer basket.
2. Rub the steak generously with red pepper flakes, salt and black pepper and coat with olive oil.
3. Transfer the steak in the Air fryer basket and cook for about 10 minutes, flipping once in between.
4. Dish out the steak and cut into desired size slices to serve.

Kielbasa Chunks With Pineapple & Peppers
Servings: 2 | Cooking Time: 10 Minutes
- ¾ pound kielbasa sausage
- 1 cup bell pepper chunks (any color)
- 1 8-ounce can pineapple chunks in juice, drained
- 1 tablespoon barbeque seasoning
- 1 tablespoon soy sauce
- cooking spray

1. Cut sausage into ½-inch slices.
2. In a medium bowl, toss all ingredients together.
3. Spray air fryer basket with nonstick cooking spray.
4. Pour sausage mixture into the basket.
5. Cook at 390°F for approximately 5minutes. Shake basket and cook an additional 5minutes.

Bjorn's Beef Steak
Servings: 1 | Cooking Time: 15 Minutes
- 1 steak, 1-inch thick
- 1 tbsp. olive oil
- Black pepper to taste
- Sea salt to taste

1. Place the baking tray inside the Air Fryer and pre-heat for about 5 minutes at 390°F.
2. Brush or spray both sides of the steak with the oil.
3. Season both sides with salt and pepper.
4. Take care when placing the steak in the baking tray and allow to cook for 3 minutes. Flip the meat over, and cook for an additional 3 minutes.
5. Take it out of the fryer and allow to sit for roughly 3 minutes before serving.

Cumin Pork Steak
Servings: 4 | Cooking Time: 25 Minutes
- 16 oz pork steak (4 oz every steak)
- ½ teaspoon ground paprika
- ½ teaspoon salt
- 1 tablespoon sesame oil
- ½ teaspoon ground cumin
- ½ teaspoon dried garlic

1. Sprinkle every pork steak with ground paprika, ground cumin, salt, and dried garlic. Then sprinkle the meat with sesame oil. Preheat the air fryer to 400F. Put the pork steak in the air fryer in one layer and cook them for 15 minutes. Then flip the steaks on another side and cook them for 10 minutes more.

Lamb Loin Chops With Lemon
Servings:4 | Cooking Time: 30 Minutes
- 2 tablespoons Dijon mustard
- 1 tablespoon fresh lemon juice
- ½ teaspoon olive oil
- 1 teaspoon dried tarragon
- Salt and ground black pepper, as required
- 8 (4-ounces) lamb loin chops

1. In a large bowl, mix together the mustard, lemon juice, oil, tarragon, salt, and black pepper.
2. Add chops and generously coat with the mixture.
3. Set the temperature of air fryer to 390 degrees F. Grease an air fryer basket.
4. Arrange chops into the prepared air fryer basket in a single layer in 2 batches.
5. Air fry for about 15 minutes, flipping once halfway through.
6. Remove the chops from air fryer and transfer onto serving plates.
7. Serve hot.

Cream Cheese Pork
Servings: 4 | Cooking Time: 20 Minutes
- 16 oz pork tenderloin
- 1 teaspoon liquid smoke
- 1 teaspoon mustard
- 1 teaspoon cream cheese
- ½ teaspoon ground paprika
- 1 teaspoon avocado oil

1. In the mixing bowl mix up liquid smoked, mustard, cream cheese, and ground paprika. Add avocado oil and. Stir the mixture. Then rub the pork tenderloin with the smoky mixture and wrap in the foil. Preheat the air fryer to 375F. Put the wrapped tenderloin in the air fryer basket and cook it for 20 minutes. Then discard the foil and slice the tenderloin into the servings.

Roasted Ribeye Steak With Rum
Servings:4 | Cooking Time: 50 Minutes
- ½ cup rum
- 2 pounds bone-in ribeye steak
- 2 tablespoons extra virgin olive oil
- Salt and black pepper to taste

1. Place all Ingredients in a Ziploc bag and allow to marinate in the fridge for at least 2 hours.
2. Preheat the air fryer to 3900F.
3. Place the grill pan accessory in the air fryer.
4. Grill for 25 minutes per piece.
5. Halfway through the cooking time, flip the meat for even grilling.

Ham Pinwheels
Servings:4 | Cooking Time:11 Minutes
- 1 puff pastry sheet
- 10 ham slices
- 1 cup Gruyere cheese, shredded plus more for sprinkling
- 4 teaspoons Dijon mustard

1. Preheat the Air fryer to 375 o F and grease an Air fryer basket.
2. Place the puff pastry onto a smooth surface and spread evenly with the mustard.
3. Top with the ham and ¾ cup cheese and roll the puff pastry.
4. Wrap the roll in plastic wrap and freeze for about 30 minutes.
5. Remove from the freezer and slice into ½-inch rounds.
6. Arrange the pinwheels in the Air fryer basket and cook for about 8 minutes.
7. Top with remaining cheese and cook for 3 more minutes.
8. Dish out in a platter and serve warm.

Pork Chops Marinate In Honey-mustard
Servings:4 | Cooking Time: 25 Minutes
- 2 tablespoons honey
- 2 tablespoons minced garlic
- 4 pork chops
- 4 tablespoons mustard
- Salt and pepper to taste

1. Preheat the air fryer to 3300F.
2. Place the air fryer basket.
3. Season the pork chops with the rest of the Ingredients.
4. Place inside the basket.
5. Cook for 20 to 25 minutes until golden.

Sausage Meatballs
Servings:4 | Cooking Time:15 Minutes
- 3½-ounce sausage, casing removed
- ½ medium onion, minced finely
- 1 teaspoon fresh sage, chopped finely
- 3 tablespoons Italian breadcrumbs
- ½ teaspoon garlic, minced
- Salt and black pepper, to taste

1. Preheat the Air fryer to 355 o F and grease an Air fryer basket.
2. Mix all the ingredients in a bowl until well combined.
3. Shape the mixture into equal-sized balls and arrange the balls in the Air fryer basket.
4. Cook for about 15 minutes and dish out to serve warm.

Easy Rib Eye Steak
Servings:4 | Cooking Time:14 Minutes
- 2 lbs. rib eye steak
- 1 tablespoon olive oil
- 1 tablespoon steak rubo

1. Preheat the Air fryer to 400 o F and grease an Air fryer basket.
2. Rub the steak generously with steak rub and coat with olive oil.
3. Transfer the steak in the Air fryer basket and cook for about 14 minutes, flipping once in between.
4. Dish out the steak and cut into desired size slices to serve.

Steak Kebabs
Servings:4 | Cooking Time: 10 Minutes Per Batch
- 1 ½ pounds sirloin steak, cut into 1" cubes
- 1 medium yellow onion, peeled and cut into 1" pieces
- 1 medium green bell pepper, seeded and cut into 1" pieces
- 1 medium red bell pepper, seeded and cut into 1" pieces
- 1 teaspoon salt
- ½ teaspoon ground black pepper
- 2 tablespoons olive oil

1. Soak twelve 6" skewers in water 10 minutes to prevent burning. Preheat the air fryer to 400°F.
2. To assemble kebabs, place one piece of steak on skewer, then a piece of onion, green bell pepper, and red bell pepper. Repeat three times per skewer.
3. Sprinkle assembled kebabs with salt and black pepper, then drizzle with oil.
4. Place kebabs in the air fryer basket in a single layer, working in batches as necessary. Cook 10 minutes, turning halfway through cooking time, until vegetables are tender, meat is brown, and internal temperature reaches at least 160°F. Serve warm.

Fantastic Leg Of Lamb
Servings:4 | Cooking Time:1 Hour 15 Minutes
- 2 pounds (3 ounce) leg of lamb
- 2 fresh rosemary sprigs
- 2 fresh thyme sprigs
- 2 tablespoons olive oil
- Salt and black pepper, to taste

1. Preheat the Air fryer to 300 o F and grease an Air fryer basket.
2. Sprinkle the leg of lamb with oil, salt and black pepper and wrap with herb sprigs.
3. Arrange the leg of lamb in the Air fryer basket and cook for about 75 minutes.
4. Dish out and serve warm.

Chili Loin Medallions
Servings: 4 | Cooking Time: 15 Minutes
- 1-pound pork loin
- 4 oz bacon, sliced
- 1 teaspoon ground cumin
- 1 teaspoon coconut oil, melted
- ½ teaspoon salt
- ½ teaspoon chili flakes

1. Slice the pork loin on the meat medallions and sprinkle them with ground cumin, salt, and chili flakes. Then wrap every meat medallion in the sliced bacon and sprinkle with coconut oil. Place the wrapped medallions in the air fryer basket in one layer and cook them for 10 minutes at 375F. Then carefully flip the meat medallions on another side and cook them for 5 minutes more.

Bourbon-bbq Sauce Marinated Beef Bbq
Servings:4 | Cooking Time: 60 Minutes
- ¼ cup bourbon
- ¼ cup barbecue sauce
- 1 tablespoon Worcestershire sauce
- 2 pounds beef steak, pounded
- Salt and pepper to taste

1. Place all ingredients in a Ziploc bag and allow to marinate in the

fridge for at least 2 hours.
2. Preheat the air fryer to 3900F.
3. Place the grill pan accessory in the air fryer.
4. Place on the grill pan and cook for 20 minutes per batch.
5. Halfway through the cooking time, give a stir to cook evenly.
6. Meanwhile, pour the marinade on a saucepan and allow to simmer until the sauce thickens.
7. Serve beef with the bourbon sauce.

Baby Back Ribs
Servings: 4 | Cooking Time: 36 Minutes

- 2¼ pounds Pork baby back rib rack(s)
- 1 tablespoon Dried barbecue seasoning blend or rub (gluten-free, if a concern)
- 1 cup Water
- 3 tablespoons Purchased smooth barbecue sauce (gluten-free, if a concern)

1. Preheat the air fryer to 350°F.
2. Cut the racks into 4- to 5-bone sections, about two sections for the small batch, three for the medium, and four for the large. Sprinkle both sides of these sections with the seasoning blend.
3. Pour the water into the bottom of the air-fryer drawer or into a tray placed under the rack. (The rack cannot then sit in water—adjust the amount of water for your machine.) Set the rib sections in the basket so that they're not touching. Air-fry for 30 minutes, turning once.
4. If using a tray with water, check it a couple of times to make sure it still has water in it or hasn't overflowed from the rendered fat.
5. Brush half the barbecue sauce on the exposed side of the ribs. Air-fry undisturbed for 3 minutes. Turn the racks over (but make sure they're still not touching), brush with the remaining sauce, and air-fry undisturbed for 3 minutes more, or until sizzling and brown.
6. Use kitchen tongs to transfer the racks to a cutting board. Let stand for 5 minutes, then slice between the bones to serve.

Butter Beef
Servings: 4 | Cooking Time: 10 Minutes

- 4 beef steaks (3 oz each steak)
- 4 tablespoons butter, softened
- 1 teaspoon ground black pepper
- ½ teaspoon salt

1. In the shallow bowl mix up softened butter, ground black pepper, and salt. Then brush the beef steaks with the butter mixture from each side. Preheat the air fryer to 400F. Put the butter steaks in the air fryer and cook them for 5 minutes from each side.

Basil Pork
Servings: 4 | Cooking Time: 25 Minutes

- 4 pork chops
- A pinch of salt and black pepper
- 2 teaspoons basil, dried
- 2 tablespoons olive oil
- ½ teaspoon chili powder

1. In a pan that fits your air fryer, mix all the ingredients, toss, introduce in the fryer and cook at 400 degrees F for 25 minutes. Divide everything between plates and serve.

Super Simple Steaks
Servings: 2 | Cooking Time: 14 Minutes

- ½ pound quality cuts steak
- Salt and black pepper, to taste

1. Preheat the Air fryer to 390 o F and grease an Air fryer basket.
2. Season the steaks evenly with salt and black pepper and transfer into the Air fryer basket.
3. Cook for about 14 minutes and dish out to serve.

Rib Eye Steak Seasoned With Italian Herb
Servings: 4 | Cooking Time: 45 Minutes

- 1 packet Italian herb mix
- 1 tablespoon olive oil
- 2 pounds bone-in rib eye steak
- Salt and pepper to taste

1. Preheat the air fryer to 3900F.
2. Place the grill pan accessory in the air fryer.
3. Season the steak with salt, pepper, Italian herb mix, and olive oil. Cover top with foil.
4. Grill for 45 minutes and flip the steak halfway through the cooking time.

Garlic Lamb Roast
Servings: 6 | Cooking Time: 1½ Hours

- 2¾ pounds half lamb leg roast
- 3 garlic cloves, cut into thin slices
- 2 tablespoons extra-virgin olive oil
- 1 tablespoon dried rosemary, crushed
- Salt and ground black pepper, as required

1. In a small bowl, mix together the oil, rosemary, salt, and black pepper.
2. With the tip of a sharp knife, make deep slits on the top of lamb roast fat.
3. Insert the garlic slices into the slits.
4. Coat the lamb roast evenly with oil mixture.
5. Set the temperature of air fryer to 390 degrees F. Grease an air fryer basket.
6. Arrange lamb into the prepared air fryer basket in a single layer.
7. Air Fry for about 15 minutes and then another 1¼ hours at 320 degrees F.
8. Remove from air fryer and transfer the roast onto a platter.
9. With a piece of foil, cover the roast for about 10 minutes before slicing.
10. Cut the roast into desired size slices and serve.

Veal Rolls
Servings: 4 | Cooking Time: 15 Minutes

- 4 (6-ounce) veal cutlets
- 2 tablespoons fresh sage leaves
- 4 cured ham slices
- 1 tablespoon unsalted butter, melted
- Salt and black pepper, to taste

1. Preheat the Air fryer to 390 o F and grease an Air fryer basket.
2. Season the veal cutlets with salt and roll them up tightly.
3. Wrap 1 ham slice around each roll and coat with 1 tablespoon of the butter.
4. Top rolls with the sage leaves and transfer into the Air fryer basket.

5. Cook for about 10 minutes, flipping once in between and set the Air fryer to 300 o F.
6. Cook for about 5 more minutes and dish out to serve hot.

Pesto Coated Rack Of Lamb
Servings:4 | Cooking Time:15 Minutes
- ½ bunch fresh mint
- 1 garlic clove
- ½ tablespoon honey
- 1 (1½-pounds) rack of lamb
- ¼ cup extra-virgin olive oil
- Salt and black pepper, to taste

1. Preheat the Air fryer to 200 o F and grease an Air fryer basket.
2. Put the mint, garlic, oil, honey, salt, and black pepper in a blender and pulse until smooth to make pesto.
3. Coat the rack of lamb with this pesto on both sides and arrange in the Air fryer basket.
4. Cook for about 15 minutes and cut the rack into individual chops to serve.

Beef And Tomato Sauce
Servings: 4 | Cooking Time: 15 Minutes
- 1-pound beef loin tri-tip
- 1 tablespoon keto tomato sauce
- 1 teaspoon avocado oil

1. Pierce the beef loin tri-tip with a fork to get many small cuts. In the shallow bowl mix up tomato sauce and avocado oil. Brush the beef loin with the BBQ sauce mixture from each side and transfer in the air fryer. Cook the meat at 400F for 15 minutes. When the beef loin is cooked, remove it from the air fryer and let it rest for 5 minutes. Slice the meat into the servings.

Beef Short Ribs
Servings:4 | Cooking Time: 25 Minutes
- 3 pounds beef short ribs
- 2 tablespoons olive oil
- 3 teaspoons salt
- 3 teaspoons ground black pepper
- ½ cup barbecue sauce

1. Preheat the air fryer to 375°F.
2. Place short ribs in a large bowl. Drizzle with oil and sprinkle both sides with salt and pepper.
3. Place in the air fryer basket and cook 20 minutes. Remove from basket and brush with barbecue sauce. Return to the air fryer basket and cook 5 additional minutes until sauce is dark brown and internal temperature reaches at least 160°F. Serve warm.

Pretzel-coated Pork Tenderloin
Servings: 4 | Cooking Time: 10 Minutes
- 1 Large egg white(s)
- 2 teaspoons Dijon mustard (gluten-free, if a concern)
- 1½ cups (about 6 ounces) Crushed pretzel crumbs (see the headnote; gluten-free, if a concern)
- 1 pound (4 sections) Pork tenderloin, cut into ¼-pound (4-ounce) sections
- Vegetable oil spray

1. Preheat the air fryer to 350°F .
2. Set up and fill two shallow soup plates or small pie plates on your counter: one for the egg white(s), whisked with the mustard until foamy; and one for the pretzel crumbs.
3. Dip a section of pork tenderloin in the egg white mixture and turn it to coat well, even on the ends. Let any excess egg white mixture slip back into the rest, then set the pork in the pretzel crumbs. Roll it several times, pressing gently, until the pork is evenly coated, even on the ends. Generously coat the pork section with vegetable oil spray, set it aside, and continue coating and spraying the remaining sections.
4. Set the pork sections in the basket with at least ¼ inch between them. Air-fry undisturbed for 10 minutes, or until an instant-read meat thermometer inserted into the center of one section registers 145°F.
5. Use kitchen tongs to transfer the pieces to a wire rack. Cool for 3 to 5 minutes before serving.

Beef & Mushrooms
Servings: 1 | Cooking Time: 3 Hours 15 Minutes
- 6 oz. beef
- ¼ onion, diced
- ½ cup mushroom slices
- 2 tbsp. favorite marinade [preferably bulgogi]

1. Slice or cube the beef and put it in a bowl.
2. Cover the meat with the marinade, place a layer of aluminum foil or saran wrap over the bowl, and place the bowl in the refrigerator for 3 hours.
3. Put the meat in a baking dish along with the onion and mushrooms
4. Air Fry at 350°F for 10 minutes. Serve hot.

Extra Crispy Country-style Pork Riblets
Servings: 3 | Cooking Time: 30 Minutes
- ⅓ cup Tapioca flour
- 2½ tablespoons Chile powder
- ¾ teaspoon Table salt (optional)
- 1¼ pounds Boneless country-style pork ribs, cut into 1½-inch chunks
- Vegetable oil spray

1. Preheat the air fryer to 375°F .
2. Mix the tapioca flour, chile powder, and salt (if using) in a large bowl until well combined. Add the country-style rib chunks and toss well to coat thoroughly.
3. When the machine is at temperature, gently shake off any excess tapioca coating from the chunks. Generously coat them on all sides with vegetable oil spray. Arrange the chunks in the basket in one (admittedly fairly tight) layer. The pieces may touch. Air-fry for 30 minutes, rearranging the pieces at the 10- and 20-minute marks to expose any touching bits, until very crisp and well browned.
4. Gently pour the contents of the basket onto a wire rack. Cool for 5 minutes before serving.

Top Loin Beef Strips With Blue Cheese
Servings:4 | Cooking Time: 50 Minutes
- 1 tablespoon pine nuts, toasted
- 2 tablespoons butter, softened
- 4 boneless beef top loin steaks
- 2 pounds crumbled blue cheese
- 2 tablespoons cream cheese
- Salt and pepper to taste

1. Preheat the air fryer to 3900F.
2. Place the grill pan accessory in the air fryer.
3. Season the beef with salt and pepper. Brush all sides with butter.
4. Grill for 25 minutes per batch making sure to flip halfway through the cooking time.
5. Slice the beef and serve with blue cheese, cream cheese and pine nuts.

Pork Tenderloin With Bacon And Veggies

Servings: 3 | Cooking Time: 28 Minutes

- 3 potatoes
- ¾ pound frozen green beans
- 6 bacon slices
- 3 (6-ounces) pork tenderloins
- 2 tablespoons olive oil

1. Preheat the Air fryer to 390 o F and grease an Air fryer basket.
2. Wrap 4-6 green beans with one bacon slice and coat the pork tenderloins with olive oil.
3. Pierce the potatoes with a fork and arrange in the Air fryer basket.
4. Cook for about 15 minutes and add the pork tenderloins.
5. Cook for about 6 minutes and dish out in a bowl.
6. Arrange the bean rolls into the Air fryer basket and top with the pork tenderloins.
7. Cook for about 7 minutes and dish out in a platter.
8. Cut each tenderloin into desired size slices to serve alongside the potatoes and green beans rolls.

Rosemary Lamb Steak

Servings: 2 | Cooking Time: 12 Minutes

- 12 oz lamb steak (6 oz each lamb steak)
- 1 teaspoon dried rosemary
- 1 teaspoon minced onion
- 1 tablespoon avocado oil
- ½ teaspoon salt

1. Rub the lamb steaks with minced onion and salt. In the shallow bowl mix up dried rosemary and avocado oil. Sprinkle the meat with rosemary mixture. After this, preheat the air fryer to 400F. Put the lamb steaks in the air fryer in one layer and cook them for 6 minutes. Then flip the meat on another side and cook it for 6 minutes more.

Grilled Sausages With Bbq Sauce

Servings: 3 | Cooking Time: 30 Minutes

- ½ cup prepared BBQ sauce
- 6 sausage links

1. Preheat the air fryer to 3900F.
2. Place the grill pan accessory in the air fryer.
3. Place the sausage links and grill for 30 minutes.
4. Flip halfway through the cooking time.
5. Before serving brush with prepared BBQ sauce.

Tonkatsu

Servings: 3 | Cooking Time: 10 Minutes

- ½ cup All-purpose flour or tapioca flour
- 1 Large egg white(s), well beaten
- ¾ cup Plain panko bread crumbs (gluten-free, if a concern)
- 3 4-ounce center-cut boneless pork loin chops (about ½ inch thick)
- Vegetable oil spray

1. Preheat the air fryer to 375°F.
2. Set up and fill three shallow soup plates or small pie plates on your counter: one for the flour, one for the beaten egg white(s), and one for the bread crumbs.
3. Set a chop in the flour and roll it to coat all sides, even the ends. Gently shake off any excess flour and set it in the egg white(s). Gently roll and turn it to coat all sides. Let any excess egg white slip back into the rest, then set the chop in the bread crumbs. Turn it several times, pressing gently to get an even coating on all sides and the ends. Generously coat the breaded chop with vegetable oil spray, then set it aside so you can dredge, coat, and spray the remaining chop(s).
4. Set the chops in the basket with as much air space between them as possible. Air-fry undisturbed for 10 minutes, or until golden brown and crisp.
5. Use kitchen tongs to transfer the chops to a wire rack and cool for a couple of minutes before serving.

Bacon With Shallot And Greens

Servings: 2 | Cooking Time: 10 Minutes

- 7 ounces mixed greens
- 8 thick slices pork bacon
- 2 shallots, peeled and diced
- Nonstick cooking spray

1. Begin by preheating the air fryer to 345 degrees F.
2. Now, add the shallot and bacon to the Air Fryer cooking basket; set the timer for 2 minutes. Spritz with a nonstick cooking spray.
3. After that, pause the Air Fryer; throw in the mixed greens; give it a good stir and cook an additional 5 minutes. Serve warm.

Japanese Miso Steak

Servings: 4 | Cooking Time: 15 Minutes + Marinating Time

- 1 ¼ pounds flank steak
- 1 ½ tablespoons sake
- 1 tablespoon brown miso paste
- 2 garlic cloves, pressed
- 1 tablespoon olive oil

1. Place all the ingredients in a sealable food bag; shake until completely coated and place in your refrigerator for at least 1 hour.
2. Then, spritz the steak with a non-stick cooking spray; make sure to coat on all sides. Place the steak in the Air Fryer baking pan.
3. Set your Air Fryer to cook at 400 degrees F. Roast for 12 minutes, flipping twice. Serve immediately.

Poultry Recipes

Mozzarella Turkey Rolls
Servings: 4 | Cooking Time: 20 Minutes
- 4 slices turkey breast
- 1 cup sliced fresh mozzarella
- 1 tomato, sliced
- ½ cup fresh basil
- 4 chive shoots

1. Pre-heat your Air Fryer to 390°F.
2. Lay the slices of mozzarella, tomato and basil on top of each turkey slice.
3. Roll the turkey up, enclosing the filling well, and secure by tying a chive shoot around each one.
4. Put in the Air Fryer and cook for 10 minutes. Serve with a salad if desired.

Texas Bbq Chicken Thighs
Servings: 4 | Cooking Time: 30 Minutes
- Salt and black pepper to taste
- 2 tsp Texas BBQ Jerky seasoning
- 1 tbsp olive oil
- 2 tbsp cilantro, chopped

1. Preheat the Air fryer to 380 F. Grease the air fryer basket with cooking spray.
2. Drizzle the chicken with olive oil, season with salt and pepper, and sprinkle over BBQ seasoning. Place in the air fryer basket. Cook for 20 minutes. Serve sprinkled with cilantro.

Poppin' Pop Corn Chicken
Servings: 1 | Cooking Time: 20 Minutes
- 1 lb. skinless, boneless chicken breast
- 1 tsp. chili flakes
- 1 tsp. garlic powder
- ½ cup flour
- 1 tbsp. olive oil cooking spray

1. Pre-heat your fryer at 365°F. Spray with olive oil.
2. Cut the chicken breasts into cubes and place in a bowl. Toss with the chili flakes, garlic powder, and additional seasonings to taste and make sure to coat entirely.
3. Add the coconut flour and toss once more.
4. Cook the chicken in the fryer for ten minutes. Turnover and cook for a further five minutes before serving.

Naked Cheese, Chicken Stuffing 'n Green Beans
Servings: 3 | Cooking Time: 20 Minutes
- 1 cup cooked, cubed chicken breast meat
- 1/2 (10.75 ounce) can condensed cream of chicken soup
- 1/2 (14.5 ounce) can green beans, drained
- 1/2 cup shredded Cheddar cheese
- 6-ounce unseasoned dry bread stuffing mix
- salt and pepper to taste

1. Mix well pepper, salt, soup, and chicken in a medium bowl.
2. Make the stuffing according to package Directions for Cooking.
3. Lightly grease baking pan of air fryer with cooking spray. Evenly spread chicken mixture on bottom of pan. Top evenly with stuffing. Sprinkle cheese on top.
4. Cover pan with foil.
5. For 15 minutes, cook on 390oF.
6. Remove foil and cook for 5 minutes at 390oF until tops are lightly browned.
7. Serve and enjoy.

Oregano Duck Spread
Servings: 6 | Cooking Time: 10 Minutes
- ½ cup butter, softened
- 12 oz duck liver
- 1 tablespoon sesame oil
- 1 teaspoon salt
- 1 tablespoon dried oregano
- ½ onion, peeled

1. Preheat the air fryer to 395F. Chop the onion. Put the duck liver in the air fryer, add onion, and cook the ingredients for 10 minutes. Then transfer the duck pate in the food processor and process it for 2-3 minutes or until the liver is smooth (it depends on the food processor power). Then add onion and blend the mixture for 2 minutes more. Transfer the liver mixture into the bowl. After this, add oregano, salt, sesame oil, and butter. Stir the duck liver with the help of the spoon and transfer it in the bowl. Refrigerate the pate for 10-20 minutes before serving.

Buffalo Chicken Strips
Servings: 1 | Cooking Time: 30 Minutes
- ¼ cup hot sauce
- 1 lb. boneless skinless chicken tenders
- 1 tsp. garlic powder
- 1 ½ oz. pork rinds, finely ground
- 1 tsp chili powder

1. Toss the hot sauce and chicken tenders together in a bowl, ensuring the chicken is completely coated.
2. In another bowl, combine the garlic powder, ground pork rinds, and chili powder. Use this mixture to coat the tenders, covering them well. Place the chicken into your fryer, taking care not to layer pieces on top of one another.
3. Cook the chicken at 375°F for twenty minutes until cooked all the way through and golden. Serve warm with your favorite dips and sides.

Almond Coconut Chicken Tenders
Servings: 4 | Cooking Time: 20 Minutes
- 4 chicken breasts, skinless, boneless and cut into tenders
- A pinch of salt and black pepper
- 1/3 cup almond flour
- 2 eggs, whisked
- 9 ounces coconut flakes

1. Season the chicken tenders with salt and pepper, dredge them in almond flour, then dip in eggs and roll in coconut flakes. Put the chicken tenders in your air fryer's basket and cook at 400 degrees F for 10 minutes on each side. Divide between plates and serve with a side salad.

Quick And Crispy Chicken

Servings:4 | Cooking Time: 15 Minutes

- 2 tbsp butter
- 2 oz breadcrumbs
- 1 large egg, whisked

1. Preheat air fryer to 380 F. Combine butter the breadcrumbs in a bowl. Keep mixing and stirring until the mixture gets crumbly. Dip the chicken in the egg wash. Then dip the chicken in the crumbs mix. Cook for 10 minutes. Serve.

Chili Chicken Cutlets

Servings: 4 | Cooking Time: 16 Minutes

- 15 oz chicken fillet
- 1 teaspoon white pepper
- 1 teaspoon ghee, melted
- ½ teaspoon onion powder
- ¼ teaspoon chili flakes

1. Chop the chicken fillet into the tiny pieces. Then sprinkle the chopped chicken with white pepper, onion powder, and chili flakes. Stir the mixture until homogenous. Make the medium-size cutlets from the mixture. Preheat the air fryer to 365F. Brush the air fryer basket with ghee and put the chicken cutlets inside. Cook them for 8 minutes and then flip on another side with the help of the spatula. Transfer the cooked chicken cutlets on the serving plate.

Quick Chicken For Filling

Servings: 2 | Cooking Time: 8 Minutes

- 1 pound chicken tenders, skinless and boneless
- ½ teaspoon ground cumin
- ½ teaspoon garlic powder
- cooking spray

1. Sprinkle raw chicken tenders with seasonings.
2. Spray air fryer basket lightly with cooking spray to prevent sticking.
3. Place chicken in air fryer basket in single layer.
4. Cook at 390°F for 4 minutes, turn chicken strips over, and cook for an additional 4 minutes.
5. Test for doneness. Thick tenders may require an additional minute or two.

Herbed Duck Legs

Servings:2 | Cooking Time:30 Minutes

- ½ tablespoon fresh thyme, chopped
- ½ tablespoon fresh parsley, chopped
- 2 duck legs
- 1 garlic clove, minced
- 1 teaspoon five spice powder
- Salt and black pepper, as required

1. Preheat the Air fryer to 340 o F and grease an Air fryer basket.
2. Mix the garlic, herbs, five spice powder, salt, and black pepper in a bowl.
3. Rub the duck legs with garlic mixture generously and arrange into the Air fryer basket.
4. Cook for about 25 minutes and set the Air fryer to 390 o F.
5. Cook for 5 more minutes and dish out to serve hot.

Chicken & Jalapeño Pepper Quesadilla

Servings:4 | Cooking Time: 20 Minutes

- 2 cups shredded Monterey Jack cheese
- ½ cup shredded and cooked chicken
- 1 cup canned fire-roasted jalapeño peppers, chopped

1. Preheat the Air Fryer to 390 F. Divide chicken, cheese, and jalapeño peppers between 4 tortillas. Top each one with the remaining tortillas. Grease with cooking spray. In batches, place in the air fryer basket and cook for 12 minutes, turning once halfway through. Serve with green salsa.

Paprika Chicken Legs With Turnip

Servings: 3 | Cooking Time: 30 Minutes

- 1 pound chicken legs
- 1 teaspoon Himalayan salt
- 1 teaspoon paprika
- 1/2 teaspoon ground black pepper
- 1 teaspoon butter, melted
- 1 turnip, trimmed and sliced

1. Spritz the sides and bottom of the cooking basket with a nonstick cooking spray.
2. Season the chicken legs with salt, paprika, and ground black pepper.
3. Cook at 370 degrees F for 10 minutes. Increase the temperature to 380 degrees F.
4. Drizzle turnip slices with melted butter and transfer them to the cooking basket with the chicken. Cook the turnips and chicken for 15 minutes more, flipping them halfway through the cooking time.
5. As for the chicken, an instant-read thermometer should read at least 165 degrees F.
6. Serve and enjoy!

Pepper Turkey Bacon

Servings: 2 | Cooking Time: 8 Minutes

- 7 oz turkey baconq
- 1 teaspoon coconut oil, melted
- ½ teaspoon ground black pepper

1. Slice the turkey bacon if needed and sprinkle it with ground black pepper and coconut oil. Preheat the air fryer to 400F. Arrange the turkey bacon in the air fryer in one layer and cook it for 4 minutes. Then flip the bacon on another side and cook for 4 minutes more.

Marjoram Chicken

Servings: 2 | Cooking Time: 1 Hr.

- 2 skinless, boneless small chicken breasts
- 2 tbsp. butter
- 1 tsp. sea salt
- ½ tsp. red pepper flakes, crushed
- 2 tsp. marjoram
- ¼ tsp. lemon pepper

1. In a bowl, coat the chicken breasts with all of the other ingredients. Set aside to marinate for 30 – 60 minutes.
2. Pre-heat your Air Fryer to 390 degrees.
3. Cook for 20 minutes, turning halfway through cooking time.
4. Check for doneness using an instant-read thermometer. Serve over jasmine rice.

Spicy Chicken Wings

Servings: 2 | Cooking Time: 20 Minutes

- 2 tbsp hot chili sauce
- ½ tbsp honey
- ½ tbsp black pepper
- ½ tbsp lime juice
- ½ tbsp kosher salt

1. Preheat the air fryer to 350 F. Mix the lime juice, honey and chili sauce. Toss the mixture over the chicken wings. Put the chicken in the air fryer basket and cook for 15 minutes.

Jalapeno Chicken Breasts

Servings: 2 | Cooking Time: 25 Minutes

- 2 oz. full-fat cream cheese, softened
- 4 slices sugar-free bacon, cooked and crumbled
- ¼ cup pickled jalapenos, sliced
- ½ cup sharp cheddar cheese, shredded and divided
- 2 x 6-oz. boneless skinless chicken breasts

1. In a bowl, mix the cream cheese, bacon, jalapeno slices, and half of the cheddar cheese until well-combined.
2. Cut parallel slits in the chicken breasts of about ¾ the length – make sure not to cut all the way down. You should be able to make between six and eight slices, depending on the size of the chicken breast.
3. Insert evenly sized dollops of the cheese mixture into the slits of the chicken breasts. Top the chicken with sprinkles of the rest of the cheddar cheese. Place the chicken in the basket of your air fryer.
4. Set the fryer to 350°F and cook the chicken breasts for twenty minutes.
5. Test with a meat thermometer. The chicken should be at 165°F when fully cooked. Serve hot and enjoy!

Buttered Duck Breasts

Servings: 4 | Cooking Time: 22 Minutes

- 2 (12-ounces) duck breasts
- 3 tablespoons unsalted butter, melted
- Salt and ground black pepper, as required
- ½ teaspoon dried thyme, crushed
- ¼ teaspoon star anise powder

1. Preheat the Air fryer to 390 o F and grease an Air fryer basket.
2. Season the duck breasts generously with salt and black pepper.
3. Arrange the duck breasts into the prepared Air fryer basket and cook for about 10 minutes.
4. Dish out the duck breasts and drizzle with melted butter.
5. Season with thyme and star anise powder and place the duck breasts again into the Air fryer basket.
6. Cook for about 12 more minutes and dish out to serve warm.

Fried Chicken Legs

Servings: 5 | Cooking Time: 50 Minutes

- 2 lemons, halved
- 5 tbsp garlic powder
- 5 tbsp oregano, dried
- ⅓ cup olive oil
- Salt and black pepper

1. Set air fryer to 350 F. Brush the chicken legs with some olive oil.
2. Sprinkle with the lemon juice and arrange on the air fryer basket. In another bowl, combine, oregano, garlic powder, salt and pepper. Sprinkle the seasoning mixture over the chicken. Cook in the air fryer for 20 minutes, shaking every 5 minutes.

Surprisingly Tasty Chicken

Servings: 4 | Cooking Time: 1 Hour

- 1 (1½ pound) whole chicken
- 1 pound small potatoes
- Salt and black pepper, to taste
- 1 tablespoon olive oil, scrubbed

1. Preheat the Air fryer to 390 o F and grease an Air fryer basket.
2. Season the chicken with salt and black pepper and transfer into the Air fryer.
3. Cook for about 40 minutes and dish out in a plate, covering with a foil paper.
4. Mix potato, oil, salt and black pepper in a bowl and toss to coat well
5. Arrange the potatoes into the Air fryer basket and cook for 20 minutes.
6. Dish out and serve warm.

Thyme Butter Turkey Breast

Servings: 8 | Cooking Time: 60 Minutes

- 2 lbs turkey breast
- ½ tsp thyme leaves, chopped
- ¼ tsp pepper
- ½ tsp sage leaves, chopped
- 1 tbsp butter
- 1 tsp salt

1. Spray air fryer basket with cooking spray.
2. Rub butter all over the turkey breast and season with pepper, sage, thyme, and salt.
3. Place turkey breast into the air fryer basket and cook at 25 F for 60 minutes. Turn turkey breast to another side halfway through.
4. Slice and serve.

Honey & Garlic Chicken Breasts

Servings: 4 | Cooking Time: 22 Minutes

- 1 tbsp honey
- 2 garlic cloves, minced
- Salt and black pepper to taste
- 1 pound boneless skinless chicken breasts
- 3 tbsp butter, melted

1. Preheat the Air fryer to 360 F.
2. In a bowl, combine together mustard, butter, garlic, honey, pepper, and salt; mix well. Rub the chicken with the mixture and place in the greased with cooking spray air fryer basket. Cook for 10 minutes. Slide out the basket and flip; cook for 10 minutes until crispy. Slice before serving.

Creamy Onion Chicken

Servings: 4 | Cooking Time: 20 Minutes

- 1 ½ cup onion soup mix
- 1 cup mushroom soup
- ½ cup cream

1. Preheat Fryer to 400 F. Add mushrooms, onion mix and cream in a frying pan. Heat on low heat for 1 minute. Pour the warm mixture over chicken slices and allow to sit for 25 minutes. Place the marinated chicken in the air fryer cooking basket and cook for 15 minutes. Serve with the remaining cream.

Honey Chicken Drumsticks

Servings: 2 | Cooking Time: 20 Minutes

- 2 tbsp olive oil
- 2 tbsp honey
- ½ tbsp garlic, minced

1. Add the ingredients to a resealable bag; massage until well-coated. Allow the chicken to marinate for 30 minutes. Preheat your air fryer to 400 F. Add the chicken to the cooking basket and cook for 15 minutes, shaking once.

Stuffed Chicken

Servings: 2 | Cooking Time: 11 Minutes

- 8 oz chicken fillet
- 3 oz Blue cheese
- ½ teaspoon salt
- ½ teaspoon thyme
- 1 teaspoon sesame oil

1. Cut the fillet into halves and beat them gently with the help of the kitchen hammer. After this, make the horizontal cut in every fillet. Sprinkle the chicken with salt and thyme. Then fill it with Blue cheese and secure the cut with the help of the toothpick. Sprinkle the stuffed chicken fillets with sesame oil. Preheat the air fryer to 385F. Put the chicken fillets in the air fryer and cook them for 7 minutes. Then carefully flip the chicken fillets on another side and cook for 4 minutes more.

Chicken Chunks

Servings: 4 | Cooking Time: 10 Minutes

- 1 pound chicken tenders cut in large chunks, about 1½ inches
- salt and pepper
- ½ cup cornstarch
- 2 eggs, beaten
- 1 cup panko breadcrumbs
- oil for misting or cooking spray

1. Season chicken chunks to your liking with salt and pepper.
2. Dip chicken chunks in cornstarch. Then dip in egg and shake off excess. Then roll in panko crumbs to coat well.
3. Spray all sides of chicken chunks with oil or cooking spray.
4. Place chicken in air fryer basket in single layer and cook at 390°F for 5minutes. Spray with oil, turn chunks over, and spray other side.
5. Cook for an additional 5minutes or until chicken juices run clear and outside is golden brown.
6. Repeat steps 4 and 5 to cook remaining chicken.

Chicken Breasts With Sweet Chili Adobo

Servings: 3 | Cooking Time: 20 Minutes

- Salt to season
- ¼ cup sweet chili sauce
- 3 tbsp turmeric

1. Preheat air fryer to 390 F. In a bowl, add salt, sweet chili sauce, and turmeric; mix with a spoon. Place the chicken on a clean flat surface and with a brush, apply the turmeric sauce lightly on the chicken.
2. Place in the fryer basket and grill for 18 minutes; turn them halfway through. Serve with a side of steamed greens.

Juicy Turkey Breast Tenderloin

Servings: 3 | Cooking Time: 25 Minutes

- 1 turkey breast tenderloin
- ½ tsp smoked paprika
- 1/2 tsp thyme
- 1/2 tsp sage
- 1/2 tsp pepper
- 1/2 tsp salt

1. Preheat the air fryer to 350 F.
2. Spray air fryer basket with cooking spray.
3. Rub turkey breast tenderloin with paprika, pepper, thyme, sage, and salt and place in the air fryer basket.
4. Cook for 25 minutes. Turn halfway through.
5. Slice and serve.

Zesty Ranch Chicken Drumsticks

Servings: 4 | Cooking Time: 20 Minutes

- 8 chicken drumsticks
- ½ teaspoon ground black pepper
- ½ cup panko bread crumbs
- 1 teaspoon salt
- ¼ cup dry ranch seasoning
- ½ cup grated Parmesan cheese

1. Preheat the air fryer to 375°F.
2. Sprinkle drumsticks with salt, pepper, and ranch seasoning.
3. In a paper lunch bag, combine bread crumbs and Parmesan. Add drumsticks to the bag and shake to coat. Spritz with cooking spray.
4. Place drumsticks in the air fryer basket and cook 20 minutes, turning halfway through cooking time, until the internal temperature reaches at least 165°F. Serve warm.

Ricotta And Thyme Chicken

Servings: 3 | Cooking Time: 18 Minutes

- 3 chicken thighs, boneless
- 1 teaspoon ricotta cheese
- Cooking spray
- 2 teaspoons adobo sauce
- 1 teaspoon dried thyme

1. In the mixing bowl mix up adobo sauce and ricotta cheese, Add dried thyme and churn the mixture. Then brush the chicken thighs with adobo sauce mixture and leave for 10 minutes to marinate. Preheat the air fryer to 385F. Spray the air fryer basket with cooking spray and put the chicken thighs inside. Cook them for 18 minutes.

Chicken Cordon Bleu

Servings: 4 | Cooking Time: 15 Minutes

- 4 boneless, skinless chicken breasts
- ¾ teaspoon salt
- ½ teaspoon ground black pepper
- 8 slices deli Black Forest ham
- 8 slices Gruyère cheese
- 1 large egg, beaten
- 2 cups panko bread crumbs

1. Preheat the air fryer to 375°F.
2. Cut each chicken breast in half lengthwise. Use a mallet to pound to ¼" thickness. Sprinkle salt and pepper on each side of chicken.
3. Place a slice of ham and a slice of cheese on each piece of chicken. Roll up chicken and secure with toothpicks.
4. In a medium bowl, add egg. In a separate medium bowl, add bread crumbs. Dip each chicken roll into egg, then into bread crumbs, pressing gently to adhere.
5. Spritz rolls with cooking spray and place in the air fryer basket. Cook 15 minutes, turning halfway through cooking time, until rolls are golden brown and internal temperature reaches at least 165°F. Serve warm.

Tarragon & Garlic Roasted Chicken
Servings: 4 | Cooking Time: 50 Minutes
- 1 sprig fresh tarragon
- 2 tbsp butter, melted
- Salt and black pepper to taste
- 1 lemon, cut into wedges
- 1 garlic bulb

1. Preheat the Air fryer to 380 F. Grease the air fryer basket with cooking spray.
2. Brush the chicken with melted butter and season with salt and pepper. Put tarragon, garlic, and lemon into the cavity of the chicken and place in the air fryer basket. Cook for 40 minutes. Cover with foil and leave to rest for 10 minutes, then carve and serve.

Roasted Chicken
Servings: 6 | Cooking Time: 90 Minutes
- 6 lb. whole chicken
- 1 tsp. olive oil
- 1 tbsp. minced garlic
- 1 white onion, peeled and halved
- 3 tbsp. butter

1. Pre-heat the fryer at 360°F.
2. Massage the chicken with the olive oil and the minced garlic.
3. Place the peeled and halved onion, as well as the butter, inside of the chicken.
4. Cook the chicken in the fryer for seventy-five minutes.
5. Take care when removing the chicken from the fryer, then carve and serve.

Chicken Enchiladas
Servings: 6 | Cooking Time: 65 Minutes
- 2 cups cheese, grated
- ½ cup salsa
- 1 can green chilies, chopped
- 12 flour tortillas
- 2 cans enchilada sauce

1. Preheat your Fryer to 400 F. In a bowl, mix salsa and enchilada sauce. Toss in the chopped chicken to coat. Place the chicken on the tortillas and roll; top with cheese. Place the prepared tortillas in the air fryer cooking basket and cook for 60 minutes. Serve with guacamole

Chicken Nuggets
Servings: 4 | Cooking Time: 10 Minutes
- 1 pound ground chicken breast
- 1 ½ teaspoons salt, divided
- ¾ teaspoon ground black pepper, divided
- 1 ½ cups plain bread crumbs, divided
- 2 large eggs

1. Preheat the air fryer to 400°F.
2. In a large bowl, mix chicken, 1 teaspoon salt, ½ teaspoon pepper, and ½ cup bread crumbs.
3. In a small bowl, whisk eggs. In a separate medium bowl, mix remaining 1 cup bread crumbs with remaining ½ teaspoon salt and ¼ teaspoon pepper.
4. Scoop 1 tablespoon chicken mixture and flatten it into a nugget shape.
5. Dip into eggs, shaking off excess before rolling in bread crumb mixture. Repeat with remaining chicken mixture to make twenty nuggets.
6. Place nuggets in the air fryer basket and spritz with cooking spray. Cook 10 minutes, turning halfway through cooking time, until internal temperature reaches 165°F. Serve warm.

Chicken Breast With Prosciutto And Brie
Servings: 2 | Cooking Time: 25 Minutes
- 1 tbsp olive oil
- Salt and pepper to season
- 1 cup semi-dried tomatoes, sliced
- ½ cup brie cheese, halved
- 4 slices thin prosciutto

1. Preheat the air fryer to 365 F. Put the chicken on a chopping board, and cut a small incision deep enough to make stuffing on both. Insert one slice of cheese and 4 to 5 tomato slices into each chicken.
2. Lay the prosciutto on the chopping board. Put the chicken on one side and roll the prosciutto over the chicken making sure that both ends of the prosciutto meet under the chicken.
3. Drizzle olive oil and sprinkle with salt and pepper. Place the chicken in the basket and cook for 10 minutes. Turn the breasts over and cook for another 5 minutes. Slice each chicken breast in half and serve with tomato salad.

Almond Flour Battered Chicken Cordon Bleu
Servings: 1 | Cooking Time: 30 Minutes
- ¼ cup almond flour
- 1 slice cheddar cheese
- 1 slice of ham
- 1 small egg, beaten
- 1 teaspoon parsley
- 2 chicken breasts, butterflied
- Salt and pepper to taste

1. Season the chicken with parsley, salt and pepper to taste.
2. Place the cheese and ham in the middle of the chicken and roll. Secure with toothpick.
3. Soak the rolled-up chicken in egg and dredge in almond flour.
4. Place in the air fryer.
5. Cook for 30 minutes at 3500F.

Paprika Duck
Servings: 6 | Cooking Time: 28 Minutes
- 10 oz duck skin
- 1 teaspoon sunflower oil
- ½ teaspoon salt
- ½ teaspoon ground paprika

1. Preheat the air fryer to 375F. Then sprinkle the duck skin with sunflower oil, salt, and ground paprika. Put the duck skin in the air fryer and cook it for 18 minutes. Then flip it on another side and cook for 10 minutes more or until it is crunchy from both sides.

Breaded Chicken Tenderloins
Servings: 4 | Cooking Time: 12 Minutes
- 1 egg, beaten
- ½ cup breadcrumbs
- 8 skinless, boneless chicken tenderloins
- 2 tablespoons vegetable oil

1. Preheat the Air fryer to 355 o F and grease an Air fryer basket.
2. Whisk the egg in a bowl and mix vegetable oil and breadcrumbs in another bowl.

3. Dip the chicken tenderloins into the whisked egg and then coat with the breadcrumb mixture.
4. Arrange the chicken tenderloins into the Air Fryer basket and cook for about 12 minutes.
5. Dish out the chicken tenderloins into a platter and serve hot.

Cilantro Drumsticks

Servings: 4 | Cooking Time: 30 Minutes
- 8 chicken drumsticks
- ½ cup chimichurri sauce
- ¼ cup lemon juice

1. Coat the chicken drumsticks with chimichurri sauce and refrigerate in an airtight container for no less than an hour, ideally overnight.
2. When it's time to cook, pre-heat your fryer to 400°F.
3. Remove the chicken from refrigerator and allow return to room temperature for roughly twenty minutes.
4. Cook for eighteen minutes in the fryer. Drizzle with lemon juice to taste and enjoy.

Vinegar Chicken

Servings: 4 | Cooking Time: 15 Minutes
- 16 oz chicken thighs, skinless
- 1 teaspoon ground celery root
- 1 teaspoon dried celery leaves
- 1 teaspoon apple cider vinegar
- ½ teaspoon salt
- 1 tablespoon sunflower oil

1. Rub the chicken thighs with the celery root, dried celery leaves, and salt. Then sprinkle the chicken with apple cider vinegar and sunflower oil. Leave it for 15 minutes to marinate. After this, preheat the air fryer to 385F. Put the chicken thighs in the air fryer and cook them for 12 minutes. Then flip the chicken on another side and cook for 3 minutes more. Transfer the cooked chicken thighs on the plate.

Paprika Liver Spread

Servings: 6 | Cooking Time: 8 Minutes
- 1-pound chicken liver
- 2 tablespoons ghee
- 1 teaspoon salt
- 1 teaspoon smoked paprika
- ¼ cup hot water

1. Preheat the air fryer to 400F. Wash and trim the chicken liver and arrange it in the air fryer basket. Cook the ingredients for 5 minutes. Then flip them on another side and cook for 3 minutes more. When the chicken liver is cooked, transfer it in the blender. Add ghee, salt, and smoked paprika. Add hot water and blend the mixture until smooth. Then transfer the cooked chicken pâté in the bowl and store it in the fridge for up to 3 days.

Strawberry Turkey

Servings: 2 | Cooking Time: 50 Minutes
- 2 lb. turkey breast
- 1 tbsp. olive oil
- Salt and pepper
- 1 cup fresh strawberries

1. Pre-heat your fryer to 375°F.
2. Massage the turkey breast with olive oil, before seasoning with a generous amount of salt and pepper.
3. Cook the turkey in the fryer for fifteen minutes. Flip the turkey and cook for a further fifteen minutes.
4. During these last fifteen minutes, blend the strawberries in a food processor until a smooth consistency has been achieved.
5. Heap the strawberries over the turkey, then cook for a final seven minutes and enjoy.

Baked Chicken Nachos

Servings: 4 | Cooking Time: 7 Minutes
- 50 tortilla chips
- 2 cups shredded cooked chicken breast, divided
- 2 cups shredded Mexican-blend cheese, divided
- ½ cup sliced pickled jalapeño peppers, divided
- ½ cup diced red onion, divided

1. Preheat the air fryer to 300°F.
2. Use foil to make a bowl shape that fits the shape of the air fryer basket. Place half tortilla chips in the bottom of foil bowl, then top with 1 cup chicken, 1 cup cheese, ¼ cup jalapeños, and ¼ cup onion. Repeat with remaining chips and toppings.
3. Place foil bowl in the air fryer basket and cook 7 minutes until cheese is melted and toppings heated through. Serve warm.

Cinnamon Balsamic Duck

Servings: 2 | Cooking Time: 20 Minutes
- 2 duck breasts, boneless and skin scored
- A pinch of salt and black pepper
- ¼ teaspoon cinnamon powder
- 4 tablespoons stevia
- 3 tablespoons balsamic vinegar

1. In a bowl, mix the duck breasts with the rest of the ingredients and rub well. Put the duck breasts in your air fryer's basket and cook at 380 degrees F for 10 minutes on each side. Divide everything between plates and serve.

Parmesan Chicken Tenders

Servings: 4 | Cooking Time: 12 Minutes
- 1 pound boneless, skinless chicken breast tenderloins
- ½ cup mayonnaise
- 1 cup grated Parmesan cheese
- 1 cup panko bread crumbs
- ½ teaspoon garlic powder
- 1 teaspoon salt
- ½ teaspoon ground black pepper

1. Preheat the air fryer to 400°F.
2. In a large bowl, add chicken and mayonnaise and toss to coat.
3. In a medium bowl, mix Parmesan, bread crumbs, garlic powder, salt, and pepper. Press chicken into bread crumb mixture to fully coat. Spritz with cooking spray and place in the air fryer basket.
4. Cook 12 minutes, turning halfway through cooking time, until tenders are golden and crisp on the edges and internal temperature reaches at least 165°F. Serve warm.

Quick 'n Easy Brekky Eggs 'n Cream

Servings: 2 | Cooking Time: 15 Minutes
- 2 eggs
- 2 tablespoons coconut cream
- A dash of Spanish paprika
- Salt and pepper to taste

1. Preheat the air fryer for 5 minutes.
2. Place the eggs and coconut cream in a bowl. Season with salt and

pepper to taste then whisk until fluffy
3. Pour into greased ramekins and sprinkle with Spanish paprika.
4. Place in the air fryer.
5. Bake for 15 minutes at 3500F.

Chicken Gruyere

Servings: 4 | Cooking Time: 20 Minutes

- ¼ cup Gruyere cheese, grated
- 1 pound chicken breasts, boneless, skinless
- ½ cup flour
- 2 eggs, beaten
- Sea salt and black pepper to taste
- 4 lemon slices

1. Preheat your Air Fryer to 370 F. Spray the air fryer basket with cooking spray.
2. Mix the breadcrumbs with Gruyere cheese in a bowl, pour the eggs in another bowl, and the flour in a third bowl. Toss the chicken in the flour, then in the eggs, and then in the breadcrumb mixture. Place in the fryer basket, close and cook for 12 minutes. At the 6-minute mark, turn the chicken over. Once golden brown, remove onto a serving plate and serve topped with lemon slices.

Goulash

Servings: 2 | Cooking Time: 20 Minutes

- 2 chopped bell peppers
- 2 diced tomatoes
- 1 lb. ground chicken
- ½ cup chicken broth
- Salt and pepper

1. Pre-heat your fryer at 365°F and spray with cooking spray.
2. Cook the bell pepper for five minutes.
3. Add in the diced tomatoes and ground chicken. Combine well, then allow to cook for a further six minutes.
4. Pour in chicken broth, and season to taste with salt and pepper. Cook for another six minutes before serving.

Bacon Chicken Mix

Servings: 2 | Cooking Time: 25 Minutes

- 2 chicken legs
- 4 oz bacon, sliced
- ½ teaspoon salt
- ½ teaspoon ground black pepper
- 1 teaspoon sesame oil

1. Sprinkle the chicken legs with salt and ground black pepper and wrap in the sliced bacon. After this, preheat the air fryer to 385F. Put the chicken legs in the air fryer and sprinkle with sesame oil. Cook the bacon chicken legs for 25 minutes.

Southern Fried Chicken

Servings: 2 | Cooking Time: 30 Minutes

- 2 x 6-oz. boneless skinless chicken breasts
- 2 tbsp. hot sauce
- ½ tsp. onion powder
- 1 tbsp. chili powder
- 2 oz. pork rinds, finely ground

1. Cut the chicken breasts in half lengthwise and rub in the hot sauce. Combine the onion powder with the chili powder, then rub into the chicken. Leave to marinate for at least a half hour.
2. Use the ground pork rinds to coat the chicken breasts in the ground pork rinds, covering them thoroughly. Place the chicken in your fryer.
3. Set the fryer at 350°F and cook the chicken for 13 minutes. Flip the chicken and cook the other side for another 13 minutes or until golden.
4. Test the chicken with a meat thermometer. When fully cooked, it should reach 165°F. Serve hot, with the sides of your choice.

Sausage Stuffed Chicken

Servings: 4 | Cooking Time: 15 Minutes

- 4 (4-ounce) skinless, boneless chicken breasts
- 4 sausages, casing removed
- 2 tablespoons mustard sauce

1. Preheat the Air fryer to 375 o F and grease an Air fryer basket.
2. Roll each chicken breast with a rolling pin for about 1 minute.
3. Arrange 1 sausage over each chicken breast and roll up.
4. Secure with toothpicks and transfer into the Air fryer basket.
5. Cook for about 15 minutes and dish out to serve warm.

Spicy Chicken

Servings: 4 | Cooking Time: 25 Minutes

- 2 garlic cloves, crushedQ
- 1 jalapeno pepper, finely chopped
- 4 tbsp chili sauce
- Salt and black pepper

1. In a bowl, add thighs, garlic, jalapeno, chili sauce, salt, and pepper, and stir to coat. Arrange the thighs in an even layer inside your air fryer and cook for 12 minutes at 360 F, turning once halfway through.

Crispy Cajun Fried Chicken

Servings: 4 | Cooking Time: 50 Minutes

- 4 boneless, skinless chicken thighs
- ¾ cup buttermilk
- ⅓ cup hot sauce
- 1 ½ tablespoons Cajun seasoning, divided
- 1 cup all-purpose flour
- 1 large egg

1. Preheat the air fryer to 375°F.
2. In a large bowl, combine chicken thighs, buttermilk, hot sauce, and ½ tablespoon Cajun seasoning, and toss to coat. Cover and let marinate in refrigerator at least 30 minutes.
3. In a large bowl, whisk flour with ½ tablespoon Cajun seasoning. In a medium bowl, whisk egg.
4. Remove chicken from marinade and sprinkle with remaining ½ tablespoon Cajun seasoning.
5. Dredge chicken by dipping into egg, then pressing into flour to fully coat. Spritz with cooking spray and place into the air fryer basket.
6. Cook 20 minutes, turning halfway through cooking time, until chicken is golden brown and internal temperature reaches at least 165°F. Serve warm.

Honey & Garlic Chicken Wings

Servings: 4 | Cooking Time: 25 Minutes

- 16 chicken wings
- ¾ cup potato starch
- 4 cloves garlic, minced
- ½ tsp. salt
- ¼ cup butter, melted
- ¼ cup honey

1. Pre-heat your Air Fryer to 370°F.

2. Put the chicken wings in a bowl and cover them well with the potato starch.
3. Spritz a baking dish with cooking spray.
4. Transfer the wings to the dish, place inside the fryer and cook for 5 minutes.
5. In the meantime, mix together the rest of the ingredients with a whisk.
6. Top the chicken with this mixture and allow to cook for another 10 minutes before serving.

Cheese Herb Chicken Wings
Servings: 4 | Cooking Time: 15 Minutes

- 2 lbs chicken wings
- 1 tsp herb de Provence
- ½ cup parmesan cheese, grated
- 1 tsp paprika
- Salt

1. Preheat the air fryer to 350 F.
2. In a small bowl, mix together cheese, herb de Provence, paprika, and salt.
3. Spray air fryer basket with cooking spray.
4. Toss chicken wings with cheese mixture and place into the air fryer basket and cook for 15 minutes. Turn halfway through.
5. Serve and enjoy.

Sweet-mustardy Thighs
Servings: 4 | Cooking Time: 30 Minutes

- 3 tbsp honey
- 2 tbsp dijon mustard
- ½ tbsp garlic powder
- Salt and pepper to taste

1. In a bowl, mix honey, mustard, garlic, salt, and black pepper. Coat the thighs in the mixture and arrange them in your air fryer. Cook for 16 minutes at 400 F, turning once halfway through.

Teriyaki Chicken Kebabs
Servings: 4 | Cooking Time: 1 Hour 15 Minutes

- ¾ cup teriyaki sauce, divided
- 4 boneless, skinless chicken thighs, cubed
- 1 teaspoon salt
- ½ teaspoon ground black pepper
- 1 cup pineapple chunks
- 1 medium red bell pepper, seeded and cut into 1" cubes
- ¼ medium yellow onion, peeled and cut into 1" cubes

1. In a large bowl, pour ½ cup teriyaki sauce over chicken and sprinkle with salt and black pepper. Cover and let marinate in refrigerator 1 hour.
2. Soak eight 6" skewers in water at least 10 minutes to prevent burning. Preheat the air fryer to 400°F.
3. Place a cube of chicken on skewer, then a piece of pineapple, bell pepper, and onion. Repeat with remaining chicken, pineapple, and vegetables.
4. Brush kebabs with remaining ¼ cup teriyaki sauce and place in the air fryer basket. Cook 15 minutes, turning twice during cooking, until chicken reaches an internal temperature of at least 165°F and vegetables are tender. Serve warm.

Garlicky Meatballs
Servings: 2 | Cooking Time: 20 Minutes

- ½ lb. boneless chicken thighs
- 1 tsp. minced garlic
- 1 ¼ cup roasted pecans
- ½ cup mushrooms
- 1 tsp. extra virgin olive oil

1. Preheat your fryer to 375°F.
2. Cube the chicken thighs.
3. Place them in the food processor along with the garlic, pecans, and other seasonings as desired. Pulse until a smooth consistency is achieved.
4. Chop the mushrooms finely. Add to the chicken mixture and combine.
5. Using your hands, shape the mixture into balls and brush them with olive oil.
6. Put the balls into the fryer and cook for eighteen minutes. Serve hot.

Lemon Pepper Chicken Legs
Servings: 4 | Cooking Time: 30 Minutes

- ½ tsp. garlic powder
- 2 tsp. baking powder
- 8 chicken legs
- 4 tbsp. salted butter, melted
- 1 tbsp. lemon pepper seasoning

1. In a small bowl combine the garlic powder and baking powder, then use this mixture to coat the chicken legs. Lay the chicken in the basket of your fryer.
2. Cook the chicken legs at 375°F for twenty-five minutes. Halfway through, turn them over and allow to cook on the other side.
3. When the chicken has turned golden brown, test with a thermometer to ensure it has reached an ideal temperature of 165°F. Remove from the fryer.
4. Mix together the melted butter and lemon pepper seasoning and toss with the chicken legs until the chicken is coated all over. Serve hot.

Bbq Chicken Wings
Servings: 4 | Cooking Time: 20 Minutes

- 1 1/2 lbs chicken wings
- 2 tbsp unsweetened BBQ sauce
- 1 tsp paprika
- 1 tbsp olive oil
- 1 tsp garlic powder
- Pepper
- Salt

1. In a large bowl, toss chicken wings with garlic powder, oil, paprika, pepper, and salt.
2. Preheat the air fryer to 360 F.
3. Add chicken wings in air fryer basket and cook for 12 minutes.
4. Turn chicken wings to another side and cook for 5 minutes more.
5. Remove chicken wings from air fryer and toss with BBQ sauce.
6. Return chicken wings in air fryer basket and cook for 2 minutes more.
7. Serve and enjoy.

Flavorful Cornish Hen

Servings: 3 | Cooking Time: 25 Minutes
- 1 Cornish hen, wash and pat dry
- 1 tbsp olive oil
- 1 tsp smoked paprika
- 1/2 tsp garlic powder
- Pepper
- Salt

1. Coat Cornish hen with olive oil and rub with paprika, garlic powder, pepper, and salt.
2. Place Cornish hen in the air fryer basket.
3. Cook at 390 F for 25 minutes. Turn halfway through.
4. Slice and serve.

Pretzel-crusted Chicken

Servings: 4 | Cooking Time: 12 Minutes
- 2 cups mini twist pretzels
- ½ cup mayonnaise
- 2 tablespoons honey
- 2 tablespoons yellow mustard
- 4 boneless, skinless chicken breasts, sliced in half lengthwise
- 1 teaspoon salt
- ½ teaspoon ground black pepper

1. Preheat the air fryer to 375°F.
2. In a food processor, place pretzels and pulse ten times.
3. In a medium bowl, mix mayonnaise, honey, and mustard.
4. Sprinkle chicken with salt and pepper, then brush with sauce mixture until well coated.
5. Pour pretzel crumbs onto a shallow plate and press each piece of chicken into them until well coated.
6. Spritz chicken with cooking spray and place in the air fryer basket. Cook 12 minutes, turning halfway through cooking time, until edges are golden brown and the internal temperature reaches at least 165°F. Serve warm.

Chicken With Mushrooms

Servings: 4 | Cooking Time: 24 Minutes
- 2 lbs chicken breasts, halved
- 1/3 cup sun-dried tomatoes
- 8 oz mushrooms, sliced
- 1/2 cup mayonnaise
- 1 tsp salt

1. Preheat the air fryer to 370 F.
2. Spray air fryer baking dish with cooking spray.
3. Place chicken breasts into the baking dish and top with sun-dried tomatoes, mushrooms, mayonnaise, and salt. Mix well.
4. Place dish in the air fryer and cook for 24 minutes.
5. Serve and enjoy.

Turkey Scotch Eggs

Servings: 4 | Cooking Time: 20 Minutes
- 1 cup panko breadcrumbs
- 1 egg
- 1 pound ground turkey
- 1 tsp ground cumin
- 1 tbsp dried tarragon
- Salt and black pepper to taste

1. Preheat the Air fryer to 400 F.
2. In a bowl, beat eggs with salt. In a separate bowl, mix panko breadcrumbs with tarragon. In a third bowl, pour the ground turkey and mix with cumin, salt, and pepper. Shape the mixture into 4 balls. Wrap the balls around the boiled eggs, so a bigger ball is formed, with the egg in the center.
3. Dip the wrapped eggs in egg and coat with breadcrumbs. Spray with cooking spray and place them in air fryer's basket and cook for 12 minutes, flipping once halfway through. Leave to cool before serving.

Greek Chicken Meatballs

Servings: 1 | Cooking Time: 15 Minutes
- ½ oz. finely ground pork rinds
- 1 lb. ground chicken
- 1 tsp. Greek seasoning
- 1/3 cup feta, crumbled
- 1/3 cup frozen spinach, drained and thawed

1. Place all the ingredients in a large bowl and combine using your hands. Take equal-sized portions of this mixture and roll each into a 2-inch ball. Place the balls in your fryer.
2. Cook the meatballs at 350°F for twelve minutes, in several batches if necessary.
3. Once they are golden, ensure they have reached an ideal temperature of 165°F and remove from the fryer. Keep each batch warm while you move on to the next one. Serve with Tzatziki if desired.

Creamy Chicken Breasts With Crumbled Bacon

Servings: 4 | Cooking Time: 25 Minutes
- ¼ cup olive oil
- 1 block cream cheese
- 4 chicken breasts
- 8 slices of bacon, fried and crumbled
- Salt and pepper to taste

1. Preheat the air fryer for 5 minutes.
2. Place the chicken breasts in a baking dish that will fit in the air fryer.
3. Add the olive oil and cream cheese. Season with salt and pepper to taste.
4. Place the baking dish with the chicken and cook for 25 minutes at 3500F.
5. Sprinkle crumbled bacon after.

Fried Chicken Halves

Servings: 4 | Cooking Time: 75 Minutes
- 16 oz whole chicken
- 1 tablespoon dried thyme
- 1 teaspoon ground cumin
- 1 teaspoon salt
- 1 tablespoon avocado oil

1. Cut the chicken into halves and sprinkle it with dried thyme, cumin, and salt. Then brush the chicken halves with avocado oil. Preheat the air fryer to 365F. Put the chicken halves in the air fryer and cook them for 60 minutes. Then flip the chicken halves on another side and cook them for 15 minutes more.

Simple Chicken Wings

Servings: 2 | Cooking Time: 25 Minutes
- 1 pound chicken wings
- Salt and black pepper, to taste

1. Preheat the Air fryer to 380 o F and grease an Air fryer basket.
2. Season the chicken wings evenly with salt and black pepper.
3. Arrange the drumsticks into the Air Fryer basket and cook for about 25 minutes.
4. Dish out the chicken drumsticks onto a serving platter and serve hot.

Lemon Grilled Chicken Breasts
Servings: 6 | Cooking Time: 40 Minutes
- 3 tablespoons fresh lemon juice
- 2 tablespoons olive oil
- 2 cloves of garlic, minced
- 6 boneless chicken breasts, halved
- Salt and pepper to taste

1. Place all ingredients in a Ziploc bag
2. Allow to marinate for at least 2 hours in the fridge.
3. Preheat the air fryer at 3750F.
4. Place the grill pan accessory in the air fryer.
5. Grill for 40 minutes and make sure to flip the chicken every 10 minutes for even cooking.

Turkey Wings
Servings: 4 | Cooking Time: 26 Minutes
- 2 pounds turkey wings
- 4 tablespoons chicken rub
- 3 tablespoons olive oil

1. In a large bowl, mix together the turkey wings, chicken rub, and oil using your hands.
2. Set the temperature of Air Fryer to 380 degrees F. Grease an Air Fryer basket.
3. Arrange turkey wings into the prepared Air Fryer basket.
4. Air Fry for about 26 minutes, flipping once halfway through.
5. Remove from Air Fryer and place the turkey wings onto the serving plates.
6. Serve hot.

Lime And Thyme Duck
Servings: 4 | Cooking Time: 17 Minutes
- 1-pound duck breast, skinless, boneless
- 2 oz preserved lime, sliced
- 1 teaspoon apple cider vinegar
- 1 tablespoon olive oil
- ½ teaspoon salt
- ½ teaspoon dried thyme

1. Cut the duck breast on 4 pieces and sprinkle with salt, dried thyme, apple cider vinegar, and oil. Mix up the duck pieces well and put on the foil. Then pot the reserved lime over the duck and wrap the foil. Preheat the air fryer to 375F and put the wrapped duck breast in the air fryer basket. Cook it for 17 minutes.

Yummy Shredded Chicken
Servings: 2 | Cooking Time: 15 Minutes
- 2 large chicken breasts
- ¼ tsp Pepper
- 1 tsp garlic puree
- 1 tsp mustard
- Salt

1. Add all ingredients to the bowl and toss well.
2. Transfer chicken into the air fryer basket and cook at 360 F for 15 minutes.
3. Remove chicken from air fryer and shred using a fork.
4. Serve and enjoy.

Buttered Spinach-egg Omelet
Servings: 4 | Cooking Time: 15 Minutes
- ¼ cup coconut milk
- 1 tablespoon melted butter
- 1-pound baby spinach, chopped finely
- 3 tablespoons olive oil
- 4 eggs, beaten
- Salt and pepper to taste

1. Preheat the air fryer for 5 minutes.
2. In a mixing bowl, combine the eggs, coconut milk, olive oil, and butter until well-combined.
3. Add the spinach and season with salt and pepper to taste.
4. Pour all ingredients in a baking dish that will fit in the air fryer.
5. Bake at 3500F for 15 minutes.

Whole Chicken
Servings: 2 | Cooking Time: 30 Minutes
- 1 lb. whole chicken
- 1 tsp. lemon zest
- 1 ½ tbsp. honey
- 1 lemon, juiced
- 1 tbsp. soy sauce

1. Place all of the ingredients in a bowl and combine well. Refrigerate for 1 hour.
2. Put the marinated chicken in the Air Fryer baking pan. Air fry at 320°F for 18 minutes.
3. Raise the heat to 350°F and cook for another 10 minutes or until chicken has turned light brown.

Creamy Duck Strips
Servings: 5 | Cooking Time: 17 Minutes
- 12 oz duck breast, skinless, boneless
- ½ cup coconut flour
- 1 teaspoon salt
- 1/3 cup heavy cream
- 1 teaspoon white pepper

1. Cut the duck breast on the small strips (fingers) and sprinkle with salt and white pepper. Then dip the duck fingers in the heavy cream and coat in the coconut flour. Preheat the air fryer to 375F. Put the duck fingers in the air fryer basket in one layer and cook them for 10 minutes. Then flip the duck fingers on another side and cook them for 7 minutes more.

Buttermilk-fried Chicken Thighs
Servings: 4 | Cooking Time: 1 Hour
- 1 cup buttermilk
- 2 tablespoons seasoned salt, divided
- 1 pound bone-in, skin-on chicken thighs
- 1 cup all-purpose flour
- ¼ cup cornstarch

1. In a large bowl, combine buttermilk and 1 tablespoon seasoned salt. Add chicken. Cover and let marinate in refrigerator 30 minutes.
2. Preheat the air fryer to 375°F.
3. In a separate bowl, mix flour, cornstarch, and remaining seasoned salt. Dredge chicken thighs, one at a time, in flour mixture, covering completely.
4. Spray chicken generously with cooking spray, being sure that no dry spots remain. Place chicken in the air fryer basket and cook 30 minutes, turning halfway through cooking time and spraying any dry spots, until chicken is dark golden brown and crispy and internal temperature reaches at least 165°F.
5. Serve warm.

Popcorn Chicken

Servings: 4 | Cooking Time: 12 Minutes
- 1 ½ teaspoons salt, divided
- 1 teaspoon ground black pepper, divided
- 1 ½ teaspoons garlic powder, divided
- 1 tablespoon mayonnaise
- 1 pound boneless, skinless chicken breast, cut into 1" cubes
- 1 cup panko bread crumbs

1. Preheat the air fryer to 350°F.
2. In a large bowl, combine 1 teaspoon salt, ½ teaspoon pepper, 1 teaspoon garlic powder, and mayonnaise. Add chicken cubes and toss to coat.
3. Place bread crumbs in a large resealable bag and add remaining ½ teaspoon salt, ½ teaspoon pepper, and ½ teaspoon garlic powder. Place chicken into the bag and toss to evenly coat.
4. Spritz chicken with cooking spray and place in the air fryer basket. Cook 12 minutes, turning halfway through cooking time, until chicken is golden brown and internal temperature reaches at least 165°F. Serve warm.

Juicy & Spicy Chicken Wings

Servings: 4 | Cooking Time: 25 Minutes
- 2 lbs chicken wings
- 12 oz hot sauce
- 1 tsp Worcestershire sauce
- 1 tsp Tabasco
- 6 tbsp butter, melted

1. Spray air fryer basket with cooking spray.
2. Add chicken wings into the air fryer basket and cook at 380 F for 25 minutes. Shake basket after every 5 minutes.
3. Meanwhile, in a bowl, mix together hot sauce, Worcestershire sauce, and butter. Set aside.
4. Add chicken wings into the sauce and toss well.
5. Serve and enjoy.

Roasted Chicken With Potatoes

Servings: 2 | Cooking Time: 1 Hour
- 1 (1½-pounds) whole chicken
- ½ pound small potatoes
- Salt and black pepper, as required
- 1 tablespoon olive oil

1. Preheat the Air fryer to 355 o F and grease an Air fryer basket.
2. Season the chicken and potatoes with salt and black pepper and drizzle with olive oil.
3. Transfer the chicken into the Air fryer basket and cook for about 45 minutes.
4. Dish out in a serving platter and transfer the potatoes in the Air fryer basket.
5. Cook for about 15 minutes and serve alongside the chicken.

Garlic Chicken Wings

Servings: 4 | Cooking Time: 30 Minutes
- 2 pounds chicken wings
- ¼ cup olive oil
- Juice of 2 lemons
- Zest of 1 lemon, grated
- A pinch of salt and black pepper
- 2 garlic cloves, minced

1. In a bowl, mix the chicken wings with the rest of the ingredients and toss well. Put the chicken wings in your air fryer's basket and cook at 400 degrees F for 30 minutes, shaking halfway. Divide between plates and serve with a side salad.

Parsley Duck

Servings: 4 | Cooking Time: 25 Minutes
- 4 duck breast fillets, boneless, skin-on and scored
- 2 tablespoons olive oil
- 2 tablespoons parsley, chopped
- Salt and black pepper to the taste
- 1 cup chicken stock
- 1 teaspoon balsamic vinegar

1. Heat up a pan that fits your air fryer with the oil over medium heat, add the duck breasts skin side down and sear for 5 minutes. Add the rest of the ingredients, toss, put the pan in the fryer and cook at 380 degrees F for 20 minutes. Divide everything between plates and serve

Lime And Mustard Marinated Chicken

Servings: 4 | Cooking Time: 30 Minutes + Marinating Time
- 1/2 teaspoon stone-ground mustard
- 1/2 teaspoon minced fresh oregano
- 1/3 cup freshly squeezed lime juice
- 2 small-sized chicken breasts, skin-on
- 1 teaspoon kosher salt
- 1 teaspoon freshly cracked mixed peppercorns

1. Preheat your Air Fryer to 345 degrees F.
2. Toss all of the above ingredients in a medium-sized mixing dish; allow it to marinate overnight.
3. Cook in the preheated Air Fryer for 26 minutes. Bon appétit!

Simple Turkey Breast

Servings: 10 | Cooking Time: 40 Minutes
- 1 (8-pounds) bone-in turkey breast
- Salt and black pepper, as required
- 2 tablespoons olive oil

1. Preheat the Air fryer to 360 o F and grease an Air fryer basket.
2. Season the turkey breast with salt and black pepper and drizzle with oil.
3. Arrange the turkey breast into the Air Fryer basket, skin side down and cook for about 20 minutes.
4. Flip the side and cook for another 20 minutes.
5. Dish out in a platter and cut into desired size slices to serve.

Breadcrumb Turkey Breasts

Servings: 6 | Cooking Time: 25 Minutes
- 6 turkey breasts
- 1 stick butter, melted
- 1 tsp. salt
- 2 cups friendly breadcrumbs
- ½ tsp. cayenne pepper
- ½ tsp. black pepper

1. Put the breadcrumbs, half a teaspoon of the salt, a quarter teaspoon of the pepper, and the cayenne pepper in a large bowl. Combine well.
2. In a separate bowl, sprinkle the melted butter with the rest of the salt and pepper.
3. Coat the turkey breasts with the butter using a brush. Roll the turkey in the bread crumbs and transfer to a lined baking dish. Place in the Air Fryer.
4. Air fry at 390°F for 15 minutes.

Sage And Chicken Escallops
Servings: 6 | Cooking Time: 10 Minutes
- 2 ½ oz panko breadcrumbs
- 1 ounce Parmesan cheese, grated
- 6 sage leaves, chopped
- 1 ¼ ounce flour
- 2 beaten eggs

1. Place the chicken breasts between a cling film, beat well using a rolling pin until a ½ cm thickness is achieved.
2. In a bowl, add Parmesan cheese, sage and breadcrumbs. Dredge the chicken into the seasoned flour and dredge into the egg. Finally, dredge into the breadcrumbs. Preheat your air fryer to 390 F. Spray both sides of chicken breasts with cooking spray and cook in the air fryer for 4 minutes, until golden.

Crispy Chicken Thighs
Servings: 1 | Cooking Time: 35 Minutes
- 1 lb. chicken thighs
- Salt and pepper
- 2 cups roasted pecans
- 1 cup water
- 1 cup flour

1. Pre-heat your fryer to 400°F.
2. Season the chicken with salt and pepper, then set aside.
3. Pulse the roasted pecans in a food processor until a flour-like consistency is achieved.
4. Fill a dish with the water, another with the flour, and a third with the pecans.
5. Coat the thighs with the flour. Mix the remaining flour with the processed pecans.
6. Dredge the thighs in the water and then press into the -pecan mix, ensuring the chicken is completely covered.
7. Cook the chicken in the fryer for twenty-two minutes, with an extra five minutes added if you would like the chicken a darker-brown color. Check the temperature has reached 165°F before serving.

Mesmerizing Honey Chicken Drumsticks
Servings: 3 | Cooking Time: 20 Minutes
- 2 tbsp olive oil
- 2 tbsp honey
- ½ tbsp garlic, minced

1. Preheat your air fryer to 400 F. Add garlic, oil and honey to a sealable zip bag. Add chicken and toss to coat; set aside for 30 minutes. Add the coated chicken to the air fryer basket, and cook for 15 minutes.

Blackened Chicken Tenders
Servings: 4 | Cooking Time: 12 Minutes
- 1 pound boneless, skinless chicken tenders
- 2 teaspoons paprika
- 1 teaspoon garlic powder
- 1 teaspoon salt
- ½ teaspoon cayenne pepper
- ½ teaspoon dried thyme
- ½ teaspoon ground black pepper

1. Preheat the air fryer to 400°F.
2. Place chicken tenders into a large bowl.
3. In a small bowl, mix paprika, garlic powder, salt, cayenne, thyme, and black pepper. Add spice mixture to chicken and toss to coat. Spritz chicken with cooking spray.
4. Place chicken in the air fryer basket and cook 12 minutes, turning halfway through cooking time, until chicken is brown at the edges and internal temperature reaches at least 165°F. Serve warm.

Sweet Chicken Breasts
Servings: 2 | Cooking Time: 35 Minutes
- 1 tablespoon maple syrup
- 2 teaspoons minced fresh rosemary
- ¼ teaspoon salt
- ⅛ teaspoon black pepper
- 2 chicken breasts, boneless, skinless
- Cooking spray

1. In a bowl, mix mustard, maple syrup, rosemary, salt, and pepper. Rub mixture onto chicken breasts. Spray generously the air fryer basket generously with cooking spray. Arrange the breasts inside and cook for 20 minutes, turning once halfway through.

Simple Paprika Duck
Servings: 4 | Cooking Time: 25 Minutes
- 1 pound duck breasts, skinless, boneless and cubed
- Salt and black pepper to the taste
- 1 tablespoon olive oil
- ½ teaspoon sweet paprika
- ¼ cup chicken stock
- 1 teaspoon thyme, chopped

1. Heat up a pan that fits your air fryer with the oil over medium heat, add the duck pieces, and brown them for 5 minutes. Add the rest of the ingredients, toss, put the pan in the machine and cook at 380 degrees F for 20 minutes. Divide between plates and serve.

Teriyaki Chicken Legs
Servings: 2 | Cooking Time: 20 Minutes
- 4 tablespoons teriyaki sauce
- 1 tablespoon orange juice
- 1 teaspoon smoked paprika
- 4 chicken legs
- cooking spray

1. Mix together the teriyaki sauce, orange juice, and smoked paprika. Brush on all sides of chicken legs.
2. Spray air fryer basket with nonstick cooking spray and place chicken in basket.
3. Cook at 360°F for 6 minutes. Turn and baste with sauce. Cook for 6 more minutes, turn and baste. Cook for 8 minutes more, until juices run clear when chicken is pierced with a fork.

Chicken Sausage In Dijon Sauce
Servings: 4 | Cooking Time: 20 Minutes
- 4 chicken sausages
- 1/4 cup mayonnaise
- 2 tablespoons Dijon mustard
- 1 tablespoon balsamic vinegar
- 1/2 teaspoon dried rosemary

1. Arrange the sausages on the grill pan and transfer it to the preheated Air Fryer.
2. Grill the sausages at 350 degrees F for approximately 13 minutes. Turn them halfway through cooking.
3. Meanwhile, prepare the sauce by mixing the remaining ingredients with a wire whisk. Serve the warm sausages with chilled Dijon sauce. Enjoy!

Chinese Chicken Wings

Servings: 4 | Cooking Time: 45 Minutes

- 8 chicken wings
- 2 tbsp. five spice
- 2 tbsp. soy sauce
- 1 tbsp. mixed spices
- Salt and pepper to taste

1. In a bowl, mix together all of the ingredients.
2. Cover the base of the fryer with an aluminum foil and pre-heat the fryer to 360°F.
3. Add in some oil and pour in the mixture. Cook for 15 minutes.
4. Turn up the heat to 390°F, turn the chicken wings and cook for another 5 minutes. Serve with mayo dip if desired.

Chicken & Prawn Paste

Servings: 2 | Cooking Time: 30 Minutes

- 2 tbsp cornflour
- ½ tbsp wine
- 1 tbsp shrimp paste
- 1 tbsp ginger
- ½ tbsp olive oil

1. Preheat your air fryer to 360 F. In a bowl, mix oil, ginger, and wine. Cover the chicken wings with the prepared marinade and top with flour. Add the floured chicken to shrimp paste and coat it. Place the chicken in your air fryer's cooking basket and cook for 20 minutes, until crispy on the outside.

Spinach 'n Bacon Egg Cups

Servings: 4 | Cooking Time: 10 Minutes

- ¼ cup spinach, chopped finely
- 1 bacon strip, fried and crumbled
- 3 tablespoons butter
- 4 eggs, beaten
- Salt and pepper to taste

1. Preheat the air fryer for 5 minutes.
2. In a mixing bowl, combine the eggs, butter, and spinach. Season with salt and pepper to taste.
3. Grease a ramekin with cooking spray and pour the egg mixture inside.
4. Sprinkle with bacon bits.
5. Place the ramekin in the air fryer.
6. Cook for 10 minutes at 350ºF.

Almond Flour Coco-milk Battered Chicken

Servings: 4 | Cooking Time: 30 Minutes

- ¼ cup coconut milk
- ½ cup almond flour
- 1 ½ tablespoons old bay Cajun seasoning
- 1 egg, beaten
- 4 small chicken thighs
- Salt and pepper to taste

1. Preheat the air fryer for 5 minutes.
2. Mix the egg and coconut milk in a bowl.
3. Soak the chicken thighs in the beaten egg mixture.
4. In a mixing bowl, combine the almond flour, Cajun seasoning, salt and pepper.
5. Dredge the chicken thighs in the almond flour mixture.
6. Place in the air fryer basket.
7. Cook for 30 minutes at 350ºF.

Shaking Tarragon Chicken Tenders

Servings: 2 | Cooking Time: 15 Minutes

- Salt and pepper to taste
- ½ cup dried tarragon
- 1 tbsp butter

1. Preheat air fryer to 390 F. Lay a 12 X 12 inch cut of foil on a flat surface. Place the chicken on the foil, sprinkle the tarragon on both, and share the butter onto both breasts. Sprinkle with salt and pepper.
2. Loosely wrap the foil around the breasts to enable airflow. Place the wrapped chicken in the basket and cook for 12 minutes. Remove the chicken and carefully unwrap the foil. Serve with the sauce extract and steamed veggies.

Family Farm's Chicken Wings

Servings: 6 | Cooking Time: 20 Minutes

- 6 chicken wings
- 2 cloves garlic, chopped
- 2 tbsp. Worcestershire sauce
- 1 tbsp. honey
- 1 tsp. red chili flakes
- Pepper and salt to taste

1. Place all the ingredients, except for the chicken wings, in a bowl and combine well.
2. Coat the chicken with the mixture and refrigerate for 1 hour.
3. Put the marinated chicken wings in the Air Fryer basket and spritz with cooking spray.
4. Air fry the chicken wings at 320°F for 8 minutes. Raise the temperature to 350°F and cook for an additional 4 minutes. Serve hot.

Easy & Crispy Chicken Wings

Servings: 8 | Cooking Time: 20 Minutes

- 1 1/2 lbs chicken wings
- 2 tbsp olive oil
- Pepper
- Salt

1. Toss chicken wings with oil and place in the air fryer basket.
2. Cook chicken wings at 370 F for 15 minutes.
3. Shake basket and cook at 400 F for 5 minutes more.
4. Season chicken wings with pepper and salt.
5. Serve and enjoy.

Fajita Style Chicken Breast

Servings: 2 | Cooking Time: 35 Minutes

- 2 x 6-oz. boneless skinless chicken breasts
- 1 green bell pepper, sliced
- 1 tbsp. coconut oil, melted
- ¼ medium white onion, sliced
- 3 tsp. taco seasoning mix

1. Cut each chicken breast in half and place each one between two sheets of cooking parchment. Using a mallet, pound the chicken to flatten to a quarter-inch thick.
2. Place the chicken on a flat surface, with the short end facing you. Place four slices of pepper and three slices of onion at the end of each piece of chicken. Roll up the chicken tightly, making sure not to let any veggies fall out. Secure with some toothpicks or with butcher's string.
3. Coat the chicken with coconut oil and then with taco seasoning. Place into your air fryer.
4. Turn the fryer to 350°F and cook the chicken for twenty-five minutes.
5. Serve the rolls immediately with your favorite dips and sides.

Lemon & Garlic Chicken
Servings: 1 | Cooking Time: 25 Minutes
- 1 chicken breast
- 1 tbsp. chicken seasoning
- Handful black peppercorns
- 1 tsp. garlic, minced
- 1 lemon juice
- Pepper and salt to taste

1. Pre-heat the Air Fryer to 350°F.
2. Sprinkle the chicken with pepper and salt. Massage the chicken seasoning into the chicken breast, coating it well, and lay the seasoned chicken on a sheet of aluminum foil.
3. Top the chicken with the garlic, lemon juice, and black peppercorns. Wrap the foil to seal the chicken tightly.
4. Cook the chicken in the fryer basket for 15 minutes.

Cheese Stuffed Turkey Breasts
Servings: 4 | Cooking Time: 18 Minutes
- 2 (8-ounces) turkey breast fillets, skinless and boneless, each cut into 2 pieces
- 4 cheddar cheese slices
- 1 tablespoon fresh parsley, minced
- 4 bacon slices
- Salt and black pepper, to taste

1. Preheat the Air fryer to 365 o F and grease an Air fryer basket.
2. Make a slit in each turkey piece horizontally and season with salt and black pepper.
3. Insert cheddar cheese slice into the slits and sprinkle with parsley.
4. Wrap each turkey piece with one bacon slice and transfer into the Air fryer basket.
5. Cook for about 18 minutes and dish out to serve warm.

Chili And Paprika Chicken Wings
Servings: 5 | Cooking Time: 12 Minutes
- 1-pound chicken wing
- 1 teaspoon ground paprika
- 1 teaspoon chili powder
- ½ teaspoon salt
- 1 tablespoon sunflower oil

1. Pour the sunflower oil in the shallow bowl. Add chili powder and ground paprika. Gently stir the mixture. Sprinkle the chicken wings with red chili mixture and salt. Preheat the air fryer to 400F. Place the chicken wings in the preheated air fryer in one layer and cook for 6 minutes. Then flip the wings on another side and cook for 6 minutes more.

Tomato Chicken Mix
Servings: 4 | Cooking Time: 18 Minutes
- 1-pound chicken breast, skinless, boneless
- 1 tablespoon keto tomato sauce
- 1 teaspoon avocado oil
- ½ teaspoon garlic powder

1. In the small bowl mix up tomato sauce, avocado oil, and garlic powder. Then brush the chicken breast with the tomato sauce mixture well. Preheat the air fryer to 385F. Place the chicken breast in the air fryer and cook it for 15 minutes. Then flip it on another side and cook for 3 minutes more. Slice the cooked chicken breast into servings.

Chicken Quarters With Broccoli And Rice
Servings: 3 | Cooking Time: 30 Minutes
- 1 package instant long grain rice
- 1 cup chopped broccoli
- 2 cups water
- 1 can condensed cream chicken soup
- 1 tbsp minced garlic

1. Preheat air fryer to 390 F, and place chicken in the air fryer. Season with salt, pepper and one tbsp oil; cook for 10 minutes. In a bowl, mix rice, water, garlic, soup and broccoli. Combine well. Remove the chicken from the air fryer and place it on a platter to drain. Spread the rice mixture on the bottom of the dish and place the chicken on top of the rice. Cook again for 10 minutes.

Grilled Chicken Wings With Curry-yogurt Sauce
Servings: 4 | Cooking Time: 35 Minutes
- ½ cup plain yogurt
- 1 tablespoons curry powder
- 2 pounds chicken wings
- Salt and pepper to taste

1. Season the chicken wings with yogurt, curry powder, salt and pepper. Toss to combine everything.
2. Allow to marinate in the fridge for at least 2 hours.
3. Preheat the air fryer to 3900F.
4. Place the grill pan accessory in the air fryer.
5. Grill the chicken for 35 minutes and make sure to flip the chicken halfway through the cooking time.

Tangy Chicken With Parsley And Lime
Servings: 2 | Cooking Time: 30 Minutes + Marinating Time
- 1 1/2 handful fresh parsley, roughly chopped
- Fresh juice of 1/2 lime
- 1 teaspoon ground black pepper
- 1 1/2 large-sized chicken breasts, cut into halves
- 1 teaspoon kosher salt
- Zest of 1/2 lime

1. Preheat your Air Fryer to 335 degrees F.
2. Toss the chicken breasts with the other ingredients and let it marinate a couple of hours.
3. Roast for 26 minutes and serve warm. Bon appétit!

Rosemary Partridge
Servings: 4 | Cooking Time: 14 Minutes
- 10 oz partridges
- 1 teaspoon dried rosemary
- 1 tablespoon butter, melted
- 1 teaspoon salt

1. Cut the partridges into the halves and sprinkle with dried rosemary and salt. Then brush them with melted butter. Preheat the air fryer to 385F. Put the partridge halves in the air fryer and cook them for 8 minutes. Then flip the poultry on another side and cook for 6 minutes more.

Italian Chicken Thighs

Servings: 4 | Cooking Time: 30 Minutes

- 4 skin-on bone-in chicken thighs
- 2 tbsp. unsalted butter, melted
- 3 tsp. Italian herbs
- ½ tsp. garlic powder
- ¼ tsp. onion powder

1. Using a brush, coat the chicken thighs with the melted butter. Combine the herbs with the garlic powder and onion powder, then massage into the chicken thighs. Place the thighs in the fryer.
2. Cook at 380°F for 20 minutes, turning the chicken halfway through to cook on the other side.
3. When the thighs have achieved a golden color, test the temperature with a meat thermometer. Once they have reached 165°F, remove from the fryer and serve.

One-tray Parmesan Wings

Servings: 4 | Cooking Time: 30 Minutes

- 1 tsp Dijon mustard
- Salt to taste
- 2 tbsp olive oil
- 2 cloves garlic, crushed
- 4 tbsp grated Parmesan cheese
- 2 tsp chopped fresh parsley

1. Preheat the Air fryer to 380 F. Grease the air fryer basket with cooking spray.
2. Season chicken with salt and pepper. Brush it with mustard. On a plate, pour 2 tbsp of the Parmesan cheese. Coat chicken with Parmesan cheese. Drizzle with olive oil and place in the air fryer basket. Cook for 20 minutes. Top with the remaining Parmesan cheese and parsley to serve.

Crumbed Sage Chicken Scallopini4

Servings: 4 | Cooking Time: 12 Minutes

- 3 oz breadcrumbs
- 2 tbsp grated Parmesan cheese
- 2 oz flour
- 2 eggs, beaten
- 1 tbsp fresh, chopped sage

1. Preheat the air fryer to 370 F. Place some plastic wrap underneath and on top of the chicken breasts. Using a rolling pin, beat the meat until it becomes really thin. In a bowl, combine the Parmesan cheese, sage and breadcrumbs.
2. Dip the chicken in the egg first, and then in the sage mixture. Spray with cooking oil and arrange the meat in the air fryer. Cook for 7 minutes.

Betty's Baked Chicken

Servings: 1 | Cooking Time: 70 Minutes

- ½ cup butter
- 1 tsp. pepper
- 3 tbsp. garlic, minced
- 1 whole chicken

1. Pre-heat your fryer at 350°F.
2. Allow the butter to soften at room temperature, then mix well in a small bowl with the pepper and garlic.
3. Massage the butter into the chicken. Any remaining butter can go inside the chicken.
4. Cook the chicken in the fryer for half an hour. Flip, then cook on the other side for another thirty minutes.
5. Test the temperature of the chicken by sticking a meat thermometer into the fat of the thigh to make sure it has reached 165°F. Take care when removing the chicken from the fryer. Let sit for ten minutes before you carve it and serve.

Herb Seasoned Turkey Breast

Servings: 4 | Cooking Time: 35 Minutes

- 2 lbs turkey breast
- 1 tsp fresh rosemary, chopped
- Pepper
- 1 tsp fresh sage, chopped
- 1 tsp fresh thyme, chopped
- Salt

1. Spray air fryer basket with cooking spray.
2. In a small bowl, mix together sage, rosemary, and thyme.
3. Season turkey breast with pepper and salt and rub with herb mixture.
4. Place turkey breast in air fryer basket and cook at 390 F for 30-35 minutes.
5. Slice and serve.

Caprese Chicken With Balsamic Sauce

Servings: 6 | Cooking Time: 25 Minutes

- 6 basil leaves
- ¼ cup balsamic vinegar
- 6 slices tomato
- 1 tbsp butter
- 6 slices mozzarella cheese

1. Preheat your Fryer to 400 F and heat butter and balsamic vinegar in a frying pan over medium heat. Cover the chicken meat with the marinade. Place the chicken in the cooking basket and cook for 20 minutes. Cover the chicken with basil, tomato slices and cheese. Serve and enjoy!

Marinated Chicken

Servings: 4 | Cooking Time: 30 Minutes

- 1 and ½ cups Keto tomato sauce
- A pinch of salt and black pepper
- ½ teaspoon chili powder
- 1 teaspoon onion powder
- 1 tablespoon coconut aminos
- 2 pounds chicken drumsticks

1. In bowl, mix the chicken drumsticks with all the other ingredients, toss and keep in the fridge for 10 minutes. Drain the drumsticks, put them in your air fryer's basket and cook at 380 degrees F for 15 minutes on each side. Divide everything between plates and serve.

Bacon-wrapped Turkey With Cheese

Servings: 12 | Cooking Time: 20 Minutes

- 1 ½ small-sized turkey breast, chop into 12 pieces
- 12 thin slices Asiago cheese
- Paprika, to taste
- Fine sea salt and ground black pepper, to savor
- 12 rashers bacon

1. Lay out the bacon rashers; place 1 slice of Asiago cheese on each bacon piece.
2. Top with turkey, season with paprika, salt, and pepper, and roll them up; secure with a cocktail stick.
3. Air-fry at 365 degrees F for 13 minutes. Bon appétit!

Grilled Chicken Recipe From Jamaica
Servings:2 | Cooking Time: 30 Minutes
- ¼ cup pineapple chunks
- 1 tablespoon vegetable oil
- 2 whole chicken thighs
- 3 teaspoons lime juice
- 4 tablespoons jerk seasoning

1. In a shallow dish, mix well all Ingredients. Marinate in the ref for 3 hours.
2. Thread chicken pieces and pineapples in skewers. Place on skewer rack in air fryer.
3. For 30 minutes, cook on 360oF. Halfway through cooking time, turnover skewers.
4. Serve and enjoy.

Fried Chicken Thighs
Servings: 4 | Cooking Time: 35 Minutes
- 4 chicken thighs
- 1 ½ tbsp. Cajun seasoning
- 1 egg, beaten
- ½ cup flour
- 1 tsp. seasoning salt

1. Pre-heat the Air Fryer to 350°F.
2. In a bowl combine the flour, Cajun seasoning, and seasoning salt.
3. Place the beaten egg in another bowl.
4. Coat the chicken with the flour before dredging it in the egg. Roll once more in the flour.
5. Put the chicken in the Air Fryer and cook for 25 minutes. Serve hot.

Five Spice Duck Legs
Servings: 4 | Cooking Time: 25 Minutes
- 4 duck legs
- 2 garlic cloves, minced
- 1 teaspoon five spice
- A pinch of salt and black pepper
- 2 tablespoons olive oil
- 1 teaspoon hot chili powder

1. In a bowl, mix the duck legs with all the other ingredients and rub them well. Put the duck legs in your air fryer's basket and cook at 380 degrees F for 25 minutes, flipping them halfway. Divide between plates and serve.

Grilled Chicken Pesto
Servings:8 | Cooking Time: 30 Minutes
- 1 ¾ cup commercial pesto
- 8 chicken thighs
- Salt and pepper to taste

1. Place all Ingredients in the Ziploc bag and allow to marinate in the fridge for at least 2 hours.
2. Preheat the air fryer to 3900F.
3. Place the grill pan accessory in the air fryer.
4. Grill the chicken for at least 30 minutes.
5. Make sure to flip the chicken every 10 minutes for even grilling.

Cajun Seasoned Chicken
Servings: 2 | Cooking Time: 15 Minutes
- 2 boneless chicken breasts
- 3 tbsp. Cajun spice

1. Coat both sides of the chicken breasts with Cajun spice. Put the seasoned chicken in Air Fryer basket.
2. Air fry at 350°F for 10 minutes, ensuring they are cooked through before slicing up and serving.

Turkey-hummus Wraps
Servings: 4 | Cooking Time: 7 Minutes Per Batch
- 4 large whole wheat wraps
- ½ cup hummus
- 16 thin slices deli turkey
- 8 slices provolone cheese
- 1 cup fresh baby spinach (or more to taste)

1. To assemble, place 2 tablespoons of hummus on each wrap and spread to within about a half inch from edges. Top with 4 slices of turkey and 2 slices of provolone. Finish with ¼ cup of baby spinach—or pile on as much as you like.
2. Roll up each wrap. You don't need to fold or seal the ends.
3. Place 2 wraps in air fryer basket, seam side down.
4. Cook at 360°F for 4minutes to warm filling and melt cheese. If you like, you can continue cooking for 3 more minutes, until the wrap is slightly crispy.
5. Repeat step 4 to cook remaining wraps.

Thyme Turkey Nuggets
Servings:2 | Cooking Time: 20 Minutes
- 1 egg, beaten
- 1 cup breadcrumbs
- 1 tbsp dried thyme
- ½ tbsp dried parsley
- Salt and pepper, to taste

1. Preheat air fryer to 350 F. In a bowl, mix ground chicken, thyme, parsley, salt and pepper. Shape the mixture into balls. Dip in the breadcrumbs, then egg, then in the breadcrumbs again. Place the nuggets in the air fryer basket, spray with cooking spray cook for 10 minutes, shaking once.

Sesame Chicken Wings
Servings:4 | Cooking Time: 25 Minutes
- 2 tbsp sesame oil
- 2 tbsp maple syrup
- Salt and black pepper
- 3 tbsp sesame seeds

1. In a bowl, add wings, oil, maple syrup, salt and pepper, and stir to coat well. In another bowl, add the sesame seeds and roll the wings in the seeds to coat thoroughly. Arrange the wings in an even layer inside your air fryer and cook for 12 minutes on 360 F, turning once halfway through.

Fish & Seafood Recipes

Mango Shrimp Skewers

Servings: 4 | Cooking Time: 20 Minutes

- 2 tbsp olive oil
- ½ tsp garlic powder
- 1 tsp dry mango powder
- 2 tbsp fresh lime juice
- Salt and black pepper to taste

1. In a bowl, mix well the garlic powder, mango powder, lime juice, salt, and pepper. Add the shrimp and toss to coat. Cover and allow to marinate for 15 minutes.
2. Preheat your Air Fryer to 390 F. Spray the air fryer basket with cooking spray. Transfer the marinated shrimp to the cooking basket and drizzle the olive oil. Cook for 5 minutes, Slide out the fryer basket and shake the shrimp; cook for 5 minutes. Leave to cool for 5 minutes and serve.

Herbed Garlic Lobster

Servings: 3 | Cooking Time: 15 Minutes

- 1 tsp garlic, minced
- 1 tbsp butter
- Salt and pepper to taste
- ½ tbsp lemon Juice

1. Add all the ingredients to a food processor, except shrimp, and blend well. Clean the skin of the lobster and cover with the marinade. Preheat your air fryer to 380 F. Place the lobster in your air fryer's cooking basket and cook for 10 minutes. Serve with fresh herbs and enjoy!

Better Fish Sticks

Servings: 3 | Cooking Time: 8 Minutes

- ¾ cup Seasoned Italian-style dried bread crumbs (gluten-free, if a concern)
- 3 tablespoons (about ½ ounce) Finely grated Parmesan cheese
- 10 ounces Skinless cod fillets, cut lengthwise into 1-inch-wide pieces
- 3 tablespoons Regular or low-fat mayonnaise (not fat-free; gluten-free, if a concern)
- Vegetable oil spray

1. Preheat the air fryer to 400°F.
2. Mix the bread crumbs and grated Parmesan in a shallow soup bowl or a small pie plate.
3. Smear the fish fillet sticks completely with the mayonnaise, then dip them one by one in the bread-crumb mixture, turning and pressing gently to make an even and thorough coating. Coat each stick on all sides with vegetable oil spray.
4. Set the fish sticks in the basket with at least ¼ inch between them. Air-fry undisturbed for 8 minutes, or until golden brown and crisp.
5. Use a nonstick-safe spatula to gently transfer them from the basket to a wire rack. Cool for only a minute or two before serving.

Potato-wrapped Salmon Fillets

Servings: 3 | Cooking Time: 8 Minutes

- 1 Large 1-pound elongated yellow potato(es), peeled
- 3 6-ounce, 1½-inch-wide, quite thick skinless salmon fillets
- Olive oil spray
- ¼ teaspoon Table salt
- ¼ teaspoon Ground black pepper

1. Preheat the air fryer to 400°F.
2. Use a vegetable peeler or mandoline to make long strips from the potato(es). You'll need anywhere from 8 to 12 strips per fillet, depending on the shape of the potato and of the salmon fillet.
3. Drape potato strips over a salmon fillet, overlapping the strips to create an even "crust." Tuck the potato strips under the fillet, overlapping the strips underneath to create as smooth a bottom as you can. Wrap the remaining fillet(s) in the same way.
4. Gently turn the fillets over. Generously coat the bottoms with olive oil spray. Turn them back seam side down and generously coat the tops with the oil spray. Sprinkle the salt and pepper over the wrapped fillets.
5. Use a nonstick-safe spatula to gently transfer the fillets seam side down to the basket. It helps to remove the basket from the machine and set it on your work surface (keeping in mind that the basket's hot). Leave as much air space as possible between the fillets. Air-fry undisturbed for 8 minutes, or until golden brown and crisp.
6. Use a nonstick-safe spatula to gently transfer the fillets to serving plates. Cool for a couple of minutes before serving.

Quick 'n Easy Tuna-mac Casserole

Servings: 4 | Cooking Time: 20 Minutes

- 1/2 (10.75 ounce) can condensed cream of chicken soup
- 1-1/2 cups cooked macaroni
- 1/2 (5 ounce) can tuna, drained
- 1/2 cup shredded Cheddar cheese
- 3/4 cup French fried onions

1. Lightly grease baking pan of air fryer with cooking spray.
2. Mix soup, tuna, and macaroni in pan. Sprinkle cheese on top.
3. For 15 minutes, cook on 360oF.
4. Remove basket and toss the mixture a bit. Sprinkle fried onions.
5. Cook for another 5 minutes.
6. Serve and enjoy.

Coconut Jerk Shrimp

Servings: 3 | Cooking Time: 8 Minutes

- 1 Large egg white(s)
- 1 teaspoon Purchased or homemade jerk dried seasoning blend (see the headnote)
- ¾ cup Plain panko bread crumbs (gluten-free, if a concern)
- ¾ cup Unsweetened shredded coconut
- 12 Large shrimp (20–25 per pound), peeled and deveined
- Coconut oil spray

1. Preheat the air fryer to 375°F.
2. Whisk the egg white(s) and seasoning blend in a bowl until foamy. Add the shrimp and toss well to coat evenly.
3. Mix the bread crumbs and coconut on a dinner plate until well combined. Use kitchen tongs to pick up a shrimp, letting the excess egg white mixture slip back into the rest. Set the shrimp in the bread-crumb mixture. Turn several times to coat evenly and thoroughly. Set on a cutting board and continue coating the remainder of the shrimp.
4. Lightly coat all the shrimp on both sides with the coconut oil spray. Set them in the basket in one layer with as much space between them as possible. (You can even stand some up along the basket's wall in some models.) Air-fry undisturbed for 6 minutes, or until the coating is lightly browned. If the air fryer is at 360°F, you may need to add 2 minutes to the cooking time.
5. Use clean kitchen tongs to transfer the shrimp to a wire rack. Cool for only a minute or two before serving.

Celery Leaves 'n Garlic-oil Grilled Turbot
Servings: 2 | Cooking Time: 20 Minutes
- ½ cup chopped celery leaves
- 1 clove of garlic, minced
- 2 tablespoons olive oil
- Salt and pepper to taste
- 2 whole turbot, scaled and head removed

1. Preheat the air fryer to 3900F.
2. Place the grill pan accessory in the air fryer.
3. Season the turbot with salt, pepper, garlic, and celery leaves.
4. Brush with oil.
5. Place on the grill pan and cook for 20 minutes until the fish becomes flaky.

Cod And Sauce
Servings: 2 | Cooking Time: 15 Minutes
- 2 cod fillets, boneless
- Salt and black pepper to the taste
- 1 bunch spring onions, chopped
- 3 tablespoons ghee, melted

1. In a pan that fits the air fryer, combine all the ingredients, toss gently, introduce in the air fryer and cook at 360 degrees F for 15 minutes. Divide the fish and sauce between plates and serve.

Char-grilled Drunken Halibut
Servings: 6 | Cooking Time: 20 Minutes
- 1 tablespoon chili powder
- 2 cloves of garlic, minced
- 3 pounds halibut fillet, skin removed
- 4 tablespoons dry white wine
- 4 tablespoons olive oil
- Salt and pepper to taste

1. Place all ingredients in a Ziploc bag.
2. Allow to marinate in the fridge for at least 2 hours.
3. Preheat the air fryer to 3900F.
4. Place the grill pan accessory in the air fryer.
5. Grill the fish for 20 minutes making sure to flip every 5 minutes.

Tilapia Teriyaki
Servings: 3 | Cooking Time: 10 Minutes
- 4 tablespoons teriyaki sauce
- 1 tablespoon pineapple juice
- 1 pound tilapia fillets
- cooking spray
- 6 ounces frozen mixed peppers with onions, thawed and drained
- 2 cups cooked rice

1. Mix the teriyaki sauce and pineapple juice together in a small bowl.
2. Split tilapia fillets down the center lengthwise.
3. Brush all sides of fish with the sauce, spray air fryer basket with nonstick cooking spray, and place fish in the basket.
4. Stir the peppers and onions into the remaining sauce and spoon over the fish. Save any leftover sauce for drizzling over the fish when serving.
5. Cook at 360°F for 10 minutes, until fish flakes easily with a fork and is done in center.
6. Divide into 3 or 4 servings and serve each with approximately ½ cup cooked rice.

Smoked Halibut And Eggs In Brioche
Servings: 4 | Cooking Time: 25 Minutes
- 4 brioche rolls
- 1 pound smoked halibut, chopped
- 4 eggs
- 1 teaspoon dried thyme
- 1 teaspoon dried basil
- Salt and black pepper, to taste

1. Cut off the top of each brioche; then, scoop out the insides to make the shells.
2. Lay the prepared brioche shells in the lightly greased cooking basket.
3. Spritz with cooking oil; add the halibut. Crack an egg into each brioche shell; sprinkle with thyme, basil, salt, and black pepper.
4. Bake in the preheated Air Fryer at 325 degrees F for 20 minutes. Bon appétit!

Grilled Scallops With Pesto
Servings: 3 | Cooking Time: 15 Minutes
- ½ cup prepared commercial pesto
- 12 large scallops, side muscles removed
- Salt and pepper to taste

1. Place all ingredients in a Ziploc bag and allow the scallops to marinate in the fridge for at least 2 hours.
2. Preheat the air fryer to 3900F.
3. Place the grill pan accessory in the air fryer.
4. Grill the scallops for 15 minutes.
5. Serve on pasta or bread if desired.

Miso Fish
Servings: 2 | Cooking Time: 10 Minutes
- 2 cod fish fillets
- 1 tbsp garlic, chopped
- 2 tsp swerve
- 2 tbsp miso

1. Add all ingredients to the zip-lock bag. Shake well place in the refrigerator for overnight.
2. Place marinated fish fillets into the air fryer basket and cook at 350 F for 10 minutes.
3. Serve and enjoy.

Crusty Pesto Salmon
Servings: 2 | Cooking Time: 15 Minutes
- ¼ cup s, roughly chopped
- ¼ cup pesto
- 2 x 4-oz. salmon fillets
- 2 tbsp. unsalted butter, melted

1. Mix the s and pesto together.
2. Place the salmon fillets in a round baking dish, roughly six inches in diameter.
3. Brush the fillets with butter, followed by the pesto mixture, ensuring to coat both the top and bottom. Put the baking dish inside the fryer.
4. Cook for twelve minutes at 390°F.
5. The salmon is ready when it flakes easily when prodded with a fork. Serve warm.

Lime 'n Chat Masala Rubbed Snapper

Servings:2 | Cooking Time: 25 Minutes
- 1/3 cup chat masala
- 2 tablespoons olive oil
- Salt to taste
- 1-1/2 pounds whole fish, cut in half
- 3 tablespoons fresh lime juice

1. Preheat the air fryer to 3900F.
2. Place the grill pan accessory in the air fryer.
3. Season the fish with salt, chat masala and lime juice.
4. Brush with oil
5. Place the fish on a foil basket and place inside the grill.
6. Cook for 25 minutes.

Egg Frittata With Smoked Trout

Servings:6 | Cooking Time: 15 Minutes
- 1 onion, chopped
- 2 tablespoons coconut oil
- 6 eggs, beaten
- 2 fillets smoked trout, shredded
- 2 tablespoons olive oil
- Salt and pepper to taste

1. Preheat the air fryer for 5 minutes.
2. Place all ingredients in a mixing bowl until well-combined.
3. Pour into a baking dish that will fit in the air fryer.
4. Cook for 15 minutes at 4000F.

Rosemary-infused Butter Scallops

Servings: 4 | Cooking Time: 1 Hour 10 Minutes
- 2 pounds sea scallops
- 4 tablespoons butter
- Sea salt and freshly cracked black pepper, to taste
- 1/2 cup beer
- 2 sprigs rosemary, only leaves

1. In a ceramic dish, mix the sea scallops with beer; let it marinate for 1 hour.
2. Meanwhile, preheat your Air Fryer to 400 degrees F. Melt the butter and add the rosemary leaves. Stir for a few minutes.
3. Discard the marinade and transfer the sea scallops to the Air Fryer basket. Season with salt and black pepper.
4. Cook the scallops in the preheated Air Fryer for 7 minutes, shaking the basket halfway through the cooking time. Work in batches.
5. Bon appétit!

Marinated Scallops With Butter And Beer

Servings: 4 | Cooking Time: 1 Hour 10 Minutes
- 2 pounds sea scallops
- 4 tablespoons butter
- Sea salt and freshly cracked black pepper, to taste
- 1/2 cup beer
- 2 sprigs rosemary, only leaves

1. In a ceramic dish, mix the sea scallops with beer; let it marinate for 1 hour.
2. Meanwhile, preheat your Air Fryer to 400 degrees F. Melt the butter and add the rosemary leaves. Stir for a few minutes.
3. Discard the marinade and transfer the sea scallops to the Air Fryer basket. Season with salt and black pepper.
4. Cook the scallops in the preheated Air Fryer for 7 minutes, shaking the basket halfway through the cooking time. Work in batches.
5. Bon appétit!

Quick And Easy Shrimp

Servings:2 | Cooking Time:5 Minutes
- ½ pound tiger shrimp
- 1 tablespoon olive oil
- ½ teaspoon old bay seasoning
- ¼ teaspoon smoked paprika
- ¼ teaspoon cayenne pepper
- Salt, to taste

1. Preheat the Air fryer to 390 o F and grease an Air fryer basket.
2. Mix all the ingredients in a large bowl until well combined.
3. Place the shrimps in the Air fryer basket and cook for about 5 minutes.
4. Dish out and serve warm.

Beer Battered Cod Filet

Servings:2 | Cooking Time: 15 Minutes
- ½ cup all-purpose flour
- 1 ¼ cup lager beer
- 2 eggs, beaten
- ¾ teaspoon baking powder
- 2 cod fillets
- Salt and pepper to taste

1. Preheat the air fryer to 3900F.
2. Pat the fish fillets dry then set aside.
3. In a bowl, combine the rest of the Ingredients to create a batter.
4. Dip the fillets on the batter and place on the double layer rack.
5. Cook for 15 minutes.

Zesty Mahi Mahi

Servings:3 | Cooking Time:8 Minutes
- 1½ pounds Mahi Mahi fillets
- 1 lemon, cut into slices
- 1 tablespoon fresh dill, chopped
- ½ teaspoon red chili powder
- Salt and ground black pepper, as required

1. Preheat the Air fryer to 375 o F and grease an Air fryer basket.
2. Season the Mahi Mahi fillets evenly with chili powder, salt, and black pepper.
3. Arrange the Mahi Mahi fillets into the Air fryer basket and top with the lemon slices.
4. Cook for about 8 minutes and dish out
5. Place the lemon slices over the salmon the salmon fillets in the serving plates.
6. Garnish with fresh dill and serve warm.

Fish Sticks For Kids

Servings: 8 | Cooking Time: 6 Minutes
- 8 ounces fish fillets (pollock or cod)
- salt (optional)
- ½ cup plain breadcrumbs
- oil for misting or cooking spray

1. Cut fish fillets into "fingers" about ½ x 3 inches. Sprinkle with salt to taste, if desired.
2. Roll fish in breadcrumbs. Spray all sides with oil or cooking spray.
3. Place in air fryer basket in single layer and cook at 390°F for 6 minutes, until golden brown and crispy.

Crab Rangoon

Servings:4 | Cooking Time: 5 Minutes
- ½ cup imitation crabmeat
- 4 ounces full-fat cream cheese, softened
- ¼ teaspoon Worcestershire sauce
- 8 wonton wrappers

1. Preheat the air fryer to 400°F.
2. In a medium bowl, mix crabmeat, cream cheese, and

Worcestershire until combined.

3. Place wonton wrappers on work surface. For each rangoon, scoop ½ tablespoon crab mixture onto center of a wonton wrapper. Press opposing edges toward the center and pinch to close. Spray with cooking spray to coat well. Repeat with remaining crab mixture and wontons.

4. Place in the air fryer basket and cook 5 minutes until brown at the edges. Serve warm.

Lemon Shrimp And Zucchinis

Servings: 4 | Cooking Time: 15 Minutes

- 1 pound shrimp, peeled and deveined
- A pinch of salt and black pepper
- 2 zucchinis, cut into medium cubes
- 1 tablespoon lemon juice
- 1 tablespoon olive oil
- 1 tablespoon garlic, minced

1. In a pan that fits the air fryer, combine all the ingredients, toss, put the pan in the machine and cook at 370 degrees F for 15 minutes. Divide between plates and serve right away.

Basil And Paprika Cod

Servings: 4 | Cooking Time: 15 Minutes

- 4 cod fillets, boneless
- 1 teaspoon red pepper flakes
- ½ teaspoon hot paprika
- 2 tablespoon olive oil
- 1 teaspoon basil, dried
- Salt and black pepper to the taste

1. In a bowl, mix the cod with all the other ingredients and toss. Put the fish in your air fryer's basket and cook at 380 degrees F for 15 minutes. Divide the cod between plates and serve.

Cajun Salmon With Lemon

Servings:1 | Cooking Time: 10 Minutes

- ¼ tsp brown sugar
- Juice of ½ lemon
- 1 tbsp cajun seasoning
- 2 lemon wedges
- 1 tbsp chopped parsley, for garnishing

1. Preheat the air fryer to 350 F, and combine sugar and lemon; coat the salmon with this mixture. Coat with the Cajun seasoning as well. Place a parchment paper into the air fryer and cook the fish for 7 minutes. Serve with lemon wedges and chopped parsley.

Buttered Scallops

Servings:2 | Cooking Time:4 Minutes

- ¾ pound sea scallops, cleaned and patted very dry
- 1 tablespoon butter, melted
- ½ tablespoon fresh thyme, minced
- Salt and black pepper, as required

1. Preheat the Air fryer to 390 o F and grease an Air fryer basket.
2. Mix scallops, butter, thyme, salt, and black pepper in a bowl.
3. Arrange scallops in the Air fryer basket and cook for about 4 minutes.
4. Dish out the scallops in a platter and serve hot.

Sweet & Sour Glazed Salmon

Servings:2 | Cooking Time: 12 Minutes

- 1/3 cup soy sauce
- 1/3 cup honey
- 3 teaspoons rice wine vinegar
- 1 teaspoon water
- 4 (3½-ounces) salmon fillets

1. In a small bowl, mix together the soy sauce, honey, vinegar, and water.
2. In another bowl, reserve about half of the mixture.
3. Add salmon fillets in the remaining mixture and coat well.
4. Cover the bowl and refrigerate to marinate for about 2 hours.
5. Set the temperature of air fryer to 355 degrees F. Grease an air fryer basket.
6. Arrange salmon fillets into the prepared air fryer basket in a single layer.
7. Air fry for about 12 minutes, flipping once halfway through and coating with the reserved marinade after every 3 minutes.
8. Remove from air fryer and place the salmon fillets onto serving plates.
9. Serve hot.

Curried Sweet-and-spicy Scallops

Servings:3 | Cooking Time: 5 Minutes

- 6 tablespoons Thai sweet chili sauce
- 2 cups (from about 5 cups cereal) Crushed Rice Krispies or other rice-puff cereal
- 2 teaspoons Yellow curry powder, purchased or homemade (see here)
- 1 pound Sea scallops
- Vegetable oil spray

1. Preheat the air fryer to 400°F.
2. Set up and fill two shallow soup plates or small pie plates on your counter: one for the chili sauce and one for crumbs, mixed with the curry powder.
3. Dip a scallop into the chili sauce, coating it on all sides. Set it in the cereal mixture and turn several times to coat evenly. Gently shake off any excess and set the scallop on a cutting board. Continue dipping and coating the remaining scallops. Coat them all on all sides with the vegetable oil spray.
4. Set the scallops in the basket with as much air space between them as possible. Air-fry undisturbed for 5 minutes, or until lightly browned and crunchy.
5. Remove the basket. Set aside for 2 minutes to let the coating set up. Then gently pour the contents of the basket onto a platter and serve at once.

Spicy Mackerel

Servings: 2 | Cooking Time: 20 Minutes

- 2 mackerel fillets
- 2 tbsp. red chili flakes
- 2 tsp. garlic, minced
- 1 tsp. lemon juice

1. Season the mackerel fillets with the red pepper flakes, minced garlic, and a drizzle of lemon juice. Allow to sit for five minutes.
2. Preheat your fryer at 350°F.
3. Cook the mackerel for five minutes, before opening the drawer, flipping the fillets, and allowing to cook on the other side for another five minutes.
4. Plate the fillets, making sure to spoon any remaining juice over them before serving.

Basil Scallops
Servings: 4 | Cooking Time: 6 Minutes
- 12 oz scallops
- 1 tablespoon dried basil
- ½ teaspoon salt
- 1 tablespoon coconut oil, melted

1. Mix up salt, coconut oil, and dried basil. Brush the scallops with basil mixture and leave for 5 minutes to marinate. Meanwhile, preheat the air fryer to 400F. Put the marinated scallops in the air fryer and sprinkle them with remaining coconut oil and basil mixture. Cook the scallops for 4 minutes. Then flip them on another side and cook for 2 minutes more.

Salmon Patties
Servings: 4 | Cooking Time: 12 Minutes
- 1 pouch cooked salmon
- 6 tablespoons panko bread crumbs
- ½ cup mayonnaise
- 2 teaspoons Old Bay Seasoning

1. Preheat the air fryer to 350°F.
2. In a large bowl, combine all ingredients.
3. Divide mixture into four equal portions. Using your hands, form into patties and spritz with cooking spray.
4. Place in the air fryer basket and cook 12 minutes, turning halfway through cooking time, until brown and firm. Serve warm.

Air Fried Cod With Basil Vinaigrette
Servings: 4 | Cooking Time: 15 Minutes
- ¼ cup olive oil
- 4 cod fillets
- A bunch of basil, torn
- Juice from 1 lemon, freshly squeezed
- Salt and pepper to taste

1. Preheat the air fryer for 5 minutes.
2. Season the cod fillets with salt and pepper to taste.
3. Place in the air fryer and cook for 15 minutes at 3500F.
4. Meanwhile, mix the rest of the ingredients in a bowl and toss to combine.
5. Serve the air fried cod with the basil vinaigrette.

Simple Salmon Patties
Servings: 2 | Cooking Time: 10 Minutes
- 14 oz salmon
- 1/2 onion, diced
- 1 egg, lightly beaten
- 1 tsp dill
- 1/2 cup almond flour

1. Spray air fryer basket with cooking spray.
2. Add all ingredients into the bowl and mix until well combined.
3. Spray air fryer basket with cooking spray.
4. Make patties from salmon mixture and place into the air fryer basket.
5. Cook at 370 F for 5 minutes.
6. Turn patties to another side and cook for 5 minutes more.
7. Serve and enjoy.

Almond Flour Coated Crispy Shrimps
Servings: 4 | Cooking Time: 10 Minutes
- ½ cup almond flour
- 1 tablespoon yellow mustard
- 1-pound raw shrimps, peeled and deveined
- 3 tablespoons olive oil
- Salt and pepper to taste

1. Place all ingredients in a Ziploc bag and give a good shake.
2. Place in the air fryer and cook for 10 minutes at 4000F.

Fish Fillets
Servings: 4 | Cooking Time: 25 Minutes
- 4 fish fillets
- 1 egg, beaten
- 1 cup bread crumbs
- 4 tbsp. olive oil
- Pepper and salt to taste

1. Pre-heat the Air Fryer at 350°F.
2. In a shallow dish, combine together the bread crumbs, oil, pepper, and salt.
3. Pour the beaten egg into a second dish.
4. Dredge each fish fillet in the egg before rolling them in the bread crumbs. Place in the Air Fryer basket.
5. Allow to cook in the Air Fryer for 12 minutes.

Fish Taco Bowl
Servings: 4 | Cooking Time: 12 Minutes
- 2 cups finely shredded cabbage
- ½ cup mayonnaise
- Juice of 1 medium lime, divided
- 4 boneless, skinless tilapia fillets
- 2 teaspoons chili powder
- 1 teaspoon salt
- ½ teaspoon ground black pepper

1. In a large bowl, mix cabbage, mayonnaise, and half of lime juice to make a slaw. Cover and refrigerate while the fish cooks.
2. Preheat the air fryer to 400°F.
3. Sprinkle tilapia with chili powder, salt, and pepper. Spritz each side with cooking spray.
4. Place fillets in the air fryer basket and cook 12 minutes, turning halfway through cooking time, until fish is opaque, flakes easily, and reaches an internal temperature of 145°F.
5. Allow fish to cool 5 minutes before chopping into bite-sized pieces. To serve, place ½ cup slaw into each bowl and top with one-fourth of fish. Squeeze remaining lime juice over fish. Serve warm.

Fish Fillet Sandwich
Servings: 4 | Cooking Time: 18 Minutes
- 4 cod fillets
- ½ teaspoon salt
- ¼ teaspoon ground black pepper
- 2 cups unsweetened cornflakes, crushed
- 1 cup Italian bread crumbs
- 2 large eggs
- 4 sandwich buns

1. Preheat the air fryer to 375°F.
2. Sprinkle cod with salt and pepper on both sides.
3. In a large bowl, combine cornflakes and bread crumbs.
4. In a medium bowl, whisk eggs. Press each piece of cod into eggs to coat, shaking off excess, then into cornflake mixture to coat evenly on both sides. Spritz with cooking spray.
5. Place in the air fryer basket and cook 18 minutes, turning halfway through cooking time, until fillets are brown and internal temperature reaches at least 145°F. Place on buns to serve.

Lemon Garlic Shrimp
Servings: 2 | Cooking Time: 15 Minutes
- 1 medium lemon
- ½ lb. medium shrimp, shelled and deveined
- ½ tsp. Old Bay seasoning
- 2 tbsp. unsalted butter, melted
- ½ tsp. minced garlic

1. Grate the rind of the lemon into a bowl. Cut the lemon in half and juice it over the same bowl. Toss in the shrimp, Old Bay, and butter, mixing everything to make sure the shrimp is completely covered.
2. Transfer to a round baking dish roughly six inches wide, then place this dish in your fryer.
3. Cook at 400°F for six minutes. The shrimp is cooked when it turns a bright pink color.
4. Serve hot, drizzling any leftover sauce over the shrimp.

Nutritious Salmon
Servings: 2 | Cooking Time: 10 Minutes
- 2 salmon fillets
- 1 tbsp olive oil
- 1/4 tsp ground cardamom
- 1/2 tsp paprika
- Salt

1. Preheat the air fryer to 350 F.
2. Coat salmon fillets with olive oil and season with paprika, cardamom, and salt and place into the air fryer basket.
3. Cook salmon for 10-12 minutes. Turn halfway through.
4. Serve and enjoy.

Sesame Seeds Coated Tuna
Servings:2 | Cooking Time:6 Minutes
- ¼ cup white sesame seeds
- 1 tablespoon black sesame seeds
- 1 egg white
- 2 (6-ounces) tuna steaks
- Salt and black pepper, as required

1. Preheat the Air fryer to 400 o F and grease an Air fryer basket.
2. Whisk the egg white in a shallow bowl.
3. Mix the sesame seeds, salt, and black pepper in another bowl.
4. Dip the tuna steaks into the whisked egg white and dredge into the sesame seeds mixture.
5. Arrange the tuna steaks into the Air fryer basket in a single layer and cook for about 6 minutes, flipping once in between.
6. Dish out the tuna steaks onto serving plates and serve hot.

Outrageous Crispy Fried Salmon Skin
Servings:4 | Cooking Time: 10 Minutes
- ½ pound salmon skin, patted dry
- 4 tablespoons coconut oil
- Salt and pepper to taste

1. Preheat the air fryer for 5 minutes.
2. In a large bowl, combine everything and mix well.
3. Place in the fryer basket and close.
4. Cook for 10 minutes at 4000F.
5. Halfway through the cooking time, give a good shake to evenly cook the skin.

Lime, Oil 'n Leeks On Grilled Swordfish
Servings:4 | Cooking Time: 20 Minutes
- 2 tablespoons olive oil
- 3 tablespoons lime juice
- 4 medium leeks, cut into an inch long
- 4 swordfish steaks
- Salt and pepper to taste

1. Preheat the air fryer to 3900F.
2. Place the grill pan accessory in the air fryer.
3. Season the swordfish with salt, pepper and lime juice.
4. Brush the fish with olive oil
5. Place fish fillets on grill pan and top with leeks.
6. Grill for 20 minutes.

Coconut Calamari
Servings: 2 | Cooking Time: 6 Minutes
- 6 oz calamari, trimmed
- 2 tablespoons coconut flakes
- 1 egg, beaten
- 1 teaspoon Italian seasonings
- Cooking spray

1. Slice the calamari into the rings and sprinkle them with Italian seasonings. Then transfer the calamari rings in the bowl with a beaten egg and stir them gently. After this, sprinkle the calamari rings with coconut flakes and shake well. Preheat the air fryer to 400F. Put the calamari rings in the air fryer basket and spray them with cooking spray. Cook the meal for 3 minutes. Then gently stir the calamari and cook them for 3 minutes more.

Juicy Salmon And Asparagus Parcels
Servings:2 | Cooking Time:13 Minutes
- 2 salmon fillets
- 4 asparagus stalks
- ¼ cup champagne
- Salt and black pepper, to taste
- ¼ cup white sauce
- 1 teaspoon olive oil

1. Preheat the Air fryer to 355 o F and grease an Air fryer basket.
2. Mix all the ingredients in a bowl and divide this mixture evenly over 2 foil papers.
3. Arrange the foil papers in the Air fryer basket and cook for about 13 minutes.
4. Dish out in a platter and serve hot.

Salmon And Blackberry Sauce
Servings: 2 | Cooking Time: 12 Minutes
- 2 salmon fillets, boneless
- 1 tablespoon honey
- ½ cup blackberries
- 1 tablespoon olive oil
- Juice of ½ lemon
- Salt and black pepper to taste

1. In a blender, mix the blackberries with the honey, oil, lemon juice, salt, and pepper; pulse well.
2. Spread the blackberry mixture over the salmon, and then place the fish in your air fryer's basket.
3. Cook at 380 degrees F for 12 minutes, flipping the fish halfway.
4. Serve hot, and enjoy!

Restaurant-style Flounder Cutlets

Servings: 2 | Cooking Time: 15 Minutes

- 1 egg
- 1 cup Pecorino Romano cheese, grated
- Sea salt and white pepper, to taste
- 1/2 teaspoon cayenne pepper
- 1 teaspoon dried parsley flakes
- 2 flounder fillets

1. To make a breading station, whisk the egg until frothy.
2. In another bowl, mix Pecorino Romano cheese, and spices.
3. Dip the fish in the egg mixture and turn to coat evenly; then, dredge in the cracker crumb mixture, turning a couple of times to coat evenly.
4. Cook in the preheated Air Fryer at 390 degrees F for 5 minutes; turn them over and cook another 5 minutes. Enjoy!

Butter Lobster

Servings: 4 | Cooking Time: 6 Minutes

- 4 lobster tails, peeled
- ½ teaspoon salt
- 1 tablespoon avocado oil
- 4 teaspoons almond butter
- ½ teaspoon dried thyme

1. Make the cut on the back of every lobster tail and sprinkle them with dried thyme and salt. After this, sprinkle the lobster tails with avocado oil. Preheat the air fryer to 380F. Place the lobster tails in the air fryer basket and cook them for 5 minutes. After this, gently spread the lobster tails with almond butter and cook for 1 minute more.

Ahi Tuna Steaks

Servings: 2 | Cooking Time: 14 Minutes

- 2 ahi tuna steaks
- 2 tablespoons olive oil
- 3 tablespoons everything bagel seasoning

1. Preheat the air fryer to 400°F.
2. Drizzle both sides of steaks with oil. Place seasoning on a medium plate and press each side of tuna steaks into seasoning to form a thick layer.
3. Place steaks in the air fryer basket and cook 14 minutes, turning halfway through cooking time, until internal temperature reaches at least 145°F for well-done. Serve warm.

Teriyaki Salmon

Servings: 4 | Cooking Time: 27 Minutes

- ½ cup teriyaki sauce
- ¼ teaspoon salt
- 1 teaspoon ground ginger
- ½ teaspoon garlic powder
- 4 boneless, skinless salmon fillets
- 2 tablespoons toasted sesame seeds

1. In a large bowl, whisk teriyaki sauce, salt, ginger, and garlic powder. Add salmon to the bowl, being sure to coat each side with marinade. Cover and let marinate in refrigerator 15 minutes.
2. Preheat the air fryer to 375°F.
3. Spritz fillets with cooking spray and place in the air fryer basket. Cook 12 minutes, turning halfway through cooking time, until glaze has caramelized to a dark brown color, salmon flakes easily, and internal temperature reaches at least 145°F. Sprinkle sesame seeds on salmon and serve warm.

Rice Flour Coated Shrimp

Servings: 3 | Cooking Time: 20 Minutes

- 3 tablespoons rice flour
- 1 pound shrimp, peeled and deveined
- 2 tablespoons olive oil
- 1 teaspoon powdered sugar
- Salt and black pepper, as required

1. Preheat the Air fryer to 325 o F and grease an Air fryer basket.
2. Mix rice flour, olive oil, sugar, salt, and black pepper in a bowl.
3. Stir in the shrimp and transfer half of the shrimp to the Air fryer basket.
4. Cook for about 10 minutes, flipping once in between.
5. Dish out the mixture onto serving plates and repeat with the remaining mixture.

Super-simple Scallops

Servings: 2 | Cooking Time: 4 Minutes

- ¾ pound sea scallops
- 1 tablespoon butter, melted
- ½ tablespoon fresh thyme, minced
- Salt and black pepper, to taste

1. Preheat the Air fryer to 390 o F and grease an Air fryer basket.
2. Mix all the ingredients in a bowl and toss to coat well.
3. Arrange the scallops in the Air fryer basket and cook for about 4 minutes.
4. Dish out and serve warm.

Salmon Topped With Creamy Avocado-cashew Sauce

Servings: 2 | Cooking Time: 15 Minutes

- ½ clove of garlic
- ½ pound salmon fillet
- 1 avocado, pitted and chopped
- 1 teaspoon olive oil
- 2 tablespoons cashew nuts, soaked in water for 10 minutes
- Salt and pepper to taste

1. Preheat the air fryer for 5 minutes
2. Season the salmon fillets with salt, pepper, and olive oil.
3. Place in the air fryer and cook for 15 minutes at 4000F.
4. Meanwhile, place the rest of the ingredients in a food processor. Season with salt and pulse until smooth.
5. Serve the salmon fillet with the creamy avocado sauce.

Sesame Tuna Steak

Servings: 2 | Cooking Time: 12 Minutes

- 1 tbsp. coconut oil, melted
- 2 x 6-oz. tuna steaks
- ½ tsp. garlic powder
- 2 tsp. black sesame seeds
- 2 tsp. white sesame seeds

1. Apply the coconut oil to the tuna steaks with a brunch, then season with garlic powder.
2. Combine the black and white sesame seeds. Embed them in the tuna steaks, covering the fish all over. Place the tuna into your air fryer.
3. Cook for eight minutes at 400°F, turning the fish halfway through.
4. The tuna steaks are ready when they have reached a temperature of 145°F. Serve straightaway.

Cilantro Cod Mix

Servings: 4 | Cooking Time: 15 Minutes

- 1 cup cherry tomatoes, halved
- Salt and black pepper to the taste
- 2 tablespoons olive oil
- 4 cod fillets, skinless and boneless
- 2 tablespoons cilantro, chopped

1. In a baking dish that fits your air fryer, mix all the ingredients, toss gently, introduce in your air fryer and cook at 370 degrees F for 15 minutes. Divide everything between plates and serve right away.

Crispy Calamari

Servings: 4 | Cooking Time: 15 Minutes

- 1 lb. fresh squid
- Salt and pepper
- 2 cups flour
- 1 cup water
- 2 cloves garlic, minced
- ½ cup mayonnaise

1. Remove the skin from the squid and discard any ink. Slice the squid into rings and season with some salt and pepper.
2. Put the flour and water in separate bowls. Dip the squid firstly in the flour, then into the water, then into the flour again, ensuring that it is entirely covered with flour.
3. Pre-heat the fryer at 400°F. Put the squid inside and cook for six minutes.
4. In the meantime, prepare the aioli by combining the garlic with the mayonnaise in a bowl.
5. Once the squid is ready, plate up and serve with the aioli.

Fish-in-chips

Servings: 4 | Cooking Time: 11 Minutes

- 1 cup All-purpose flour or potato starch
- 2 Large egg(s), well beaten
- 1½ cups (6 ounces) Crushed plain potato chips, preferably thick-cut or ruffled (gluten-free, if a concern)
- 4 4-ounce skinless cod fillets

1. Preheat the air fryer to 400°F.
2. Set up and fill three shallow soup plates or small pie plates on your counter: one for the flour, one for the beaten egg(s), and one for the crushed potato chips.
3. Dip a piece of cod in the flour, turning it to coat on all sides, even the ends and sides. Gently shake off any excess flour, then dip it in the beaten egg(s). Gently turn to coat it on all sides, then let any excess egg slip back into the rest. Set the fillet in the crushed potato chips and turn several times and onto all sides, pressing gently to coat the fish. Dip it back in the egg(s), coating all sides but taking care that the coating doesn't slip off; then dip it back in the potato chips for a thick, even coating. Set it aside and coat more fillets in the same way.
4. When the machine is at temperature, set the fillets in the basket with as much air space between them as possible. Air-fry undisturbed for 11 minutes, until golden brown and firm but not hard.
5. Use kitchen tongs to transfer the fillets to a wire rack. Cool for just a minute or two before serving.

Beer-battered Cod

Servings: 3 | Cooking Time: 12 Minutes

- 1½ cups All-purpose flour
- 1 Large egg(s)
- 3 4-ounce skinless cod fillets
- 3 tablespoons Old Bay seasoning
- ¼ cup Amber beer, pale ale, or IPA
- Vegetable oil spray

1. Preheat the air fryer to 400°F.
2. Set up and fill two shallow soup plates or small pie plates on your counter: one with the flour, whisked with the Old Bay until well combined; and one with the egg(s), whisked with the beer until foamy and uniform.
3. Dip a piece of cod in the flour mixture, turning it to coat on all sides (not just the top and bottom). Gently shake off any excess flour and dip the fish in the egg mixture, turning it to coat. Let any excess egg mixture slip back into the rest, then set the fish back in the flour mixture and coat it again, then back in the egg mixture for a second wash, then back in the flour mixture for a third time. Coat the fish on all sides with vegetable oil spray and set it aside. "Batter" the remaining piece(s) of cod in the same way.
4. Set the coated cod fillets in the basket with as much space between them as possible. They should not touch. Air-fry undisturbed for 12 minutes, or until brown and crisp.
5. Use kitchen tongs to gently transfer the fish to a wire rack. Cool for only a couple of minutes before serving.

Parmesan Walnut Salmon

Servings: 4 | Cooking Time: 12 Minutes

- 4 salmon fillets
- 1/4 cup parmesan cheese, grated
- 1/2 cup walnuts
- 1 tsp olive oil
- 1 tbsp lemon rind

1. Preheat the air fryer to 370 F.
2. Spray an air fryer baking dish with cooking spray.
3. Place salmon on a baking dish.
4. Add walnuts into the food processor and process until finely ground.
5. Mix ground walnuts with parmesan cheese, oil, and lemon rind. Stir well.
6. Spoon walnut mixture over the salmon and press gently.
7. Place in the air fryer and cook for 12 minutes.
8. Serve and enjoy.

Bacon-wrapped Cajun Scallops

Servings: 4 | Cooking Time: 13 Minutes

- 8 slices bacon
- 8 sea scallops, rinsed and patted dry
- 1 teaspoon Cajun seasoning
- 4 tablespoons salted butter, melted

1. Preheat the air fryer to 375°F.
2. Place bacon in the air fryer basket and cook 3 minutes. Remove bacon and wrap each scallop in one slice bacon before securing with a toothpick.
3. Sprinkle Cajun seasoning evenly over scallops. Spritz scallops lightly with cooking spray and place in the air fryer basket in a single layer. Cook 10 minutes, turning halfway through cooking time, until scallops are opaque and firm and internal temperature reaches at least 130°F. Drizzle with butter. Serve warm.

Buttery Cod

Servings: 2 | Cooking Time: 12 Minutes

- 2 x 4-oz. cod fillets
- 2 tbsp. salted butter, melted
- 1 tsp. Old Bay seasoning
- ½ medium lemon, sliced

1. Place the cod fillets in a baking dish.
2. Brush with melted butter, season with Old Bay, and top with some lemon slices.
3. Wrap the fish in aluminum foil and put into your fryer.
4. Cook for eight minutes at 350°F.
5. The cod is ready when it flakes easily. Serve hot.

Fish Sticks

Servings: 4 | Cooking Time: 20 Minutes

- 1 lb. tilapia fillets, cut into strips
- 1 large egg, beaten
- 2 tsp. Old Bay seasoning
- 1 tbsp. olive oil
- 1 cup friendly bread crumbs

1. Pre-heat the Air Fryer at 400°F.
2. In a shallow dish, combine together the bread crumbs, Old Bay, and oil. Put the egg in a small bowl.
3. Dredge the fish sticks in the egg. Cover them with bread crumbs and put them in the fryer's basket.
4. Cook the fish for 10 minutes or until they turn golden brown.
5. Serve hot.

Breaded Hake

Servings: 2 | Cooking Time: 12 Minutes

- 1 egg
- 4 ounces breadcrumbs
- 4 (6-ounces) hake fillets
- 1 lemon, cut into wedges
- 2 tablespoons vegetable oil

1. Preheat the Air fryer to 350 o F and grease an Air fryer basket.
2. Whisk the egg in a shallow bowl and mix breadcrumbs and oil in another bowl.
3. Dip hake fillets into the whisked egg and then, dredge in the breadcrumb mixture.
4. Arrange the hake fillets into the Air fryer basket in a single layer and cook for about 12 minutes.
5. Dish out the hake fillets onto serving plates and serve, garnished with lemon wedges.

Crispy Fish Fingers

Servings: 8 | Cooking Time: 20 Minutes

- 1 egg, beaten
- ½ cup buttermilk
- 1 cup panko breadcrumbs
- Salt and black pepper
- Cooking spray

1. In a bowl, mix egg and buttermilk. On a plate, mix and spread crumbs, salt, and pepper. Dip each finger into the egg mixture, then roll it up in the crumbs, and spray with cooking spray. Arrange on the air fryer basket and cook for 10 minutes at 380 F, turning once halfway through. Serve with aioli.

Honey-glazed Salmon

Servings: 4 | Cooking Time: 30 Minutes

- 2 tablespoons soy sauce
- 1 teaspoon sriracha
- ½ teaspoon minced garlic
- 4 skin-on salmon fillets
- 2 teaspoons honey

1. In a large bowl, whisk together soy sauce, sriracha, and garlic. Place salmon in bowl. Cover and let marinate in refrigerator at least 20 minutes.
2. Preheat the air fryer to 375°F.
3. Place salmon in the air fryer basket and cook 8 minutes. Open air fryer and brush honey on salmon. Continue cooking 2 more minutes until salmon flakes easily and internal temperature reaches at least 145°F. Serve warm.

Chili Squid Rings

Servings: 2 | Cooking Time: 10 Minutes

- 8 oz squid tube, trimmed, washed
- 4 oz chorizo, chopped
- 1 teaspoon olive oil
- 1 teaspoon chili flakes
- 1 tablespoon keto mayonnaise

1. Preheat the air fryer to 400F and put the chopped chorizo in the air fryer basket. Sprinkle it with chili flakes and olive oil and cook for 6 minutes. Then shake chorizo well. Slice the squid tube into the rings and add in the air fryer. Cook the meal for 4 minutes at 400F. Shake the cooked meal well and transfer it in the plates. Sprinkle the meal with keto mayonnaise.

Chili-lime Shrimp

Servings: 4 | Cooking Time: 10 Minutes

- 1 pound medium shrimp, peeled and deveined
- ½ cup lime juice
- 2 tablespoons olive oil
- 2 tablespoons sriracha
- 1 teaspoon salt
- ¼ teaspoon ground black pepper

1. Preheat the air fryer to 375°F.
2. In an 6" round cake pan, combine all ingredients.
3. Place pan in the air fryer and cook 10 minutes, stirring halfway through cooking time, until the inside of shrimp are pearly white and opaque and internal temperature reaches at least 145°F. Serve warm.

Easy Grilled Pesto Scallops

Servings: 3 | Cooking Time: 15 Minutes

- 12 large scallops, side muscles removed
- Salt and pepper to taste
- ½ cup prepared commercial pesto

1. Place all ingredients in a Ziploc bag and allow the scallops to marinate in the fridge for at least 2 hours.
2. Preheat the air fryer at 3900F.
3. Place the grill pan accessory in the air fryer.
4. Grill the scallops for 15 minutes.
5. Serve on pasta or bread if desired.

Japanese Citrus Soy Squid
Servings: 4 | Cooking Time: 10 Minutes

- ½ cup mirin
- 1 cup soy sauce
- 1/3 cup yuzu or orange juice, freshly squeezed
- 2 cups water
- 2 pounds squid body, cut into rings

1. Place all ingredients in a Ziploc bag and allow the squid rings to marinate in the fridge for at least 2 hours.
2. Preheat the air fryer at 3900F.
3. Place the grill pan accessory in the air fryer.
4. Grill the squid rings for 10 minutes.
5. Meanwhile, pour the marinade over a sauce pan and allow to simmer for 10 minutes or until the sauce has reduced.
6. Baste the squid rings with the sauce before serving.

Breaded Scallops
Servings: 6 | Cooking Time: 5 Minutes

- 3 tbsp flour
- 4 salt and black pepper
- 1 egg, lightly beaten
- 1 cup breadcrumbs
- Cooking spray

1. Coat the scallops with flour. Dip into the egg, then into the breadcrumbs. Spray them with olive oil and arrange them in the air fryer. Cook for 6 minutes at 360 F, turning once halfway through cooking.

Quick & Easy Air Fried Salmon
Servings: 1 | Cooking Time: 13 Minutes

- 1 tbsp soy sauce
- ¼ tsp garlic powder
- Salt and pepper

1. Preheat air fryer to 350 F, and combine soy sauce, garlic powder, salt and pepper. Brush the mixture over salmon. Place salmon onto the air fryer; cook for 10 minutes, until crispy.

Butter Flounder Fillets
Servings: 4 | Cooking Time: 20 Minutes

- 4 flounder fillets, boneless
- A pinch of salt and black pepper
- 1 cup parmesan, grated
- 4 tablespoons butter, melted
- 2 tablespoons olive oil

1. In a bowl, mix the parmesan with salt, pepper, butter and the oil and stir well. Arrange the fish in a pan that fits the air fryer, spread the parmesan mix all over, introduce in the fryer and cook at 400 degrees F for 20 minutes. Divide between plates and serve with a side salad.

Air Fried Dilly Trout
Servings: 3 | Cooking Time: 30 Minutes

- 3 tbsp olive oil
- Salt to taste
- ½ cup greek yogurt
- ½ cup sour cream
- 2 tbsp finely chopped dill

1. Preheat the air fryer to 300 F. Drizzle the trout with oil and season with a pinch of salt. Place the seasoned trout into the air fryer's cooking basket. Cook for 20 minutes and top with the dill sauce before serving. For the dill sauce, in a large bowl, mix yogurt, sour cream, chopped dill and salt.

Lemon-roasted Salmon Fillets
Servings: 3 | Cooking Time: 7 Minutes

- 3 6-ounce skin-on salmon fillets
- Olive oil spray
- 9 Very thin lemon slices
- ¾ teaspoon Ground black pepper
- ¼ teaspoon Table salt

1. Preheat the air fryer to 400°F.
2. Generously coat the skin of each of the fillets with olive oil spray. Set the fillets skin side down on your work surface. Place three overlapping lemon slices down the length of each salmon fillet. Sprinkle them with the pepper and salt. Coat lightly with olive oil spray.
3. Use a nonstick-safe spatula to transfer the fillets one by one to the basket, leaving as much air space between them as possible. Air-fry undisturbed for 7 minutes, or until cooked through.
4. Use a nonstick-safe spatula to transfer the fillets to serving plates. Cool for only a minute or two before serving.

Shrimp And Parsley Olives
Servings: 4 | Cooking Time: 12 Minutes

- 1 pound shrimp, peeled and deveined
- 4 garlic clove, minced
- 1 cup black olives, pitted and chopped
- 3 tablespoons parsley
- 1 tablespoon olive oil

1. In a pan that fits the air fryer, combine all the ingredients, toss, put the pan in the machine and cook at 380 degrees F for 12 minutes. Divide between plates and serve.

Cajun Seasoned Salmon Filet
Servings: 1 | Cooking Time: 15 Minutes

- 1 salmon fillet
- 1 teaspoon juice from lemon, freshly squeezed
- 3 tablespoons extra virgin olive oil
- A dash of Cajun seasoning mix
- Salt and pepper to taste

1. Preheat the air fryer for 5 minutes.
2. Place all ingredients in a bowl and toss to coat.
3. Place the fish fillet in the air fryer basket.
4. Bake for 15 minutes at 3250F.
5. Once cooked drizzle with olive oil

Fried Catfish Fillets
Servings: 2 | Cooking Time: 40 Minutes

- 3 tbsp breadcrumbs
- 1 tsp cayenne pepper
- 1 tsp dry fish seasoning, of choice
- 2 sprigs parsley, chopped
- Salt to taste, optional
- Cooking spray

1. Preheat air fryer to 400 F. Pour all the dry ingredients, except the parsley, in a zipper bag. Pat dry and add the fish pieces. Close the bag and shake to coat the fish well. Do this with one fish piece at a time.
2. Lightly spray the fish with olive oil. Arrange them in the fryer basket, one at a time depending on the size of the fish. Close the air fryer and cook for 10 minutes. Flip the fish and cook further for 10 minutes. For extra crispiness, cook for 3 more minutes. Garnish with parsley and serve.

Cajun Flounder Fillets
Servings: 2 | Cooking Time: 5 Minutes
- 2 4-ounce skinless flounder fillet(s)
- 2 teaspoons Peanut oil
- 1 teaspoon Purchased or homemade Cajun dried seasoning blend (see the headnote)

1. Preheat the air fryer to 400°F.
2. Oil the fillet(s) by drizzling on the peanut oil, then gently rubbing in the oil with your clean, dry fingers. Sprinkle the seasoning blend evenly over both sides of the fillet(s).
3. When the machine is at temperature, set the fillet(s) in the basket. If working with more than one fillet, they should not touch, although they may be quite close together, depending on the basket's size. Air-fry undisturbed for 5 minutes, or until lightly browned and cooked through.
4. Use a nonstick-safe spatula to transfer the fillets to a serving platter or plate(s). Serve at once.

Swordfish With Capers And Tomatoes
Servings: 2 | Cooking Time: 10 Minutes
- 2 1-inch thick swordfish steaks
- A pinch of salt and black pepper
- 30 ounces tomatoes, chopped
- 2 tablespoons capers, drained
- 1 tablespoon red vinegar
- 2 tablespoons oregano, chopped

1. In a pan that fits the air fryer, combine all the ingredients, toss, put the pan in the fryer and cook at 390 degrees F for 10 minutes, flipping the fish halfway. Divide the mix between plates and serve.

Horseradish-crusted Salmon Fillets
Servings: 3 | Cooking Time: 8 Minutes
- ½ cup Fresh bread crumbs (see the headnote)
- 4 tablespoons (¼ cup/½ stick) Butter, melted and cooled
- ¼ cup Jarred prepared white horseradish
- Vegetable oil spray
- 4 6-ounce skin-on salmon fillets (for more information, see here)

1. Preheat the air fryer to 400°F.
2. Mix the bread crumbs, butter, and horseradish in a bowl until well combined.
3. Take the basket out of the machine. Generously spray the skin side of each fillet. Pick them up one by one with a nonstick-safe spatula and set them in the basket skin side down with as much air space between them as possible. Divide the bread-crumb mixture between the fillets, coating the top of each fillet with an even layer. Generously coat the bread-crumb mixture with vegetable oil spray.
4. Return the basket to the machine and air-fry undisturbed for 8 minutes, or until the topping has lightly browned and the fish is firm but not hard.
5. Use a nonstick-safe spatula to transfer the salmon fillets to serving plates. Cool for 5 minutes before serving. Because of the butter in the topping, it will stay very hot for quite a while. Take care, especially if you're serving these fillets to children.

Crispy Prawn In Bacon Wraps
Servings: 4 | Cooking Time: 30 Minutes
- 8 jumbo prawns, peeled and deveined
- Lemon Wedges for garnishing

1. Wrap each prawn from head to tail with each bacon slice overlapping to keep the bacon in place. Secure the end of the bacon with a toothpick. It's ok not to cover the ends of the cheese with bacon. Refrigerate for 15 minutes.
2. Preheat air fryer to 400 F. Arrange the bacon-wrapped prawns on the fryer's basket, cook for 7 minutes or until the bacon is crispy. Transfer prawns to a paper towel to cool. Remove the toothpicks and serve the bacon-wrapped prawns with lemon wedges and a side of steamed green vegetables.

Lime Cod
Servings: 4 | Cooking Time: 14 Minutes
- 4 cod fillets, boneless
- 1 tablespoon olive oil
- Salt and black pepper to the taste
- 2 teaspoons sweet paprika
- Juice of 1 lime

1. In a bowl, mix all the ingredients, transfer the fish to your air fryer's basket and cook 350 degrees F for 7 minutes on each side. Divide the fish between plates and serve with a side salad.

French Clams
Servings: 5 | Cooking Time: 3 Minutes
- 2-pounds clams, raw, shells removed
- 1 tablespoon Herbs de Provence
- 1 tablespoon sesame oil
- 1 garlic clove, diced

1. Put the clams in the bowl and sprinkle with Herbs de Provence, sesame oil, and diced garlic. Shake the seafood well. Preheat the air fryer to 390F. Put the clams in the air fryer and cook them for 3 minutes. When the clams are cooked, shake them well and transfer in the serving plates.

Air Fried Catfish
Servings: 4 | Cooking Time: 20 Minutes
- 4 catfish fillets
- 1 tbsp olive oil
- 1/4 cup fish seasoning
- 1 tbsp fresh parsley, chopped

1. Preheat the air fryer to 400 F.
2. Spray air fryer basket with cooking spray.
3. Seasoned fish with seasoning and place into the air fryer basket.
4. Drizzle fish fillets with oil and cook for 10 minutes.
5. Turn fish to another side and cook for 10 minutes more.
6. Garnish with parsley and serve.

Foil Packet Lobster Tail
Servings: 2 | Cooking Time: 15 Minutes
- 2 x 6-oz. lobster tail halves
- 2 tbsp. salted butter, melted
- ½ medium lemon, juiced
- ½ tsp. Old Bay seasoning
- 1 tsp. dried parsley

1. Lay each lobster on a sheet of aluminum foil. Pour a light drizzle of melted butter and lemon juice over each one, and season with Old Bay.
2. Fold down the sides and ends of the foil to seal the lobster. Place

each one in the fryer.
3. Cook at 375°F for twelve minutes.
4. Just before serving, top the lobster with dried parsley.

Mahi-mahi "burrito" Fillets
Servings: 3 | Cooking Time: 10 Minutes
- 1 Large egg white
- 1½ cups (6 ounces) Crushed corn tortilla chips (gluten-free, if a concern)
- 1 tablespoon Chile powder
- 3 5-ounce skinless mahi-mahi fillets
- 6 tablespoons Canned refried beans
- Vegetable oil spray

1. Preheat the air fryer to 400°F.
2. Set up and fill two shallow soup plates or small pie plates on your counter: one with the egg white, beaten until foamy; and one with the crushed tortilla chips.
3. Gently rub ½ teaspoon chile powder on each side of each fillet.
4. Spread (or maybe smear) 1 tablespoon refried beans over both sides and the edges of a fillet. Dip the fillet in the egg white, turning to coat it on both sides. Let any excess egg white slip back into the rest, then set the fillet in the crushed tortilla chips. Turn several times, pressing gently to coat it evenly. Coat the fillet on all sides with the vegetable oil spray, then set it aside. Prepare the remaining fillet(s) in the same way.
5. When the machine is at temperature, set the fillets in the basket with as much air space between them as possible. Air-fry undisturbed for 10 minutes, or until crisp and browned.
6. Use a nonstick-safe spatula to transfer the fillets to a serving platter or plates. Cool for only a minute or so, then serve hot.

Lemon Butter Scallops
Servings: 1 | Cooking Time: 30 Minutes
- 1 lemon
- 1 lb. scallops
- ½ cup butter
- ¼ cup parsley, chopped

1. Juice the lemon into a Ziploc bag.
2. Wash your scallops, dry them, and season to taste. Put them in the bag with the lemon juice. Refrigerate for an hour.
3. Remove the bag from the refrigerator and leave for about twenty minutes until it returns to room temperature. Transfer the scallops into a foil pan that is small enough to be placed inside the fryer.
4. Pre-heat the fryer at 400°F and put the rack inside.
5. Place the foil pan on the rack and cook for five minutes.
6. In the meantime, melt the butter in a saucepan over a medium heat. Zest the lemon over the saucepan, then add in the chopped parsley. Mix well.
7. Take care when removing the pan from the fryer. Transfer the contents to a plate and drizzle with the lemon-butter mixture. Serve hot.

Fried Shrimps With Sweet Chili Sauce
Servings: 1 | Cooking Time: 6 Minutes
- ½ cup flour
- ½ cup sweet chili sauce
- ½ pound raw shrimps, peeled and deveined
- 1 egg, beaten
- 1 teaspoon chili powder
- Salt and pepper to taste

1. Mix together the shrimps and eggs in a bowl. Season with salt and pepper to taste.
2. In another bowl, mix the chili powder and flour.
3. Dredge the shrimps in the flour mixture.
4. Preheat the air fryer to 3300F.
5. Place the shrimps on the double layer rack.
6. Cook for 6 minutes.
7. Serve with chili sauce.

Miso-rubbed Salmon Fillets
Servings: 3 | Cooking Time: 5 Minutes
- ¼ cup White (shiro) miso paste (usually made from rice and soy beans)
- 1½ tablespoons Mirin or a substitute (see here)
- 2½ teaspoons Unseasoned rice vinegar (see here)
- Vegetable oil spray
- 3 6-ounce skin-on salmon fillets (for more information, see here)

1. Preheat the air fryer to 400°F.
2. Mix the miso, mirin, and vinegar in a small bowl until uniform.
3. Remove the basket from the machine. Generously spray the skin side of each fillet. Pick them up one by one with a nonstick-safe spatula and set them in the basket skin side down with as much air space between them as possible. Coat the top of each fillet with the miso mixture, dividing it evenly between them.
4. Return the basket to the machine. Air-fry undisturbed for 5 minutes, or until lightly browned and firm.
5. Use a nonstick-safe spatula to transfer the fillets to serving plates. Cool for only a minute or so before serving.

Fried Tilapia Bites
Servings: 4 | Cooking Time: 20 Minutes
- ½ cup cornflakes
- 3 tbsp flour
- 1 egg, beaten
- Salt to taste
- Lemon wedges for serving

1. Preheat your Air Fryer to 390 F. Spray the air fryer basket with cooking spray.
2. Put the flour, egg, and conflakes each into a different bowl, three bowls in total. Add salt egg bowl and mix well. Dip the tilapia first in the flour, then in the egg, and lastly, coat in the cornflakes. Lay on the air fryer basket. Spray with cooking spray and cook for 5 minutes. Slide out the fryer basket and shake the shrimp; cook further for 5 minutes. Serve with lemon wedges.

Air Fried Calamari
Servings: 3 | Cooking Time: 30 Minutes
- ½ cup cornmeal or cornstarch
- 2 large eggs, beaten
- 2 mashed garlic cloves
- 1 cup breadcrumbs
- lemon juice

1. Coat calamari with the cornmeal. The first mixture is prepared by mixing the eggs and garlic. Dip the calamari in the eggs' mixture. Then dip them in the breadcrumbs. Put the rings in the fridge for 2 hours.
2. Then, line them in the air fryer and add oil generously. Fry for 10 to 13 minutes at 390 F, shaking once halfway through. Serve with garlic mayonnaise and top with lemon juice.

Hot Prawns
Servings:8 | Cooking Time: 12 Minutes
- Salt and black pepper
- ½ tsp ground cayenne
- ½ tsp chili flakes
- ½ tsp ground cumin
- ½ tsp garlic powder

1. In a bowl, season the prawns with salt and black pepper. Sprinkle cayenne, flakes, cumin and garlic and stir to coat. Spray the air fryer's basket with oil and arrange the prawns in an even layer. Cook for 8 minutes at 340 F, turning once halfway through. Serve with fresh lettuce leaves or sweet chili sauce.

Cajun Lemon Salmon
Servings: 1 | Cooking Time: 15 Minutes
- 1 salmon fillet
- 1 tsp. Cajun seasoning
- ½ lemon, juiced
- ¼ tsp. sugar
- 2 lemon wedges, for serving

1.1 Pre-heat the Air Fryer to 350°F.
2.2 Combine the lemon juice and sugar.
3.3 Cover the salmon with the sugar mixture.
4.4 Coat the salmon with the Cajun seasoning.
5.5 Line the base of your fryer with a sheet of parchment paper.
6.6 Transfer the salmon to the fryer and allow to cook for 7 minutes.

Maple Glazed Salmon
Servings:2 | Cooking Time:8 Minutes
- 2 (6-ounces) salmon fillets
- Salt, to taste
- 2 tablespoons maple syrup

1. Preheat the Air fryer to 355 o F and grease an Air fryer basket.
2. Coat the salmon fillets evenly with maple syrup and season with salt.
3. Arrange the salmon fillets into the Air fryer basket and cook for about 8 minutes.
4. Remove from the Air fryer and dish out the salmon fillets to serve hot.

Citrusy Branzini On The Grill
Servings:2 | Cooking Time: 15 Minutes
- 2 branzini fillets
- Salt and pepper to taste
- 3 lemons, juice freshly squeezed
- 2 oranges, juice freshly squeezed

1. Place all ingredients in a Ziploc bag. Allow to marinate in the fridge for 2 hours.
2. Preheat the air fryer at 3900F.
3. Place the grill pan accessory in the air fryer.
4. Place the fish on the grill pan and cook for 15 minutes until the fish is flaky.

Healthy And Easy To Make Salmon
Servings:2 | Cooking Time: 10 Minutes
- ½ of lemon
- 2 teaspoons avocado oil
- 2 teaspoons paprika
- 2 wild caught salmon fillets
- Salt and pepper to taste

1. Preheat the air fryer to 3900F.
2. Season the salmon fillets with avocado oil, paprika, salt, and pepper. Drizzle with lemon juice on both sides.
3. Place the grill pan accessory in the air fryer.
4. Place the salmon fillets and cook for 10 minutes.
5. Be sure to flip the fillets halfway through the cooking time.

Bacon Wrapped Shrimp
Servings:4 | Cooking Time: 14 Minutes
- 1 pound bacon
- 1½ pounds tiger shrimp, peeled and deveined

1. With a slice of bacon, wrap each shrimp.
2. Refrigerate for about 20 minutes.
3. Set the temperature of air fryer to 390 degrees F. Grease an air fryer basket.
4. Arrange shrimp into the prepared air fryer basket in 2 batches in a single layer.
5. Air fry for about 5-7 minutes.
6. Remove from air fryer and transfer the shrimp onto serving plates.
7. Serve hot.

Tilapia Fish Fillets
Servings: 2 | Cooking Time: 7 Minutes
- 2 tilapia fillets
- 1 tsp old bay seasoning
- 1/2 tsp butter
- 1/4 tsp lemon pepper
- Pepper
- Salt

1. Spray air fryer basket with cooking spray.
2. Place fish fillets into the air fryer basket and season with lemon pepper, old bay seasoning, pepper, and salt.
3. Spray fish fillets with cooking spray and cook at 400 F for 7 minutes.
4. Serve and enjoy.

Prawns
Servings: 4 | Cooking Time: 30 Minutes
- 1 lb. prawns, peeled
- 1 lb. bacon slices

1. Pre-heat the Air Fryer to 400°F.
2. Wrap the bacon slices around the prawns and put them in fryer's basket.
3. Air fry for 5 minutes and serve hot.

Crispy Smelts

Servings:3 | Cooking Time: 20 Minutes

- 1 pound Cleaned smelts
- 3 tablespoons Tapioca flour
- Vegetable oil spray
- To taste Coarse sea salt or kosher salt

1. Preheat the air fryer to 400°F.
2. Toss the smelts and tapioca flour in a large bowl until the little fish are evenly coated.
3. Lay the smelts out on a large cutting board. Lightly coat both sides of each fish with vegetable oil spray.
4. When the machine is at temperature, set the smelts close together in the basket, with a few even overlapping on top. Air-fry undisturbed for 20 minutes, until lightly browned and crisp.
5. Remove the basket from the machine and turn out the fish onto a wire rack. The smelts will most likely come out as one large block, or maybe in a couple of large pieces. Cool for a minute or two, then sprinkle the smelts with salt and break the block(s) into much smaller sections or individual fish to serve.

Bacon Wrapped Scallops

Servings:4 | Cooking Time:12 Minutes

- 5 center-cut bacon slices, cut each in 4 pieces
- 20 sea scallops, cleaned and patted very dry
- Olive oil cooking spray
- 1 teaspoon lemon pepper seasoning
- ½ teaspoon paprika
- Salt and ground black pepper, to taste

1. Preheat the Air fryer to 400 o F and grease an Air fryer basket.
2. Wrap each scallop with a piece of bacon and secure each with a toothpick.
3. Season the scallops evenly with lemon pepper seasoning and paprika.
4. Arrange half of the scallops into the Air fryer basket and spray with cooking spray.
5. Season with salt and black pepper and cook for about 6 minutes.
6. Repeat with the remaining half and serve warm.

Ghee Shrimp And Green Beans

Servings: 4 | Cooking Time: 15 Minutes

- 1 pound shrimp, peeled and deveined
- A pinch of salt and black pepper
- ½ pound green beans, trimmed and halved
- Juice of 1 lime
- 2 tablespoons cilantro, chopped
- ¼ cup ghee, melted

1. In a pan that fits your air fryer, mix all the ingredients, toss, introduce in the fryer and cook at 360 degrees F for 15 minutes shaking the fryer halfway. Divide into bowls and serve.

Sweet And Sour Glazed Cod

Servings:2 | Cooking Time:12 Minutes

- 1 teaspoon water
- 4 (3½-ounces) cod fillets
- 1/3 cup soy sauce
- 1/3 cup honey
- 3 teaspoons rice wine vinegar

1. Preheat the Air fryer to 355 o F and grease an Air fryer basket.
2. Mix the soy sauce, honey, vinegar and water in a small bowl.
3. Reserve about half of the mixture in another bowl.
4. Stir the cod fillets in the remaining mixture until well coated.
5. Cover and refrigerate to marinate for about 3 hours.
6. Arrange the cod fillets into the Air fryer basket and cook for about 12 minutes, flipping once in between.
7. Coat with the reserved marinade and dish out the cod to serve hot.

Salmon Cakes

Servings:4 | Cooking Time: 15 Minutes

- 14 oz boiled and mashed potatoes
- 2 oz flour
- A handful of capers
- A handful of chopped parsley
- 1 tsp olive oil
- zest of 1 lemon

1. Place the mashed potatoes in a large bowl and flake the salmon over. Stir in capers, parsley, and lemon zest. Shape small cakes out of the mixture. Dust them with flour and place in the fridge to set, for 1 hour. Preheat the air fryer to 350 F. Brush the olive oil over the basket's bottom and add the cakes. Cook for 7 minutes.

Authentic Alaskan Crab Legs

Servings:3 | Cooking Time: 15 Minutes

- 2 cups butter, melted
- 1 cup salted water

1. Preheat air fryer to 380 F, and dip the crab legs in salted water; let stay for a few minutes. Place them in the basket and cook for 10 minutes. Pour the butter over crab legs to serve.

Greek-style Grilled Scallops

Servings:3 | Cooking Time: 15 Minutes

- ¼ cup Greek yogurt
- A pinch of saffron threads
- 1 ½ teaspoons rice vinegar
- Salt and pepper to taste
- 12 large sea scallops
- 2 tablespoons olive oil

1. Place all ingredients in a Ziploc bag and allow the scallops to marinate in the fridge for at least 2 hours.
2. Preheat the air fryer at 3900F.
3. Place the grill pan accessory in the air fryer.
4. Grill the scallops for 15 minutes.
5. Serve on bread and drizzle with more olive oil if desired.

Coriander Cod And Green Beans

Servings: 4 | Cooking Time: 15 Minutes

- 12 oz cod fillet
- ½ cup green beans, trimmed and halved
- 1 tablespoon avocado oil
- 1 teaspoon salt
- 1 teaspoon ground coriander

1. Cut the cod fillet on 4 servings and sprinkle every serving with salt and ground coriander. After this, place the fish on 4 foil squares. Top them with green beans and avocado oil and wrap them into parcels. Preheat the air fryer to 400F. Place the cod parcels in the air fryer and cook them for 15 minutes.

Ham Tilapia

Servings: 4 | Cooking Time: 10 Minutes

- 16 oz tilapia fillet
- 4 ham slices
- 1 teaspoon sunflower oil
- ½ teaspoon salt
- 1 teaspoon dried rosemary

1. Cut the tilapia on 4 servings. Sprinkle every fish serving with salt, dried rosemary, and sunflower oil. Then carefully wrap the fish fillets in the ham slices and secure with toothpicks. Preheat the air fryer to 400F. Put the wrapped tilapia in the air fryer basket in one layer and cook them for 10 minutes. Gently flip the fish on another side after 5 minutes of cooking.

Cajun Spiced Veggie-shrimp Bake

Servings: 4 | Cooking Time: 20 Minutes

- 1 Bag of Frozen Mixed Vegetables
- 1 Tbsp Gluten Free Cajun Seasoning
- Olive Oil Spray
- Season with salt and pepper
- Small Shrimp Peeled & Deveined (Regular Size Bag about 50-80 Small Shrimp)

1. Lightly grease baking pan of air fryer with cooking spray. Add all Ingredients and toss well to coat. Season with pepper and salt, generously.
2. For 10 minutes, cook on 330oF. Halfway through cooking time, stir.
3. Cook for 10 minutes at 330oF.
4. Serve and enjoy.

Nacho Chips Crusted Prawns

Servings: 2 | Cooking Time: 8 Minutes

- ¾ pound prawns, peeled and deveined
- 1 large egg
- 5 ounces Nacho flavored chips, finely crushed

1. In a shallow bowl, beat the egg.
2. In another bowl, place the nacho chips
3. Dip each prawn into the beaten egg and then, coat with the crushed nacho chips.
4. Set the temperature of air fryer to 350 degrees F. Grease an air fryer basket.
5. Arrange prawns into the prepared air fryer basket.
6. Air fry for about 8 minutes.
7. Remove from air fryer and transfer the prawns onto serving plates.
8. Serve hot.

Breaded Flounder

Servings: 3 | Cooking Time: 12 Minutes

- 1 egg
- 1 cup dry breadcrumbs
- 3 (6-ounces) flounder fillets
- 1 lemon, sliced
- ¼ cup vegetable oil

1. Preheat the Air fryer to 360 o F and grease an Air fryer basket.
2. Whisk the egg in a shallow bowl and mix breadcrumbs and oil in another bowl.
3. Dip flounder fillets into the whisked egg and coat with the breadcrumb mixture.
4. Arrange flounder fillets into the Air fryer basket and cook for about 12 minutes.
5. Dish out the flounder fillets onto serving plates and garnish with the lemon slices to serve.

Broiled Tilapia

Servings: 4 | Cooking Time: 10 Minutes

- 1 lb. tilapia fillets
- ½ tsp. lemon pepper
- Salt to taste

1. Spritz the Air Fryer basket with some cooking spray.
2. Put the tilapia fillets in basket and sprinkle on the lemon pepper and salt.
3. Cook at 400°F for 7 minutes.
4. Serve with a side of vegetables.

Amazing Salmon Fillets

Servings: 2 | Cooking Time: 7 Minutes

- 2 (7-ounce) (¾-inch thick) salmon fillets
- 1 tablespoon Italian seasoning
- 1 tablespoon fresh lemon juice

1. Preheat the Air fryer to 355 o F and grease an Air fryer grill pan.
2. Rub the salmon evenly with Italian seasoning and transfer into the Air fryer grill pan, skin-side up.
3. Cook for about 7 minutes and squeeze lemon juice on it to serve.

Snow Crab Legs

Servings: 6 | Cooking Time: 15 Minutes Per Batch

- 8 pounds fresh shell-on snow crab legs
- 2 tablespoons olive oil
- 2 teaspoons Old Bay Seasoning
- 4 tablespoons salted butter, melted
- 2 teaspoons lemon juice

1. Preheat the air fryer to 400°F.
2. Drizzle crab legs with oil and sprinkle with Old Bay. Place in the air fryer basket, working in batches as necessary. Cook 15 minutes, turning halfway through cooking time, until crab turns a bright red-orange.
3. In a small bowl, whisk together butter and lemon juice. Serve as a dipping sauce with warm crab legs.

Thyme Scallops

Servings: 1 | Cooking Time: 12 Minutes

- 1 lb. scallops
- Salt and pepper
- ½ tbsp. butter
- ½ cup thyme, chopped

1. Wash the scallops and dry them completely. Season with pepper and salt, then set aside while you prepare the pan.
2. Grease a foil pan in several spots with the butter and cover the bottom with the thyme. Place the scallops on top.
3. Pre-heat the fryer at 400°F and set the rack inside.
4. Place the foil pan on the rack and allow to cook for seven minutes.
5. Take care when removing the pan from the fryer and transfer the scallops to a serving dish. Spoon any remaining butter in the pan over the fish and enjoy.

Crab Legs
Servings: 3 | Cooking Time: 20 Minutes
- 3 lb. crab legs
- ¼ cup salted butter, melted and divided
- ½ lemon, juiced
- ¼ tsp. garlic powder

1. In a bowl, toss the crab legs and two tablespoons of the melted butter together. Place the crab legs in the basket of the fryer.
2. Cook at 400°F for fifteen minutes, giving the basket a good shake halfway through.
3. Combine the remaining butter with the lemon juice and garlic powder.
4. Crack open the cooked crab legs and remove the meat. Serve with the butter dip on the side and enjoy!

Creamy Salmon
Servings: 2 | Cooking Time: 20 Minutes
- ¾ lb. salmon, cut into 6 pieces
- ¼ cup yogurt
- 1 tbsp. olive oil
- 1 tbsp. dill, chopped
- 3 tbsp. sour cream
- Salt to taste

1.1 Sprinkle some salt on the salmon.
2.2 Put the salmon slices in the Air Fryer basket and add in a drizzle of olive oil.
3.3 Air fry the salmon at 285°F for 10 minutes.
4.4 In the meantime, combine together the cream, dill, yogurt, and salt.
5.5 Plate up the salmon and pour the creamy sauce over it. Serve hot.

Salmon Croquettes
Servings: 4 | Cooking Time: 15 Minutes
- 1 lb. can red salmon, drained and mashed
- ⅓ cup olive oil
- 2 eggs, beaten
- 1 cup friendly bread crumbs
- ½ bunch parsley, chopped

1.1 Pre-heat the Air Fryer to 400°F.
2.2 In a mixing bowl, combine together the drained salmon, eggs, and parsley.
3.3 In a shallow dish, stir together the bread crumbs and oil to combine well.
4.4 Mold equal-sized amounts of the mixture into small balls and coat each one with bread crumbs.
5.5 Put the croquettes in the fryer's basket and air fry for 7 minutes.

Rosemary Garlic Prawns
Servings: 2 | Cooking Time: 15 Minutes
- 3 garlic cloves, minced
- 1 rosemary sprig, chopped
- ½ tbsp melted butter
- Salt and pepper, to taste

1. Combine garlic, butter, rosemary, salt and pepper, in a bowl. Add the prawns to the bowl and mix to coat them well. Cover the bowl and refrigerate for an hour. Preheat the air fryer to 350 F, and cook for 6 minutes. Increase the temperature to 390 degrees, and cook for one more minute.

Salmon And Olives
Servings: 4 | Cooking Time: 15 Minutes
- 1 tablespoon lemon zest, grated
- 1/3 cup olive oil
- 4 salmon fillets, boneless
- 1 cup green olives, pitted and sliced
- Juice of 2 limes
- Salt and black pepper to the taste

1. In a baking dish that fits your air fryer, mix all the ingredients, toss, put the pan in the fryer and cook at 370 degrees F for 15 minutes. Divide everything between plates and serve.

Shrimp Skewers
Servings: 5 | Cooking Time: 5 Minutes
- 4-pounds shrimps, peeled
- 2 tablespoons fresh cilantro, chopped
- 2 tablespoons apple cider vinegar
- 1 teaspoon ground coriander
- 1 tablespoon avocado oil
- Cooking spray

1. In the shallow bowl mix up avocado oil, ground coriander, apple cider vinegar, and fresh cilantro. Then put the shrimps in the big bowl and sprinkle with avocado oil mixture. Mix them well and leave for 10 minutes to marinate. After this, string the shrimps on the skewers. Preheat the air fryer to 400F. Arrange the shrimp skewers in the air fryer and cook them for 5 minutes.

Butter Paprika Swordfish
Servings: 4 | Cooking Time: 12 Minutes
- 4 swordfish fillets, boneless
- 1 tablespoon olive oil
- ¾ teaspoon sweet paprika
- 2 teaspoons basil, dried
- Juice of 1 lemon
- 2 tablespoons butter, melted

1. In a bowl, mix the oil with the other ingredients except the fish fillets and whisk. Brush the fish with this mix, place it in your air fryer's basket and cook for 6 minutes on each side. Divide between plates and serve with a side salad.

Perfect Soft-shelled Crabs
Servings: 2 | Cooking Time: 12 Minutes
- ½ cup All-purpose flour
- 1 tablespoon Old Bay seasoning
- 1 Large egg(s), well beaten
- 1 cup (about 3 ounces) Ground oyster crackers
- 2 2½-ounce cleaned soft-shelled crab(s), about 4 inches across
- Vegetable oil spray

1. Preheat the air fryer to 375°F (or 380°F or 390°F, if one of these is the closest setting).
2. Set up and fill three shallow soup plates or small pie plates on your counter: one for the flour, whisked with the Old Bay until well combined; one for the beaten egg(s); and one for the cracker crumbs.
3. Set a soft-shelled crab in the flour mixture and turn to coat evenly and well on all sides, even inside the legs. Dip the crab into the egg(s) and coat well, turning at least once, again getting some of the egg between the legs. Let any excess egg slip back into the rest,

then set the crab in the cracker crumbs. Turn several times, pressing very gently to get the crab evenly coated with crumbs, even between the legs. Generously coat the crab on all sides with vegetable oil spray. Set it aside if you're making more than one and coat these in the same way.

4. Set the crab(s) in the basket with as much air space between them as possible. They may overlap slightly, particularly at the ends of their legs, depending on the basket's size. Air-fry undisturbed for 12 minutes, or until very crisp and golden brown. If the machine is at 390°F, the crabs may be done in only 10 minutes.

5. Use kitchen tongs to gently transfer the crab(s) to a wire rack. Cool for a couple of minutes before serving.

Clams And Sauce

Servings: 4 | Cooking Time: 20 Minutes

- 15 small clams
- 1 tablespoon spring onions, chopped
- Juice of 1 lime
- 10 ounces coconut cream
- 2 tablespoons cilantro, chopped
- 1 teaspoon olive oil

1. Heat up a pan that fits your air fryer with the oil over medium heat, add the spring onions and sauté for 2 minutes. Add lime juice, coconut cream and the cilantro, stir and cook for 2 minutes more. Add the clams, toss, introduce in the fryer and cook at 390 degrees F for 15 minutes. Divide into bowls and serve hot.

Italian Mackerel

Servings: 2 | Cooking Time: 15 Minutes

- 8 oz mackerel, trimmed
- 1 tablespoon Italian seasonings
- 1 teaspoon keto tomato sauce
- 2 tablespoons ghee, melted
- ½ teaspoon salt

1. Rub the mackerel with Italian seasonings, and tomato sauce. After this, rub the fish with salt and leave for 15 minutes in the fridge to marinate. Meanwhile, preheat the air fryer to 390F. When the time of marinating is finished, brush the fish with ghee and wrap in the baking paper. Place the wrapped fish in the air fryer and cook it for 15 minutes.

Vegetable & Side Dishes

Artichokes Sauté
Servings: 4 | Cooking Time: 15 Minutes
- 10 ounces artichoke hearts, halved
- 3 garlic cloves
- 2 cups baby spinach
- ¼ cup veggie stock
- 2 teaspoons lime juice
- Salt and black pepper to the taste

1. In a pan that fits your air fryer, mix all the ingredients, toss, introduce in the fryer and cook at 370 degrees F for 15 minutes. Divide between plates and serve as a side dish.

Cumin Artichokes
Servings: 4 | Cooking Time: 15 Minutes
- 12 ounces artichoke hearts
- ½ teaspoon olive oil
- 1 teaspoon coriander, ground
- ½ teaspoon cumin seeds
- Salt and black pepper to the taste
- 1 tablespoon lemon juice

1. In a pan that fits your air fryer, mix all the ingredients, toss, introduce the pan in the fryer and cook at 370 degrees F for 15 minutes. Divide the mix between plates and serve as a side dish.

Carrot Crisps
Servings: 2 | Cooking Time: 20 Minutes
- Salt to taste

1. Put the carrot strips in a bowl and season with salt to taste. Grease the fryer basket lightly with cooking spray, and add the carrot strips. Cook at 350 F for 10 minutes, stirring once halfway through.

Bacon-wrapped Avocados
Servings: 6 | Cooking Time: 40 Minutes
- 3 large avocados, sliced
- ⅓ tsp salt
- ⅓ tsp chili powder
- ⅓ tsp cumin powder

1. Stretch the bacon strips to elongate and cut in half to make 24 pieces. Wrap each bacon piece around a slice of avocado. Tuck the end of bacon into the wrap. Season with salt, chili and cumin.
2. Arrange wrapped pieces on the fryer and cook at 350 F for 8 minutes, flipping halfway through to cook evenly. Remove onto a wire rack and repeat the process for the remaining avocado pieces.

Homemade Potato Puffs
Servings: 3 | Cooking Time: 22 Minutes
- 3 6-ounce red beets
- Vegetable oil spray
- To taste Coarse sea salt or kosher salt

1. Preheat the air fryer to 375°F.
2. Remove the stems from the beets and peel them with a knife or vegetable peeler. Slice them into ½-inch-thick circles. Lay these flat on a cutting board and slice them into ½-inch-thick sticks. Generously coat the sticks on all sides with vegetable oil spray.
3. When the machine is at temperature, drop them into the basket, shake the basket to even the sticks out into as close to one layer as possible, and air-fry for 20 minutes, tossing and rearranging the beet matchsticks every 5 minutes, or until brown and even crisp at the ends. If the machine is at 360°F, you may need to add 2 minutes to the cooking time.
4. Pour the fries into a big bowl, add the salt, toss well, and serve warm.

Asian Green Beans
Servings: 2 | Cooking Time: 10 Minutes
- 8 oz green beans, trimmed and cut in half
- 1 tsp sesame oil
- 1 tbsp tamari

1. Add all ingredients into the large mixing bowl and toss well.
2. Spray air fryer basket with cooking spray.
3. Transfer green beans in air fryer basket and cook at 400 F for 10 minutes. Toss halfway through.
4. Serve and enjoy.

Steak Fries
Servings: 4 | Cooking Time: 25 Minutes
- 2 pounds Medium Yukon Gold or other yellow potatoes (peeled or not—your choice)
- 2 tablespoons Olive oil
- ½ teaspoon, or more to taste Table salt
- ½ teaspoon, or more to taste Ground black pepper

1. Preheat the air fryer to 350°F.
2. Cut the potatoes lengthwise into wedges about 1 inch wide at the outer edge. Toss these wedges in a bowl with the oil, salt, and pepper until the wedges are evenly coated in the oil. (Start with the minimum amounts of salt and pepper we recommend—you can always add more later.)
3. When the machine is at temperature, set the wedges in the basket in a crisscross stack, with about half of the wedges first lining in the basket's bottom, then others set on top of those at a 45-degree angle. Air-fry undisturbed for 15 minutes.
4. Increase the machine's temperature to 400°F. Toss the fries so they're no longer in a crisscross pattern but more like a mound. Air-fry for 10 minutes more (from the moment you raise the temperature), tossing and rearranging the fries once, until they're crisp and brown.
5. Pour them onto a wire rack and cool for a few minutes before serving hot.

Herbed Garlic Radishes
Servings: 2 | Cooking Time: 15 Minutes
- 1 lb. radishes
- 2 tbsp. unsalted butter, melted
- ¼ tsp. dried oregano
- ½ tsp. dried parsley
- ½ tsp. garlic powder

1. Prepare the radishes by cutting off their tops and bottoms and quartering them.
2. In a bowl, combine the butter, dried oregano, dried parsley, and garlic powder. Toss with the radishes to coat.
3. Transfer the radishes to your air fryer and cook at 350°F for ten

minutes, shaking the basket at the halfway point to ensure the radishes cook evenly through. The radishes are ready when they begin to turn brown.

Chicken Wings With Alfredo Sauce
Servings:4 | Cooking Time: 60 Minutes
- Salt to taste
- ½ cup Alfredo sauce

1. Preheat the air fryer to 370°F.
2. Season the wings with salt. Arrange them in the air fryer, without touching. Cook in batches if needed, for 20 minutes, until no longer pink in the center. Increase the temperature to 390 F and cook for 5 minutes more. Remove to a big bowl and coat well with the sauce to serve.

Cheesy Cauliflower Tots
Servings:4 | Cooking Time: 12 Minutes Per Batch
- 1 steamer bag riced cauliflower
- ⅓ cup Italian bread crumbs
- ¼ cup all-purpose flour
- 1 large egg
- ¾ cup shredded sharp Cheddar cheese
- ½ teaspoon salt
- ¼ teaspoon ground black pepper

1. Cook cauliflower according to the package directions. Let cool, then squeeze in a cheesecloth or kitchen towel to drain excess water.
2. Preheat the air fryer to 400°F. Cut parchment paper to fit the air fryer basket.
3. In a large bowl, mix drained cauliflower, bread crumbs, flour, egg, and Cheddar. Sprinkle in salt and pepper, then mix until well combined.
4. Roll 2 tablespoons of mixture into a tot shape. Repeat to use all of the mixture.
5. Place tots on parchment in the air fryer basket, working in batches as necessary. Spritz with cooking spray. Cook 12 minutes, turning tots halfway through cooking time, until golden brown. Serve warm.

Yellow Squash And Zucchinis Dish
Servings: 4 | Cooking Time:45 Minutes
- 1 yellow squash; halved, deseeded and cut into chunks
- 6 tsp. olive oil
- 1 lb. zucchinis; sliced
- 1/2 lb. carrots; cubed
- 1 tbsp. tarragon; chopped
- Salt and white pepper to the taste

1. In your air fryer's basket; mix zucchinis with carrots, squash, salt, pepper and oil; toss well and cook at 400 °F, for 25 minutes. Divide them on plates and serve as a side dish with tarragon sprinkled on top.

Zucchinis And Arugula Mix
Servings: 4 | Cooking Time: 20 Minutes
- 1 pound zucchinis, sliced
- 1 tablespoon olive oil
- Salt and white pepper to the taste
- 4 ounces arugula leaves
- ¼ cup chives, chopped
- 1 cup walnuts, chopped

1. In a pan that fits the air fryer, combine all the ingredients except the arugula and walnuts, toss, put the pan in the machine and cook at 360 degrees F for 20 minutes. Transfer this to a salad bowl, add the arugula and the walnuts, toss and serve as a side salad.

Collard Greens Sauté
Servings: 4 | Cooking Time: 12 Minutes
- 1 pound collard greens, trimmed
- 2 fennel bulbs, trimmed and quartered
- 2 tablespoons olive oil
- Salt and black pepper to the taste
- ½ cup keto tomato sauce

1. In a pan that fits your air fryer, mix the collard greens with the fennel and the rest of the ingredients, toss, put the pan in the fryer and cook at 350 degrees F for 12 minutes. Divide everything between plates and serve.

Air-fried Brussels Sprouts
Servings:2 | Cooking Time: 15 Minutes
- 1 tbsp butter, melted
- Salt and black pepper to taste
- ¼ tsp cayenne pepper

1. In a bowl, mix Brussels sprouts, butter, cayenne pepper, salt, and pepper. Place Brussels sprouts in air fryer basket. Cook for 10 minutes at 380 F. Serve with sautéed onion rings.

Mozzarella Green Beans
Servings: 4 | Cooking Time: 6 Minutes
- 1 cup green beans, trimmed
- 2 oz Mozzarella, shredded
- 1 teaspoon butter
- ½ teaspoon chili flakes
- ¼ cup beef broth

1. Sprinkle the green beans with chili flakes and put in the air fryer baking pan. Add beef broth and butter. Then top the vegetables with shredded Mozzarella. Preheat the air fryer to 400F. Put the pan with green beans in the air fryer and cook the meal for 6 minutes.

Simple Stuffed Bell Peppers
Servings: 2 | Cooking Time: 20 Minutes
- 2 bell peppers, tops and seeds removed
- Salt and pepper, to taste
- 2/3 cup cream cheese
- 2 tablespoons mayonnaise
- 1 tablespoon fresh celery stalks, chopped

1. Arrange the peppers in the lightly greased cooking basket. Cook in the preheated Air Fryer at 400 degrees F for 15 minutes, turning them over halfway through the cooking time.
2. Season with salt and pepper.
3. Then, in a mixing bowl, combine the cream cheese with the mayonnaise and chopped celery. Stuff the pepper with the cream cheese mixture and serve.

Mustard Greens Mix
Servings: 6 | Cooking Time: 12 Minutes
- 1 pound collard greens, trimmed
- ¼ pound bacon, cooked and chopped
- A drizzle of olive oil
- Salt and black pepper to taste
- ½ cup veggie stock

1. Place all ingredients in a pan that fits your air fryer and mix well.
2. Put the pan in the fryer and cook at 260 degrees F for 12 minutes.
3. Divide everything between plates and serve.

Roasted Potatoes & Cheese
Servings: 4 | Cooking Time: 55 Minutes
- 4 medium potatoes
- 1 asparagus bunch
- ⅓ cup cottage cheese
- ⅓ cup low-fat crème fraiche
- 1 tbsp. wholegrain mustard

1. Pour some oil into your Air Fryer and pre-heat to 390°F.
2. Cook potatoes for 20 minutes.
3. Boil the asparagus in salted water for 3 minutes.
4. Remove the potatoes and mash them with rest of ingredients. Sprinkle on salt and pepper.
5. Serve with rice.

Maple Glazed Corn
Servings: 4 | Cooking Time: 6 Minutes
- 4 ears of corn
- 1 tablespoon maple syrup
- Black pepper to taste
- 1 tablespoon butter, melted

1. Combine the black pepper, butter, and the maple syrup in a bowl.
2. Rub the corn with the mixture, and then put it in your air fryer.
3. Cook at 390 degrees F for 6 minutes.
4. Divide the corn between plates and serve.

Lemon Tempeh
Servings: 4 | Cooking Time: 12 Minutes
- 1 teaspoon lemon juice
- 1 tablespoon sunflower oil
- ¼ teaspoon ground coriander
- 6 oz tempeh, chopped

1. Sprinkle the tempeh with lemon juice, sunflower oil, and ground coriander. Massage the tempeh gently with the help of the fingertips. After this, preheat the air fryer to 325F. Put the tempeh in the air fryer and cook it for 12 minutes. Flip the tempeh every 2 minutes during cooking.

Roasted Brussels Sprouts With Bacon
Servings: 4 | Cooking Time: 20 Minutes
- 4 slices thick-cut bacon, chopped (about ¼ pound)
- 1 pound Brussels sprouts, halved (or quartered if large)
- freshly ground black pepper

1. Preheat the air fryer to 380°F.
2. Air-fry the bacon for 5 minutes, shaking the basket once or twice during the cooking time.
3. Add the Brussels sprouts to the basket and drizzle a little bacon fat from the bottom of the air fryer drawer into the basket. Toss the sprouts to coat with the bacon fat. Air-fry for an additional 15 minutes, or until the Brussels sprouts are tender to a knifepoint.
4. Season with freshly ground black pepper.

Coconut Mushrooms Mix
Servings: 4 | Cooking Time: 15 Minutes
- 1 pound brown mushrooms, sliced
- 1 pound kale, torn
- Salt and black pepper to the taste
- 2 tablespoons olive oil
- 14 ounces coconut milk

1. In a pan that fits your air fryer, mix the kale with the rest of ingredients and toss. Put the pan in the fryer, cook at 380 degrees F for 15 minutes, divide between plates and serve.

Jicama Fries
Servings: 1 | Cooking Time: 25 Minutes
- 1 small jicama, peeled
- ¼ tsp. onion powder
- ¾ tsp. chili powder
- ¼ tsp. garlic powder
- ¼ tsp. ground black pepper

1. To make the fries, cut the jicama into matchsticks of your desired thickness.
2. In a bowl, toss them with the onion powder, chili powder, garlic powder, and black pepper to coat. Transfer the fries into the basket of your air fryer.
3. Cook at 350°F for twenty minutes, giving the basket an occasional shake throughout the cooking process. The fries are ready when they are hot and golden in color. Enjoy!

Mozzarella Asparagus Mix
Servings: 4 | Cooking Time: 10 Minutes
- 1 pound asparagus, trimmed
- 2 tablespoons olive oil
- A pinch of salt and black pepper
- 2 cups mozzarella, shredded
- ½ cup balsamic vinegar
- 2 cups cherry tomatoes, halved

1. In a pan that fits your air fryer, mix the asparagus with the rest of the ingredients except the mozzarella and toss. Put the pan in the air fryer and cook at 400 degrees F for 10 minutes. Divide between plates and serve.

Air-fried Crispy Chicken Thighs
Servings: 4 | Cooking Time: 30 Minutes
- ½ tsp salt
- ¼ tsp black pepper
- ¼ tsp garlic powder

1. Season the thighs with salt, pepper, and garlic powder. Arrange thighs, skin side down, in the air fryer and cook until golden brown, for 20 minutes at 350 F.

Cheesy Onion Rings
Servings:3 | Cooking Time: 20 Minutes
- ¾ cup Parmesan cheese, shredded
- 2 medium eggs, beaten
- 1 tsp garlic powder
- A pinch of salt
- 1 cup flour
- 1 tsp paprika powder

1. Add eggs to a bowl. In another bowl, mix cheese, garlic powder, salt, flour, and paprika. Dip onion rings in egg, then in the cheese mixture, in the egg again and finally in the cheese mixture. Add the rings to the basket and cook them for 8 minutes at 350 F. Serve with a cheese or tomato dip.

Paprika Jicama
Servings: 5 | Cooking Time: 7 Minutes
- 15 oz jicama, peeled
- ½ teaspoon salt
- ½ teaspoon ground paprika
- ½ teaspoon chili flakes
- 1 teaspoon sesame oil

1. Preheat the air fryer to 400F. Cut Jicama into the small sticks and sprinkle with salt, ground paprika, and chili flakes. Then put the Jicama stick in the air fryer and sprinkle with sesame oil. Cook the vegetables for 4 minutes. Then shake them well and cook for 3 minutes.

Spanish Chorizo With Brussels Sprouts
Servings:4 | Cooking Time: 15 Minutes
- 2 pounds Brussels sprouts, trimmed and halved
- 2 tbsp canola oil
- Salt and black pepper to taste
- 1 tsp garlic puree
- 1 thyme sprig, chopped

1. Preheat the Air fryer to 390 F. Grease the air fryer basket with cooking spray.
2. In a bowl, mix together canola oil, garlic puree, salt, and pepper. Add the Brussels sprouts and toss to coat. Arrange chorizo and Brussels sprouts on the air fryer basket and cook for 10 minutes, turning halfway. Scatter over thyme and serve.

Tasty Herb Tomatoes
Servings: 4 | Cooking Time: 15 Minutes
- 2 large tomatoes, halved
- 1 tbsp olive oil
- 1/2 tsp thyme, chopped
- 2 garlic cloves, minced
- Pepper
- Salt

1. Add all ingredients into the bowl and toss well.
2. Transfer tomatoes into the air fryer basket and cook at 390 F for 15 minutes.
3. Serve and enjoy.

Turmeric Cauliflower Rice
Servings: 4 | Cooking Time: 20 Minutes
- 1 big cauliflower, florets separated and riced
- 1 and ½ cups chicken stock
- 1 tablespoon olive oil
- Salt and black pepper to the taste
- ½ teaspoon turmeric powder

1. In a pan that fits the air fryer, combine the cauliflower with the oil and the rest of the ingredients, toss, introduce in the air fryer and cook at 360 degrees F for 20 minutes. Divide between plates and serve as a side dish.

Beet Fries
Servings: 3 | Cooking Time: 22 Minutes
- 3 6-ounce red beets
- Vegetable oil spray
- To taste Coarse sea salt or kosher salt

1. Preheat the air fryer to 375°F.
2. Remove the stems from the beets and peel them with a knife or vegetable peeler. Slice them into ½-inch-thick circles. Lay these flat on a cutting board and slice them into ½-inch-thick sticks. Generously coat the sticks on all sides with vegetable oil spray.
3. When the machine is at temperature, drop them into the basket, shake the basket to even the sticks out into as close to one layer as possible, and air-fry for 20 minutes, tossing and rearranging the beet matchsticks every 5 minutes, or until brown and even crisp at the ends. If the machine is at 360°F, you may need to add 2 minutes to the cooking time.
4. Pour the fries into a big bowl, add the salt, toss well, and serve warm.

Green Bean Crisps
Servings:4 | Cooking Time: 15 Minutes
- 1 tbsp olive oil
- 1 tsp garlic powder
- 1 tsp onion powder
- 1 tsp paprika
- Salt and black pepper to taste

1. Preheat the Air fryer to 390 F. Grease the air fryer basket with cooking spray.
2. In a bowl, mix olive oil, garlic and onion powder, paprika, salt, and pepper. Coat green beans in the mixture. Place in air fryer basket; cook for 10 minutes, shaking once. Allow to cool before serving.

Corn Muffins
Servings:12 | Cooking Time: 10 Minutes
- ½ cup all-purpose flour
- ½ cup cornmeal
- ¼ cup granulated sugar
- ½ teaspoon baking powder
- ¼ cup salted butter, melted
- ½ cup buttermilk
- 1 large egg

1. Preheat the air fryer to 350°F.
2. In a large bowl, whisk together flour, cornmeal, sugar, and baking powder.
3. Add butter, buttermilk, and egg to dry mixture. Stir until well combined.

4. Divide batter evenly among twelve silicone or aluminum muffin cups, filling cups about halfway. Working in batches as needed, place in the air fryer and cook 10 minutes until golden brown. Let cool 5 minutes before serving.

Elegant Carrot Cookies

Servings: 8 | Cooking Time: 30 Minutes
- Salt and pepper to taste
- 1 tbsp parsley
- 1¼ oz oats
- 1 whole egg, beaten
- 1 tbsp thyme

1. Preheat your air fryer to 360 F.
2. In a bowl, combine carrots with salt, pepper, beaten egg, oats, thyme, and parsley and mix well. Form the batter into cookie shapes. Place in air fryer's basket and cook for 15 minutes.

Perfect Crispy Tofu

Servings: 4 | Cooking Time: 20 Minutes
- 1 block firm tofu, pressed and cut into 1-inch cubes
- 1 tbsp arrowroot flour
- 2 tsp sesame oil
- 1 tsp vinegar
- 2 tbsp soy sauce

1. In a bowl, toss tofu with oil, vinegar, and soy sauce and let sit for 15 minutes.
2. Toss marinated tofu with arrowroot flour.
3. Spray air fryer basket with cooking spray.
4. Add tofu in air fryer basket and cook for 20 minutes at 370 F. Shake basket halfway through.
5. Serve and enjoy.

Garlic Radishes

Servings: 4 | Cooking Time: 15 Minutes
- 20 radishes, halved
- 1 teaspoon chives, chopped
- 1 tablespoon garlic, minced
- Salt and black pepper to the taste
- 2 tablespoons olive oil

1. In your air fryer's pan, combine all the ingredients and toss. Introduce the pan in the machine and cook at 370 degrees F for 15 minutes. Divide between plates and serve as a side dish.

Balsamic Radishes

Servings: 4 | Cooking Time: 15 Minutes
- 2 bunches red radishes, halved
- 1 tablespoon olive oil
- 2 tablespoons balsamic vinegar
- 2 tablespoons parsley, chopped
- Salt and black pepper to the taste

1. In a bowl, mix the radishes with the remaining ingredients except the parsley, toss and put them in your air fryer's basket. Cook at 400 degrees F for 15 minutes, divide between plates, sprinkle the parsley on top and serve as a side dish.

Cheesy Texas Toast

Servings: 2 | Cooking Time: 4 Minutes
- 2 1-inch-thick slice(s) Italian bread (each about 4 inches across)
- 4 teaspoons Softened butter
- 2 teaspoons Minced garlic
- ¼ cup (about ¾ ounce) Finely grated Parmesan cheese

1. Preheat the air fryer to 400°F.
2. Spread one side of a slice of bread with 2 teaspoons butter. Sprinkle with 1 teaspoon minced garlic, followed by 2 tablespoons grated cheese. Repeat this process if you're making one or more additional toasts.
3. When the machine is at temperature, put the bread slice(s) cheese side up in the basket (with as much air space between them as possible if you're making more than one). Air-fry undisturbed for 4 minutes, or until browned and crunchy.
4. Use a nonstick-safe spatula to transfer the toasts cheese side up to a wire rack. Cool for 5 minutes before serving.

Easy Celery Root Mix

Servings: 4 | Cooking Time: 15 Minutes
- 2 cups celery root, roughly cubed
- A pinch of salt and black pepper
- ½ tablespoon butter, melted

1. Put all of the ingredients in your air fryer and toss.
2. Cook at 350 degrees F for 15 minutes.
3. Divide between plates and serve.

Lemon Kale

Servings: 4 | Cooking Time: 15 Minutes
- 10 cups kale, torn
- 2 tablespoons olive oil
- Salt and black pepper to the taste
- 2 tablespoons lemon zest, grated
- 1 tablespoon lemon juice
- 1/3 cup pine nuts

1. In a pan that fits the air fryer, combine all the ingredients, toss, introduce the pan in the machine and cook at 380 degrees F for 15 minutes. Divide between plates and serve as a side dish.

Beet Wedges Dish

Servings: 4 | Cooking Time: 25 Minutes
- 4 beets; washed, peeled and cut into large wedges
- 1 tbsp. olive oil
- 2 garlic cloves; minced
- 1 tsp. lemon juice
- Salt and black to the taste

1. In a bowl; mix beets with oil, salt, pepper, garlic and lemon juice; toss well, transfer to your air fryer's basket and cook them at 400 °F, for 15 minutes. Divide beets wedges on plates and serve as a side dish.

Butter Broccoli

Servings: 4 | Cooking Time: 15 Minutes
- 1 pound broccoli florets
- A pinch of salt and black pepper
- 1 teaspoons sweet paprika
- ½ tablespoon butter, melted

1. In a bowl, mix the broccoli with the rest of the ingredients, and toss. Put the broccoli in your air fryer's basket, cook at 350 degrees F for 15 minutes, divide between plates and serve.

Perfect Broccolini
Servings: 4 | Cooking Time: 15 Minutes
- 1 pound Broccolini
- Olive oil spray
- Coarse sea salt or kosher salt

1. Preheat the air fryer to 375°F.
2. Place the broccolini on a cutting board. Generously coat it with olive oil spray, turning the vegetables and rearranging them before spraying a couple of times more, to make sure everything's well coated, even the flowery bits in their heads.
3. When the machine is at temperature, pile the broccolini in the basket, spreading it into as close to one layer as you can. Air-fry for 5 minutes, tossing once to get any covered or touching parts exposed to the air currents, until the leaves begin to get brown and even crisp. Watch carefully and use this visual cue to know the moment to stop the cooking.
4. Transfer the broccolini to a platter. Spread out the pieces and sprinkle them with salt to taste.

Roasted Acorn Squash
Servings: 4 | Cooking Time: 25 Minutes
- 1 large acorn squash, cut in half lengthwise
- 2 tbsp olive oil
- 1/4 cup parmesan cheese, grated
- 1/4 tsp pepper
- 8 fresh thyme sprigs

1. Preheat the air fryer to 370 F.
2. Remove seed from squash and cut into 3/4-inch slices.
3. Add squash slices, olive oil, thyme, parmesan cheese, pepper, and salt in a bowl and toss to coat.
4. Add squash slices into the air fryer basket and cook for 25 minutes. Turn halfway through.
5. Serve and enjoy.

Ghee Savoy Cabbage
Servings: 4 | Cooking Time: 15 Minutes
- 1 Savoy cabbage head, shredded
- Salt and black pepper to the taste
- 1 and ½ tablespoons ghee, melted
- ¼ cup coconut cream
- 1 tablespoon dill, chopped

1. In a pan that fits the air fryer, combine all the ingredients except the coconut cream, toss, put the pan in the air fryer and cook at 390 degrees F for 10 minutes. Add the cream, toss, cook for 5 minutes more, divide between plates and serve.

Garlic-parmesan French Fries
Servings: 4 | Cooking Time: 45 Minutes
- 3 large russet potatoes, peeled, trimmed, and sliced into ½" × 4" sticks
- 2 ½ tablespoons olive oil, divided
- 2 teaspoons minced garlic
- ½ teaspoon salt
- ¼ teaspoon ground black pepper
- 1 teaspoon dried parsley
- ¼ cup grated Parmesan cheese

1. Place potato sticks in a large bowl of cold water and let soak 30 minutes.
2. Preheat the air fryer to 350°F.
3. Drain potatoes and gently pat dry. Place in a large, dry bowl.
4. Pour 2 tablespoons oil over potatoes. Add garlic, salt, and pepper, then toss to fully coat.
5. Place fries in the air fryer basket and cook 15 minutes, shaking the basket twice during cooking, until fries are golden and crispy on the edges.
6. Place fries into a clean medium bowl and drizzle with remaining ½ tablespoon oil. Sprinkle parsley and Parmesan over fries and toss to coat. Serve warm.

Garlic Tomatoes Recipe
Servings: 4 | Cooking Time: 25 Minutes
- 4 garlic cloves; crushed
- 1 lb. mixed cherry tomatoes
- 3 thyme springs; chopped.
- 1/4 cup olive oil
- Salt and black pepper to the taste

1. In a bowl; mix tomatoes with salt, black pepper, garlic, olive oil and thyme, toss to coat, introduce in your air fryer and cook at 360 °F, for 15 minutes. Divide tomatoes mix on plates and serve

Cheesy Sticks With Sweet Thai Sauce
Servings: 4 | Cooking Time: 20 Minutes + Freezing Time
- 2 cups breadcrumbs
- 3 eggs
- 1 cup sweet Thai sauce
- 4 tbsp skimmed milk

1. Pour crumbs in a bowl. Beat eggs into another bowl with milk. One after the other, dip sticks in the egg mixture, in the crumbs, then egg mixture again and then in the crumbs again. Freeze for 1 hour.
2. Preheat air fryer to 380 F. Arrange the sticks on the fryer. Cook for 5 minutes, flipping them halfway through cooking to brown evenly. Cook in batches. Serve with a sweet Thai sauce.

Duck Fat Roasted Red Potatoes
Servings: 4 | Cooking Time: 15 Minutes
- 1 tbsp garlic powder
- Salt and black pepper to taste
- 2 tbsp thyme, chopped
- 3 tbsp duck fat, melted

1. Preheat the Air fryer to 380 F. In a bowl, mix duck fat, garlic powder, salt, and pepper. Add the potatoes and shake to coat. Place in the air fryer cooking basket and cook for 12 minutes, then shake and continue cooking for another 10 minutes. Serve warm sprinkled with thyme.

Parsley Savoy Cabbage Mix
Servings: 4 | Cooking Time: 15 Minutes
- 1 Savoy cabbage, shredded
- 2 spring onions, chopped
- 2 tablespoons keto tomato sauce
- Salt and black pepper to the taste
- 1 tablespoon parsley, chopped

1. In a pan that fits your air fryer, mix the cabbage the rest of the ingredients except the parsley, toss, put the pan in the fryer and cook at 360 degrees F for 15 minutes. Divide between plates and serve with parsley sprinkled on top.

Air-frier Baked Potatoes

Servings: 4 | Cooking Time: 45 Minutes

- 2 tbsp olive oil
- Salt and ground black pepper to taste

1. Rub potatoes with half tbsp of olive oil. Season with salt and pepper, and arrange them on the air fryer. Cook for 40 minutes at 400 F. Let cool slightly, then make a slit on top. Use a fork to fluff the insides of the potatoes. Fill the potato with cheese or garlic mayo.

Roasted Mushrooms

Servings: 4 | Cooking Time: 15 Minutes

- 2 lbs mushrooms, clean and quarters
- 2 tbsp vermouth
- 2 tsp herb de Provence
- 1/2 tsp garlic powder
- 1 tbsp butter, melted

1. Add mushrooms in a bowl with remaining ingredients and toss well.
2. Transfer mushrooms into the air fryer basket and cook at 320 F for 15 minutes. Toss halfway through.
3. Serve and enjoy.

Cheesy Ranch Broccoli

Servings: 6 | Cooking Time: 24 Minutes

- 4 cups broccoli florets
- 1/2 cup cheddar cheese, shredded
- 1/4 cup ranch dressing
- 1/4 cup heavy whipping cream
- Pepper
- Salt

1. Add all ingredients into the large bowl and toss well to coat.
2. Spread broccoli mixture into the air fryer baking dish and place into the air fryer.
3. Cook at 350 F for 24 minutes.
4. Stir well and serve.

Fried Agnolotti

Servings: 6 | Cooking Time: 25 Minutes

- 1 cup flour
- 4 eggs, beaten
- Cooking spray
- Salt and black pepper
- 2 cups breadcrumbs

1. Mix flour with salt and pepper. Dip pasta into the flour, then into the egg, and finally in the breadcrumbs. Spray with oil and arrange in the air fryer in an even layer. Set to 400 F and cook for 14 minutes, turning once halfway through cooking. Cook until nice and golden. Serve with goat cheese.

Paprika Green Beans

Servings: 4 | Cooking Time: 20 Minutes

- 6 cups green beans, trimmed
- 2 tablespoons olive oil
- 1 tablespoon hot paprika
- A pinch of salt and black pepper

1. In a bowl, mix the green beans with the other ingredients, toss, put them in the air fryer's basket and cook at 370 degrees F for 20 minutes. Divide between plates and serve as a side dish.

Herbed Croutons With Brie Cheese

Servings: 1 | Cooking Time: 20 Minutes

- 1 tbsp french herbs
- 7 oz brie cheese, chopped
- 2 slices bread, halved

1. Preheat air fryer to 340 F. In a bowl, mix oil with herbs. Brush the bread slices with oil mixture. Place on a flat surface. Top with brie cheese. Place in air fryer's basket; cook for 7 minutes. Cut into cubes.

Cheddar Asparagus

Servings: 4 | Cooking Time: 10 Minutes

- 2 pounds asparagus, trimmed
- 2 tablespoons olive oil
- 1 cup cheddar cheese, shredded
- 4 garlic cloves, minced
- 4 bacon slices, cooked and crumbled

1. In a bowl, mix the asparagus with the other ingredients except the bacon, toss and put in your air fryer's basket. Cook at 400 degrees F for 10 minutes, divide between plates, sprinkle the bacon on top and serve.

Sriracha Chili Chicken Wings

Servings: 4 | Cooking Time: 30 Minutes

- Salt to taste
- ¼ cup sriracha chili sauce
- 1 tsp garlic powder

1. Preheat the Air fryer to 370 F.
2. Season chicken with salt and garlic powder. Spray with cooking spray and place in the air fryer basket. Cook for 25 minutes, flipping once halfway through. When ready, coat in the sriracha sauce and serve.

Roasted Broccoli

Servings: 4 | Cooking Time: 8 Minutes

- 12 ounces broccoli florets
- 2 tablespoons olive oil
- ½ teaspoon salt
- ¼ teaspoon ground black pepper

1. Preheat the air fryer to 360°F.
2. In a medium bowl, place broccoli and drizzle with oil. Sprinkle with salt and pepper.
3. Place in the air fryer basket and cook 8 minutes, shaking the basket twice during cooking, until the edges are brown and the center is tender. Serve warm.

Mushrooms, Sautéed

Servings: 4 | Cooking Time: 4 Minutes

- 8 ounces sliced white mushrooms, rinsed and well drained
- ¼ teaspoon garlic powder
- 1 tablespoon Worcestershire sauce

1. Place mushrooms in a large bowl and sprinkle with garlic powder and Worcestershire. Stir well to distribute seasonings evenly.
2. Place in air fryer basket and cook at 390°F for 4 minutes, until tender.

Lemon And Butter Artichokes
Servings: 4 | Cooking Time: 15 Minutes
- 12 ounces artichoke hearts
- Juice of ½ lemon
- 4 tablespoons butter, melted
- 2 tablespoons tarragon, chopped
- Salt and black pepper to the taste

1. In a bowl, mix all the ingredients, toss, transfer the artichokes to your air fryer's basket and cook at 370 degrees F for 15 minutes. Divide between plates and serve as a side dish.

Pop Corn Broccoli
Servings: 1 | Cooking Time: 10 Minutes
- 4 egg yolks
- ¼ cup butter, melted
- 2 cups coconut flower
- Salt and pepper
- 2 cups broccoli florets

1. In a bowl, whisk the egg yolks and melted butter together. Throw in the coconut flour, salt and pepper, then stir again to combine well.
2. Pre-heat the fryer at 400°F.
3. Dip each broccoli floret into the mixture and place in the fryer. Cook for six minutes, in multiple batches if necessary. Take care when removing them from the fryer and enjoy!

Tomato Candy
Servings: 12 | Cooking Time: 120 Minutes
- 6 Small Roma or plum tomatoes, halved lengthwise
- 1½ teaspoons Coarse sea salt or kosher salt

1. Before you turn the machine on, set the tomatoes cut side up in a single layer in the basket (or the basket attachment). They can touch each other, but try to leave at least a fraction of an inch between them (depending, of course, on the size of the basket or basket attachment). Sprinkle the cut sides of the tomatoes with the salt.
2. Set the machine to cook at 225°F (or 230°F, if that's the closest setting). Put the basket in the machine and air-fry for 2 hours, or until the tomatoes are dry but pliable, with a little moisture down in their centers.
3. Remove the basket from the machine and cool the tomatoes in it for 10 minutes before gently transferring them to a plate for serving, or to a shallow dish that you can cover and store in the refrigerator for up to 1 week.

Skinny Pumpkin Chips
Servings: 2 | Cooking Time: 20 Minutes
- 1 pound pumpkin, cut into sticks
- 1 tablespoon coconut oil
- 1/2 teaspoon rosemary
- 1/2 teaspoon basil
- Salt and ground black pepper, to taste

1. Start by preheating the Air Fryer to 395 degrees F. Brush the pumpkin sticks with coconut oil; add the spices and toss to combine.
2. Cook for 13 minutes, shaking the basket halfway through the cooking time.
3. Serve with mayonnaise. Bon appétit!

Hot Chicken Wingettes
Servings:3 | Cooking Time: 30 Minutes
- Salt and pepper to taste
- ⅓ cup hot sauce
- ½ tbsp vinegar

1. Preheat air fryer to 360 F. Season the chicken with pepper and salt. Add to the air fryer and cook for 25 minutes. Toss every 5 minutes. Mix vinegar and hot sauce. Pour the sauce over the chicken to serve.

Simple Cheese Sandwich
Servings:1 | Cooking Time: 20 Minutes
- 2 scallions
- 2 tbsp butter
- 2 slices bread
- ¾ cup Cheddar cheese

1. Preheat your air fryer to 360 F.
2. Lay the bread slices on a flat surface. On one slice, spread the exposed side with butter, followed by cheddar and scallions. On the other slice, spread butter and then sprinkle cheese.
3. Bring the buttered sides together to form sand. Place the sandwich in your air fryer's cooking basket and cook for 10 minutes. Serve with berry sauce.

Yeast Rolls
Servings:16 | Cooking Time: 1 Hour 10 Minutes
- 4 tablespoons salted butter
- ¼ cup granulated sugar
- 1 cup hot water
- 1 tablespoon quick-rise yeast
- 1 large egg
- 1 teaspoon salt
- 2 ½ cups all-purpose flour, divided

1. In a microwave-safe bowl, microwave butter 30 seconds until melted. Pour 2 tablespoons of butter into a large bowl. Add sugar, hot water, and yeast. Mix until yeast is dissolved.
2. Using a rubber spatula, mix in egg, salt, and 2 ¼ cups flour. Dough will be very sticky.
3. Cover bowl with plastic wrap and let rise in a warm place 1 hour.
4. Sprinkle remaining ¼ cup flour on dough and turn onto a lightly floured surface. Knead 2 minutes, then cut into sixteen even pieces.
5. Preheat the air fryer to 350°F. Spray a 6" round cake pan with cooking spray.
6. Sprinkle each roll with flour and arrange in pan. Brush with remaining melted butter. Place pan in the air fryer basket and cook 10 minutes until fluffy and golden on top. Serve warm.

Cheesy Bacon Fries
Servings:4 | Cooking Time: 25 Minutes
- 5 slices bacon, chopped
- 2 tbsp vegetable oil
- 2½ cups Cheddar cheese, shredded
- 3 oz melted cream cheese
- Salt and pepper to taste
- ¼ cup scallions, chopped

1. Preheat your air fryer to 400 F.
2. Add bacon to air fryer's basket and cook for 4, shaking once; set aside. Add in potatoes and drizzle oil on top to coat. Cook for 25

minutes, shaking the basket every 5 minutes. Season with salt and pepper.
3. In a bowl, mix cheddar cheese and cream cheese. Pour over the potatoes and cook for 5 more minutes at 340 F. Sprinkle chopped scallions on top and serve.

Curry Cabbage Sauté
Servings: 4 | Cooking Time: 20 Minutes
- 30 ounces green cabbage, shredded
- 1 tablespoon red curry paste
- 3 tablespoons coconut oil, melted
- A pinch of salt and black pepper

1. In a pan that fits the air fryer, combine the cabbage with the rest of the ingredients, toss, introduce the pan in the machine and cook at 380 degrees F for 20 minutes. Divide between plates and serve as a side dish.

Garlic Asparagus
Servings: 3 | Cooking Time: 5 Minutes
- 9 oz Asparagus
- ¼ teaspoon chili powder
- ¼ teaspoon garlic powder
- 1 teaspoon olive oil
- 4 Provolone cheese slices

1. Trim the asparagus and sprinkle with chili powder and garlic powder. The preheat the air fryer to 400F. Put the asparagus in the air fryer basket and sprinkle with olive oil. Cook the vegetables for 3 minutes. Then top the asparagus with Provolone cheese and cook for 3 minutes more.

Perfect French Fries
Servings: 3 | Cooking Time: 37 Minutes
- 1 pound Large russet potato(es)
- Vegetable oil or olive oil spray
- ½ teaspoon Table salt

1. Cut each potato lengthwise into ¼-inch-thick slices. Cut each of these lengthwise into ¼-inch-thick matchsticks.
2. Set the potato matchsticks in a big bowl of cool water and soak for 5 minutes. Drain in a colander set in the sink, then spread the matchsticks out on paper towels and dry them very well.
3. Preheat the air fryer to 225°F (or 230°F, if that's the closest setting).
4. When the machine is at temperature, arrange the matchsticks in an even layer (if overlapping but not compact) in the basket. Air-fry for 20 minutes, tossing and rearranging the fries twice.
5. Pour the contents of the basket into a big bowl. Increase the air fryer's temperature to 325°F (or 330°F, if that's the closest setting).
6. Generously coat the fries with vegetable or olive oil spray. Toss well, then coat them again to make sure they're covered on all sides, tossing (and maybe spraying) a couple of times to make sure.
7. When the machine is at temperature, pour the fries into the basket and air-fry for 12 minutes, tossing and rearranging the fries at least twice.
8. Increase the machine's temperature to 375°F (or 380°F or 390°F, if one of these is the closest setting). Air-fry for 5 minutes more (from the moment you raise the temperature), tossing and rearranging the fries at least twice to keep them from burning and to make sure they all get an even measure of the heat, until brown and crisp.
9. Pour the contents of the basket into a serving bowl. Toss the fries with the salt and serve hot.

Sweet Butternut Squash
Servings: 8 | Cooking Time: 15 Minutes
- 1 medium butternut squash, peeled and cubed
- 2 tablespoons salted butter, melted
- ½ teaspoon salt
- 1 ½ tablespoons brown sugar
- ½ teaspoon ground cinnamon

1. Preheat the air fryer to 400°F.
2. In a large bowl, place squash and add butter. Toss to coat. Sprinkle salt, brown sugar, and cinnamon over squash and toss to fully coat.
3. Place squash in the air fryer basket and cook 15 minutes, shaking the basket three times during cooking, until the edges are golden and the center is fork-tender. Serve warm.

Mediterranean Bruschetta
Servings: 10 | Cooking Time: 25 Minutes
- Olive oil
- 3 garlic cloves, minced
- 1 cup grated cheddar cheese
- 1 tsp dried oregano
- Salt and pepper to taste

1. Brush the bread with oil and sprinkle with garlic. Scatter the cheese on top, then oregano, salt and pepper. Arrange the slices on the fryer and cook for 14 minutes at 360 F, turning once. Serve.

Crispy Bacon With Butterbean Dip
Servings: 2 | Cooking Time: 10 Minutes
- 1 tbsp chives
- 3 ½ oz feta
- Pepper to taste
- 1 tsp olive oil
- 3 ½ oz bacon, sliced

1. Preheat your air fryer to 340 F. Blend beans, oil and pepper using a blender. Arrange bacon slices on your air fryer's cooking basket. Sprinkle chives on top and cook for 10 minutes. Add feta cheese to the butter bean blend and stir. Serve bacon with the dip.

Crispy Chicken Nuggets
Servings: 4 | Cooking Time: 25 Minutes
- Salt and black pepper to taste
- 2 tbsp olive oil
- 5 tbsp plain breadcrumbs
- 2 tbsp panko breadcrumbs
- 2 tbsp grated Parmesan cheese

1. Preheat air fryer to 380 F. and grease. Season the chicken with pepper and salt. In a bowl, pour olive oil. In a separate bowl, add crumb, and Parmesan cheese. Place the chicken pieces in the oil to coat, then dip into breadcrumb mixture, and transfer to the air fryer. Work in batches if needed. Lightly spray chicken with cooking spray. Cook for 10 minutes, flipping once halfway through.

Mustard Endives
Servings: 4 | Cooking Time: 15 Minutes
- 4 endives, trimmed
- A pinch of salt and black pepper
- 2 tablespoons white vinegar
- 3 tablespoons olive oil
- 1 teaspoon mustard
- ½ cup walnuts, chopped

1. In a bowl, mix the oil with salt, pepper, mustard and vinegar and whisk really well. Add the endives, toss and transfer them to your air fryer's basket. Cook at 350 degrees F for 15 minutes, divide between plates and serve with walnuts sprinkled on top.

Spicy Cheese Lings
Servings: 3 | Cooking Time: 25 Minutes
- 1 cup flour + extra for kneading
- ¼ tsp chili powder
- ½ tsp baking powder
- 3 tsp butter
- A pinch of salt

1. In a bowl, mix cheese, flour, baking powder, chili powder, butter, and salt. Add some water and mix well to get a dough. Remove the dough on a flat floured surface. Using a rolling pin, roll the dough out into a thin sheet. Cut the dough into lings' shape. Add the cheese lings to the basket, and cook for 6 minutes at 350 F, flipping once halfway through.

Taco Okra
Servings: 3 | Cooking Time: 10 Minutes
- 9 oz okra, chopped
- 1 teaspoon taco seasoning
- 1 teaspoon sunflower oil

1. In the mixing bowl mix up chopped okra, taco seasoning, and sunflower oil. Then preheat the air fryer to 385F. Put the okra mixture in the air fryer and cook it for 5 minutes. Then shake the vegetables well and cook them for 5 minutes more.

Dill Tomato
Servings: 2 | Cooking Time: 8 Minutes
- 1 oz Parmesan, sliced
- 1 tomato
- 1 teaspoon fresh dill, chopped
- 1 teaspoon olive oil
- ¼ teaspoon dried thyme

1. Trim the tomato and slice it on 2 pieces. Then preheat the air fryer to 350F. Top the tomato slices with sliced Parmesan, chopped fresh dill, and thyme. Sprinkle the tomatoes with olive oil and put in the air fryer. Cook the meal for 8 minutes. Remove cooked tomato parm from the air fryer with the help of the spatula.

Simple Taro Fries
Servings: 2 | Cooking Time: 20 Minutes
- 8 small taro, peel and cut into fries shape
- 1 tbsp olive oil
- 1/2 tsp salt

1. Add taro slice in a bowl and toss well with olive oil and salt.
2. Transfer taro slices into the air fryer basket.
3. Cook at 360 F for 20 minutes. Toss halfway through.
4. Serve and enjoy.

Low-carb Pita Chips
Servings: 1 | Cooking Time: 15 Minutes
- 1 cup mozzarella cheese, shredded
- 1 egg
- ¼ cup blanched finely ground flour
- ½ oz. pork rinds, finely ground

1. Melt the mozzarella in the microwave. Add the egg, flour, and pork rinds and combine together to form a smooth paste. Microwave the cheese again if it begins to set.
2. Put the dough between two sheets of parchment paper and use a rolling pin to flatten it out into a rectangle. The thickness is up to you. With a sharp knife, cut into the dough to form triangles. It may be necessary to complete this step-in multiple batches.
3. Place the chips in the fryer and cook for five minutes at 350°F. Turn them over and cook on the other side for another five minutes, or until the chips are golden and firm.
4. Allow the chips to cool and harden further. They can be stored in an airtight container.

Classic French Fries
Servings: 2 | Cooking Time: 25 Minutes
- 2 russet potatoes, washed, dried, cut strips
- 2 tbsp olive oil
- Salt and black pepper to taste

1. Spray air fryer basket with cooking spray. In a bowl, toss the strips with olive oil, and season with salt and pepper. Arrange in the air fryer and cook for 18 minutes at 400 F, turning once halfway through. Check for crispiness and serve immediately, with garlic aioli, ketchup or crumbled cheese.

Paprika Asparagus
Servings: 4 | Cooking Time: 10 Minutes
- 1 pound asparagus, trimmed
- 3 tablespoons olive oil
- A pinch of salt and black pepper
- 1 tablespoon sweet paprika

1. In a bowl, mix the asparagus with the rest of the ingredients and toss. Put the asparagus in your air fryer's basket and cook at 400 degrees F for 10 minutes. Divide between plates and serve.

Fried Mashed Potato Balls
Servings: 4 | Cooking Time: 10 Minutes
- 2 cups mashed potatoes
- ¾ cup sour cream, divided
- 1 teaspoon salt
- ½ teaspoon ground black pepper
- 1 cup shredded sharp Cheddar cheese
- 4 slices bacon, cooked and crumbled
- 1 cup panko bread crumbs

1. Preheat the air fryer to 400°F. Cut parchment paper to fit the air fryer basket.
2. In a large bowl, mix mashed potatoes, ½ cup sour cream, salt, pepper, Cheddar, and bacon. Form twelve balls using 2 tablespoons of the potato mixture per ball.
3. Divide remaining ¼ cup sour cream evenly among mashed potato balls, coating each before rolling in bread crumbs.
4. Place balls on parchment in the air fryer basket and spritz with cooking spray. Cook 10 minutes until brown. Serve warm.

Delicious Chicken Taquitos
Servings:4 | Cooking Time: 25 Minutes
- 1 cup shredded mozzarella cheese
- ¼ cup salsa
- ¼ cup Greek yogurt
- Salt and ground black pepper
- 8 flour tortillas

1. In a bowl, mix chicken, cheese, salsa, sour cream, salt, and pepper. Spray one side of the tortilla with cooking spray. Lay 2 tbsp of the chicken mixture at the center of the non-oiled side the tortillas. Roll tightly around the mixture. Arrange taquitos on your air fryer basket. Cook for 12 minutesat 380 F.

Roasted Coconut Carrots
Servings:4 | Cooking Time: 15 Minutes
- 1 pound horse carrots, sliced
- Salt and black pepper to taste
- ½ tsp chili powder

1. Preheat the Air fryer to 400 F.
2. In a bowl, mix the carrots with coconut oil, chili powder, salt, and pepper. Place in the air fryer and cook for 7 minutes. Slide out the basket and shake; cook for another 5 minutes until golden brown.

Balsamic Greens Sauté
Servings: 4 | Cooking Time: 15 Minutes
- 1 pound collard greens
- ¼ cup cherry tomatoes, halved
- 1 tablespoon balsamic vinegar
- A pinch of salt and black pepper
- 2 tablespoons chicken stock

1. In a pan that fits your air fryer, mix the collard greens with the other ingredients, toss gently, introduce in the air fryer and cook at 360 degrees F for 15 minutes. Divide between plates and serve as a side dish.

Parmesan Veggie Mix
Servings: 4 | Cooking Time: 15 Minutes
- 1 broccoli head, florets separated
- ½ pound asparagus, trimmed
- Juice of 1 lime
- Salt and black pepper to the taste
- 2 tablespoons olive oil
- 3 tablespoons parmesan, grated

1. In a bowl, mix the asparagus with the broccoli and all the other ingredients except the parmesan, toss, transfer to your air fryer's basket and cook at 400 degrees F for 15 minutes. Divide between plates, sprinkle the parmesan on top and serve.

Bacon & Asparagus Spears
Servings:4 | Cooking Time: 25 Minutes
- 4 bacon slices
- 1 tbsp olive oil
- 1 tbsp sesame oil
- 1 tbsp brown sugar
- 1 garlic clove, crushed

1. Preheat your air fryer to 380 F. In a bowl, mix the oils, sugar and crushed garlic. Separate the asparagus into 4 bunches (5 spears in 1 bunch) and wrap each bunch with a bacon slice. Coat the bunches with the sugar and oil mix. Place the bunches in your air fryer's cooking basket and cook for 8 minutes.

Corn-crusted Chicken Tenders
Servings:4 | Cooking Time: 25 Minutes
- Salt and black pepper to taste
- 1 egg
- 1 cup ground cornmeal

1. Preheat the Air Fryer to 390 F.
2. In a bowl, mix ground cornmeal, salt, and pepper. In another bowl, beat egg; season with salt and pepper. Dip the chicken in the egg and then coat in cornmeal; shake off. Spray the prepared sticks with cooking spray and place them in the air fryer basket in a single layer. Cook for 6 minutes. Slide out the basket and flip; cook for another 6 minutes until golden brown. Serve with your favorite dip.

Avocado And Green Beans
Servings: 4 | Cooking Time: 15 Minutes
- 1 pint mixed cherry tomatoes, halved
- 1 avocado, peeled, pitted and cubed
- ¼ pound green beans, trimmed and halved
- 2 tablespoons olive oil

1. In a pan that fits your air fryer, mix the tomatoes with the rest of the ingredients, toss, put the pan in the machine and cook at 360 degrees F for 15 minutes. Transfer to bowls and serve.

Crispy Cauliflower Bites
Servings:4 | Cooking Time: 20 Minutes
- 1 cup flour
- 1 egg, beaten
- 1 cup milk
- 1 head cauliflower, cut into florets

1. Preheat the Air fryer to 390 F. Grease the air fryer basket with cooking spray. In a bowl, mix flour, milk, egg, and Italian seasoning. Coat the cauliflower in the mixture, then drain the excess liquid.
2. Place the florets in the air fryer cooking basket, spray them with cooking spray, and cook for 7 minutes, shake and continue cooking for another 5 minutes. Allow to cool before serving.

Tandoori Cauliflower
Servings: 4 | Cooking Time: 10 Minutes
- ½ cup Plain full-fat yogurt (not Greek yogurt)
- 1½ teaspoons Yellow curry powder, purchased or homemade (see the headnote)
- 1½ teaspoons Lemon juice
- ¾ teaspoon Table salt (optional)
- 4½ cups (about 1 pound 2 ounces) 2-inch cauliflower florets

1. Preheat the air fryer to 400°F.
2. Whisk the yogurt, curry powder, lemon juice, and salt (if using) in a large bowl until uniform. Add the florets and stir gently to coat the florets well and evenly. Even better, use your clean, dry hands to get the yogurt mixture down into all the nooks of the florets.
3. When the machine is at temperature, transfer the florets to the basket, spreading them gently into as close to one layer as you can. Air-fry for 10 minutes, tossing and rearranging the florets twice so that any covered or touching parts are exposed to the air currents, until lightly browned and tender if still a bit crunchy.
4. Pour the contents of the basket onto a wire rack. Cool for at least 5 minutes before serving, or serve at room temperature.

Coconut Chives Sprouts
Servings: 4 | Cooking Time: 20 Minutes
- 1 pound Brussels sprouts, trimmed and halved
- Salt and black pepper to the taste
- 2 tablespoons ghee, melted
- ½ cup coconut cream
- 2 tablespoons garlic, minced
- 1 tablespoon chives, chopped

1. In your air fryer, mix the sprouts with the rest of the ingredients except the chives, toss well, introduce in the air fryer and cook them at 370 degrees F for 20 minutes. Divide the Brussels sprouts between plates, sprinkle the chives on top and serve as a side dish.

Macaroni And Cheese
Servings:4 | Cooking Time: 25 Minutes
- 1 ½ cups dry elbow macaroni
- 1 cup chicken broth
- ½ cup whole milk
- 2 tablespoons salted butter, melted
- 8 ounces sharp Cheddar cheese, shredded, divided
- ½ teaspoon ground black pepper

1. Preheat the air fryer to 350°F.
2. In a 6" baking dish, combine macaroni, broth, milk, butter, half the Cheddar, and pepper. Stir to combine.
3. Place in the air fryer basket and cook 12 minutes.
4. Stir in remaining Cheddar, then return the basket to the air fryer and cook 13 additional minutes.
5. Stir macaroni and cheese until creamy. Let cool 10 minutes before serving.

Garlic Mushrooms
Servings: 4 | Cooking Time: 5 Minutes
- 4 Portobello mushroom caps
- 4 teaspoons olive oil
- 1 teaspoon garlic, diced

1. Trim the mushrooms if needed. Preheat the air fryer to 400F. In the mixing bowl mix up oil and garlic. Sprinkle the mushrooms with garlic mixture and put in the how air fryer. Cook the mushroom steaks for 5 minutes.

Cheese Zucchini Rolls
Servings: 2 | Cooking Time: 10 Minutes
- 1 large zucchini, trimmed
- 3 oz Mozzarella, sliced
- 1 teaspoon keto tomato sauce
- 1 teaspoon olive oil

1. Slice the zucchini on the long thin slices. Then sprinkle every zucchini slice with marinara sauce and top with sliced Mozzarella. Roll the zucchini and secure it with toothpicks. Preheat the air fryer to 385F. Put the zucchini rolls in the air fryer and sprinkle them with olive oil. Cook the zucchini rolls for 10 minutes.

Baked Potato For One
Servings:1 | Cooking Time: 35 Minutes
- 1 medium russet potato
- 1 teaspoon canola oil
- ¼ teaspoon onion powder
- Salt and pepper, to taste
- 1 tablespoon cream cheese
- 1 tablespoon chopped chives

1. Scrub the potato under running water to remove debris.
2. Place the baking dish in the air fryer and add the potato.
3. Brush with oil over entire surface and season with onion powder, salt, and pepper.
4. Close the air fryer and cook for 35 minutes at 350°F.
5. Once cooked, slice through the potato and serve with cream cheese and chives.

Green Beans
Servings: 4 | Cooking Time: 12 Minutes
- 1 pound fresh green beans
- 2 tablespoons Italian salad dressing
- salt and pepper

1. Wash beans and snap off stem ends.
2. In a large bowl, toss beans with Italian dressing.
3. Cook at 330°F for 5minutes. Shake basket or stir and cook 5minutes longer. Shake basket again and, if needed, continue cooking for 2 minutes, until as tender as you like. Beans should shrivel slightly and brown in places.
4. Sprinkle with salt and pepper to taste.

Parmesan Artichoke Hearts
Servings:4 | Cooking Time: 15 Minutes
- 1 egg
- ¼ Parmesan cheese, grated
- 1 tsp garlic powder
- ¼ cup flour
- ⅓ cup panko breadcrumbs
- Salt and black pepper to taste

1. Preheat the Air fryer to 390 F. Grease the air fryer basket with cooking spray.
2. Pat dry the artichokes with paper towels and cut them into wedges. In a bowl, whisk the egg white with salt. In another bowl, combine Parmesan cheese, breadcrumbs, and garlic powder. In a third pour the flour; mix with salt and pepper.
3. Dip the artichokes in the flour, followed by a dip in the egg, and finally coat with breadcrumb mixture. Place in your air fryer's cooking basket and cook for 10 minutes, flipping once. Let cool before serving.

Balsamic Garlic Kale
Servings: 6 | Cooking Time: 12 Minutes
- 2 tablespoons olive oil
- 3 garlic cloves, minced
- 2 and ½ pounds kale leaves
- Salt and black pepper to the taste
- 2 tablespoons balsamic vinegar

1. In a pan that fits the air fryer, combine all the ingredients and toss. Put the pan in your air fryer and cook at 300 degrees F for 12 minutes. Divide between plates and serve.

Garlicky Chips With Herbs
Servings:2 | Cooking Time: 60 Minutes
- 2 tbsp olive oil
- 3 garlic cloves, crushed
- 1 tsp each of fresh rosemary, thyme, oregano, chopped
- Salt and black pepper to taste

1. In a bowl, mix oil, garlic, herbs, salt and pepper. Arrange potatoes in the air fryer's basket and cook for 14 minutes at 360 F, shaking it every 4-5 minutes.

Turmeric Kale Mix

Servings: 2 | Cooking Time: 12 Minutes

- 3 tablespoons butter, melted
- 2 cups kale leaves
- Salt and black pepper to taste
- ½ cup yellow onion, chopped
- 2 teaspoons turmeric powder

1. Place all ingredients in a pan that fits your air fryer and mix well.
2. Put the pan in the fryer and cook at 250 degrees F for 12 minutes.
3. Divide between plates and serve.

Collard Greens And Bacon Recipe

Servings: 4 | Cooking Time: 22 Minutes

- 1 lb. collard greens
- 1 tbsp. apple cider vinegar
- 2 tbsp. chicken stock
- 3 bacon strips; chopped
- 1/4 cup cherry tomatoes; halved
- Salt and black pepper to the taste

1. Heat up a pan that fits your air fryer over medium heat, add bacon; stir and cook 1-2 minutes
2. Add tomatoes, collard greens, vinegar, stock, salt and pepper; stir, introduce in your air fryer and cook at 320 °F, for 10 minutes. Divide among plates and serve

Parmesan Crusted Pickles

Servings: 4 | Cooking Time: 35 Minutes

- 2 eggs
- 2 tsp water
- 1 cup grated Parmesan cheese
- 1 ½ cups breadcrumbs, smooth
- Black pepper to taste

1. Add breadcrumbs and pepper to a bowl and mix well. In another bowl, beat eggs with water. Add cheese to a separate bowl. Spray fryer basket and spray with cooking spray.
2. Preheat the air fryer to 400 F. Dredge the pickle slices in the egg mixture, then in breadcrumbs and then in cheese. Place them in the fryer. Cook for 4 minutes. Turn and cook for further for 5 minutes.

Mouth-watering Salami Sticks

Servings: 3 | Cooking Time: 10 Minutes

- 3 tbsp sugar
- A pinch garlic powder
- A pinch chili powder
- Salt to taste
- 1 tsp liquid smoke

1. Place the meat, sugar, garlic powder, chili powder, salt and liquid smoke in a bowl. Mix with a spoon. Mold out 4 sticks with your hands, place them on a plate, and refrigerate for 2 hours. Cook at 350 F. for 10 minutes, flipping once halfway through.

Rosemary Roasted Potatoes With Lemon

Servings: 4 | Cooking Time: 12 Minutes

- 1 pound small red-skinned potatoes, halved or cut into bite-sized chunks
- 1 tablespoon olive oil
- 1 teaspoon finely chopped fresh rosemary
- ¼ teaspoon salt
- freshly ground black pepper
- 1 tablespoon lemon zest

1. Preheat the air fryer to 400°F.
2. Toss the potatoes with the olive oil, rosemary, salt and freshly ground black pepper.
3. Air-fry for 12 minutes (depending on the size of the chunks), tossing the potatoes a few times throughout the cooking process.
4. As soon as the potatoes are tender to a knifepoint, toss them with the lemon zest and more salt if desired.

Ghee Lemony Endives

Servings: 4 | Cooking Time: 15 Minutes

- 3 tablespoons ghee, melted
- 12 endives, trimmed
- A pinch of salt and black pepper
- 1 tablespoon lemon juice

1. In a bowl, mix the endives with the ghee, salt, pepper and lemon juice and toss. Put the endives in the fryer's basket and cook at 350 degrees F for 15 minutes. Divide between plates and serve.

Balsamic And Garlic Cabbage Mix

Servings: 4 | Cooking Time: 15 Minutes

- 4 garlic cloves, minced
- 1 tablespoon olive oil
- 6 cups red cabbage, shredded
- 1 tablespoon balsamic vinegar
- Salt and black pepper to the taste

1. In a pan that fits the air fryer, combine all the ingredients, toss, introduce the pan in the air fryer and cook at 380 degrees F for 15 minutes. Divide between plates and serve as a side dish.

Tender Eggplant Fries

Servings: 2 | Cooking Time: 20 Minutes

- 1 tsp olive oil
- 1 tsp soy sauce
- Salt to taste

1. Preheat your air fryer to 400 F. Make a marinade of 1 tsp oil, soy sauce and salt. Mix well. Add in the eggplant slices and let stand for 5 minutes. Place the prepared eggplant slices in your air fryer's cooking basket and cook for 5 minutes. Serve with a drizzle of maple syrup.

Air-fried Cheesy Broccoli With Garlic

Servings: 2 | Cooking Time: 25 Minutes

- 1 egg white
- 1 garlic clove, grated
- Salt and black pepper to taste
- ½ lb broccoli florets
- ⅓ cup grated Parmesan cheese

1. In a bowl, whisk together the butter, egg, garlic, salt, and black pepper. Toss in broccoli to coat well. Top with Parmesan cheese and; toss to coat. Arrange broccoli in a single layer in the air fryer, without overcrowding. Cook for 10 minutes at 360 F. Remove to a plate and sprinkle with Parmesan cheese.

Roasted Belgian Endive With Pistachios And Lemon
Servings: 2 | Cooking Time: 7 Minutes
- 2 Medium 3-ounce Belgian endive head(s)
- 2 tablespoons Olive oil
- ½ teaspoon Table salt
- ¼ cup Finely chopped unsalted shelled pistachios
- Up to 2 teaspoons Lemon juice

1. Preheat the air fryer to 325°F (or 330°F, if that's the closest setting).
2. Trim the Belgian endive head(s), removing the little bit of dried-out stem end but keeping the leaves intact. Quarter the head(s) through the stem (which will hold the leaves intact). Brush the endive quarters with oil, getting it down between the leaves. Sprinkle the quarters with salt.
3. When the machine is at temperature, set the endive quarters cut sides up in the basket with as much air space between them as possible. They should not touch. Air-fry undisturbed for 7 minutes, or until lightly browned along the edges.
4. Use kitchen tongs to transfer the endive quarters to serving plates or a platter. Sprinkle with the pistachios and lemon juice. Serve warm or at room temperature.

Roasted Almond Delight
Servings: 12 | Cooking Time: 20 Minutes
- 3 tbsp liquid smoke
- 2 tsp salt
- 2 tbsp molasses

1. Preheat your air fryer to 360 F. In a bowl, add salt, liquid, molasses, and cashews; toss to coat. Place in your air fryer's cooking basket and cook for 10 minutes, shaking the basket every 5 minutes.

Calamari With Olives
Servings: 3 | Cooking Time: 25 Minutes
- ½ piece cilantro, chopped
- 2 strips chili pepper, chopped
- 1 tbsp olive oil
- 1 cup pimiento-stuffed green olives, sliced
- Salt and black pepper to taste

1. In a bowl, add rings, chili pepper, salt, pepper, oil, and cilantor. Marinate for 10 minutes. Pour the calamari into a baking dish. Place in the fryer basket and cook for 15 minutes stirring every 5 minutes at 400 F. Serve warm with olives.

Zesty Salmon Jerky
Servings: 2 | Cooking Time: 6 Hours
- 1 lb. boneless skinless salmon
- ½ tsp. ground ginger
- ¼ tsp. red pepper flakes
- ½ tsp. liquid smoke
- ¼ cup soy sauce

1. Cut the salmon into strips about four inches long and a quarter-inch thick.
2. Put the salmon in an airtight container or bag along with the liquid smoke, ginger, soy sauce, and red pepper flakes, combining everything to coat the salmon completely. Leave the salmon in the refrigerator for at least two hours.
3. Transfer the salmon slices in the fryer, taking care not to overlap any pieces. This step may need to be completed in multiple batches.
4. Cook at 140°F for four hours.
5. Take care when removing the salmon from the fryer and leave it to cool. This jerky makes a good snack and can be stored in an airtight container.

Flatbread
Servings: 1 | Cooking Time: 20 Minutes
- 1 cup mozzarella cheese, shredded
- ¼ cup blanched finely ground flour
- 1 oz. full-fat cream cheese, softened

1. Microwave the mozzarella for half a minute until melted. Combine with the flour to achieve a smooth consistency, before adding the cream cheese. Keep mixing to create a dough, microwaving the mixture again if the cheese begins to harden.
2. Divide the dough into two equal pieces. Between two sheets of parchment paper, roll out the dough until it is about a quarter-inch thick. Cover the bottom of your fryer with another sheet of parchment.
3. Transfer the dough into the fryer and cook at 320°F for seven minutes. You may need to complete this step in two batches. Make sure to turn the flatbread halfway through cooking. Take care when removing it from the fryer and serve warm.

Super Cabbage Canapes
Servings: 2 | Cooking Time: 15 Minutes
- 1 cube Amul cheese
- ½ carrot, cubed
- ¼ onion, cubed
- ¼ capsicum, cubed
- Fresh basil to garnish

1. Preheat your air fryer to 360 F. Using a bowl, mix onion, carrot, capsicum and cheese. Toss to coat everything evenly. Add cabbage rounds to the air fryer's cooking basket. Top with the veggie mixture and cook for 5 minutes. Serve with a garnish of fresh basil.

Cauliflower Tots
Servings: 8 | Cooking Time: 20 Minutes
- 1 large head cauliflower
- ½ cup parmesan cheese, grated
- 1 cup mozzarella cheese, shredded
- 1 tsp. seasoned salt
- 1 egg

1. Place a steamer basket over a pot of boiling water, ensuring the water is not high enough to enter the basket.
2. Cut up the cauliflower into florets and transfer to the steamer basket. Cover the pot with a lid and leave to steam for seven minutes, making sure the cauliflower softens.
3. Place the florets on a cheesecloth and leave to cool. Remove as much moisture as possible. This is crucial as it ensures the cauliflower will harden.
4. In a bowl, break up the cauliflower with a fork.
5. Stir in the parmesan, mozzarella, seasoned salt, and egg, incorporating the cauliflower well with all of the other ingredients. Make sure the mixture is firm enough to be moldable.
6. Using your hand, mold about two tablespoons of the mixture into tots and repeat until you have used up all of the mixture. Put each tot into your air fryer basket. They may need to be cooked in multiple batches.
7. Cook at 320°F for twelve minutes, turning them halfway through. Ensure they are brown in color before serving.

Basic Pepper French Fries

Servings: 4 | Cooking Time: 33 Minutes

- 1 teaspoon fine sea salt
- 1/2 teaspoon freshly ground black pepper
- 2 ½ tablespoons canola oil
- 6 Russet potatoes, cut them into fries
- 1/2 teaspoon crushed red pepper flakes

1. Start by preheating your air fryer to 340 degrees F.
2. Place the fries in your air fryer and toss them with the oil. Add the seasonings and toss again.
3. Cook for 30 minutes, shaking your fries several times. Taste for doneness and eat warm.

Cabbage Slaw

Servings: 4 | Cooking Time: 20 Minutes

- 1 green cabbage head, shredded
- Juice of ½ lemon
- A pinch of salt and black pepper
- ½ cup coconut cream
- ½ teaspoon fennel seeds
- 1 tablespoon mustard

1. In a pan that fits the air fryer, combine the cabbage with the rest of the ingredients, toss, introduce the pan in the machine and cook at 350 degrees F for 20 minutes. Divide between plates and serve right away as a side dish.

Basil Squash

Servings: 4 | Cooking Time: 10 Minutes

- 1 teaspoon sesame oil
- 1 teaspoon dried basil
- 6 oz Kabocha squash, roughly chopped

1. Sprinkle the squash with dried basil and sesame oil and place it in the air fryer basket. Cook the vegetables at 400F for 4 minutes. Then shake them well and cook for 6 minutes more. The time of cooking depends on kabocha squash size.

Cheddar-garlic Drop Biscuits

Servings: 10 | Cooking Time: 10 Minutes Per Batch

- 2 cups all-purpose flour
- 1 tablespoon baking powder
- 1 teaspoon salt
- ½ teaspoon garlic powder
- ¾ cup sour cream
- ¾ cup salted butter, melted, divided
- 1 cup shredded Cheddar cheese

1. Preheat the air fryer to 400°F.
2. In a large bowl, mix flour, baking powder, salt, garlic powder, sour cream, and ½ cup butter until well combined. Gently stir in Cheddar.
3. Using your hands, form dough into ten even-sized balls.
4. Place balls in the air fryer basket, working in batches as necessary. Cook 10 minutes until golden and crispy on the edges.
5. Remove biscuits from the air fryer and brush with remaining ¼ cup melted butter to serve.

Green Peas With Mint

Servings: 4 | Cooking Time: 5 Minutes

- 1 cup shredded lettuce
- 1 10-ounce package frozen green peas, thawed
- 1 tablespoon fresh mint, shredded
- 1 teaspoon melted butter

1. Lay the shredded lettuce in the air fryer basket.
2. Toss together the peas, mint, and melted butter and spoon over the lettuce.
3. Cook at 360°F for 5 minutes, until peas are warm and lettuce wilts.

Green Beans And Tomatoes Recipe

Servings: 4 | Cooking Time: 25 Minutes

- 1-pint cherry tomatoes
- 2 tbsp. olive oil
- 1 lb. green beans
- Salt and black pepper to the taste

1. In a bowl; mix cherry tomatoes with green beans, olive oil, salt and pepper, toss, transfer to your air fryer and cook at 400 °F, for 15 minutes. Divide among plates and serve right away

Super-crispy Asparagus Fries

Servings: 4 | Cooking Time: 20 Minutes

- 2 eggs
- 1 teaspoon Dijon mustard
- 1 cup Parmesan cheese, grated
- Sea salt and ground black pepper, to taste
- 18 asparagus spears, trimmed
- 1/2 cup sour cream

1. Start by preheating your Air Fryer to 400 degrees F.
2. In a shallow bowl, whisk the eggs and mustard. In another shallow bowl, combine the Parmesan cheese, salt, and black pepper.
3. Dip the asparagus spears in the egg mixture, then in the parmesan mixture; press to adhere.
4. Cook for 5 minutes; work in three batches. Serve with sour cream on the side. Enjoy!

Vegan & Vegetarian Recipes

Hearty Carrots

Servings: 4 | Cooking Time: 25 Minutes

- 2 shallots, chopped
- 3 carrots, sliced
- Salt to taste
- ¼ cup yogurt
- 2 garlic cloves, minced
- 3 tbsp parsley, chopped

1. Preheat air fryer to 370 F. In a bowl, mix carrots, salt, garlic, shallots, parsley and yogurt. Sprinkle with oil. Place the veggies in air fryer basket and cook for 15 minutes. Serve with basil and garlic mayo.

Garlic-roasted Brussels Sprouts With Mustard

Servings: 3 | Cooking Time: 20 Minutes

- 1 pound Brussels sprouts, halved
- 2 tablespoons olive oil
- Sea salt and freshly ground black pepper, to taste
- 2 garlic cloves, minced
- 1 tablespoon Dijon mustard

1. Toss the Brussels sprouts with the olive oil, salt, black pepper, and garlic.
2. Roast in the preheated Air Fryer at 380 degrees F for 15 minutes, shaking the basket occasionally.
3. Serve with Dijon mustard and enjoy!

Curried Cauliflower Florets

Servings: 4 | Cooking Time: 34 Minutes

- Salt to taste
- 1 ½ tbsp curry powder
- ½ cup olive oil
- ⅓ cup fried pine nuts

1. Preheat the air fryer to 390 F, and mix the pine nuts and 1 tsp of olive oil, in a medium bowl. Pour them in the air fryer's basket and cook for 2 minutes; remove to cool.
2. Place the cauliflower on a cutting board. Use a knife to cut them into 1-inch florets. Place them in a large mixing bowl. Add the curry powder, salt, and the remaining olive oil; mix well. Place the cauliflower florets in the fryer's basket in 2 batches, and cook each batch for 10 minutes. Remove the curried florets onto a serving platter, sprinkle with the pine nuts, and toss. Serve the florets with tomato sauce or as a side to a meat dish.

Potato, Eggplant, And Zucchini Chips

Servings: 4 | Cooking Time: 45 Minutes

- 5 potatoes, cut into strips
- ½ cup cornstarch
- ½ cup olive oil
- 3 zucchinis, cut into strips
- ½ cup water
- Salt to season

1. Preheat air fryer to 390 F. In a bowl, stir in cornstarch, water, salt, pepper, oil, eggplants, zucchini, and potatoes. Place one-third of the veggie strips in the fryer's basket and cook them for 12 minutes, shaking once. Once ready, transfer them to a serving platter. Serve warm.

Traditional Jacket Potatoes

Servings: 4 | Cooking Time: 30 Minutes

- 2 garlic cloves, minced
- Salt and pepper to taste
- 1 tsp rosemary
- 1 tsp butter

1. Wash the potatoes thoroughly under water. Preheat your air fryer to 360 F, and prick the potatoes with a fork. Place them into your air fryer's cooking basket and cook for 25 minutes. Cut the potatoes in half and top with butter and rosemary; season with salt and pepper. Serve immediately.

Sweet And Spicy Barbecue Tofu

Servings: 4 | Cooking Time: 1 Hour 15 Minutes

- 1 package extra-firm tofu, drained
- ½ cup barbecue sauce
- ½ cup brown sugar
- 1 teaspoon liquid smoke
- 1 teaspoon crushed red pepper flakes
- ½ teaspoon salt

1. Press tofu block to remove excess moisture. If you don't have a tofu press, line a baking sheet with paper towels and set tofu on top. Set a second baking sheet on top of tofu and weight it with a heavy item such as a skillet. Let tofu sit at least 30 minutes, changing paper towels if necessary.
2. Cut pressed tofu into twenty-four equal pieces. Set aside.
3. In a large bowl, combine barbecue sauce, brown sugar, liquid smoke, red pepper flakes, and salt. Mix well and add tofu, coating completely. Cover and let marinate at least 30 minutes on the counter.
4. Preheat the air fryer to 400°F.
5. Spray the air fryer basket with cooking spray and add marinated tofu. Cook 15 minutes, shaking the basket twice during cooking.
6. Let cool 10 minutes before serving warm.

Cinnamon Sugar Tortilla Chips

Servings: 4 | Cooking Time: 20 Minutes

- 4 (10-inch) flour tortillas
- 1/4 cup vegan margarine, melted
- 1 ½ tablespoons ground cinnamon
- 1/4 cup caster sugar

1. Slice each tortilla into eight slices. Brush the tortilla pieces with the melted margarine.
2. In a mixing bowl, thoroughly combine the cinnamon and sugar. Toss the cinnamon mixture with the tortillas.
3. Transfer to the cooking basket and cook at 360 degrees F for 8 minutes or until lightly golden. Work in batches.
4. They will crisp up as they cool. Serve and enjoy!

Roasted Cauliflower

Servings: 2 | Cooking Time: 20 Minutes

- medium head cauliflower
- 2 tbsp. salted butter, melted
- 1 medium lemon
- 1 tsp. dried parsley
- ½ tsp. garlic powder

1. Having removed the leaves from the cauliflower head, brush it with the melted butter. Grate the rind of the lemon over it and then drizzle some juice. Finally add the parsley and garlic powder on top.
2. Transfer the cauliflower to the basket of the fryer.
3. Cook for fifteen minutes at 350°F, checking regularly to ensure it doesn't overcook. The cauliflower is ready when it is hot and fork tender.
4. Take care when removing it from the fryer, cut up and serve.

Cottage Cheese And Potatoes

Servings:5 | Cooking Time: 30 Minutes

- 1 bunch asparagus, trimmed
- ¼ cup fresh cream
- ¼ cup cottage cheese, cubed
- 1 tbsp whole-grain mustard

1. Preheat the air fryer to 400 F and place the potatoes in the basket; cook for 25 minutes. Boil salted water in a pot over medium heat. Add asparagus and cook for 3 minutes until tender.
2. In a bowl, mix cooked potatoes, cottage cheese, cream, asparagus and mustard. Toss well and season with salt and black pepper. Transfer the mixture to the potato skin shells and serve.

Pineapple Appetizer Ribs

Servings:4 | Cooking Time: 30 Minutes

- 7 oz salad dressing
- 5 oz can pineapple juice
- 2 cups water
- garlic salt
- salt and black pepper

1. Sprinkle the ribs with salt and pepper, and place them in a saucepan. Pour water and cook the ribs for 12 minutes on high heat. Drain the ribs and arrange them in the fryer; sprinkle with garlic salt. Cook for 15 minutes at 390 F. Prepare the sauce by combining the salad dressing and the pineapple juice. Serve the ribs drizzled with the sauce.

Easy Roast Winter Vegetable Delight

Servings:2 | Cooking Time: 30 Minutes

- 1 cup chopped butternut squash
- 2 small red onions, cut in wedges
- 1 cup chopped celery
- 1 tbsp chopped fresh thyme
- Salt and pepper to taste
- 2 tsp olive oil

1. Preheat the air fryer to 200 F, and in a bowl, add turnip, squash, red onions, celery, thyme, pepper, salt, and olive oil; mix well. Pour the vegetables into the fryer's basket and cook for 16 minutes, tossing once halfway through.

Parsley-loaded Mushrooms

Servings:2 | Cooking Time: 15 Minutes

- 2 slices white bread
- 1 garlic clove, crushed
- 2 tsp olive oil
- 2 tbsp parsley, finely chopped
- salt and black pepper

1. Preheat air fryer to 360 F. In a food processor, grind the bread into crumbs. Add garlic, parsley and pepper; mix and stir in the olive oil. Cut off the mushroom stalks and fill the caps with the breadcrumbs. Place the mushroom caps in the air fryer basket Cook for 10 minutes or until golden and crispy.

Brussels Sprouts With Balsamic Oil

Servings:4 | Cooking Time: 15 Minutes

- ¼ teaspoon salt
- 1 tablespoon balsamic vinegar
- 2 cups Brussels sprouts, halved
- 2 tablespoons olive oil

1. Preheat the air fryer for 5 minutes.
2. Mix all ingredients in a bowl until the zucchini fries are well coated.
3. Place in the air fryer basket.
4. Close and cook for 15 minutes for 3500F.

Breadcrumbs Stuffed Mushrooms

Servings:4 | Cooking Time:10 Minutes

- 1½ spelt bread slices
- 1 tablespoon flat-leaf parsley, finely chopped
- 16 small button mushrooms, stemmed and gills removed
- 1½ tablespoons olive oil
- 1 garlic clove, crushed
- Salt and black pepper, to taste

1. Preheat the Air fryer to 390 o F and grease an Air fryer basket.
2. Put the bread slices in a food processor and pulse until fine crumbs form.
3. Transfer the crumbs into a bowl and stir in the olive oil, garlic, parsley, salt, and black pepper.
4. Stuff the breadcrumbs mixture in each mushroom cap and arrange the mushrooms in the Air fryer basket.
5. Cook for about 10 minutes and dish out in a bowl to serve warm.

Air Fried Halloumi With Veggies

Servings:2 | Cooking Time: 15 Minutes

- 2 zucchinis, cut into even chunks
- 1 large carrot, cut into chunks
- 1 large eggplant, peeled, cut into chunks
- 2 tsp olive oil
- 1 tsp dried mixed herbs
- Salt and black pepper

1. In a bowl, add halloumi, zucchini, carrot, eggplant, olive oil, herbs, salt and pepper. Sprinkle with oil, salt and pepper. Arrange halloumi and veggies on the air fryer basket and drizzle with olive oil. Cook for 14 minutes at 340 F, shaking once. Sprinkle with mixed herbs to serve.

Spinach And Feta Pinwheels
Servings:4 | Cooking Time: 15 Minutes
- 1 sheet frozen puff pastry, thawed
- 3 ounces full-fat cream cheese, softened
- 1 bag frozen spinach, thawed and drained
- ¼ teaspoon salt
- ⅓ cup crumbled feta cheese
- 1 large egg, whisked

1. Preheat the air fryer to 320°F. Unroll puff pastry into a flat rectangle.
2. In a medium bowl, mix cream cheese, spinach, and salt until well combined.
3. Spoon cream cheese mixture onto pastry in an even layer, leaving a ½" border around the edges.
4. Sprinkle feta evenly across dough and gently press into filling to secure. Roll lengthwise to form a log shape.
5. Cut the roll into twelve 1" pieces. Brush with egg. Place in the air fryer basket and cook 15 minutes, turning halfway through cooking time.
6. Let cool 5 minutes before serving.

Easy Crispy Shawarma Chickpeas
Servings: 4 | Cooking Time: 25 Minutes
- 1 (12-ounce) can chickpeas, drained and rinsed
- 2 tablespoons canola oil
- 1 teaspoon cayenne pepper
- 1 teaspoon sea salt
- 1 tablespoon Shawarma spice blend

1. Toss all ingredients in a mixing bowl.
2. Roast in the preheated Air Fryer at 380 degrees F for 10 minutes, shaking the basket halfway through the cooking time.
3. Work in batches. Bon appétit!

Spicy Celery Sticks
Servings: 4 | Cooking Time: 20 Minutes
- 1 pound celery, cut into matchsticks
- 2 tablespoons peanut oil
- 1 jalapeño, seeded and minced
- 1/4 teaspoon dill
- 1/2 teaspoon basil
- Salt and white pepper to taste

1. Start by preheating your Air Fryer to 380 degrees F.
2. Toss all ingredients together and place them in the Air Fryer basket.
3. Cook for 15 minutes, shaking the basket halfway through the cooking time. Transfer to a serving platter and enjoy!

Caprese Eggplant Stacks
Servings:4 | Cooking Time: 8 Minutes
- 1 medium eggplant, cut into 4 (½") slices
- ½ teaspoon salt
- ¼ teaspoon ground black pepper
- 4 (¼") slices tomato
- 2 ounces fresh mozzarella cheese, cut into 4 slices
- 1 tablespoon olive oil
- ¼ cup fresh basil, sliced

1. Preheat the air fryer to 320°F.
2. In a 6" round pan, place eggplant slices. Sprinkle with salt and pepper. Top each with a tomato slice, then a mozzarella slice, and drizzle with oil.
3. Place in the air fryer basket and cook 8 minutes until eggplant is tender and cheese is melted. Garnish with fresh basil to serve.

Baked Green Beans
Servings:6 | Cooking Time: 20 Minutes
- 2 whole eggs, beaten
- ½ cup Parmesan cheese, grated
- ½ cup flour
- 1 tsp cayenne pepper
- 1 ½ pounds green beans
- Salt to taste

1. Preheat your air fryer to 400 F, and in a bowl, mix panko, Parmesan cheese, cayenne pepper, season with salt and pepper. Cover the green beans in flour and dip in eggs.
2. Dredge beans in the Parmesan-panko mix. Place the prepared beans in your air fryer's cooking basket and cook for 15 minutes. Serve

Bell Peppers Cups
Servings:4 | Cooking Time:8 Minutes
- 8 mini red bell peppers, tops and seeds removed
- 1 teaspoon fresh parsley, chopped
- ¾ cup feta cheese, crumbled
- ½ tablespoon olive oil
- Freshly ground black pepper, to taste

1. Preheat the Air fryer to 390 o F and grease an Air fryer basket.
2. Mix feta cheese, parsley, olive oil and black pepper in a bowl.
3. Stuff the bell peppers with feta cheese mixture and arrange in the Air fryer basket.
4. Cook for about 8 minutes and dish out to serve hot.

Spinach & Feta Crescent Triangles
Servings:4 | Cooking Time: 20 Minutes
- 1 cup steamed spinach
- 1 cup crumbled feta cheese
- ¼ tsp garlic powder
- 1 tsp chopped oregano
- ¼ tsp salt

1. Preheat the air fryer to 350 F, and roll the dough onto a lightly floured flat surface. Combine the feta, spinach, oregano, salt, and garlic powder together in a bowl. Cut the dough into 4 equal pieces.
2. Divide the spinach/feta mixture between the dough pieces. Fold the dough and secure with a fork. Place onto a lined baking dish, and then in the air fryer. Cook for 12 minutes, until lightly browned.

Classic Baked Banana
Servings: 2 | Cooking Time: 20 Minutes
- 2 just-ripe bananas
- 2 teaspoons lime juice
- 2 tablespoons honey
- 1/4 teaspoon grated nutmeg
- 1/2 teaspoon ground cinnamon
- A pinch of salt

1. Toss the banana with all ingredients until well coated. Transfer your bananas to the parchment-lined cooking basket.
2. Bake in the preheated Air Fryer at 370 degrees F for 12 minutes, turning them over halfway through the cooking time. Enjoy!

Family Favorite Potatoes

Servings:4 | Cooking Time:20 Minutes

- 1¾ pound waxy potatoes, cubed and boiled
- ½ cup Greek plain yoghurt
- 2 tablespoons olive oil, divided
- 1 tablespoon paprika, divided
- Salt and black pepper, to taste

1. Preheat the Air fryer to 355 o F and grease an Air fryer basket.
2. Mix 1 tablespoon olive oil, 1/3 tablespoon of paprika and black pepper in a bowl and toss to coat well.
3. Transfer into the Air fryer basket and cook for about 20 minutes.
4. Mix yogurt, remaining oil, salt and black pepper in a bowl and serve with potatoes.

Cool Mini Zucchini's

Servings:4 | Cooking Time: 25 Minutes

- 4 large eggs, beaten
- 1 medium zucchini, sliced
- 4 ounces feta cheese, drained and crumbled
- 2 tbsp fresh dill, chopped
- Cooking spray
- Salt and pepper as needed

1. Preheat the air fryer to 360 F, and un a bowl, add the beaten eggs and season with salt and pepper.
2. Stir in zucchini, dill and feta cheese. Grease 8 muffin tins with cooking spray. Roll pastry and arrange them to cover the sides of the muffin tins. Divide the egg mixture evenly between the holes. Place the prepared tins in your air fryer and cook for 15 minutes. Serve and enjoy!

Layered Ravioli Bake

Servings:4 | Cooking Time: 20 Minutes

- 2 cups marinara sauce, divided
- 2 packages fresh cheese ravioli
- 12 slices provolone cheese
- ½ cup Italian bread crumbs
- ½ cup grated vegetarian Parmesan cheese

1. Preheat the air fryer to 350°F.
2. In the bottom of a 3-quart baking pan, spread ⅓ cup marinara. Place 6 ravioli on top of the sauce, then add 3 slices provolone on top, then another layer of ⅓ cup marinara. Repeat these layers three times to use up remaining ravioli, provolone, and sauce.
3. In a small bowl, mix bread crumbs and Parmesan. Sprinkle over the top of dish.
4. Cover pan with foil, being sure to tuck foil under the bottom of the pan to ensure the air fryer fan does not blow it off. Place pan in the air fryer basket and cook 15 minutes.
5. Remove foil and cook an additional 5 minutes until the top is brown and bubbling. Serve warm.

Zucchini Gratin

Servings: 2 | Cooking Time: 15 Minutes

- 5 oz. parmesan cheese, shredded
- 1 tbsp. coconut flour
- 1 tbsp. dried parsley
- 2 zucchinis
- 1 tsp. butter, melted

1. Mix the parmesan and coconut flour together in a bowl, seasoning with parsley to taste.
2. Cut the zucchini in half lengthwise and chop the halves into four slices.
3. Pre-heat the fryer at 400°F.
4. Pour the melted butter over the zucchini and then dip the zucchini into the parmesan-flour mixture, coating it all over. Cook the zucchini in the fryer for thirteen minutes.

Swiss Cheese And Eggplant Crisps

Servings: 4 | Cooking Time: 45 Minutes

- 1/2 pound eggplant, sliced
- 1/4 cup almond meal
- 2 tablespoons flaxseed meal
- Coarse sea salt and ground black pepper, to taste
- 1 teaspoon paprika
- 1 cup parmesan, freshly grated

1. Toss the eggplant with 1 tablespoon of salt and let it stand for 30 minutes. Drain and rinse well.
2. Mix the almond meal, flaxseed meal, salt, black pepper, and paprika in a bowl. Then, pour in the water and whisk to combine well.
3. Then, place parmesan in another shallow bowl.
4. Dip the eggplant slices in the almond meal mixture, then in parmesan; press to coat on all sides. Transfer to the lightly greased Air Fryer basket.
5. Cook at 370 degrees F for 6 minutes. Turn each slice over and cook an additional 5 minutes.
6. Serve garnished with spicy ketchup if desired. Bon appétit!

Salted Beet Chips

Servings:2 | Cooking Time:6 Minutes

- 1 tablespoon cooking oil
- 1-pound beets, peeled and sliced
- Salt and pepper to taste

1. Place all Ingredients in a bowl and toss to coat everything.
2. Place the sliced beets in the double layer rack.
3. Place the rack with the beets in the air fryer.
4. Close the air fryer and cook for 6 minutes at 3900F.

Healthy Avocado Fries

Servings:2 | Cooking Time: 20 Minutes

- Salt as needed
- 1 avocado, cubed
- ¼ cup aquafaba

1. In a bowl, mix crumbs, aquafaba and salt. Preheat your air fryer to 390 F, and roll the avocado cubes in the crumbs mixture to coat evenly. Place the prepared cubes in your air fryer's cooking basket and cook for 10 minutes.

Corn Cakes

Servings:8 | Cooking Time: 25 Minutes

- 2 eggs, lightly beaten
- ⅓ cup finely chopped green onions
- ¼ cup roughly chopped parsley
- 1 cup flour
- ½ tsp baking powder
- Salt and black pepper

1. In a bowl, add corn, eggs, parsley and green onions, and season with salt and pepper; mix well to combine. Sift flour and baking

powder into the bowl and stir. Line the air fryer's basket with baking paper and spoon batter dollops, making sure they are separated by at least an inch. Cook for 10 minutes at 400 F, turning once halfway through. Serve with sour cream.

Broccoli Salad
Servings: 2 | Cooking Time: 15 Minutes
- 3 cups fresh broccoli florets
- 2 tbsp. coconut oil, melted
- ¼ cup sliced s
- ½ medium lemon, juiced

1. Take a six-inch baking dish and fill with the broccoli florets. Pour the melted coconut oil over the broccoli and add in the sliced s. Toss together. Put the dish in the air fryer.
2. Cook at 380°F for seven minutes, stirring at the halfway point.
3. Place the broccoli in a bowl and drizzle the lemon juice over it.

Caribbean-style Fried Plantains
Servings: 2 | Cooking Time: 20 Minutes
- 2 plantains, peeled and cut into slices
- 2 tablespoons avocado oil
- 2 teaspoons Caribbean Sorrel Rum Spice Mix

1. Toss the plantains with the avocado oil and spice mix.
2. Cook in the preheated Air Fryer at 400 degrees F for 10 minutes, shaking the cooking basket halfway through the cooking time.
3. Adjust the seasonings to taste and enjoy!

Rosemary Olive-oil Over Shrooms N Asparagus
Servings:6 | Cooking Time: 15 Minutes
- ½ pound fresh mushroom, quartered
- 1 bunch fresh asparagus, trimmed and cleaned
- 2 sprigs of fresh rosemary, minced
- 2 teaspoon olive oil
- salt and pepper to taste

1. Preheat the air fryer to 4000F.
2. Place the asparagus and mushrooms in a bowl and pour the rest of the ingredients.
3. Toss to coat the asparagus and mushrooms.
4. Place inside the air fryer and cook for 15 minutes.

Stuffed Mushrooms With Bacon & Cheese
Servings:4 | Cooking Time: 20 Minutes
- 1 clove garlic, minced
- alt and pepper to taste
- 4 slices bacon, chopped
- ¼ cup grated Cheddar cheese
- 1 tbsp olive oil
- 1 tbsp chopped parsley

1. Preheat air fryer to 390 F. In a bowl, add oil, bacon, cheddar cheese, parsley, salt, pepper, and garlic. Mix well with a spoon. Cut the stalks of the mushroom off and fill each cup with the bacon mixture.
2. Press the bacon mixture into the caps. Place the stuffed mushrooms in the fryer's basket and cook at 390 F for 8 minutes. Once golden and crispy, plate them and serve with a green salad.

Spiced Up Potato Wedges
Servings:6 | Cooking Time: 30 Minutes
- 2 tbsp olive oil
- 2 tsp smoked paprika
- 2 tbsp sriracha hot chili sauce
- ½ cup Greek yogurt

1. Soak potatoes under cold water for 30 minutes; pat dry with a towel. Preheat your air fryer to 340 F, and coat potatoes with oil and paprika. Cook them for 20 minutes, shaking once halfway through. Remove to a paper to let them dry; season with salt and pepper. Serve with the yogurt and chili sauce.

Radish And Mozzarella Salad With Balsamic Vinaigrette
Servings:4 | Cooking Time:30 Minutes
- 1½ pounds radishes, trimmed and halved
- ½ pound fresh mozzarella, sliced
- Salt and freshly ground black pepper, to taste
- 3 tablespoons olive oil
- 1 teaspoon honey
- 1 tablespoon balsamic vinegar

1. Preheat the Air fryer to 350 o F and grease an Air fryer basket.
2. Mix radishes, salt, black pepper and 2 tablespoons of olive oil in a bowl and toss to coat well.
3. Arrange the radishes in the Air fryer basket and cook for about 30 minutes, flipping twice in between.
4. Dish out in a bowl and top with the remaining ingredients to serve.

Croissant Rolls
Servings:8 | Cooking Time: 6 Minutes
- 1 (8-ounces) can croissant rolls
- 4 tablespoons butter, melted

1. Set the temperature of air fryer to 320 degrees F. Grease an air fryer basket.
2. Arrange croissant rolls into the prepared air fryer basket.
3. Air fry for about 4 minutes.
4. Flip the side and air fry for 1-2 more minutes.
5. Remove from the air fryer and transfer onto a platter.
6. Drizzle with the melted butter and serve hot.

Crispy Marinated Tofu
Servings:3 | Cooking Time: 20 Minutes
- 1 (14-ounces) block firm tofu, pressed and cut into 1-inch cubes
- 2 tablespoons low sodium soy sauce
- 2 teaspoons sesame oil, toasted
- 1 teaspoon seasoned rice vinegar
- 1 tablespoon cornstarch

1. In a bowl, mix well tofu, soy sauce, sesame oil, and vinegar.
2. Set aside to marinate for about 25-30 minutes.
3. Coat the tofu cubes evenly with cornstarch.
4. Set the temperature of air fryer to 370 degrees F. Grease an air fryer basket.
5. Arrange tofu pieces into the prepared air fryer basket in a single layer.
6. Air fry for about 20 minutes, shaking once halfway through.
7. Remove from air fryer and transfer the tofu onto serving plates.
8. Serve warm.

Cottage And Mayonnaise Stuffed Peppers

Servings: 2 | Cooking Time: 20 Minutes

- 1 red bell pepper, top and seeds removed
- 1 yellow bell pepper, top and seeds removed
- Salt and pepper, to taste
- 1 cup Cottage cheese
- 4 tablespoons mayonnaise
- 2 pickles, chopped

1. Arrange the peppers in the lightly greased cooking basket. Cook in the preheated Air Fryer at 400 degrees F for 15 minutes, turning them over halfway through the cooking time.
2. Season with salt and pepper.
3. Then, in a mixing bowl, combine the cream cheese with the mayonnaise and chopped pickles. Stuff the pepper with the cream cheese mixture and serve. Enjoy!

Sweet And Spicy Parsnips

Servings:6 | Cooking Time:44 Minutes

- 2 pounds parsnip, peeled and cut into 1-inch chunks
- 1 tablespoon butter, melted
- 2 tablespoons honey
- 1 tablespoon dried parsley flakes, crushed
- ¼ teaspoon red pepper flakes, crushed
- Salt and ground black pepper, to taste

1. Preheat the Air fryer to 355 o F and grease an Air fryer basket.
2. Mix the parsnips and butter in a bowl and toss to coat well.
3. Arrange the parsnip chunks in the Air fryer basket and cook for about 40 minutes.
4. Mix the remaining ingredients in another large bowl and stir in the parsnip chunks.
5. Transfer the parsnip chunks in the Air fryer basket and cook for about 4 minutes.
6. Dish out the parsnip chunks onto serving plates and serve hot.

Cheesy Bbq Tater Tot

Servings:6 | Cooking Time: 20 Minutes

- ½ cup shredded Cheddar
- 12 slices bacon
- 1-lb frozen tater tots, defrosted
- 2 tbsp chives
- Ranch dressing, for serving

1. Thread one end of bacon in a skewer, followed by one tater, snuggly thread the bacon around tater like a snake, and then another tater, and then snake the bacon again until you reach the end. Repeat with the rest of the Ingredients.
2. For 10 minutes, cook on 360oF. Halfway through cooking time, turnover skewers. If needed cook in batches.
3. Place skewers on a serving platter and sprinkle cheese and chives on top.
4. Serve and enjoy with ranch dressing on the side.

Turmeric Crispy Chickpeas

Servings:4 | Cooking Time: 22 Minutes

- 1 tbsp butter, melted
- ¼ tsp turmeric
- ½ tsp dried rosemary
- Salt to taste

1. Preheat the Air fryer to 380 F.
2. In a bowl, combine together chickpeas, butter, rosemary, turmeric, and salt; toss to coat. Place the prepared chickpeas in your Air Fryer's cooking basket and cook for 6 minutes. Slide out the basket and shake; cook for another 6 minutes until crispy.

Cheesy Cauliflower Crust Pizza

Servings:2 | Cooking Time: 12 Minutes Per Batch

- 2 steamer bags cauliflower florets
- 1 large egg
- 1 cup grated vegetarian Parmesan cheese
- 3 cups shredded mozzarella cheese, divided
- 1 cup pizza sauce

1. Preheat the air fryer to 375°F. Cut two pieces of parchment paper to fit the air fryer basket, one for each crust.
2. Cook cauliflower in the microwave according to package instructions, then drain in a colander. Run under cold water until cool to the touch. Use a cheesecloth to squeeze the excess water from cauliflower, removing as much as possible.
3. In a food processor, combine cauliflower, egg, Parmesan, and 1 cup mozzarella. Process on low about 15 seconds until a sticky ball forms.
4. Separate dough into two pieces. Working with damp hands to prevent dough from sticking, press each dough ball into a 6" round.
5. Place crust on parchment in the air fryer basket, working in batches as necessary. Cook 6 minutes, then flip over with a spatula and top the crust with ½ cup pizza sauce and 1 cup mozzarella. Cook an additional 6 minutes until edges are dark brown and cheese is brown and bubbling. Let cool at least 5 minutes before serving. The crust firms up as it cools.

Scrumptiously Healthy Chips

Servings:2 | Cooking Time: 10 Minutes

- 1 bunch kale
- 1 teaspoon garlic powder
- 2 tablespoons almond flour
- 2 tablespoons olive oil
- Salt and pepper to taste

1. Preheat the air fryer for 5 minutes.
2. In a bowl, combine all ingredients until the kale leaves are coated with the other ingredients.
3. Place in a fryer basket and cook for 10 minutes until crispy.

Delightful Mushrooms

Servings:4 | Cooking Time:22 Minutes

- 2 cups mushrooms, sliced
- 2 tablespoons cheddar cheese, shredded
- 1 tablespoon fresh chives, chopped
- 2 tablespoons olive oil

1. Preheat the Air fryer to 355 o F and grease an Air fryer basket.
2. Coat the mushrooms with olive oil and arrange into the Air fryer basket.
3. Cook for about 20 minutes and dish out in a platter.
4. Top with chives and cheddar cheese and cook for 2 more minutes.
5. Dish out and serve warm.

Feta Cheese Triangles

Servings:4 | Cooking Time: 20 Minutes

- 2 sheets filo pastry
- 1 egg yolk
- 2 tbsp parsley, finely chopped
- 1 scallion, finely chopped
- 2 tbsp olive oil
- salt and black pepper

1. In a large bowl, beat the yolk and mix with the cheese, the chopped parsley and scallion. Season with salt and black pepper. Cut each filo sheet in three parts or strips. Put a teaspoon of the feta mixture on the bottom.
2. Roll the strip in a spinning spiral way until the filling of the inside mixture is completely wrapped in a triangle. Preheat the air fryer to 360 F, and brush the surface of the filo with oil. Place up to 5 triangles in the Air frier's basket and cook for 5 minutes. Lower the temperature to 330 F, cook for 3 more minutes or until golden brown.

Caramelized Brussels Sprout

Servings:4 | Cooking Time:35 Minutes

- 1 pound Brussels sprouts, trimmed and halved
- 4 teaspoons butter, melted
- Salt and black pepper, to taste

1. Preheat the Air fryer to 400 o F and grease an Air fryer basket.
2. Mix all the ingredients in a bowl and toss to coat well.
3. Arrange the Brussels sprouts in the Air fryer basket and cook for about 35 minutes.
4. Dish out and serve warm.

Sesame Seeds Bok Choy(1)

Servings:4 | Cooking Time:6 Minutes

- 4 bunches baby bok choy, bottoms removed and leaves separated
- 1 teaspoon sesame seeds
- Olive oil cooking spray
- 1 teaspoon garlic powder

1. Preheat the Air fryer to 325 o F and grease an Air fryer basket.
2. Arrange the bok choy leaves into the Air fryer basket and spray with the cooking spray.
3. Sprinkle with garlic powder and cook for about 6 minutes, shaking twice in between.
4. Dish out in the bok choy onto serving plates and serve garnished with sesame seeds.

Herbed Potatoes

Servings:4 | Cooking Time:15 Minutes

- 6 small potatoes, chopped
- 2 tablespoons fresh parsley, chopped
- 3 tablespoons olive oil
- 2 teaspoons mixed dried herbs
- Salt and black pepper, to taste

1. Preheat the Air fryer to 360 o F and grease an Air fryer basket.
2. Mix the potatoes, oil, herbs, salt and black pepper in a bowl.
3. Arrange the chopped potatoes into the Air fryer basket and cook for about 15 minutes, tossing once in between.
4. Dish out the potatoes onto serving plates and serve garnished with parsley.

Red Wine Infused Mushrooms

Servings:6 | Cooking Time:30 Minutes

- 1 tablespoon butter
- 2 pounds fresh mushrooms, quartered
- 2 teaspoons Herbs de Provence
- ½ teaspoon garlic powder
- 2 tablespoons red wine

1. Preheat the Air fryer to 325 o F and grease an Air fryer pan.
2. Mix the butter, Herbs de Provence, and garlic powder in the Air fryer pan and toss to coat well.
3. Cook for about 2 minutes and stir in the mushrooms and red wine.
4. Cook for about 28 minutes and dish out in a platter to serve hot.

Tender Butternut Squash Fry

Servings:2 | Cooking Time: 10 Minutes

- 1 tablespoon cooking oil
- 1-pound butternut squash, seeded and sliced
- Salt and pepper to taste

1. Place the grill pan accessory in the air fryer.
2. In a bowl, place all Ingredients and toss to coat and season the squash.
3. Place in the grill pan.
4. Close the air fryer and cook for 10 minutes at 3300F.

Easy Fried Tomatoes

Servings:3 | Cooking Time: 15 Minutes

- ¼ tbsp creole seasoning
- Salt and pepper to taste
- ¼ cup flour
- ½ cup buttermilk
- breadcrumbs as needed

1. Add flour to one bowl and buttermilk to another. Season tomatoes with salt and pepper. Make a mix of creole seasoning and breadcrumbs. Cover tomato slices with flour, dip in buttermilk and then into the breadcrumbs. Cook the tomato slices in your air fryer for 5 minutes at 400 F. Serve.

Broccoli With Olives

Servings:4 | Cooking Time:19 Minutes

- 2 pounds broccoli, stemmed and cut into 1-inch florets
- 1/3 cup Kalamata olives, halved and pitted
- ¼ cup Parmesan cheese, grated
- 2 tablespoons olive oil
- Salt and ground black pepper, as required
- 2 teaspoons fresh lemon zest, grated

1. Preheat the Air fryer to 400 o F and grease an Air fryer basket.
2. Boil the broccoli for about 4 minutes and drain well.
3. Mix broccoli, oil, salt, and black pepper in a bowl and toss to coat well.
4. Arrange broccoli into the Air fryer basket and cook for about 15 minutes.
5. Stir in the olives, lemon zest and cheese and dish out to serve.

Cauliflower Steaks Gratin
Servings: 2 | Cooking Time: 13 Minutes
- 1 head cauliflower
- 1 tablespoon olive oil
- salt and freshly ground black pepper
- ½ teaspoon chopped fresh thyme leaves
- 3 tablespoons grated Parmigiano-Reggiano cheese
- 2 tablespoons panko breadcrumbs

1. Preheat the air-fryer to 370°F.
2. Cut two steaks out of the center of the cauliflower. To do this, cut the cauliflower in half and then cut one slice about 1-inch thick off each half. The rest of the cauliflower will fall apart into florets, which you can roast on their own or save for another meal.
3. Brush both sides of the cauliflower steaks with olive oil and season with salt, freshly ground black pepper and fresh thyme. Place the cauliflower steaks into the air fryer basket and air-fry for 6 minutes. Turn the steaks over and air-fry for another 4 minutes. Combine the Parmesan cheese and panko breadcrumbs and sprinkle the mixture over the tops of both steaks and air-fry for another 3 minutes until the cheese has melted and the breadcrumbs have browned. Serve this with some sautéed bitter greens and air-fried blistered tomatoes.

Twice-baked Broccoli-cheddar Potatoes
Servings: 4 | Cooking Time: 35 Minutes
- 4 large russet potatoes
- 2 tablespoons plus 2 teaspoons ranch dressing
- 1 teaspoon salt
- ½ teaspoon ground black pepper
- ¼ cup chopped cooked broccoli florets
- 1 cup shredded sharp Cheddar cheese

1. Preheat the air fryer to 400°F.
2. Using a fork, poke several holes in potatoes. Place in the air fryer basket and cook 30 minutes until fork-tender.
3. Once potatoes are cool enough to handle, slice lengthwise and scoop out the cooked potato into a large bowl, being careful to maintain the structural integrity of potato skins. Add ranch dressing, salt, pepper, broccoli, and Cheddar to potato flesh and stir until well combined.
4. Scoop potato mixture back into potato skins and return to the air fryer basket. Cook an additional 5 minutes until cheese is melted. Serve warm.

Eggplant Caviar
Servings: 3 | Cooking Time: 20 Minutes
- ½ red onion, chopped and blended
- 2 tbsp balsamic vinegar
- 1 tbsp olive oil
- salt

1. Arrange the eggplants in the basket and cook them for 15 minutes at 380 F. Remove them and let them cool. Then cut the eggplants in half, lengthwise, and empty their insides with a spoon.
2. Blend the onion in a blender. Put the inside of the eggplants in the blender and process everything. Add the vinegar, olive oil and salt, then blend again. Serve cool with bread and tomato sauce or ketchup.

Easy Fry Portobello Mushroom
Servings: 2 | Cooking Time: 10 Minutes
- 1 tablespoon cooking oil
- 1-pound Portobello mushroom, sliced
- Salt and pepper to taste

1. Place the grill pan accessory in the air fryer.
2. In a bowl, place all Ingredients and toss to coat and season the mushrooms.
3. Place in the grill pan.
4. Close the air fryer and cook for 10 minutes at 3300F.

Curried Eggplant
Servings: 2 | Cooking Time: 10 Minutes
- 1 large eggplant, cut into ½-inch thick slices
- 1 garlic clove, minced
- ½ fresh red chili, chopped
- 1 tablespoon vegetable oil
- ¼ teaspoon curry powder
- Salt, to taste

1. Preheat the Air fryer to 300 o F and grease an Air fryer basket.
2. Mix all the ingredients in a bowl and toss to coat well.
3. Arrange the eggplant slices in the Air fryer basket and cook for about 10 minutes, tossing once in between.
4. Dish out onto serving plates and serve hot.

Chipotle Chickpea Tacos
Servings: 4 | Cooking Time: 10 Minutes
- 2 cans chickpeas, drained and rinsed
- ¼ cup adobo sauce
- ¾ teaspoon salt
- ¼ teaspoon ground black pepper
- 8 medium flour tortillas, warmed
- 1 ½ cups chopped avocado
- ½ cup chopped fresh cilantro

1. Preheat the air fryer to 375°F.
2. In a large bowl, toss chickpeas, adobo, salt, and pepper to fully coat.
3. Using a slotted spoon, place chickpeas in the air fryer basket and cook 10 minutes, shaking the basket twice during cooking, until tender.
4. To assemble, scoop ¼ cup chickpeas into a tortilla, then top with avocado and cilantro. Repeat with remaining tortillas and filling. Serve warm.

Roasted Brussels Sprouts & Pine Nuts
Servings: 6 | Cooking Time: 20 Minutes
- 1 tbsp olive oil
- 1 ¾ oz raisins, soaked
- Juice of 1 orange
- salt to taste
- 1 ¾ oz toasted pine nuts

1. Preheat your air fryer to 392 F. In a bowl, pop the sprouts with oil and salt and stir to combine well. Add the sprouts to the air fryer and roast for 15 minutes. Mix with toasted pine nuts and soaked raisins. Drizzle with orange juice to serve.

Spicy Corn Fritters
Servings:4 | Cooking Time: 22 Minutes
- 1 can yellow corn, drained
- ½ cup all-purpose flour
- ¾ cup shredded pepper jack cheese
- 1 large egg
- ½ teaspoon chili powder
- ¼ teaspoon garlic powder
- ½ teaspoon salt
- ¼ teaspoon ground black pepper

1. Cut parchment paper to fit the air fryer basket.
2. In a large bowl, mix all ingredients until well combined. Using a ½-cup scoop, separate mixture into four portions.
3. Gently press each into a 4" round and spritz with cooking spray. Place in freezer 10 minutes.
4. Preheat the air fryer to 400°F.
5. Place fritters in the air fryer basket and cook 12 minutes, turning halfway through cooking time, until fritters are brown on the top and edges and firm to the touch. Serve warm.

Zucchini Topped With Coconut Cream 'n Bacon
Servings:3 | Cooking Time: 20 Minutes
- 1 tablespoon lemon juice
- 3 slices bacon, fried and crumbled
- 3 tablespoons olive oil
- 3 zucchini squashes
- 4 tablespoons coconut cream
- Salt and pepper to taste

1. Preheat the air fryer for 5 minutes.
2. Line up chopsticks on both sides of the zucchini and slice thinly until you hit the stick. Brush the zucchinis with olive oil. Set aside.
3. Place the zucchini in the air fryer. Bake for 20 minutes at 350oF.
4. Meanwhile, combine the coconut cream and lemon juice in a mixing bowl. Season with salt and pepper to taste.
5. Once the zucchini is cooked, scoop the coconut cream mixture and drizzle on top.
6. Sprinkle with bacon bits.

Zucchini Garlic-sour Cream Bake
Servings:5 | Cooking Time: 20 Minutes
- 1 (8 ounce) package cream cheese, softened
- 1 cup sour cream
- 1 large zucchini, cut lengthwise then in half
- 1 tablespoon minced garlic
- 1/4 cup grated Parmesan cheese
- paprika to taste

1. Lightly grease baking pan of air fryer with cooking spray.
2. Place zucchini slices in a single layer in pan.
3. In a bowl whisk well, remaining Ingredients except for paprika. Spread on top of zucchini slices. Sprinkle paprika.
4. Cover pan with foil.
5. For 10 minutes, cook on 390oF.
6. Remove foil and cook for 10 minutes at 330oF.
7. Serve and enjoy.

Cheese Stuffed Tomatoes
Servings:2 | Cooking Time: 15 Minutes
- 2 large tomatoes
- ½ cup broccoli, finely chopped
- ½ cup cheddar cheese, shredded
- 1 tablespoon unsalted butter, melted
- ½ teaspoon dried thyme, crushed

1. Slice the top of each tomato and scoop out pulp and seeds.
2. In a bowl, mix together the chopped broccoli and cheese.
3. Stuff each tomato evenly with broccoli mixture.
4. Set the temperature of air fryer to 355 degrees F. Grease an air fryer basket.
5. Arrange tomatoes into the prepared air fryer basket.
6. Drizzle evenly with butter.
7. Air fry for about 12-15 minutes.
8. Remove from air fryer and transfer the tomatoes onto a serving platter.
9. Set aside to cool slightly.
10. Garnish with thyme and serve.

Lemony Green Beans
Servings:3 | Cooking Time:12 Minutes
- 1 pound green beans, trimmed and halved
- 1 teaspoon butter, melted
- 1 tablespoon fresh lemon juice
- ¼ teaspoon garlic powder

1. Preheat the Air fryer to 400 o F and grease an Air fryer basket.
2. Mix all the ingredients in a bowl and toss to coat well.
3. Arrange the green beans into the Air fryer basket and cook for about 12 minutes.
4. Dish out in a serving plate and serve hot.

Portobello Mini Pizzas
Servings:4 | Cooking Time: 10 Minutes
- 4 large portobello mushrooms, stems removed
- 2 cups shredded mozzarella cheese, divided
- ½ cup full-fat ricotta cheese
- 1 teaspoon salt, divided
- ½ teaspoon ground black pepper
- 1 teaspoon Italian seasoning
- 1 cup pizza sauce

1. Preheat the air fryer to 350°F.
2. Use a spoon to hollow out mushroom caps. Spritz mushrooms with cooking spray. Place ¼ cup mozzarella into each mushroom cap.
3. In a small bowl, mix ricotta, ½ teaspoon salt, pepper, and Italian seasoning. Divide mixture evenly and spoon into mushroom caps.
4. Pour ¼ cup pizza sauce into each mushroom cap, then top each with ¼ cup mozzarella. Sprinkle tops of pizzas with remaining salt.
5. Place mushrooms in the air fryer basket and cook 10 minutes until cheese is brown and bubbling. Serve warm.

Hasselback Potatoes
Servings:4 | Cooking Time:30 Minutes
- 4 potatoes
- 2 tablespoons Parmesan cheese, shredded
- 1 tablespoon fresh chives, chopped
- 2 tablespoons olive oil

1. Preheat the Air fryer to 355 o F and grease an Air fryer basket.

2. Cut slits along each potato about ¼-inch apart with a sharp knife, making sure slices should stay connected at the bottom.
3. Coat the potatoes with olive oil and arrange into the Air fryer basket.
4. Cook for about 30 minutes and dish out in a platter.
5. Top with chives and Parmesan cheese to serve.

Gourmet Wasabi Popcorn

Servings: 2 | Cooking Time: 30 Minutes

- 1/2 teaspoon brown sugar
- 1 teaspoon salt
- 1/2 teaspoon wasabi powder, sifted
- 1 tablespoon avocado oil
- 3 tablespoons popcorn kernels

1. Add the dried corn kernels to the Air Fryer basket; toss with the remaining ingredients.
2. Cook at 395 degrees F for 15 minutes, shaking the basket every 5 minutes. Work in two batches.
3. Taste, adjust the seasonings and serve immediately. Bon appétit!

Okra With Green Beans

Servings:2 | Cooking Time:20 Minutes

- ½ (10-ounces) bag frozen cut okra
- ½ (10-ounces) bag frozen cut green beans
- ¼ cup nutritional yeast
- 3 tablespoons balsamic vinegar
- Salt and black pepper, to taste

1. Preheat the Air fryer to 400 o F and grease an Air fryer basket.
2. Mix the okra, green beans, nutritional yeast, vinegar, salt, and black pepper in a bowl and toss to coat well.
3. Arrange the okra mixture into the Air fryer basket and cook for about 20 minutes.
4. Dish out in a serving dish and serve hot.

Crispy Brussels Sprout Chips

Servings: 2 | Cooking Time: 20 Minutes

- 10 Brussels sprouts, separated into leaves
- 1 teaspoon canola oil
- 1 teaspoon coarse sea salt
- 1 teaspoon paprika

1. Toss all ingredients in the lightly greased Air Fryer basket.
2. Bake at 380 degrees F for 15 minutes, shaking the basket halfway through the cooking time to ensure even cooking.
3. Serve and enjoy!

Roasted Brussels Sprouts

Servings:4 | Cooking Time: 25 Minutes

- ½ tsp garlic, chopped
- 2 tbsp olive oil
- Salt and black pepper to taste

1. Wash the Brussels sprouts thoroughly under cold water and trim off the outer leaves, keeping only the head of the sprouts. In a bowl, mix oil, garlic, salt, and pepper. Add sprouts to this mixture and let rest for 5 minutes. Place the coated sprouts in your air fryer's cooking basket and cook for 15 minutes.

Healthy Apple-licious Chips

Servings:1 | Cooking Time: 6 Minutes

- ½ teaspoon ground cumin
- 1 apple, cored and sliced thinly
- 1 tablespoon sugar
- A pinch of salt

1. Place all ingredients in a bowl and toss to coat everything.
2. Put the grill pan accessory in the air fryer and place the sliced apples on the grill pan.
3. Close the air fryer and cook for 6 minutes at 3900F.

Italian Seasoned Easy Pasta Chips

Servings:2 | Cooking Time:10 Minutes

- ½ teaspoon salt
- 1 ½ teaspoon Italian seasoning blend
- 1 tablespoon nutritional yeast
- 1 tablespoon olive oil
- 2 cups whole wheat bowtie pasta

1. Place the baking dish accessory in the air fryer.
2. Give a good stir.
3. Close the air fryer and cook for 10 minutes at 3900F.

Kurkuri Bhindi (indian Fried Okra)

Servings:4 | Cooking Time: 20 Minutes

- 2 tbsp garam masala
- 1 cup cornmeal
- ¼ cup flour
- Salt to taste
- ½ pound okra, trimmed and halved lengthwise
- 1 egg

1. Preheat the Air Fryer to 380 F.
2. In a bowl, mix cornmeal, flour, chili powder, garam masala, salt, and pepper. In another bowl, whisk the egg; season with salt and pepper. Dip the okra in the egg and then coat in cornmeal mixture. Spray okra with cooking spray and place in the air fryer basket in a single layer. Cook for 6 minutes. Slide out the basket and shake; cook for another 6 minutes until golden brown. Serve with your favorite dip.

Sweet And Sour Brussel Sprouts

Servings:2 | Cooking Time:10 Minutes

- 2 cups Brussels sprouts, trimmed and halved lengthwise
- 1 tablespoon balsamic vinegar
- 1 tablespoon maple syrup
- Salt, as required

1. Preheat the Air fryer to 400 o F and grease an Air fryer basket.
2. Mix all the ingredients in a bowl and toss to coat well.
3. Arrange the Brussel sprouts in the Air fryer basket and cook for about 10 minutes, shaking once halfway through.
4. Dish out in a bowl and serve hot.

Easy Glazed Carrots

Servings:4 | Cooking Time:12 Minutes

- 3 cups carrots, peeled and cut into large chunks
- 1 tablespoon olive oil
- 1 tablespoon honey
- Salt and black pepper, to taste

1. Preheat the Air fryer to 390 o F and grease an Air fryer basket.
2. Mix all the ingredients in a bowl and toss to coat well.
3. Transfer into the Air fryer basket and cook for about 12 minutes.
4. Dish out and serve hot.

Sweet Potato French Fries
Servings:4 | Cooking Time: 30 Minutes
- ½ tsp garlic powder
- ½ tsp chili powder
- ¼ tsp cumin
- 3 tbsp olive oil
- 3 sweet potatoes, cut into thick strips

1. In a bowl, mix salt, garlic powder, chili powder, and cumin, and whisk in oil. Coat the strips well in this mixture and arrange them on the air fryer's basket. Cook for 20 minutes at 380 F until crispy. Serve.

Baked Polenta With Chili-cheese
Servings:3 | Cooking Time: 10 Minutes
- 1 commercial polenta roll, sliced
- 1 cup cheddar cheese sauce
- 1 tablespoon chili powder

1. Place the baking dish accessory in the air fryer.
2. Arrange the polenta slices in the baking dish.
3. Add the chili powder and cheddar cheese sauce.
4. Close the air fryer and cook for 10 minutes at 3900F.

Poblano & Tomato Stuffed Squash
Servings:3 | Cooking Time: 50 Minutes
- 6 grape tomatoes, halved
- 1 poblano pepper, cut into strips
- ¼ cup grated mozzarella, optional
- 2 tsp olive oil divided
- Salt and pepper, to taste

1. Preheat the air fryer to 350 F. Trim the ends and cut the squash lengthwise. You will only need one half for this recipe Scoop the flash out, so you make room for the filling. Brush 1 tsp of oil over the squash.
2. Place in the air fryer and roast for 30 minutes. Combine the remaining olive oil with tomatoes and poblanos, season with salt and pepper. Place the peppers and tomatoes into the squash. Cook for 15 more minutes. If using mozzarella, add it on top of the squash, two minutes before the end.

Tacos
Servings: 24 | Cooking Time: 8 Minutes Per Batch
- 1 24-count package 4-inch corn tortillas
- 1½ cups refried beans (about ¾ of a 15-ounce can)
- 4 ounces sharp Cheddar cheese, grated
- ½ cup salsa
- oil for misting or cooking spray

1. Preheat air fryer to 390°F.
2. Wrap refrigerated tortillas in damp paper towels and microwave for 30 to 60 seconds to warm. If necessary, rewarm tortillas as you go to keep them soft enough to fold without breaking.
3. Working with one tortilla at a time, top with 1 tablespoon of beans, 1 tablespoon of grated cheese, and 1 teaspoon of salsa. Fold over and press down very gently on the center. Press edges firmly all around to seal. Spray both sides with oil or cooking spray.
4. Cooking in two batches, place half the tacos in the air fryer basket. To cook 12 at a time, you may need to stand them upright and lean some against the sides of basket. It's okay if they're crowded as long as you leave a little room for air to circulate around them.
5. Cook for 8 minutes or until golden brown and crispy.
6. Repeat steps 4 and 5 to cook remaining tacos.

Sautéed Spinach
Servings:2 | Cooking Time:9 Minutes
- 1 small onion, chopped
- 6 ounces fresh spinach
- 2 tablespoons olive oil
- 1 teaspoon ginger, minced
- Salt and black pepper, to taste

1. Preheat the Air fryer to 360 o F and grease an Air fryer pan.
2. Put olive oil, onions and ginger in the Air fryer pan and place in the Air fryer basket.
3. Cook for about 4 minutes and add spinach, salt, and black pepper.
4. Cook for about 4 more minutes and dish out in a bowl to serve.

Air-fried Sweet Potato
Servings:4 | Cooking Time: 30 Minutes
- ½ tsp garlic powder
- ½ tsp cayenne pepper
- ¼ tsp cumin
- 3 tbsp olive oil
- 3 sweet potatoes, cut into ½-inch thick wedges
- A handful of chopped fresh parsley
- Sea salt

1. In a bowl, mix salt, garlic powder, chili powder, and cumin. Whisk in oil, and coat the potatoes. Arrange in the air fryer, without overcrowding, and cook for 20 minutes at 380 F; toss regularly to get crispy on all sides. Sprinkle with parsley and sea salt, and serve!

Almond Asparagus
Servings:3 | Cooking Time:6 Minutes
- 1 pound asparagus
- 1/3 cup almonds, sliced
- 2 tablespoons olive oil
- 2 tablespoons balsamic vinegar
- Salt and black pepper, to taste

1. Preheat the Air fryer to 400 o F and grease an Air fryer basket.
2. Mix asparagus, oil, vinegar, salt, and black pepper in a bowl and toss to coat well.
3. Arrange asparagus into the Air fryer basket and sprinkle with the almond slices.
4. Cook for about 6 minutes and dish out to serve hot.

Roasted Mushrooms In Herb-garlic Oil
Servings:4 | Cooking Time: 25 Minutes
- ½ teaspoon minced garlic
- 2 pounds mushrooms
- 2 teaspoons herbs de Provence
- 3 tablespoons coconut oil
- Salt and pepper to taste

1. Preheat the air fryer for 5 minutes.
2. Place all ingredients in a baking dish that will fit in the air fryer.
3. Mix to combine.
4. Place the baking dish in the air fryer.
5. Cook for 25 minutes at 3500F.

Cheesy Vegetarian Lasagna
Servings:4 | Cooking Time: 40 Minutes
- 1 ¼ cups shredded Italian-blend cheese, divided
- ½ cup grated vegetarian Parmesan cheese, divided
- ½ cup full-fat ricotta cheese
- ½ teaspoon salt
- ¼ teaspoon ground black pepper
- 2 cups tomato pasta sauce, divided
- 5 no-boil lasagna noodles

1. Preheat the air fryer to 360°F. Spritz a 6" round baking pan with cooking spray.
2. In a medium bowl, mix 1 cup Italian-blend cheese, ¼ cup Parmesan, ricotta, salt, and pepper.
3. Pour ½ cup pasta sauce into the bottom of the prepared pan. Break the noodles into pieces to fit the pan. Place a layer of noodles into the pan.
4. Separate ricotta mixture into three portions. Spread one-third of the mixture over noodles in the pan. Pour ½ cup pasta sauce over ricotta mixture. Repeat layers of noodles, cheese mixture, and pasta sauce twice more until all ingredients are used, topping the final layer with remaining Italian-blend cheese.
5. Cover pan tightly with foil, being sure to tuck foil under the bottom of the pan to ensure the air fryer fan does not blow it off. Place in the air fryer basket. Cook 35 minutes, then remove foil and cook an additional 5 minutes until the top is golden brown and noodles are fork-tender.
6. Remove from the air fryer basket and top with remaining Parmesan and let cool 5 minutes before serving.

Pesto Vegetable Kebabs
Servings:4 | Cooking Time: 8 Minutes
- 12 ounces button mushrooms
- 12 ounces cherry tomatoes
- 2 medium zucchini, cut into ¼" slices
- 1 medium red onion, peeled and cut into 1" cubes
- 1 cup pesto, divided
- ½ teaspoon salt
- ¼ teaspoon ground black pepper

1. Soak eight 6" skewers in water 10 minutes to avoid burning. Preheat the air fryer to 350°F.
2. Place a mushroom on a skewer, followed by a tomato, zucchini slice, and red onion piece. Repeat to fill up the skewer, then follow the same pattern for remaining skewers.
3. Brush each skewer evenly using ½ cup pesto. Sprinkle kebabs with salt and pepper. Place in the air fryer basket and cook 10 minutes, turning halfway through cooking time, until vegetables are tender. Brush kebabs with remaining ½ cup pesto before serving.

Air-fried Cauliflower
Servings:4 | Cooking Time: 20 Minutes
- 2 tbsp olive oil
- ½ tsp salt
- ¼ tsp freshly ground black pepper

1. In a bowl, toss cauliflower, oil, salt, and black pepper, until the florets are well-coated. Arrange the florets in the air fryer and cook for 8 minutes at 360 F; work in batches if needed. Serve the crispy cauliflower in lettuce wraps with chicken, cheese or mushrooms.

Indian Plantain Chips
Servings: 2 | Cooking Time: 30 Minutes
- 1 pound plantain, thinly sliced
- 1 tablespoon turmeric
- 2 tablespoons coconut oil

1. Fill a large enough cup with water and add the turmeric to the water.
2. Soak the plantain slices in the turmeric water for 15 minutes. Brush with coconut oil and transfer to the Air Fryer basket.
3. Cook in the preheated Air Fryer at 400 degrees F for 10 minutes, shaking the cooking basket halfway through the cooking time.
4. Serve at room temperature. Enjoy!

Crispy 'n Healthy Avocado Fingers
Servings:4 | Cooking Time: 10 Minutes
- ½ cup panko breadcrumbs
- ½ teaspoon salt
- 1 pitted Haas avocado, peeled and sliced
- liquid from 1 can white beans or aquafaba

1. Preheat the air fryer at 3500F.
2. In a shallow bowl, toss the breadcrumbs and salt until well combined.
3. Dredge the avocado slices first with the aquafaba then in the breadcrumb mixture.
4. Place the avocado slices in a single layer inside the air fryer basket.
5. Cook for 10 minutes and shake halfway through the cooking time.

Cheesy Broccoli With Eggs
Servings:4 | Cooking Time: 15 Minutes
- 4 eggs
- 1 cup cheese, shredded
- 1 cup cream
- 1 pinch nutmeg
- 1 tsp ginger powder
- salt and pepper to taste

1. Steam the broccoli for 5 minutes. Then drain them and add 1 egg, cream, nutmeg, ginger, salt and pepper. Butter small ramekins and spread the mixture. Sprinkle the shredded cheese on top. Cook for 10 minutes at 280 F.

Crispy Air-fried Tofu
Servings:4 | Cooking Time: 25 Minutes
- 2 tbsp olive oil
- ½ cup flour
- ½ cup crushed cornflakes
- Salt and black pepper to taste
- Cooking spray

1. Sprinkle oil over tofu and massage gently until well-coated. On a plate, mix flour, cornflakes, salt, and black pepper. Dip each strip into the mixture to coat, spray with oil and arrange the strips in your air fryer lined with baking paper. Cook for 14 minutes at 360 F, turning once halfway through.

Chewy Glazed Parsnips

Servings:6 | Cooking Time:44 Minutes

- 2 pounds parsnips, peeled and cut into 1-inch chunks
- 1 tablespoon butter, melted
- 2 tablespoons maple syrup
- 1 tablespoon dried parsley flakes, crushed
- ¼ teaspoon red pepper flakes, crushed

1. Preheat the Air fryer to 355 o F and grease an Air fryer basket.
2. Mix parsnips and butter in a bowl and toss to coat well.
3. Arrange the parsnips in the Air fryer basket and cook for about 40 minutes.
4. Meanwhile, mix remaining ingredients in a large bowl.
5. Transfer this mixture into the Air fryer basket and cook for about 4 more minutes.
6. Dish out and serve warm.

Jalapeno Stuffed With Bacon 'n Cheeses

Servings:8 | Cooking Time: 15 Minutes

- ¼ cup cheddar cheese, shredded
- 1 teaspoon paprika
- 16 fresh jalapenos, sliced lengthwise and seeded
- 16 strips of uncured bacon, cut into half
- 4-ounce cream cheese
- Salt to taste

1. In a mixing bowl, mix together the cream cheese, cheddar cheese, salt, and paprika until well-combined.
2. Scoop half a teaspoon onto each half of jalapeno peppers.
3. Use a thin strip of bacon and wrap it around the cheese-filled jalapeno half. Wear gloves when doing this step because jalapeno is very spicy.
4. Place in the air fryer basket and cook for 15 minutes in a 3500F preheated air fryer.

Feisty Baby Carrots

Servings:4 | Cooking Time: 20 Minutes

- 1 tsp dried dill
- 1 tbsp olive oil
- 1 tbsp honey
- Salt and pepper to taste

1. Preheat air fryer to 350 F. In a bowl, mix oil, carrots and honey; stir to coat. Season with dill, pepper and salt. Place the prepared carrots in your air fryer's cooking basket and cook for 12 minutes.

Toasted Ravioli

Servings:4 | Cooking Time: 8 Minutes

- 1 cup Italian bread crumbs
- 2 tablespoons grated vegetarian Parmesan cheese
- 1 large egg
- ¼ cup whole milk
- 1 package fresh cheese ravioli

1. Preheat the air fryer to 400°F.
2. In a large bowl, whisk together bread crumbs and Parmesan.
3. In a medium bowl, whisk together egg and milk.
4. Dip each ravioli into egg mixture, shaking off the excess, then press into bread crumb mixture until well coated. Spritz each side with cooking spray.
5. Place in the air fryer basket and cook 8 minutes, turning halfway through cooking time, until ravioli is brown at the edges and crispy. Serve warm.

Mushroom 'n Bell Pepper Pizza

Servings:10 | Cooking Time: 10 Minutes

- ¼ red bell pepper, chopped
- 1 cup oyster mushrooms, chopped
- 1 shallot, chopped
- 1 vegan pizza dough
- 2 tablespoons parsley
- salt and pepper

1. Preheat the air fryer to 4000F.
2. Slice the pizza dough into squares. Set aside.
3. In a mixing bowl, mix together the oyster mushroom, shallot, bell pepper and parsley.
4. Season with salt and pepper to taste.
5. Place the topping on top of the pizza squares.
6. Place inside the air fryer and cook for 10 minutes.

Green Bean Casserole

Servings: 2 | Cooking Time: 10 Minutes

- tbsp. butter, melted
- 1 cup green beans
- 6 oz. cheddar cheese, shredded
- 7 oz. parmesan cheese, shredded
- ¼ cup heavy cream

1. Pre-heat your fryer at 400°F.
2. Take a baking dish small enough to fit inside the fryer and cover the bottom with melted butter. Throw in the green beans, cheddar cheese, and any seasoning as desired, then give it a stir. Add the parmesan on top and finally the heavy cream.
3. Cook in the fryer for six minutes. Allow to cool before serving.

Spaghetti Squash

Servings:4 | Cooking Time: 45 Minutes

- 1 large spaghetti squash, halved lengthwise and seeded
- 1 teaspoon salt
- ½ teaspoon ground black pepper
- 1 teaspoon garlic powder
- 1 teaspoon dried parsley
- 2 tablespoons salted butter, melted

1. Preheat the air fryer to 350°F.
2. Sprinkle squash with salt, pepper, garlic powder, and parsley. Spritz with cooking spray.
3. Place skin side down in the air fryer basket and cook 30 minutes.
4. Turn squash skin side up and cook an additional 15 minutes until fork-tender. You should be able to easily use a fork to scrape across the surface to separate the strands.
5. Place strands in a medium bowl, top with butter, and toss. Serve warm.

Crispy Ham Rolls

Servings:3 | Cooking Time: 17 Minutes

- 3 packages Pepperidge farm rolls
- 1 tbsp softened butter
- 1 tsp mustard seeds
- 1 tsp poppy seeds
- 1 small chopped onion

1. Mix butter, mustard, onion and poppy seeds. Spread the mixture on top of the rolls. Cover with the chopped ham. Roll up and arrange them on the basket of the air fryer; cook at 350 F for 15 minutes.

Sautéed Green Beans

Servings: 2 | Cooking Time: 10 Minutes

- 8 ounces fresh green beans, trimmed and cut in half
- 1 teaspoon sesame oil
- 1 tablespoon soy sauce

1. Preheat the Air fryer to 390 o F and grease an Air fryer basket.
2. Mix green beans, soy sauce, and sesame oil in a bowl and toss to coat well.
3. Arrange green beans into the Air fryer basket and cook for about 10 minutes, tossing once in between.
4. Dish out onto serving plates and serve hot.

Cinnamon Pear Chips

Servings: 1 | Cooking Time: 25 Minutes

- 1 medium pear, cored and thinly sliced
- 2 tablespoons cinnamon & sugar mixture

1. Toss the pear slices with the cinnamon & sugar mixture. Transfer them to the lightly greased Air Fryer basket.
2. Bake in the preheated Air Fryer at 380 degrees F for 8 minutes, turning them over halfway through the cooking time.
3. Transfer to wire rack to cool. Bon appétit!

Crispy Shawarma Broccoli

Servings: 4 | Cooking Time: 25 Minutes

- 1 pound broccoli, steamed and drained
- 2 tablespoons canola oil
- 1 teaspoon cayenne pepper
- 1 teaspoon sea salt
- 1 tablespoon Shawarma spice blend

1. Toss all ingredients in a mixing bowl.
2. Roast in the preheated Air Fryer at 380 degrees F for 10 minutes, shaking the basket halfway through the cooking time.
3. Work in batches. Bon appétit!

Cheesy Kale

Servings: 2 | Cooking Time: 15 Minutes

- lb. kale
- 8 oz. parmesan cheese, shredded
- 1 onion, diced
- 1 tsp. butter
- 1 cup heavy cream

1. Dice up the kale, discarding any hard stems. In a baking dish small enough to fit inside the fryer, combine the kale with the parmesan, onion, butter and cream.
2. Pre-heat the fryer at 250°F.
3. Set the baking dish in the fryer and cook for twelve minutes. Make sure to give it a good stir before serving.

Basil Tomatoes

Servings: 2 | Cooking Time: 10 Minutes

- 2 tomatoes, halved
- 1 tablespoon fresh basil, chopped
- Olive oil cooking spray
- Salt and black pepper, as required

1. Preheat the Air fryer to 320 o F and grease an Air fryer basket.
2. Spray the tomato halves evenly with olive oil cooking spray and season with salt, black pepper and basil.
3. Arrange the tomato halves into the Air fryer basket, cut sides up.
4. Cook for about 10 minutes and dish out onto serving plates.

Grilled 'n Glazed Strawberries

Servings: 2 | Cooking Time: 20 Minutes

- 1 tbsp honey
- 1 tsp lemon zest
- 1-lb large strawberries
- 3 tbsp melted butter
- Lemon wedges
- Pinch kosher salt

1. Thread strawberries in 4 skewers.
2. In a small bowl, mix well remaining Ingredients except for lemon wedges. Brush all over strawberries.
3. Place skewer on air fryer skewer rack.
4. For 10 minutes, cook on 360oF. Halfway through cooking time, brush with honey mixture and turnover skewer.
5. Serve and enjoy with a squeeze of lemon.

Crispy Wings With Lemony Old Bay Spice

Servings: 4 | Cooking Time: 25 Minutes

- ½ cup butter
- ¾ cup almond flour
- 1 tablespoon old bay spices
- 1 teaspoon lemon juice, freshly squeezed
- 3 pounds chicken wings
- Salt and pepper to taste

1. Preheat the air fryer for 5 minutes.
2. In a mixing bowl, combine all ingredients except for the butter.
3. Place in the air fryer basket.
4. Cook for 25 minutes at 3500F.
5. Halfway through the cooking time, shake the fryer basket for even cooking.
6. Once cooked, drizzle with melted butter.

Roasted Vegetable Grilled Cheese

Servings: 4 | Cooking Time: 6 Minutes

- 8 slices sourdough bread
- 4 slices provolone cheese
- ½ cup chopped roasted red peppers
- ¼ cup chopped yellow onion
- 4 slices white American cheese

1. Preheat the air fryer to 300°F.
2. Place a slice of bread on a work surface. Top with a slice of provolone, then with 2 tablespoons roasted red peppers and 1 tablespoon onion. Repeat with three more bread slices and remaining provolone and vegetables.
3. Place loaded bread slices in the air fryer basket and cook 1 minute until cheese is melted and onion is softened.
4. Remove the air fryer basket and carefully place 1 slice of American cheese on top of each slice of bread, finishing each with a second slice of bread to complete each sandwich.
5. Spritz the top with cooking spray. Increase the air fryer temperature to 400°F and cook 5 minutes, turning carefully after 3 minutes, until bread is golden and cheese is melted. Serve warm.

Cheese And Bean Enchiladas
Servings:4 | Cooking Time: 9 Minutes
- 1 can pinto beans, drained and rinsed
- 1 ½ tablespoons taco seasoning
- 1 cup red enchilada sauce, divided
- 1 ½ cups shredded Mexican-blend cheese, divided
- 4 fajita-size flour tortillas

1. Preheat the air fryer to 320°F.
2. In a large microwave-safe bowl, microwave beans for 1 minute. Mash half the beans and fold into whole beans. Mix in taco seasoning, ¼ cup enchilada sauce, and 1 cup cheese until well combined.
3. Place ¼ cup bean mixture onto each tortilla. Fold up one end about 1", then roll to close.
4. Place enchiladas into a 3-quart baking pan, pushing together as needed to make them fit. Pour remaining ¾ cup enchilada sauce over enchiladas and top with remaining ½ cup cheese.
5. Place pan in the air fryer basket and cook 8 minutes until cheese is brown and bubbling and the edges of tortillas are brown. Serve warm.

Rice Flour Crusted Tofu
Servings:3 | Cooking Time: 28 Minutes
- 1 (14-ounces) block firm tofu, pressed and cubed into ½-inch size
- 2 tablespoons cornstarch
- ¼ cup rice flour
- Salt and ground black pepper, as required
- 2 tablespoons olive oil

1. In a bowl, mix together cornstarch, rice flour, salt, and black pepper.
2. Coat the tofu evenly with flour mixture.
3. Drizzle the tofu with oil.
4. Set the temperature of air fryer to 360 degrees F. Grease an air fryer basket.
5. Arrange tofu cubes into the prepared air fryer basket in a single layer.
6. Air fry for about 14 minutes per side.
7. Remove from air fryer and transfer the tofu onto serving plates.
8. Serve warm.

Black Bean And Rice Burrito Filling
Servings:4 | Cooking Time: 20 Minutes
- 1 cup uncooked instant long-grain white rice
- 1 cup salsa
- ½ cup vegetable broth
- 1 cup black beans
- ½ cup corn

1. Preheat the air fryer to 400°F.
2. Mix all ingredients in a 3-quart baking dish until well combined.
3. Cover with foil, being sure to tuck foil under the bottom of the pan to ensure the air fryer fan does not blow it off.
4. Cook 20 minutes, stirring twice during cooking. Serve warm.

Hearty Apple Chips
Servings:2 | Cooking Time: 25 Minutes
- 1 tsp salt
- 1 whole apple, sauce and sliced
- ½ tsp cinnamon
- Confectioners' sugar for serving

1. Preheat air fryer to 400 F. In a bowl, mix cinnamon, salt and sugar; add apple slices. Place the prepared apple spices in your fryer's cooking basket and bake for 8 minutes. Dust with confectioners' sugar.

Crunchy Parmesan Zucchini
Servings:4 | Cooking Time: 20 Minutes
- ½ cup grated Parmesan cheese
- ½ cup breadcrumbs
- ¼ cup melted butter
- ¼ cup chopped parsley
- 4 garlic cloves, minced
- Salt and pepper, to taste

1. Preheat air fryer to 350 F. In a bowl, mix breadcrumbs, Parmesan cheese, garlic, and parsley. Season with salt and pepper, to taste; stir in the melted butter. Arrange the zucchinis with the cut side up. Spread the mixture onto the zucchini evenly. Place half of the zucchinis in the air fryer and cook for 10 minutes. Increase the temperature to 370 F, and cook for 3 more minutes for extra crunchiness. Repeat, and serve hot.

Vegetable Nuggets
Servings:6 | Cooking Time: 10 Minutes Per Batch
- 1 cup shredded carrots
- 2 cups broccoli florets
- 2 large eggs
- 1 cup shredded Cheddar cheese
- 1 cup Italian bread crumbs
- 1 teaspoon salt
- ½ teaspoon ground black pepper

1. Preheat the air fryer to 400°F.
2. In a food processor, combine carrots and broccoli and pulse five times. Add eggs, Cheddar, bread crumbs, salt, and pepper, and pulse ten times.
3. Carefully scoop twenty-four balls, about 1 heaping tablespoon each, out of the mixture. Spritz balls with cooking spray.
4. Place balls in the air fryer basket, working in batches as necessary, and cook 10 minutes, shaking the basket twice during cooking to ensure even browning. Serve warm.

Extreme Zucchini Fries
Servings:4 | Cooking Time: 25 Minutes
- 2 egg whites
- ½ cup seasoned breadcrumbs
- 2 tbsp grated Parmesan cheese
- Cooking spray as needed
- ¼ tsp garlic powder
- Salt and pepper to taste

1. Preheat your air fryer to 420 F, and coat cooling rack with cooking spray; place it in the fryer's basket. In a bowl, beat the egg whites and season with salt and pepper. In another bowl, mix garlic powder, cheese and breadcrumbs.

2. Take zucchini slices and dredge them in eggs, followed by breadcrumbs. Add zucchini to the rack (in the cooking basket) and spray more oil. cook for 20 minutes. Serve and enjoy!

Perfectly Roasted Mushrooms

Servings:4 | Cooking Time:32 Minutes

- 1 tablespoon butter
- 2 pounds mushrooms, quartered
- 2 tablespoons white vermouth
- 2 teaspoons herbs de Provence
- ½ teaspoon garlic powder

1. Preheat the Air fryer to 320 o F and grease an Air fryer pan.
2. Mix herbs de Provence, garlic powder and butter in the Air fryer pan and transfer into the Air fryer basket.
3. Cook for about 2 minutes and stir in the mushrooms.
4. Cook for about 25 minutes and add white vermouth.
5. Cook for 5 more minutes and dish out to serve warm.

Avocado Rolls

Servings:5 | Cooking Time: 15 Minutes

- 10 egg roll wrappers
- 1 tomato, diced
- ¼ tsp pepper
- ½ tsp salt

1. Place all filling ingredients in a bowl; mash with a fork until somewhat smooth. There should be chunks left. Divide the feeling between the egg wrappers. Wet your finger and brush along the edges, so the wrappers can seal well. Roll and seal the wrappers.
2. Arrange them on a baking sheet lined dish, and place in the air fryer. Cook at 350 F for 5 minutes. Serve with sweet chili dipping and enjoy.

Herbed Eggplant

Servings:2 | Cooking Time:15 Minutes

- 1 large eggplant, cubed
- ½ teaspoon dried marjoram, crushed
- ½ teaspoon dried oregano, crushed
- ½ teaspoon dried thyme, crushed
- ½ teaspoon garlic powder
- Salt and black pepper, to taste
- Olive oil cooking spray

1. Preheat the Air fryer to 390 o F and grease an Air fryer basket.
2. Mix herbs, garlic powder, salt, and black pepper in a bowl.
3. Spray the eggplant cubes with cooking spray and rub with the herb mixture.
4. Arrange the eggplant cubes in the Air fryer basket and cook for about 15 minutes, flipping twice in between.
5. Dish out onto serving plates and serve hot.

Salted Garlic Zucchini Fries

Servings:6 | Cooking Time: 15 Minutes

- ¼ teaspoon garlic powder
- ½ cup almond flour
- 2 large egg whites, beaten
- 3 medium zucchinis, sliced into fry sticks
- Salt and pepper to taste

1. Preheat the air fryer for 5 minutes.
2. Mix all ingredients in a bowl until the zucchini fries are well coated.
3. Place in the air fryer basket.
4. Close and cook for 15 minutes for 4250F.

Melted Cheese 'n Almonds On Tomato

Servings:3 | Cooking Time: 20 Minutes

- ¼ cup toasted almonds
- 1 yellow red bell pepper, chopped
- 3 large tomatoes
- 4 ounces Monterey Jack cheese
- Salt and pepper to taste

1. Preheat the air fryer to 3300F.
2. Place the grill pan accessory in the air fryer.
3. Slice the tops of the tomatoes and remove the seeds to create hollow "cups."
4. In a mixing bowl, combine the cheese, bell pepper, and almonds. Season with salt and pepper to taste.
5. Stuff the tomatoes with the cheese filling.
6. Place the stuffed tomatoes on the grill pan and cook for 15 to 20 minutes.

Parmesan Asparagus

Servings:3 | Cooking Time:10 Minutes

- 1 pound fresh asparagus, trimmed
- 1 tablespoon Parmesan cheese, grated
- 1 tablespoon butter, melted
- 1 teaspoon garlic powder
- Salt and black pepper, to taste

1. Preheat the Air fryer to 400 o F and grease an Air fryer basket.
2. Mix the asparagus, cheese, butter, garlic powder, salt, and black pepper in a bowl and toss to coat well.
3. Arrange the asparagus into the Air fryer basket and cook for about 10 minutes.
4. Dish out in a serving plate and serve hot.

Spicy Potatoes

Servings:6 | Cooking Time:20 Minutes

- 1¾ pounds waxy potatoes, peeled and cubed
- 1 tablespoon olive oil
- ½ teaspoon ground cumin
- ½ teaspoon ground coriander
- ½ teaspoon paprika
- Salt and black pepper, to taste

1. Preheat the Air fryer to 355 o F and grease an Air fryer basket.
2. Mix the potatoes, olive oil, and spices in a bowl and toss to coat well.
3. Transfer into the Air fryer basket and cook for about 20 minutes.
4. Dish out the potato cubes onto serving plates and serve hot.

Tangy Asparagus And Broccoli
Servings: 4 | Cooking Time: 25 Minutes
- 1/2 pound asparagus, cut into 1 1/2-inch pieces
- 1/2 pound broccoli, cut into 1 1/2-inch pieces
- 2 tablespoons peanut oil
- Some salt and white pepper, to taste
- 1/2 cup chicken broth
- 2 tablespoons apple cider vinegar

1. Place the vegetables in a single layer in the lightly greased cooking basket. Drizzle the peanut oil over the vegetables.
2. Sprinkle with salt and white pepper.
3. Cook at 380 degrees F for 15 minutes, shaking the basket halfway through the cooking time.
4. Add 1/2 cup of chicken broth to a saucepan; bring to a rapid boil and add the vinegar. Cook for 5 to 7 minutes or until the sauce has reduced by half.
5. Spoon the sauce over the warm vegetables and serve immediately. Bon appétit!

Chili Fried Okra
Servings:4 | Cooking Time: 15 Minutes
- 3 tbsp sour cream
- 2 tbsp flour
- 2 tbsp semolina
- ½ tsp red chili powder
- Salt and black pepper to taste

1. Preheat the Air fryer to 400 F. Spray the air fryer basket with cooking spray.
2. In a bowl, pour sour cream. In a separate bowl, mix flour, semolina, chili powder, salt, and pepper. Dip okra in the sour cream, followed by a dip in the flour mixture. Place in your air fryer's basket and cook for 5 minutes. Slide out the basket and shake. Cook for 5 more minutes. Allow to cool and serve.

Garden Fresh Green Beans
Servings:4 | Cooking Time:12 Minutes
- 1 pound green beans, washed and trimmed
- 1 teaspoon butter, melted
- 1 tablespoon fresh lemon juice
- ¼ teaspoon garlic powder
- Salt and freshly ground pepper, to taste

1. Preheat the Air fryer to 400 o F and grease an Air fryer basket.
2. Put all the ingredients in a large bowl and transfer into the Air fryer basket.
3. Cook for about 8 minutes and dish out in a bowl to serve warm.

Desserts Recipes

Hot Coconut 'n Cocoa Buns
Servings: 8 | Cooking Time: 15 Minutes
- ¼ cup cacao nibs
- 1 cup coconut milk
- 1/3 cup coconut flour
- 3 tablespoons cacao powder
- 4 eggs, beaten

1. Preheat the air fryer for 5 minutes.
2. Combine all ingredients in a mixing bowl.
3. Form buns using your hands and place in a baking dish that will fit in the air fryer.
4. Bake for 15 minutes for 3750F.
5. Once air fryer turns off, leave the buns in the air fryer until it cools completely.

Grilled Banana Boats
Servings: 3 | Cooking Time: 15 Minutes
- 3 large bananas
- 1 tablespoon ginger snaps
- 2 tablespoons mini chocolate chips
- 3 tablespoons mini marshmallows
- 3 tablespoons crushed vanilla wafers

1. In the peel, slice your banana lengthwise; make sure not to slice all the way through the banana. Divide the remaining ingredients between the banana pockets.
2. Place in the Air Fryer grill pan. Cook at 395 degrees F for 7 minutes.
3. Let the banana boats cool for 5 to 6 minutes, and then eat with a spoon. Bon appétit!

Dark Chocolate Peanut Butter S'mores
Servings: 4 | Cooking Time: 6 Minutes
- 4 graham cracker sheets
- 4 marshmallows
- 4 teaspoons chunky peanut butter
- 4 ounces dark chocolate
- ½ teaspoon ground cinnamon

1. Preheat the air fryer to 390°F. Break the graham crackers in half so you have 8 pieces.
2. Place 4 pieces of graham cracker on the bottom of the air fryer. Top each with one of the marshmallows and bake for 6 or 7 minutes, or until the marshmallows have a golden brown center.
3. While cooking, slather each of the remaining graham crackers with 1 teaspoon peanut butter.
4. When baking completes, carefully remove each of the graham crackers, add 1 ounce of dark chocolate on top of the marshmallow, and lightly sprinkle with cinnamon. Top with the remaining peanut butter graham cracker to make the sandwich. Serve immediately.

Chocolate Molten Lava Cake
Servings: 4 | Cooking Time: 25 Minutes
- 3 ½ oz. butter, melted
- 3 ½ tbsp. sugar
- 3 ½ oz. chocolate, melted
- 1 ½ tbsp. flour
- 2 eggs

1. Pre-heat the Air Fryer to 375°F.
2. Grease four ramekins with a little butter.
3. Rigorously combine the eggs and butter before stirring in the melted chocolate.
4. Slowly fold in the flour.
5. Spoon an equal amount of the mixture into each ramekin.
6. Put them in the Air Fryer and cook for 10 minutes
7. Place the ramekins upside-down on plates and let the cakes fall out. Serve hot.

Apple Tart
Servings: 2 | Cooking Time: 25 Minutes
- 2½-ounce butter, chopped and divided
- 3 ½-ounce flour
- 1 egg yolk
- 1 large apple, peeled, cored and cut into 12 wedges
- 1-ounce sugar

1. Preheat the Air fryer to 390 o F and grease a baking pan lightly.
2. Mix half of the butter and flour in a bowl until a soft dough is formed.
3. Roll the dough into 6-inch round on a floured surface.
4. Place the remaining butter and sugar in a baking pan and arrange the apple wedges in a circular pattern.
5. Top with rolled dough and press gently along the edges of the pan.
6. Transfer the baking pan in the Air fryer basket and cook for about 25 minutes.
7. Dish out and serve hot.

Nutella And Banana Pastries
Servings: 4 | Cooking Time: 12 Minutes
- 1 puff pastry sheet, cut into 4 equal squares
- ½ cup Nutella
- 2 bananas, sliced
- 2 tablespoons icing sugar

1. Preheat the Air fryer to 375 o F and grease an Air fryer basket.
2. Spread Nutella on each pastry square and top with banana slices and icing sugar.
3. Fold each square into a triangle and slightly press the edges with a fork.
4. Arrange the pastries in the Air fryer basket and cook for about 12 minutes.
5. Dish out and serve immediately.

Lemon Cookies
Servings: 4 | Cooking Time: 42 Minutes
- 4 ounces full-fat cream cheese, softened
- ½ cup salted butter, softened
- ½ cup granulated sugar
- 1 teaspoon vanilla extract
- 1 cup all-purpose flour
- Zest and juice of 1 medium lemon plus 1 tablespoon lemon juice, divided
- 1 cup confectioners' sugar

1. In a large bowl using a handheld electric mixer, combine cream cheese, butter, granulated sugar, and vanilla. Gradually add flour, lemon zest, and juice of 1 lemon.
2. Chill dough in the refrigerator 30 minutes. While dough is chilling, in a medium bowl, mix confectioners' sugar with remaining 1 tablespoon lemon juice to make a glaze. Set aside.
3. Preheat the air fryer to 300°F. Cut parchment paper to fit the air fryer basket.
4. Form dough into eight 1" balls. Place on parchment paper in the air fryer basket, working in batches as necessary, and cook 12 minutes until edges of the cookies are lightly brown.
5. Spoon glaze over cookies. Cool 10 minutes before serving.

Apple Fritters
Servings: 6 | Cooking Time: 15 Minutes
- 1 cup self-rising flour
- ½ cup granulated sugar
- 1 ½ teaspoons ground cinnamon
- ¼ cup whole milk
- 1 large egg
- 1 cup diced Granny Smith apples

1. Preheat the air fryer to 375°F. Cut parchment paper to fit the air fryer basket.
2. In a large bowl, combine flour, sugar, cinnamon, and milk.
3. Stir in egg and gently fold in apples.
4. Scoop dough in ¼-cup portions onto parchment paper. Place in the air fryer basket and cook 15 minutes, turning halfway through cooking time, until golden brown and a toothpick inserted into the center comes out clean. Let cool 5 minutes before serving.

Apple Crumble
Servings: 4 | Cooking Time: 25 Minutes
- 1 (14-ounces) can apple pie filling
- ¼ cup butter, softened
- 9 tablespoons self-rising flour
- 7 tablespoons caster sugar
- Pinch of salt

1. Set the temperature of air fryer to 320 degrees F. Lightly, grease a baking dish.
2. Place apple pie filling evenly into the prepared baking dish.
3. In a medium bowl, add the remaining ingredients and mix until a crumbly mixture forms.
4. Spread the mixture evenly over apple pie filling.
5. Arrange the baking dish in an air fryer basket.
6. Air fry for about 25 minutes.
7. Remove the baking dish from air fryer and place onto a wire rack to cool for about 10 minutes.
8. Serve warm.

Strawberry Frozen Dessert
Servings: 1 | Cooking Time: 45 Minutes
- ½ cup sugar-free strawberry preserves
- ½ cup Sugar in the Raw or Splenda
- 2 cups Fage Total 0% Greek Yogurt
- Ice cream maker

1. In a food processor, purée the strawberries. Add the strawberry preserves.
2. Add the Greek yogurt and fully mix.
3. Put into the ice cream maker for 25-30 minute.
4. Serve!

Blueberry Cookies
Servings: 2 | Cooking Time: 30 Minutes
- 3 oz blueberries
- ½ teaspoon avocado oil

1. Put the blueberries in the blender and grind them until smooth. Then line the air fryer basket with baking paper. Brush it with the avocado oil. After this, pour the blended blueberries on the prepared baking paper and flatten it in one layer with the help of the spatula. Cook the blueberry leather for 30 minutes at 300F. Cut into cookies and serve.

Bacon Cookies
Servings: 2 | Cooking Time: 15 Minutes
- ¼ tsp. ginger
- 1/5 tsp. baking soda
- 2/3 cup peanut butter
- 2 tbsp. Swerve
- 3 slices bacon, cooked and chopped

1. In a bowl, mix the ginger, baking soda, peanut butter, and Swerve together, making sure to combine everything well.
2. Stir in the chopped bacon.
3. With clean hands, shape the mixture into a cylinder and cut in six. Press down each slice into a cookie with your palm.
4. Pre-heat your fryer at 350°F.
5. When the fryer is warm, put the cookies inside and cook for seven minutes. Take care when taking them out of the fryer and allow to cool before serving.

Cauliflower Rice Pudding
Servings: 4 | Cooking Time: 25 Minutes
- 1 and ½ cups cauliflower rice
- 2 cups coconut milk
- 3 tablespoons stevia
- 2 tablespoons ghee, melted
- 4 plums, pitted and roughly chopped

1. In a bowl, mix all the ingredients, toss, divide into ramekins, put them in the air fryer, and cook at 340 degrees F for 25 minutes. Cool down and serve.

Keto Butter Balls
Servings: 4 | Cooking Time: 10 Minutes
- 1 tablespoon butter, softened1 tablespoon Erythritol
- ½ teaspoon ground cinnamon
- 1 tablespoon coconut flour
- 1 teaspoon coconut flakes
- Cooking spray

1. Put the butter, Erythritol, ground cinnamon, coconut flour, and coconut flakes. Then stir the mixture with the help of the fork until homogenous. Make 4 balls. Preheat the air fryer to 375F. Spray the air fryer basket with cooking spray and place the balls inside. Cook the dessert for 10 minutes.

Cinnamon Fried Plums
Servings: 6 | Cooking Time: 20 Minutes
- 6 plums, cut into wedges
- 1 teaspoon ginger, ground
- ½ teaspoon cinnamon powder
- Zest of 1 lemon, grated
- 2 tablespoons water
- 10 drops stevia

1. In a pan that fits the air fryer, combine the plums with the rest of the ingredients, toss gently, put the pan in the air fryer and cook at 360 degrees F for 20 minutes. Serve cold.

Moon Pie
Servings: 4 | Cooking Time: 10 Minutes
- 8 large marshmallows
- 8 squares each of dark, milk and white chocolate

1. Arrange the cracker halves on a cutting board. Put 2 marshmallows onto half of the graham cracker halves. Place 2 squares of chocolate onto the cracker with the marshmallows. Put the remaining crackers on top to create 4 sandwiches. Wrap each one in the baking paper so it resembles a parcel. Cook in the fryer for 5 minutes at 340 F.

Cocoa Spread
Servings: 4 | Cooking Time: 5 Minutes
- 2 oz walnuts, chopped
- ½ teaspoon vanilla extract
- 1 teaspoon of cocoa powder
- 5 teaspoons coconut oil
- 1 tablespoon Erythritol

1. Preheat the air fryer to 350F. Put the walnuts in the mason jar. Add coconut oil, vanilla extract, Erythritol, and cocoa powder. Stir the mixture until smooth with the help of the spoon. Then place the mason jar with Nutella in the preheated air fryer and cook it for 5 minutes. Stir Nutella before serving.

Swedish Chocolate Mug Cake
Servings: 1 | Cooking Time: 15 Minutes
- 1 tbsp. cocoa powder
- 3 tbsp. coconut oil
- ¼ cup flour
- 3 tbsp. whole milk
- 5 tbsp. sugar

1. In a bowl, stir together all of the ingredients to combine them completely.
2. Take a short, stout mug and pour the mixture into it.
3. Put the mug in your Air Fryer and cook for 10 minutes at 390°F.

Delicious Apple Pie
Servings: 9 | Cooking Time: 25 Minutes
- 5 tbsp sugar
- 1 ¼ oz butter
- 3 tbsp cinnamon
- 2 whole apple, sliced

1. Preheat the air fryer to 360 F. In a bowl, mix 3 tbsp sugar, butter and flour; form pastry using the batter.
2. Roll out the pastry on a floured surface and transfer to the fryer's basket. Top with apple slices. Cover apples with sugar and cinnamon; cook for 20 minutes. Sprinkle with powdered sugar to serve.

Apple Jam
Servings: 8 | Cooking Time: 20 Minutes
- 8 apples, peeled, cored and blended
- 1 cup apple juice
- 1 teaspoon cinnamon powder

1. In a pan that fits your air fryer, mix the apples with the cinnamon and apple juice; stir.
2. Place the pan in the fryer and cook at 340 degrees F for 20 minutes.
3. Blend using an immersion blender.
4. Divide the jam into cups and serve.

Currant Cream Ramekins
Servings: 6 | Cooking Time: 20 Minutes
- 1 cup red currants, blended
- 1 cup black currants, blended
- 3 tablespoons stevia
- 1 cup coconut cream

1. In a bowl, combine all the ingredients and stir well. Divide into ramekins, put them in the fryer and cook at 340 degrees F for 20 minutes. Serve the pudding cold.

Sage Cream
Servings: 4 | Cooking Time: 30 Minutes
- 7 cups red currants
- 1 cup swerve
- 1 cup water
- 6 sage leaves

1. In a pan that fits your air fryer, mix all the ingredients, toss, put the pan in the fryer and cook at 330 degrees F for 30 minutes. Discard sage leaves, divide into cups and serve cold.

Butter Custard
Servings: 2 | Cooking Time: 35 Minutes
- ¼ cup heavy cream
- 1 tablespoon Erythritol
- 3 egg yolks
- 1 teaspoon coconut flour
- 1 teaspoon butter

1. Whip the heavy cream and them mix it up with Erythritol and coconut flour. Whisk the egg yolks and add them in the whipped cream mixture. Then grease 2 ramekins with butter and transfer the whipped cream mixture in the ramekins. Preheat the air fryer to 300F. Put the ramekins with custard in the air fryer and cook them for 35 minutes.

Chocolate Banana Pastries

Servings:4 | Cooking Time: 12 Minutes

- 1 puff pastry sheet
- ½ cup Nutella
- 2 bananas, peeled and sliced

1. Cut the pastry sheet into 4 equal-sized squares.
2. Spread Nutella evenly on each square of pastry.
3. Divide the banana slices over Nutella.
4. Fold each square into a triangle and with wet fingers, slightly press the edges.
5. Then with a fork, press the edges firmly.
6. Set the temperature of air fryer to 375 degrees F. Lightly, grease an air fryer basket.
7. Arrange pastries into the prepared air fryer basket in a single layer.
8. Air fry for about 10-12 minutes.
9. Remove from air fryer and transfer the pastries onto a platter.
10. Serve warm.

Cream Cheese Muffins

Servings: 10 | Cooking Time: 16 Minutes

- 2 eggs
- 1/2 cup erythritol
- 8 oz cream cheese
- 1 tsp ground cinnamon
- 1/2 tsp vanilla

1. Preheat the air fryer to 325 F.
2. In a bowl, mix together cream cheese, vanilla, erythritol, and eggs until soft.
3. Pour batter into the silicone muffin molds and sprinkle cinnamon on top.
4. Place muffin molds into the air fryer basket and cook for 16 minutes.
5. Serve and enjoy.

Molten Lava Cakes

Servings:3 | Cooking Time: 10 Minutes

- 2 large eggs
- 1 teaspoon vanilla extract
- ¼ teaspoon salt
- 3 tablespoons unsalted butter
- ¾ cup milk chocolate chips
- ¼ cup all-purpose flour

1. Preheat the air fryer to 350°F. Spray three 4" ramekins with cooking spray.
2. In a medium bowl, whisk eggs, vanilla, and salt until well combined.
3. In a large microwave-safe bowl, microwave butter and chocolate chips in 20-second intervals, stirring after each interval, until mixture is fully melted, smooth, and pourable.
4. Whisk chocolate and slowly add egg mixture. Whisk until fully combined.
5. Sprinkle flour into bowl and whisk into chocolate mixture. It should be easily pourable.
6. Divide batter evenly among prepared ramekins. Place in the air fryer basket and cook 5 minutes until the edges and top are set.
7. Let cool 5 minutes and use a butter knife to loosen the edges from ramekins.
8. To serve, place a small dessert plate upside down on top of each ramekin. Quickly flip ramekin and plate upside down so lava cake drops to the plate. Let cool 5 minutes. Serve.

Chocolate Peanut Butter Cups

Servings: 2 | Cooking Time: 70 Minutes

- 1 stick unsalted butter
- 1 oz / 1 cube unsweetened chocolate
- 5 packets Sugar in the Raw
- 1 tbsp heavy cream
- 4 tbsp peanut butter

1. In a microwave, melt the butter and chocolate.
2. Add the Sugar.
3. Stir in the cream and peanut butter.
4. Line the muffin tins. Fill the muffin cups.
5. Freeze for 60 minutes.
6. Serve!

Cinnamon Apple Chips

Servings: 6 | Cooking Time: 8 Minutes

- 3 Granny Smith apples, wash, core and thinly slice
- 1 tsp ground cinnamon
- Pinch of salt

1. Rub apple slices with cinnamon and salt and place into the air fryer basket.
2. Cook at 390 F for 8 minutes. Turn halfway through.
3. Serve and enjoy.

Cream Cups

Servings: 6 | Cooking Time: 10 Minutes

- 2 tablespoons butter, melted
- 8 ounces cream cheese, soft
- 3 tablespoons coconut, shredded and unsweetened
- 3 eggs
- 4 tablespoons swerve

1. In a bowl, mix all the ingredients and whisk really well. Divide into small ramekins, put them in the fryer and cook at 320 degrees F and bake for 10 minutes. Serve cold.

Fried Twinkies

Servings:6 | Cooking Time: 5 Minutes

- 2 Large egg white(s)
- 2 tablespoons Water
- 1½ cups (about 9 ounces) Ground gingersnap cookie crumbs
- 6 Twinkies
- Vegetable oil spray

1. Preheat the air fryer to 400°F.
2. Set up and fill two shallow soup plates or small pie plates on your counter: one for the egg white(s), whisked with the water until foamy; and one for the gingersnap crumbs.
3. Dip a Twinkie in the egg white(s), turning it to coat on all sides, even the ends. Let the excess egg white mixture slip back into the rest, then set the Twinkie in the crumbs. Roll it to coat on all sides, even the ends, pressing gently to get an even coating. Then repeat this process: egg white(s), followed by crumbs. Lightly coat the prepared Twinkie on all sides with vegetable oil spray. Set aside and coat each of the remaining Twinkies with the same double-dipping technique, followed by spraying.
4. Set the Twinkies flat side up in the basket with as much air space between them as possible. Air-fry for 5 minutes, or until browned and crunchy.
5. Use a nonstick-safe spatula to gently transfer the Twinkies to a wire rack. Cool for at least 10 minutes before serving.

Chocolate Raspberry Wontons

Servings: 6 | Cooking Time: 15 Minutes

- 1 (12-ounce) package wonton wrappers
- 6 ounces chocolate chips
- 1/2 cup raspberries, mashed
- 1 egg, lightly whisked + 1 tablespoon of water (egg wash)
- 1/4 cup caster sugar

1. Divide the chocolate chips and raspberries among the wonton wrappers. Now, fold the wrappers diagonally in half over the filling; press the edges with a fork.
2. Brush with the egg wash and seal the edges.
3. Bake at 370 degrees F for 8 minutes, flipping them halfway through the cooking time.
4. Work in batches. Sprinkle the caster sugar over your wontons and enjoy!

Lemon Mousse

Servings:6 | Cooking Time:10 Minutes

- 12-ounces cream cheese, softened
- ¼ teaspoon salt
- 1 teaspoon lemon liquid stevia
- 1/3 cup fresh lemon juice
- 1½ cups heavy cream

1. Preheat the Air fryer to 345 degrees F and grease a large ramekin lightly.
2. Mix all the ingredients in a large bowl until well combined.
3. Pour into the ramekin and transfer into the Air fryer.
4. Cook for about 10 minutes and pour into the serving glasses.
5. Refrigerate to cool for about 3 hours and serve chilled.

Crème Brulee

Servings:3 | Cooking Time: 60 Minutes

- 1 cup milk
- 2 vanilla pods
- 10 egg yolks
- 4 tbsp sugar + extra for topping

1. In a pan, add the milk and cream. Cut the vanilla pods open and scrape the seeds into the pan with the vanilla pods also. Place the pan over medium heat on a stovetop until almost boiled while stirring regularly. Turn off the heat. Add the egg yolks to a bowl and beat it. Add the sugar and mix well but not too bubbly.
2. Remove the vanilla pods from the milk mixture; pour the mixture onto the eggs mixture while stirring constantly. Let it sit for 25 minutes. Fill 2 to 3 ramekins with the mixture. Place the ramekins in the fryer basket and cook them at 190 F for 50 minutes. Once ready, remove the ramekins and let sit to cool. Sprinkle the remaining sugar over and use a torch to melt the sugar, so it browns at the top.

Sugar Pork Rinds

Servings: 2 | Cooking Time: 10 Minutes

- 2 oz. pork rinds
- ¼ cup powdered erythritol
- 2 tsp. unsalted butter, melted
- ½ tsp. ground cinnamon

1. Coat the rinds with the melted butter.
2. In a separate bowl, combine the erythritol and cinnamon and pour over the pork rinds, ensuring the rinds are covered completely and evenly.
3. Transfer the pork rinds into the fryer and cook at 400°F for five minutes.

Coconut Sunflower Cookies

Servings: 8 | Cooking Time: 10 Minutes

- 5 oz sunflower seed butter
- 6 tbsp coconut flour
- 1 tsp vanilla
- ¼ tsp olive oil
- 2 tbsp swerve
- Pinch of salt

1. Add all ingredients into the bowl and mix until dough is formed.
2. Preheat the air fryer to 360 F.
3. Make cookies from mixture and place into the air fryer and cook for 10 minutes.
4. Serve and enjoy.

Fruity Tacos

Servings:2 | Cooking Time: 5 Minutes

- 2 soft shell tortillas
- 4 tablespoons strawberry jelly
- ¼ cup blueberries
- ¼ cup raspberries
- 2 tablespoons powdered sugar

1. Set the temperature of air fryer to 300 degrees F. Lightly, grease an air fryer basket.
2. Arrange the tortillas onto a smooth surface.
3. Spread two tablespoons of strawberry jelly over each tortilla and top each with berries.
4. Sprinkle each with the powdered sugar.
5. Arrange tortillas into the prepared air fryer basket.
6. Air fry for about 5 minutes or until crispy.
7. Remove from the air fryer and transfer the tortillas onto a platter.
8. Serve warm.

Creamy Pudding

Servings: 6 | Cooking Time: 25 Minutes

- 2 cups fresh cream
- 6 egg yolks, whisked
- 6 tablespoons white sugar
- Zest of 1 orange

1. Combine all ingredients in a bowl and whisk well.
2. Divide the mixture between 6 small ramekins.
3. Place the ramekins in your air fryer and cook at 340 degrees F for 25 minutes.
4. Place in the fridge for 1 hour before serving.

Chocolate Soufflé

Servings:2 | Cooking Time: 25 Minutes

- ¼ cup butter, melted
- 2 tbsp flour
- 3 tbsp sugar
- 3 oz chocolate, melted
- ½ tsp vanilla extract

1. Preheat the air fryer to 330 F.
2. Beat the yolks along with the sugar and vanilla extract; stir in butter, chocolate, and flour. and whisk the whites until a stiff peak forms.
3. Working in batches, gently combine the egg whites with the chocolate mixture. Divide the batter between two greased ramekins. Cook for 14 minutes.

Cherry Pie
Servings: 8 | Cooking Time: 35 Minutes
- 1 tbsp. milk
- 2 ready-made pie crusts
- 21 oz. cherry pie filling
- 1 egg yolk

1. Pre-heat the Air Fryer to 310°F.
2. Coat the inside of a pie pan with a little oil or butter and lay one of the pie crusts inside. Use a fork to pierce a few holes in the pastry.
3. Spread the pie filling evenly over the crust.
4. Slice the other crust into strips and place them on top of the pie filling to make the pie look more homemade.
5. Place in the Air Fryer and cook for 15 minutes.

Sweet Potato Pie Rolls
Servings: 3 | Cooking Time: 8 Minutes
- 6 Spring roll wrappers
- 1½ cups Canned yams in syrup, drained
- 2 tablespoons Light brown sugar
- ¼ teaspoon Ground cinnamon
- 1 Large egg(s), well beaten
- Vegetable oil spray

1. Preheat the air fryer to 400°F.
2. Set a spring roll wrapper on a clean, dry work surface. Scoop up ¼ cup of the pulpy yams and set along one edge of the wrapper, leaving 2 inches on each side of the yams. Top the yams with about 1 teaspoon brown sugar and a pinch of ground cinnamon. Fold the sides of the wrapper perpendicular to the yam filling up and over the filling, partially covering it. Brush beaten egg(s) over the side of the wrapper farthest from the yam. Starting with the yam end, roll the wrapper closed, ending at the part with the beaten egg that you can press gently to seal. Lightly coat the roll on all sides with vegetable oil spray. Set it aside seam side down and continue filling, rolling, and spraying the remaining wrappers in the same way.
3. Set the rolls seam side down in the basket with as much air space between them as possible. Air-fry undisturbed for 8 minutes, or until crisp and golden brown.
4. Use a nonstick-safe spatula and perhaps kitchen tongs for balance to gently transfer the rolls to a wire rack. Cool for at least 5 minutes or up to 30 minutes before serving.

Lemon Bars Recipe
Servings: 6 | Cooking Time: 35 Minutes
- 4 eggs
- 1 cup butter; soft
- 2 ¼ cups flour
- Juice from 2 lemons
- 2 cups sugar

1. In a bowl; mix butter with 1/2 cup sugar and 2 cups flour; stir well, press on the bottom of a pan that fits your air fryer, introduce in the fryer and cook at 350 °F, for 10 minutes
2. In another bowl, mix the rest of the sugar with the rest of the flour, eggs and lemon juice, whisk well and spread over crust. Introduce in the fryer at 350 °F, for 15 minutes more, leave aside to cool down, cut bars and serve them.

Lemon Curd
Servings: 2 | Cooking Time: 30 Minutes
- 3 tbsp sugar
- 1 egg
- 1 egg yolk
- ¾ lemon, juiced

1. Add sugar and butter in a medium ramekin and beat evenly. Add egg and yolk slowly while still whisking the fresh yellow color will be attained. Add the lemon juice and mix. Place the bowl in the fryer basket and cook at 250 F for 6 minutes. Increase the temperature again to 320 F and cook for 15 minutes.
2. Remove the bowl onto a flat surface; use a spoon to check for any lumps and remove. Cover the ramekin with a plastic wrap and refrigerate overnight or serve immediately.

Lemon Berries Stew
Servings: 4 | Cooking Time: 20 Minutes
- 1 pound strawberries, halved
- 4 tablespoons stevia
- 1 tablespoon lemon juice
- 1 and ½ cups water

1. In a pan that fits your air fryer, mix all the ingredients, toss, put it in the fryer and cook at 340 degrees F for 20 minutes. Divide the stew into cups and serve cold.

Caramel Baked Apples
Servings: 4 | Cooking Time: 16 Minutes
- 4 medium Pink Lady apples
- ½ cup salted butter
- 8 soft caramel chews
- ½ cup rolled oats
- ¼ cup granulated sugar
- 1 teaspoon ground cinnamon

1. Preheat the air fryer to 350°F.
2. Using a sharp knife, carefully core apples by cutting a large, deep square into the center from the top down. Scoop out seeds and insides, leaving about one-fourth of apple intact at the bottom.
3. In a medium microwave-safe bowl, microwave butter 30 seconds. Add caramels and microwave 15 seconds more. Stir quickly to finish melting caramels into butter.
4. Add oats, sugar, and cinnamon to caramel mixture. Mix until well combined and crumbly.
5. Scoop mixture into cored apples. Place in the air fryer basket and cook 15 minutes until apples are wrinkled and softened. Serve warm.

White Chocolate Chip Cookies
Servings: 8 | Cooking Time: 30 Minutes
- 3 oz brown sugar
- 2 oz white chocolate chips
- 1 tbsp honey
- 1 ½ tbsp milk
- 4 oz butter

1. Preheat the air fryer to 350 F, and beat the butter and sugar until fluffy. Beat in the honey, milk, and flour. Gently fold in the chocolate cookies. Drop spoonfuls of the mixture onto a prepared cookie sheet. Cook for 18 minutes.

Apple Pie Crumble
Servings:4 | Cooking Time:25 Minutes
- 1 (14-ounce) can apple pie
- ¼ cup butter, softened
- 9 tablespoons self-rising flour
- 7 tablespoons caster sugar
- Pinch of salt

1. Preheat the Air fryer to 320 o F and grease a baking dish.
2. Mix all the ingredients in a bowl until a crumbly mixture is formed.
3. Arrange the apple pie in the baking dish and top with the mixture.
4. Transfer the baking dish into the Air fryer basket and cook for about 25 minutes.
5. Dish out in a platter and serve.

Coconut Cupcakes
Servings:12 | Cooking Time: 15 Minutes Per Batch
- 1 cup all-purpose flour
- ½ cup granulated sugar
- 1 teaspoon baking powder
- ¼ cup salted butter, melted
- 1 large egg
- ½ cup full-fat canned coconut milk
- ½ cup sweetened shredded coconut

1. Preheat the air fryer to 300°F.
2. In a large bowl, whisk together flour, sugar, and baking powder.
3. Add butter, egg, and coconut milk to dry mixture. Stir until well combined.
4. Fold in shredded coconut. Divide evenly among twelve silicone or aluminum muffin cups, filling each halfway full.
5. Place in the air fryer basket, working in batches as necessary. Cook 15 minutes until brown at the edges and a toothpick inserted into the center comes out clean. Let cool for 5 minutes before serving.

Shortbread Fingers
Servings: 10 | Cooking Time: 20 Minutes
- 1 ½ cups butter
- 1 cup flour
- ¾ cup sugar
- Cooking spray

1. Pre-heat your Air Fryer to 350°F.
2. In a bowl. combine the flour and sugar.
3. Cut each stick of butter into small chunks. Add the chunks into the flour and the sugar.
4. Blend the butter into the mixture to combine everything well.
5. Use your hands to knead the mixture, forming a smooth consistency.
6. Shape the mixture into 10 equal-sized finger shapes, marking them with the tines of a fork for decoration if desired.
7. Lightly spritz the Air Fryer basket with the cooking spray. Place the cookies inside, spacing them out well.
8. Bake the cookies for 12 minutes.
9. Let cool slightly before serving. Alternatively, you can store the cookies in an airtight container for up to 3 days.

Grape Stew
Servings: 4 | Cooking Time: 14 Minutes
- 1 pound red grapes
- Juice and zest of 1 lemon
- 26 ounces grape juice

1. In a pan that fits your air fryer, add all ingredients and toss.
2. Place the pan in the fryer and cook at 320 degrees F for 14 minutes.
3. Divide into cups, refrigerate, and serve cold.

Apple Pastry Pouch
Servings:2 | Cooking Time: 25 Minutes
- 1 tablespoon brown sugar
- 2 tablespoons raisins
- 2 small apples, peeled and cored
- 2 puff pastry sheets
- 2 tablespoons butter, melted

1. In a bowl, mix together the sugar and raisins.
2. Fill the core of each apple with raisins mixture.
3. Place one apple in the center of each pastry sheet and fold dough to cover the apple completely.
4. Then, pinch the edges to seal.
5. Coat each apple evenly with butter.
6. Set the temperature of air fryer to 355 degrees F. Lightly, grease an air fryer basket.
7. Arrange apple pouches into the prepared air fryer basket in a single layer.
8. Air fry for about 25 minutes.
9. Remove from air fryer and transfer the apple pouches onto a platter.
10. Serve warm.

Roasted Pumpkin Seeds & Cinnamon
Servings: 2 | Cooking Time: 35 Minutes
- 1 cup pumpkin raw seeds
- 1 tbsp. ground cinnamon
- 2 tbsp. sugar
- 1 cup water
- 1 tbsp. olive oil

1. In a frying pan, combine the pumpkin seeds, cinnamon and water.
2. Boil the mixture over a high heat for 2 - 3 minutes.
3. Pour out the water and place the seeds on a clean kitchen towel, allowing them to dry for 20 - 30 minutes.
4. In a bowl, mix together the sugar, dried seeds, a pinch of cinnamon and one tablespoon of olive oil.
5. Pre-heat the Air Fryer to 340°F.
6. Place the seed mixture in the fryer basket and allow to cook for 15 minutes, shaking the basket periodically throughout.

Butter Plums
Servings: 4 | Cooking Time: 20 Minutes
- 2 teaspoons cinnamon powder
- 4 plums, halved
- 4 tablespoons butter, melted
- 3 tablespoons swerve

1. In a pan that fits your air fryer, mix the plums with the rest of the ingredients, toss, put the pan in the air fryer and cook at 300 degrees F for 20 minutes. Divide into cups and serve cold.

Baked Plum Cream
Servings: 4 | Cooking Time: 20 Minutes
- 1 pound plums, pitted and chopped
- ¼ cup swerve
- 1 tablespoon lemon juice
- 1 and ½ cups heavy cream

1. In a bowl, mix all the ingredients and whisk really well. Divide this into 4 ramekins, put them in the air fryer and cook at 340 degrees F for 20 minutes. Serve cold.

Peanut Cookies
Servings: 4 | Cooking Time: 5 Minutes
- 4 tablespoons peanut butter
- 4 teaspoons Erythritol
- 1 egg, beaten
- ¼ teaspoon vanilla extract

1. In the mixing bowl mix up peanut butter, Erythritol, egg, and vanilla extract. Stir the mixture with the help of the fork. Then make 4 cookies. Preheat the air fryer to 355F. Place the cookies in the air fryer and cook them for 5 minutes.

Chocolate Candies
Servings: 4 | Cooking Time: 2 Minutes
- 1 oz almonds, crushed
- 1 oz dark chocolate
- 2 tablespoons peanut butter
- 2 tablespoons heavy cream

1. Preheat the air fryer to 390F. Chop the dark chocolate and put it in the air fryer mold. Add peanut butter and heavy cream. Stir the mixture and transfer in the air fryer. Cook it for 2 minutes or until it starts to be melt. Then line the air tray with parchment. Put the crushed almonds on the tray in one layer. Then pour the cooked chocolate mixture over the almonds. Flatten gently if needed and let it cool. Crack the cooked chocolate layer into the candies.

Peanut Butter Cookies
Servings:9 | Cooking Time: 10 Minutes Per Batch
- 1 cup creamy peanut butter
- 1 cup brown sugar
- ½ cup unsalted butter, melted
- 2 large eggs
- 2 cups all-purpose flour
- 1 ½ teaspoons baking powder

1. Preheat the air fryer to 325°F. Cut two pieces of parchment paper to fit the air fryer basket, one for each batch.
2. In a large bowl, mix peanut butter and brown sugar until combined.
3. Add butter and eggs, stirring until smooth.
4. In a medium bowl, mix flour and baking powder. Slowly add flour mixture, about a third at a time, to peanut butter mixture. Fold in to combine.
5. Roll dough into balls, about 2 tablespoons each, to make eighteen balls.
6. Place on parchment 2" apart in the air fryer, working in batches as necessary, and cook 10 minutes until the edges are golden brown. Let cool 5 minutes before serving.

Macaroon Bites
Servings: 2 | Cooking Time: 30 Minutes
- 4 egg whites
- ½ tsp vanilla
- ½ tsp EZ-Sweet (or equivalent of 1 cup artificial sweetener)
- 4½ tsp water
- 1 cup unsweetened coconut

1. Preheat your fryer to 375°F/190°C.
2. Combine the egg whites, liquids and coconut.
3. Put into the fryer and reduce the heat to 325°F/160°C.
4. Bake for 15 minutes.
5. Serve!

Oreo-coated Peanut Butter Cups
Servings:8 | Cooking Time: 4 Minutes
- 8 Standard ¾-ounce peanut butter cups, frozen
- ⅓ cup All-purpose flour
- 2 Large egg white(s), beaten until foamy
- 16 Oreos or other creme-filled chocolate sandwich cookies, ground to crumbs in a food processor
- Vegetable oil spray

1. Set up and fill three shallow soup plates or small pie plates on your counter: one for the flour, one for the beaten egg white(s), and one for the cookie crumbs.
2. Dip a frozen peanut butter cup in the flour, turning it to coat all sides. Shake off any excess, then set it in the beaten egg white(s). Turn it to coat all sides, then let any excess egg white slip back into the rest. Set the candy bar in the cookie crumbs. Turn to coat on all parts, even the sides. Dip the peanut butter cup back in the egg white(s) as before, then into the cookie crumbs as before, making sure you have a solid, even coating all around the cup. Set aside while you dip and coat the remaining cups.
3. When all the peanut butter cups are dipped and coated, lightly coat them on all sides with the vegetable oil spray. Set them on a plate and freeze while the air fryer heats.
4. Preheat the air fryer to 400°F.
5. Set the dipped cups wider side up in the basket with as much air space between them as possible. Air-fry undisturbed for 4 minutes, or until they feel soft but the coating is set.
6. Turn off the machine and remove the basket from it. Set aside the basket with the fried cups for 10 minutes. Use a nonstick-safe spatula to transfer the fried cups to a wire rack. Cool for at least another 5 minutes before serving.

Banana Fritters
Servings:8 | Cooking Time: 15 Minutes
- 3 tbsp vegetable oil
- 3 tbsp cornflour
- 1 egg white
- ¾ cup breadcrumbs

1. Preheat air fryer to 350 F.
2. Combine the oil and breadcrumbs, in a small bowl. Coat the bananas with the cornflour first, brush them with egg white, and dip them in the breadcrumb mixture. Arrange on a lined baking sheet and cook for 8 minutes.

Berry Layer Cake
Servings: 1 | Cooking Time: 8 Minutes
- ¼ lemon pound cake
- ¼ cup whipping cream
- ½ tsp Truvia
- 1/8 tsp orange flavor
- 1 cup of mixed berries

1. Using a sharp knife, divide the lemon cake into small cubes.
2. Dice the strawberries.
3. Combine the whipping cream, Truvia, and orange flavor.
4. Layer the fruit, cake and cream in a glass.
5. Serve!

Midnight Nutella® Banana Sandwich
Servings: 2 | Cooking Time: 8 Minutes
- butter, softened
- 4 slices white bread*
- ¼ cup chocolate hazelnut spread (Nutella®)
- 1 banana

1. Preheat the air fryer to 370°F.
2. Spread the softened butter on one side of all the slices of bread and place the slices buttered side down on the counter. Spread the chocolate hazelnut spread on the other side of the bread slices. Cut the banana in half and then slice each half into three slices lengthwise. Place the banana slices on two slices of bread and top with the remaining slices of bread (buttered side up) to make two sandwiches. Cut the sandwiches in half (triangles or rectangles) – this will help them all fit in the air fryer at once. Transfer the sandwiches to the air fryer.
3. Air-fry at 370°F for 5 minutes. Flip the sandwiches over and air-fry for another 2 to 3 minutes, or until the top bread slices are nicely browned. Pour yourself a glass of milk or a midnight nightcap while the sandwiches cool slightly and enjoy!

Cranberry Cream Surprise
Servings: 1 | Cooking Time: 30 Minutes
- 1 cup mashed cranberries
- ½ cup Confectioner's Style Swerve
- 2 tsp natural cherry flavoring
- 2 tsp natural rum flavoring
- 1 cup organic heavy cream

1. Combine the mashed cranberries, sweetener, cherry and rum flavorings.
2. Cover and refrigerate for 20 minutes.
3. Whip the heavy cream until soft peaks form.
4. Layer the whipped cream and cranberry mixture.
5. Top with fresh cranberries, mint leaves or grated dark chocolate.
6. Serve!

Chocolate And Avocado Cream
Servings: 4 | Cooking Time: 20 Minutes
- 2 avocados, peeled, pitted and mashed
- 3 tablespoons chocolate, melted
- 4 tablespoons erythritol
- 3 tablespoons cream cheese, soft

1. In a pan that fits the air fryer, combine all the ingredients, whisk, put the pan in the fryer and cook at 340 degrees F for 20 minutes. Divide into bowls and serve cold.

Coconut Pillow
Servings: 4 | Cooking Time: 1-2 Days
- 1 can unsweetened coconut milk
- Berries of choice
- Dark chocolate

1. Refrigerate the coconut milk for 24 hours.
2. Remove it from your refrigerator and whip for 2-3 minutes.
3. Fold in the berries.
4. Season with the chocolate shavings.
5. Serve!

Crispy Fruit Tacos
Servings: 2 | Cooking Time: 5 Minutes
- 2 soft shell tortillas
- 4 tablespoons strawberry jelly
- ¼ cup blueberries
- ¼ cup raspberries
- 2 tablespoons powdered sugar

1. Preheat the Air fryer to 300 o F and grease an Air fryer basket.
2. Put 2 tablespoons of strawberry jelly over each tortilla and top with blueberries and raspberries.
3. Sprinkle with powdered sugar and transfer into the Air fryer basket.
4. Cook for about 5 minutes until crispy and serve.

Chocolate Brownie
Servings: 4 | Cooking Time: 16 Minutes
- 1 cup bananas, overripe
- 1 scoop protein powder
- 2 tbsp unsweetened cocoa powder
- 1/2 cup almond butter, melted

1. Preheat the air fryer to 325 F.
2. Spray air fryer baking pan with cooking spray.
3. Add all ingredients into the blender and blend until smooth.
4. Pour batter into the prepared pan and place in the air fryer basket.
5. Cook brownie for 16 minutes.
6. Serve and enjoy.

Marshmallow Pastries
Servings: 8 | Cooking Time: 5 Minutes
- 4-ounce butter, melted
- 8 phyllo pastry sheets, thawed
- ½ cup chunky peanut butter
- 8 teaspoons marshmallow fluff
- Pinch of salt

1. Preheat the Air fryer to 360 o F and grease an Air fryer basket.
2. Brush butter over 1 filo pastry sheet and top with a second filo sheet.
3. Brush butter over second filo pastry sheet and repeat with all the remaining sheets.
4. Cut the phyllo layers in 8 strips and put 1 tablespoon of peanut butter and 1 teaspoon of marshmallow fluff on the underside of a filo strip.
5. Fold the tip of the sheet over the filling to form a triangle and fold repeatedly in a zigzag manner.
6. Arrange the pastries into the Air fryer basket and cook for about 5 minutes.
7. Season with a pinch of salt and serve warm.

Air Fried Snickerdoodle Poppers
Servings:6 | Cooking Time: 30 Minutes
- 1 can of Pillsbury Grands Flaky Layers Biscuits
- 1 ½ cups cinnamon sugar
- melted butter, for brushing

1. Preheat air fryer to 350 F. Unroll the flaky biscuits; cut them into fourths. Roll each ¼ into a ball. Arrange the balls on a lined baking sheet, and cook in the air fryer for 7 minutes, or until golden.
2. Prepare the Jell-O following the package's instructions. Using an injector, inject some of the vanilla pudding into each ball. Brush the balls with melted butter and then coat them with cinnamon sugar.

Raspberry Pudding Surprise
Servings: 1 | Cooking Time: 40 Minutes
- 3 tbsp chia seeds
- ½ cup unsweetened milk
- 1 scoop chocolate protein powder
- ¼ cup raspberries, fresh or frozen
- 1 tsp honey

1. Combine the milk, protein powder and chia seeds together.
2. Let rest for 5 minutes before stirring.
3. Refrigerate for 30 minutes.
4. Top with raspberries.
5. Serve!

Ricotta Lemon Cake
Servings: 8 | Cooking Time: 40 Minutes
- 1 lb ricotta
- 4 eggs
- 1 lemon juice
- 1 lemon zest
- ¼ cup erythritol

1. Preheat the air fryer to 325 F.
2. Spray air fryer baking dish with cooking spray.
3. In a bowl, beat ricotta cheese until smooth.
4. Whisk in the eggs one by one.
5. Whisk in lemon juice and zest.
6. Pour batter into the prepared baking dish and place into the air fryer.
7. Cook for 40 minutes.
8. Allow to cool completely then slice and serve.

Cheesecake Cups
Servings: 4 | Cooking Time: 10 Minutes
- 8 oz cream cheese, softened
- 2 oz heavy cream
- 1 tsp Sugar Glycerite
- 1 tsp Splenda
- 1 tsp vanilla flavoring (Frontier Organic)

1. Combine all the ingredients.
2. Whip until a pudding consistency is achieved.
3. Divide in cups.
4. Refrigerate until served!

Chocolate Mug Cake
Servings:1 | Cooking Time:13 Minutes
- ¼ cup self-rising flour
- 1 tablespoon cocoa powder
- 3 tablespoons whole milk
- 5 tablespoons caster sugar
- 3 tablespoons coconut oil

1. Preheat the Air fryer to 390 o F and grease a large mug lightly.
2. Mix all the ingredients in a shallow mug until well combined.
3. Arrange the mug into the Air fryer basket and cook for about 13 minutes.
4. Dish out and serve warm.

Pineapple Sticks
Servings: 4 | Cooking Time: 20 Minutes
- ½ fresh pineapple, cut into sticks
- ¼ cup desiccated coconut

1. Pre-heat the Air Fryer to 400°F.
2. Coat the pineapple sticks in the desiccated coconut and put each one in the Air Fryer basket.
3. Air fry for 10 minutes.

Chocolate Banana Sandwiches
Servings:2 | Cooking Time: 30 Minutes
- 1 tbsp butter, melted
- 6 oz milk chocolate, broken into chunks
- 1 banana, sliced

1. Brush the brioche slices with butter. Spread chocolate and banana on 2 brioche slices. Top with the remaining 2 slices to create 2 sandwiches. Arrange the sandwiches into your air fryer and cook for 14 minutes at 400 F, turning once halfway through. Slice in half and serve with vanilla ice cream.

Baked Apple
Servings: 6 | Cooking Time: 20 Minutes
- 3 small Honey Crisp or other baking apples
- 3 tablespoons maple syrup
- 3 tablespoons chopped pecans
- 1 tablespoon firm butter, cut into 6 pieces

1. Put ½ cup water in the drawer of the air fryer.
2. Wash apples well and dry them.
3. Split apples in half. Remove core and a little of the flesh to make a cavity for the pecans.
4. Place apple halves in air fryer basket, cut side up.
5. Spoon 1½ teaspoons pecans into each cavity.
6. Spoon ½ tablespoon maple syrup over pecans in each apple.
7. Top each apple with ½ teaspoon butter.
8. Cook at 360°F for 20 minutes, until apples are tender.

Brownies Muffins
Servings:12 | Cooking Time:10 Minutes
- 1 package Betty Crocker fudge brownie mix
- ¼ cup walnuts, chopped
- 1 egg
- 2 teaspoons water
- 1/3 cup vegetable oil

1. Preheat the Air fryer to 300 o F and grease 12 muffin molds lightly.

2. Mix all the ingredients in a bowl and divide evenly into the muffin molds.
3. Arrange the molds in the Air Fryer basket and cook for about 10 minutes.
4. Dish out and invert the muffins onto wire rack to completely cool before serving.

Fried Banana S'mores
Servings: 4 | Cooking Time: 6 Minutes
- 4 bananas
- 3 tablespoons mini semi-sweet chocolate chips
- 3 tablespoons mini peanut butter chips
- 3 tablespoons mini marshmallows
- 3 tablespoons graham cracker cereal

1. Preheat the air fryer to 400°F.
2. Slice into the un-peeled bananas lengthwise along the inside of the curve, but do not slice through the bottom of the peel. Open the banana slightly to form a pocket.
3. Fill each pocket with chocolate chips, peanut butter chips and marshmallows. Poke the graham cracker cereal into the filling.
4. Place the bananas in the air fryer basket, resting them on the side of the basket and each other to keep them upright with the filling facing up. Air-fry for 6 minutes, or until the bananas are soft to the touch, the peels have blackened and the chocolate and marshmallows have melted and toasted.
5. Let them cool for a couple of minutes and then simply serve with a spoon to scoop out the filling.

Crusty
Servings: 3 | Cooking Time: 60 Minutes
- 2 cups flour
- 4 tsp melted butter
- 2 large eggs
- ½ tsp salt

1. Mix together the flour and butter.
2. Add in the eggs and salt and combine well to form a dough ball.
3. Place the dough between two pieces of parchment paper. Roll out to 10" by 16" and ¼ inch thick.
4. Serve!

Monkey Bread
Servings: 6 | Cooking Time: 20 Minutes
- 1 can refrigerated biscuit dough
- ½ cup granulated sugar
- 1 tablespoon ground cinnamon
- ¼ cup salted butter, melted
- ¼ cup brown sugar

1. Preheat the air fryer to 325°F. Spray a 6" round cake pan with cooking spray. Separate biscuits and cut each into four pieces.
2. In a large bowl, stir granulated sugar with cinnamon. Toss biscuit pieces in the cinnamon and sugar mixture until well coated. Place each biscuit piece in prepared pan.
3. In a medium bowl, stir together butter and brown sugar. Pour mixture evenly over the biscuit pieces.
4. Place pan in the air fryer basket and cook 20 minutes until brown. Let cool 10 minutes before flipping bread out of the pan and serving.

Almond Meringue Cookies
Servings: 4 | Cooking Time: 145 Minutes
- ½ tsp almond extract
- 1 ⅓ cups sugar
- ¼ tsp salt
- 2 tsp lemon juice
- 1 ½ tsp vanilla extract
- Melted dark chocolate to drizzle

1. In a mixing bowl, add egg whites, salt, and lemon juice. Beat using an electric mixer until foamy. Slowly add the sugar and continue beating until completely combined; add the almond and vanilla extracts. Beat until stiff peaks form and glossy.
2. Line a round baking sheet with parchment paper. Fill a piping bag with the meringue mixture and pipe as many mounds on the baking sheet as you can leaving 2-inch spaces between each mound.
3. Place the baking sheet in the fryer basket and bake at 250 F for 5 minutes. Reduce the temperature to 220 F and bake for 15 more minutes. Then, reduce the temperature once more to 190 F and cook for 15 minutes. Let the meringues cool for 2 hours. Drizzle with the dark chocolate before serving.

Blackberry Cream
Servings: 6 | Cooking Time: 20 Minutes
- 2 cups blackberries
- Juice of ½ lemon
- 2 tablespoons water
- 1 teaspoon vanilla extract
- 2 tablespoons swerve

1. In a bowl, mix all the ingredients and whisk well. Divide this into 6 ramekins, put them in the air fryer and cook at 340 degrees F for 20 minutes Cool down and serve.

Almond Shortbread Cookies
Servings: 8 | Cooking Time: 1 Hour 10 Minutes
- ½ cup salted butter, softened
- ¼ cup granulated sugar
- 1 teaspoon almond extract
- 1 teaspoon vanilla extract
- 2 cups all-purpose flour

1. In a large bowl, cream butter, sugar, and extracts. Gradually add flour, mixing until well combined.
2. Roll dough into a 12" x 2" log and wrap in plastic. Chill in refrigerator at least 1 hour.
3. Preheat the air fryer to 300°F.
4. Slice dough into ¼"-thick cookies. Place in the air fryer basket 2" apart, working in batches as needed, and cook 10 minutes until the edges start to brown. Let cool completely before serving.

Orange Marmalade
Servings: 4 | Cooking Time: 20 Minutes
- 4 oranges, peeled and chopped
- 3 cups sugar
- 1½ cups water

1. In a pan that fits your air fryer, mix the oranges with the sugar and the water; stir.
2. Place the pan in the fryer and cook at 340 degrees F for 20 minutes.
3. Stir well, divide into cups, refrigerate, and serve cold.

Apple Dumplings
Servings: 4 | Cooking Time: 10 Minutes
- 4 Small tart apples, preferably McIntosh, peeled and cored
- ¼ cup Granulated white sugar
- 1½ tablespoons Ground cinnamon
- 1 sheet, thawed and cut into four quarters A 17.25-ounce box frozen puff pastry (vegetarian, if a concern)

1. Set the apples (former) stem side up on a microwave-safe plate, preferably a glass pie plate. Microwave on high for 3 minutes, or until somewhat tender (but not soft) when poked with the point of a knife. Cool to room temperature, about 30 minutes.
2. Preheat the air fryer to 400°F.
3. Combine the sugar and cinnamon in a small bowl. Roll the apples in this mixture, coating them completely on their outsides. Also sprinkle this cinnamon sugar into each hole where the core was.
4. Roll the puff pastry squares into 6 x 6-inch squares. Slice the corners off each rolled square so that it's sort of like a circle (with four otherwise straight edges, of course). Place an apple in the center of one of these squares and fold it up and all around the apple, sealing it at the top by pressing the pastry together. The apple must be completely sealed in the pastry. Repeat for the remaining apples.
5. Set the pastry-covered apples in the basket with at least ½ inch between them. Air-fry undisturbed for 10 minutes, or until puffed and golden brown.
6. Use a nonstick-safe spatula, and maybe a flatware tablespoon for balance, to transfer the apples to a wire rack. Cool for at least 5 minutes or up to 15 minutes before serving warm.

Yummy Banana Cookies
Servings: 6 | Cooking Time: 10 Minutes
- 1 cup dates, pitted and chopped
- 1 teaspoon vanilla
- 1/3 cup vegetable oil
- 2 cups rolled oats
- 3 ripe bananas

1. Preheat the air fryer to 3500F.
2. In a bowl, mash the bananas and add in the rest of the ingredients.
3. Let it rest inside the fridge for 10 minutes.
4. Drop a teaspoonful on cut parchment paper.
5. Place the cookies on parchment paper inside the air fryer basket. Make sure that the cookies do not overlap.
6. Cook for 20 minutes or until the edges are crispy.
7. Serve with almond milk.

Delicious Vanilla Custard
Servings: 2 | Cooking Time: 20 Minutes
- 5 eggs
- 2 tbsp swerve
- 1 tsp vanilla
- ½ cup unsweetened almond milk
- ½ cup cream cheese

1. Add eggs in a bowl and beat using a hand mixer.
2. Add cream cheese, sweetener, vanilla, and almond milk and beat for 2 minutes more.
3. Spray two ramekins with cooking spray.
4. Pour batter into the prepared ramekins.
5. Preheat the air fryer to 350 F.
6. Place ramekins into the air fryer and cook for 20 minutes.
7. Serve and enjoy.

Choco-coconut Puddin
Servings: 1 | Cooking Time: 65 Minutes
- 1 cup coconut milk
- 2 tbsp cacao powder or organic cocoa
- ½ tsp Sugar powder extract or 2 tbsp honey/maple syrup
- ½ tbsp quality gelatin
- 1 tbsp water

1. On a medium heat, combine the coconut milk, cocoa and sweetener.
2. In a separate bowl, mix in the gelatin and water.
3. Add to the pan and stir until fully dissolved.
4. Pour into small dishes and refrigerate for 1 hour.
5. Serve!

Coconut Berry Pudding
Servings: 6 | Cooking Time: 15 Minutes
- 2 cups coconut cream
- 1 lime zest, grated
- 3 tbsp erythritol
- ¼ cup blueberries
- 1/3 cup blackberries

1. Add all ingredients into the blender and blend until well combined.
2. Spray 6 ramekins with cooking spray.
3. Pour blended mixture into the ramekins and place in the air fryer.
4. Cook at 340 F for 15 minutes.
5. Serve and enjoy.

Chocolate Cheesecake
Servings: 4 | Cooking Time: 60 Minutes
- 4 oz cream cheese
- ½ oz heavy cream
- 1 tsp Sugar Glycerite
- 1 tsp Splenda
- 1 oz Enjoy Life mini chocolate chips

1. Combine all the ingredients except the chocolate to a thick consistency.
2. Fold in the chocolate chips.
3. Refrigerate in serving cups.
4. Serve!

Chocolate-covered Maple Bacon
Servings: 4 | Cooking Time: 25 Minutes
- 8 slices sugar-free bacon
- 1 tbsp. granular erythritol
- 1/3 cup low-carb sugar-free chocolate chips
- 1 tsp. coconut oil
- ½ tsp. maple extract

1. Place the bacon in the fryer's basket and add the erythritol on top. Cook for six minutes at 350°F and turn the bacon over. Leave to cook another six minutes or until the bacon is sufficiently crispy.
2. Take the bacon out of the fryer and leave it to cool.
3. Microwave the chocolate chips and coconut oil together for half a minute. Remove from the microwave and mix together before stirring in the maple extract.
4. Set the bacon flat on a piece of parchment paper and pour the mixture over. Allow to harden in the refrigerator for roughly five minutes before serving.

Cream Cheese Pound Cake
Servings: 8 | Cooking Time: 25 Minutes
- 1 ½ cups all-purpose flour
- 1 teaspoon baking powder
- ½ cup salted butter, melted
- 4 ounces full-fat cream cheese, softened
- 1 cup granulated sugar
- 2 teaspoons vanilla extract
- 3 large eggs

1. Preheat the air fryer to 300°F. Spray a 6" round cake pan with cooking spray.
2. In a large bowl, combine flour and baking powder. In a separate large bowl, mix butter, cream cheese, sugar, and vanilla.
3. Stir wet ingredients into dry ingredients and add eggs one at a time, making sure each egg is fully incorporated before adding the next.
4. Pour batter into prepared pan. Place in the air fryer basket and cook 25 minutes until a toothpick inserted into the center comes out clean. If cake begins to brown too quickly, cover pan with foil and cut two slits in the top of foil to encourage heat circulation. Be sure to tuck foil under the bottom of the pan to ensure the air fryer fan does not blow it off.
5. Allow cake to cool completely before serving.

No Flour Lime Muffins
Servings: 6 | Cooking Time: 30 Minutes
- Juice and zest of 2 limes
- ¼ cup superfine sugar
- 1 tsp vanilla extract
- 1 cup yogurt
- 8 oz cream cheese

1. Preheat the air fryer to 330 F, and with a spatula, gently combine the yogurt and cheese. In another bowl, beat together the rest of the ingredients. Gently fold the lime with the cheese mixture. Divide the batter between 6 lined muffin tins. Cook in the air fryer for 10 minutes.

Nutty Fudge Muffins
Servings: 10 | Cooking Time: 10 Minutes
- 1 package fudge brownie mix
- 1 egg
- 2 teaspoons water
- ¼ cup walnuts, chopped
- 1/3 cup vegetable oil

1. Preheat the Air fryer to 300 o F and grease 10 muffin tins lightly.
2. Mix brownie mix, egg, oil and water in a bowl.
3. Fold in the walnuts and pour the mixture in the muffin cups.
4. Transfer the muffin tins in the Air fryer basket and cook for about 10 minutes.
5. Dish out and serve immediately.

Avocado Pudding
Servings: 1 | Cooking Time: 5 Minutes
- Avocado
- 1 tbsp. cocoa powder
- ¼ tsp. vanilla extract
- 3 tsp. liquid Sugar
- 4 tsp. unsweetened milk

1. Pre-heat your fryer at 360°F.
2. Halve the avocado, twist to open, and scoop out the pit.
3. Spoon the flesh into a bowl and mash it with a fork. Throw in the Sugar, cocoa powder, milk, and vanilla extract, and combine everything with a hand mixer.
4. Transfer this mixture to the basket of your fryer and cook for three minutes.

Choco-berry Fudge Sauce
Servings: 2 | Cooking Time: 30 Minutes
- 4 oz cream cheese, softened
- 1-3.5 oz 90% chocolate Lindt bar, chopped
- ¼ cup powdered erythritol
- ¼ cup heavy cream
- 1 tbsp Monin sugar-free raspberry syrup

1. In a large skillet, melt together the cream cheese and chocolate.
2. Stir in the sweetener.
3. Remove from the heat and allow to cool.
4. Once cool, mix in the cream and syrup.
5. Serve!

Chocolate Apple Chips
Servings: 2 | Cooking Time: 15 Minutes
- 1 large Pink Lady apple, cored and sliced
- 1 tablespoon light brown sugar
- A pinch of kosher salt
- 2 tablespoons lemon juice
- 2 teaspoons cocoa powder

1. Toss the apple slices with the other ingredients.
2. Bake at 350 degrees F for 5 minutes; shake the basket to ensure even cooking and continue to cook an additional 5 minutes.
3. Bon appétit!

Cranberry Jam
Servings: 8 | Cooking Time: 20 Minutes
- 2 pounds cranberries
- 4 ounces black currant
- 2 pounds sugar
- Zest of 1 lime
- 3 tablespoons water

1. In a pan that fits your air fryer, add all the ingredients and stir.
2. Place the pan in the fryer and cook at 360 degrees F for 20 minutes.
3. Stir the jam well, divide into cups, refrigerate, and serve cold.

Dark Chocolate Cake
Servings: 4 | Cooking Time: 10 Minutes
- 1½ tablespoons almond flour
- 3½ oz. unsalted butter
- 3½ oz. sugar free dark chocolate, chopped
- 2 eggs
- 3½ tablespoons swerve

1. Preheat the Air fryer to 375 o F and grease 4 regular sized ramekins.
2. Microwave all chocolate bits with butter in a bowl for about 3 minutes.
3. Remove from the microwave and whisk in the eggs and swerve.
4. Stir in the flour and mix well until smooth.
5. Transfer the mixture into the ramekins and arrange in the Air fryer basket.
6. Cook for about 10 minutes and dish out to serve.

Bananas & Ice Cream
Servings: 2 | Cooking Time: 25 Minutes
- 2 large bananas
- 1 tbsp. butter
- 1 tbsp. sugar
- 2 tbsp. friendly bread crumbs
- Vanilla ice cream for serving

1. Place the butter in the Air Fryer basket and allow it to melt for 1 minute at 350°F.
2. Combine the sugar and bread crumbs in a bowl.
3. Slice the bananas into 1-inch-round pieces. Drop them into the sugar mixture and coat them well.
4. Place the bananas in the Air Fryer and cook for 10 – 15 minutes.
5. Serve warm, with ice cream on the side if desired.

Chia Chocolate Cookies
Servings: 20 | Cooking Time: 8 Minutes
- 2 1/2 tbsp ground chia
- 2 tbsp chocolate protein powder
- 1 cup sunflower seed butter
- 1 cup almond flour

1. Preheat the air fryer to 325 F.
2. In a large bowl, add all ingredients and mix until combined.
3. Make cookies from bowl mixture and place into the air fryer and cook for 8 minutes.
4. Serve and enjoy.

Chocolate Chip Cookies
Servings: 12 | Cooking Time: 20 Minutes
- ½ cup salted butter, melted
- ½ cup brown sugar
- 1 cup all-purpose flour
- 1 large egg
- 1 teaspoon baking powder
- 1 teaspoon vanilla extract
- ⅓ cup semisweet chocolate chips

1. In a large bowl, stir butter, brown sugar, flour, egg, baking powder, and vanilla until well combined.
2. Gently fold in chocolate chips. Chill dough in refrigerator 10 minutes.
3. Preheat the air fryer to 350°F. Cut parchment paper to fit the air fryer basket.
4. Scoop the batter into portions to make twelve 2" balls. Place on parchment paper in the air fryer basket 2" apart and cook 10 minutes until golden brown on the edges and bottom. Serve warm.

Ricotta And Lemon Cake Recipe
Servings: 4 | Cooking Time: 1 Hour And 10 Minutes
- 8 eggs; whisked
- Zest from 1 lemon; grated
- 1/2 lb. sugar
- 3 lbs. ricotta cheese
- Zest from 1 orange; grated
- Butter for the pan

1. In a bowl; mix eggs with sugar, cheese, lemon and orange zest and stir very well
2. Grease a baking pan that fits your air fryer with some batter, spread ricotta mixture, introduce in the fryer at 390 °F and bake for 30 minutes
3. Reduce heat at 380 °F and bake for 40 more minutes. Take out of the oven, leave cake to cool down and serve!

Molten Lava Cake
Servings: 4 | Cooking Time: 20 Minutes
- 3 ½ tbsp sugar
- 1 ½ tbsp self-rising flour
- 3 ½ oz dark chocolate, melted
- 2 eggs

1. Grease 4 ramekins with butter. Preheat the air fryer to 375 F and beat the eggs and sugar until frothy. Stir in the butter and chocolate; gently fold in the flour. Divide the mixture between the ramekins and bake in the air fryer for 10 minutes. Let cool for 2 minutes before turning the lava cakes upside down onto serving plates.

Chocolate Pudding
Servings: 1 | Cooking Time: 50 Minutes
- 3 tbsp chia seeds
- 1 cup unsweetened milk
- 1 scoop cocoa powder
- ¼ cup fresh raspberries
- ½ tsp honey

1. Mix together all of the ingredients in a large bowl.
2. Let rest for 15 minutes but stir halfway through.
3. Stir again and refrigerate for 30 minutes. Garnish with raspberries.
4. Serve!

Strawberry Cups
Servings: 8 | Cooking Time: 10 Minutes
- 16 strawberries, halved
- 2 tablespoons coconut oil
- 2 cups chocolate chips, melted

1. In a pan that fits your air fryer, mix the strawberries with the oil and the melted chocolate chips, toss gently, put the pan in the air fryer and cook at 340 degrees F for 10 minutes. Divide into cups and serve cold.

Baked Apples
Servings: 2 | Cooking Time: 35 Minutes
- 2 tbsp butter, cold
- 3 tbsp sugar
- 3 tbsp crushed walnuts
- 2 tbsp raisins
- 1 tsp cinnamon

1. Preheat the Air fryer to 400 F.
2. In a bowl, add butter, sugar, walnuts, raisins and cinnamon; mix with fingers until you obtain a crumble. Arrange the apples in the air fryer. Stuff the apples with the filling mixture. Cook for 30 minutes.

Tortilla Fried Pies
Servings: 12 | Cooking Time: 5 Minutes
- 12 small flour tortillas (4-inch diameter)
- ½ cup fig preserves
- ¼ cup sliced almonds
- 2 tablespoons shredded, unsweetened coconut
- oil for misting or cooking spray

1. Wrap refrigerated tortillas in damp paper towels and heat in microwave 30 seconds to warm.
2. Working with one tortilla at a time, place 2 teaspoons fig preserves, 1 teaspoon sliced almonds, and ½ teaspoon coconut in the center of

each.
3. Moisten outer edges of tortilla all around.
4. Fold one side of tortilla over filling to make a half-moon shape and press down lightly on center. Using the tines of a fork, press down firmly on edges of tortilla to seal in filling.
5. Mist both sides with oil or cooking spray.
6. Place hand pies in air fryer basket close but not overlapping. It's fine to lean some against the sides and corners of the basket. You may need to cook in 2 batches.
7. Cook at 390°F for 5 minutes or until lightly browned. Serve hot.
8. Refrigerate any leftover pies in a closed container. To serve later, toss them back in the air fryer basket and cook for 2 or 3 minutes to reheat.

Air Fried Doughnuts
Servings:4 | Cooking Time: 25 Minutes
- 1 tsp baking powder
- ½ cup milk
- 2 ½ tbsp butter
- 1 egg
- 2 oz brown sugar

1. Preheat the air fryer to 350 F, and beat the butter with the sugar, until smooth. Beat in eggs, and milk. In a bowl, combine the flour with the baking powder. Gently fold the flour into the butter mixture.
2. Form donut shapes and cut off the center with cookie cutters. Arrange on a lined baking sheet and cook in the fryer for 15 minutes. Serve with whipped cream or icing.

Lemon Bars
Servings:8 | Cooking Time: 20 Minutes
- 6 tablespoons salted butter, softened
- ¾ cup granulated sugar, divided
- 1 teaspoon vanilla extract
- 1 cup plus 2 tablespoons all-purpose flour, divided
- ¼ cup lemon juice
- 2 large eggs
- 1 teaspoon lemon zest

1. Preheat the air fryer to 350°F. Spray a 6" round cake pan with cooking spray.
2. In a large bowl, cream together butter and ¼ cup sugar.
3. Stir in vanilla and 1 cup flour. Press this mixture into prepared pan and place in the air fryer basket. Cook 5 minutes until golden brown.
4. In a separate bowl, mix remaining ½ cup sugar, lemon juice, eggs, remaining 2 tablespoons flour, and lemon zest. Pour mixture over baked crust and return to the air fryer to cook for 15 minutes.
5. Let cool completely before cutting into eight sections and serving.

White Chocolate Berry Cheesecake
Servings: 4 | Cooking Time: 5-10 Minutes
- 8 oz cream cheese, softened
- 2 oz heavy cream
- ½ tsp Splenda
- 1 tsp raspberries
- 1 tbsp Da Vinci Sugar-Free syrup, white chocolate flavor

1. Whip together the ingredients to a thick consistency.
2. Divide in cups.
3. Refrigerate.
4. Serve!

Hearty Banana Pastry
Servings:2 | Cooking Time: 15 Minutes
- 3 tbsp honey
- 2 puff pastry sheets, cut into thin strips
- fresh berries to serve

1. Preheat your air fryer up to 340 F.
2. Place the banana slices into the cooking basket. Cover with the pastry strips and top with honey. Cook for 10 minutes. Serve with fresh berries.

Black & White Brownies
Servings:2 | Cooking Time: 25 Minutes
- ¼ cup chocolate chips
- 2 tbsp white sugar
- ⅓ cup flour
- 2 tbsp safflower oil
- ¼ cup cocoa powder

1. Preheat the air fryer to 320 F. In a bowl, mix egg, sugar, and oil. In another bowl, mix cocoa powder and flour. Add the flour mixture to the vanilla mixture and stir until fully incorporated.
2. Prepare a baking form for your air fryer and pour the mixture into the form; sprinkle chocolate chips on top. Add the baking form in the cooking basket and cook for 20 minutes.

S'mores Pockets
Servings: 6 | Cooking Time: 5 Minutes
- 12 sheets phyllo dough, thawed
- 1½ cups butter, melted
- ¾ cup graham cracker crumbs
- 1 (7-ounce) Giant Hershey's® milk chocolate bar
- 12 marshmallows, cut in half

1. Place one sheet of the phyllo on a large cutting board. Keep the rest of the phyllo sheets covered with a slightly damp, clean kitchen towel. Brush the phyllo sheet generously with some melted butter. Place a second phyllo sheet on top of the first and brush it with more butter. Repeat with one more phyllo sheet until you have a stack of 3 phyllo sheets with butter brushed between the layers. Cover the phyllo sheets with one quarter of the graham cracker crumbs leaving a 1-inch border on one of the short ends of the rectangle. Cut the phyllo sheets lengthwise into 3 strips.
2. Take 2 of the strips and crisscross them to form a cross with the empty borders at the top and to the left. Place 2 of the chocolate rectangles in the center of the cross. Place 4 of the marshmallow halves on top of the chocolate. Now fold the pocket together by folding the bottom phyllo strip up over the chocolate and marshmallows. Then fold the right side over, then the top strip down and finally the left side over. Brush all the edges generously with melted butter to seal shut. Repeat with the next three sheets of phyllo, until all the sheets have been used. You will be able to make 2 pockets with every second batch because you will have an extra graham cracker crumb strip from the previous set of sheets.
3. Preheat the air fryer to 350°F.
4. Transfer 3 pockets at a time to the air fryer basket. Air-fry at 350°F for 4 to 5 minutes, until the phyllo dough is light brown in color. Flip the pockets over halfway through the cooking process. Repeat with the remaining 3 pockets.
5. Serve warm.

Banana Oatmeal Cookies
Servings: 6 | Cooking Time: 20 Minutes
- 2 cups quick oats
- ¼ cup milk
- 4 ripe bananas, mashed
- ¼ cup coconut, shredded

1. Pre-heat the Air Fryer to 350°F.
2. Combine all of the ingredients in a bowl.
3. Scoop equal amounts of the cookie dough onto a baking sheet and put it in the Air Fryer basket.
4. Bake the cookies for 15 minutes.

Berry Pudding
Servings: 6 | Cooking Time: 15 Minutes
- 2 cups coconut cream
- 1/3 cup blackberries
- 1/3 cup blueberries
- 3 tablespoons swerve
- Zest of 1 lime, grated

1. In a blender, combine all the ingredients and pulse well. Divide this into 6 small ramekins, put them in your air fryer and cook at 340 degrees F for 15 minutes. Serve cold.

Basic Butter Cookies
Servings:8 | Cooking Time:10 Minutes
- 4-ounce unsalted butter
- 1 cup all-purpose flour
- ¼ teaspoon baking powder
- 1¼-ounce icing sugar

1. Preheat the Air fryer to 340 o F and grease a baking sheet lightly.
2. Mix butter, icing sugar, flour and baking powder in a large bowl.
3. Mix well until a dough is formed and transfer into the piping bag fitted with a fluted nozzle.
4. Pipe the dough onto a baking sheet and arrange the baking sheet in the Air fryer.
5. Cook for about 10 minutes until golden brown and serve with tea.

Chocolate Mayonnaise Cake
Servings:6 | Cooking Time: 25 Minutes
- 1 cup all-purpose flour
- ½ cup granulated sugar
- 1 teaspoon baking powder
- ¼ cup cocoa powder
- 1 cup mayonnaise
- 1 teaspoon vanilla extract
- ½ cup whole milk

1. Preheat the air fryer to 300°F. Spray a 6" round cake pan with cooking spray.
2. In a large bowl, combine flour, sugar, baking powder, and cocoa powder.
3. Stir in mayonnaise, vanilla, and milk. Batter will be thick, but pourable.
4. Pour batter into prepared cake pan. Place in the air fryer basket and cook 25 minutes until a toothpick inserted into the center comes out clean. Serve warm.

Delicious Spiced Apples
Servings: 6 | Cooking Time: 10 Minutes
- 4 small apples, sliced
- 1 tsp apple pie spice
- 1/2 cup erythritol
- 2 tbsp coconut oil, melted

1. Add apple slices in a mixing bowl and sprinkle sweetener, apple pie spice, and coconut oil over apple and toss to coat.
2. Transfer apple slices in air fryer dish. Place dish in air fryer basket and cook at 350 F for 10 minutes.
3. Serve and enjoy.

Fiesta Pastries
Servings:8 | Cooking Time:20 Minutes
- ½ of apple, peeled, cored and chopped
- 1 teaspoon fresh orange zest, grated finely
- 7.05-ounce prepared frozen puff pastry, cut into 16 squares
- ½ tablespoon white sugar
- ½ teaspoon ground cinnamon

1. Preheat the Air fryer to 390 o F and grease an Air fryer basket.
2. Mix all ingredients in a bowl except puff pastry.
3. Arrange about 1 teaspoon of this mixture in the center of each square.
4. Fold each square into a triangle and slightly press the edges with a fork.
5. Arrange the pastries in the Air fryer basket and cook for about 10 minutes.
6. Dish out and serve immediately.

Glazed Chocolate Doughnut Holes
Servings:5 | Cooking Time: 22 Minutes
- 1 cup self-rising flour
- 1 ¼ cups plain full-fat Greek yogurt
- ¼ cup cocoa powder
- ½ cup granulated sugar
- 1 cup confectioners' sugar
- ¼ cup heavy cream
- 1 teaspoon vanilla extract

1. Preheat the air fryer to 350°F. Spray the inside of the air fryer basket with cooking spray.
2. In a large bowl, combine flour, yogurt, cocoa powder, and granulated sugar. Knead by hand 5 minutes until a large, sticky ball of dough is formed.
3. Roll mixture into balls, about 2 tablespoons each, to make twenty doughnut holes. Place doughnut holes in the air fryer basket and cook 12 minutes, working in batches as necessary.
4. While doughnut holes are cooking, in a medium bowl, mix confectioners' sugar, cream, and vanilla. Allow doughnut holes 5 minutes to cool before rolling each in the glaze. Chill in the refrigerator 5 minutes to allow glaze to set before serving.

Vanilla Bean Dream
Servings: 1 | Cooking Time: 35 Minutes
- ½ cup extra virgin coconut oil, softened
- ½ cup coconut butter, softened
- Juice of 1 lemon
- Seeds from ½ a vanilla bean

1. Whisk the ingredients in an easy-to-pour cup.
2. Pour into a lined cupcake or loaf pan.
3. Refrigerate for 20 minutes. Top with lemon zest.
4. Serve!

English Lemon Tarts
Servings: 4 | Cooking Time: 30 Minutes
- ½ cup butter
- ½ lb. flour
- 2 tbsp. sugar
- 1 large lemon, juiced and zested
- 2 tbsp. lemon curd
- Pinch of nutmeg

1. In a large bowl, combine the butter, flour and sugar until a crumbly consistency is achieved.
2. Add in the lemon zest and juice, followed by a pinch of nutmeg. Continue to combine. If necessary, add a couple tablespoons of water to soften the dough.
3. Sprinkle the insides of a few small pastry tins with flour. Pour equal portions of the dough into each one and add sugar or lemon zest on top.
4. Pre-heat the Air Fryer to 360°F.
5. Place the lemon tarts inside the fryer and allow to cook for 15 minutes.

Lemon Berry Jam
Servings: 12 | Cooking Time: 20 Minutes
- ¼ cup swerve
- 8 ounces strawberries, sliced
- 1 tablespoon lemon juice
- ¼ cup water

1. In a pan that fits the air fryer, combine all the ingredients, put the pan in the machine and cook at 380 degrees F for 20 minutes. Divide the mix into cups, cool down and serve.

Chocolate Macaroons
Servings: 16 | Cooking Time: 8 Minutes
- 2 Large egg white(s), at room temperature
- ⅛ teaspoon Table salt
- ½ cup Granulated white sugar
- 1½ cups Unsweetened shredded coconut
- 3 tablespoons Unsweetened cocoa powder

1. Preheat the air fryer to 375°F.
2. Using an electric mixer at high speed, beat the egg white(s) and salt in a medium or large bowl until stiff peaks can be formed when the turned-off beaters are dipped into the mixture.
3. Still working with the mixer at high speed, beat in the sugar in a slow stream until the meringue is shiny and thick.
4. Scrape down and remove the beaters. Fold in the coconut and cocoa with a rubber spatula until well combined, working carefully to deflate the meringue as little as possible.
5. Scoop up 2 tablespoons of the mixture. Wet your clean hands and roll that little bit of coconut bliss into a ball. Set it aside and continue making more balls: 7 more for a small batch, 15 more for a medium batch, or 23 more for a large one.
6. Line the bottom of the machine's basket or the basket attachment with parchment paper. Set the balls on the parchment with as much air space between them as possible. Air-fry undisturbed for 8 minutes, or until dry, set, and lightly browned.
7. Use a nonstick-safe spatula to transfer the macaroons to a wire rack. Cool for at least 10 minutes before serving. Or cool to room temperature, about 30 minutes, then store in a sealed container at room temperature for up to 3 days.

Pumpkin Pie
Servings: 6 | Cooking Time: 2 Hours 25 Minutes
- 1 can pumpkin pie mix
- 1 large egg
- 1 teaspoon vanilla extract
- ⅓ cup sweetened condensed milk
- 1 premade graham cracker piecrust

1. Preheat the air fryer to 325°F.
2. In a large bowl, whisk together pumpkin pie mix, egg, vanilla, and sweetened condensed milk until well combined. Pour mixture into piecrust.
3. Place in the air fryer basket and cook 25 minutes until pie is brown, firm, and a toothpick inserted into the center comes out clean.
4. Chill in the refrigerator until set, at least 2 hours, before serving.

RECIPE INDEX

A

Adobo Oregano Beef 38
Ahi Tuna Steaks 76
Air Fried Calamari 81
Air Fried Catfish 80
Air Fried Cod With Basil Vinaigrette 74
Air Fried Dilly Trout 79
Air Fried Doughnuts 133
Air Fried Grilled Steak 40
Air Fried Halloumi With Veggies 103
Air Fried Snickerdoodle Poppers 128
Air Fry Bacon 26
Air Fryer Bacon 7
Air Fryer Plantains 33
Air Fryer Sausage 8
Air-fried Brussels Sprouts 88
Air-fried Cauliflower 113
Air-fried Cheesy Broccoli With Garlic 99
Air-fried Crispy Chicken Thighs 89
Air-fried Sweet Potato 112
Air-frier Baked Potatoes 93
All-in-one Breakfast Toast 11
Almond Asparagus 112
Almond Coconut Chicken Tenders 54
Almond Crust Chicken 19
Almond Flour Battered Chicken Cordon Bleu 58
Almond Flour Coated Crispy Shrimps 74
Almond Flour Coco-milk Battered Chicken 66
Almond Meringue Cookies 129
Almond Oatmeal 15
Almond Pesto Salmon 10
Almond Shortbread Cookies 129
Amazing Blooming Onion 20
Amazing Salmon Fillets 84
Another Easy Teriyaki Bbq Recipe 42
Apple Crumble 120
Apple Dumplings 130
Apple Fritters 120
Apple Jam 121
Apple Pastry Pouch 125
Apple Pie Crumble 125
Apple Rollups 28
Apple Tart 119
Artichokes And Parsley Frittata 14
Artichokes Sauté 87

Asian Green Beans 87
Asparagus 33
Authentic Alaskan Crab Legs 83
Avocado And Cabbage Salad 14
Avocado And Green Beans 97
Avocado Eggs 13
Avocado Pudding 131
Avocado Rolls 117
Avocado Sticks 23

B

Baby Back Ribs 51
Bacon & Asparagus Spears 97
Bacon & Egg Muffins 18
Bacon & Eggs 17
Bacon & Hot Dogs Omelet 8
Bacon And Hot Dogs Omelet 11
Bacon Avocado Wraps 22
Bacon Blue Cheese Burger 39
Bacon Chicken Mix 60
Bacon Cookies 120
Bacon Cups 14
Bacon Jalapeno Poppers 24
Bacon With Shallot And Greens 53
Bacon Wrapped Filet Mignon 40
Bacon Wrapped Filets Mignons 37
Bacon Wrapped Pork Tenderloin 48
Bacon Wrapped Scallops 83
Bacon Wrapped Shrimp 82
Bacon-wrapped Avocados 87
Bacon-wrapped Cajun Scallops 77
Bacon-wrapped Sausage Skewers 28
Bacon-wrapped Turkey With Cheese 68
Baked Apple 128
Baked Apples 132
Baked Chicken Nachos 59
Baked Eggs 12
Baked Green Beans 104
Baked Plum Cream 126
Baked Polenta With Chili-cheese 112
Baked Potato For One 98
Baked Tortillas 30
Balsamic And Garlic Cabbage Mix 99
Balsamic Garlic Kale 98
Balsamic Greens Sauté 97

Balsamic Pork Chops 41
Balsamic Radishes 91
Banana Chia Seed Pudding 16
Banana Fritters 126
Banana Oatmeal Cookies 134
Banana-nut Muffins 19
Bananas & Ice Cream 132
Barbecue Little Smokies 33
Barbecue-style Beef Cube Steak 42
Basic Butter Cookies 134
Basic Pepper French Fries 101
Basil And Paprika Cod 73
Basil Pork 51
Basil Scallops 74
Basil Squash 101
Basil Tomatoes 115
Bbq Chicken Wings 61
Bbq Lil Smokies 22
Beef & Mushrooms 52
Beef And Tomato Sauce 52
Beef Bulgogi 42
Beef Short Ribs 52
Beef With Tomato Sauce And Fennel 38
Beer Battered Cod Filet 72
Beer-battered Cod 77
Beet Fries 90
Beet Wedges Dish 91
Bell Peppers Cups 104
Berry Layer Cake 127
Berry Pudding 134
Better Fish Sticks 70
Betty's Baked Chicken 68
Bjorn's Beef Steak 49
Black & White Brownies 133
Black Bean And Rice Burrito Filling 116
Black's Bangin' Casserole 5
Blackberry Cream 129
Blackened Chicken Tenders 65
Blistered Shishito Peppers 25
Blueberry Cookies 120
Bourbon-bbq Sauce Marinated Beef Bbq 50
Bow Tie Pasta Chips 25
Bread Cups Omelette 9
Breadcrumb Turkey Breasts 64
Breadcrumbs Stuffed Mushrooms 103
Breaded Chicken Tenderloins 58
Breaded Flounder 84
Breaded Hake 78

Breaded Scallops 79
Breakfast Chimichangas 5
Breakfast Muffins 19
Breakfast Sandwich 11
Breakfast Sausage Casserole 10
Breakfast Tea 7
Broccoli Casserole 15
Broccoli Cheese Nuggets 27
Broccoli Florets 27
Broccoli Salad 106
Broccoli With Olives 108
Broiled Tilapia 84
Brownies Muffins 128
Brussels Sprout Crisps 35
Brussels Sprouts 23
Brussels Sprouts With Balsamic Oil 103
Buffalo Bites 22
Buffalo Chicken Strips 54
Butter Beef 51
Butter Broccoli 91
Butter Custard 121
Butter Flounder Fillets 79
Butter Lobster 76
Butter Paprika Swordfish 85
Butter Plums 125
Buttered Duck Breasts 56
Buttered Eggs In Hole 6
Buttered Scallops 73
Buttered Spinach-egg Omelet 63
Buttered Striploin Steak 48
Buttermilk-fried Chicken Thighs 63
Buttery Cod 78
Buttery Pork Chops 37
Buttery Scallops 15

C
Cabbage Chips 29
Cabbage Slaw 101
Cajun Flounder Fillets 80
Cajun Kale Chips 25
Cajun Lemon Salmon 82
Cajun Salmon With Lemon 73
Cajun Seasoned Chicken 69
Cajun Seasoned Salmon Filet 79
Cajun Spiced Veggie-shrimp Bake 84
Cajun Sweet-sour Grilled Pork 41
Calamari With Olives 100
Caprese Chicken With Balsamic Sauce 68

Caprese Eggplant Stacks 104
Caramel Baked Apples 124
Caramelized Brussels Sprout 108
Caramelized Pork 44
Caribbean-style Fried Plantains 106
Carrot Crisps 87
Cashew Bowls 21
Cauliflower Poppers 29
Cauliflower Rice Pudding 120
Cauliflower Steaks Gratin 109
Cauliflower Tots 100
Celery Leaves 'n Garlic-oil Grilled Turbot 71
Champagne-vinegar Marinated Skirt Steak 48
Char-grilled Drunken Halibut 71
Char-grilled Skirt Steak With Fresh Herbs 47
Charred Onions 'n Steak Cube Bbq 37
Cheddar Asparagus 93
Cheddar Bacon Ranch Pinwheels 47
Cheddar Cheese Lumpia Rolls 24
Cheddar-garlic Drop Biscuits 101
Cheese And Bean Enchiladas 116
Cheese Crackers 28
Cheese Dip 30
Cheese Herb Chicken Wings 61
Cheese Sandwich 32
Cheese Stuffed Tomatoes 110
Cheese Stuffed Turkey Breasts 67
Cheese Wafers 26
Cheese Zucchini Rolls 98
Cheeseburgers 44
Cheesecake Cups 128
Cheesy Bacon Bread 24
Cheesy Bacon Fries 94
Cheesy Bbq Tater Tot 107
Cheesy Broccoli With Eggs 113
Cheesy Cauliflower Crust Pizza 107
Cheesy Cauliflower Tots 88
Cheesy Kale 115
Cheesy Omelet 18
Cheesy Onion Rings 90
Cheesy Polenta Sticks 20
Cheesy Ranch Broccoli 93
Cheesy Sandwich 14
Cheesy Sausage Sticks 7
Cheesy Sticks With Sweet Thai Sauce 92
Cheesy Texas Toast 91
Cheesy Vegetarian Lasagna 113
Cherry Pie 124

Chewy Glazed Parsnips 114
Chi Spacca's Bistecca 9
Chia Chocolate Cookies 132
Chicken & Jalapeño Pepper Quesadilla 55
Chicken & Prawn Paste 66
Chicken Bites 13
Chicken Breast With Prosciutto And Brie 58
Chicken Breasts With Sweet Chili Adobo 57
Chicken Chunks 57
Chicken Cordon Bleu 57
Chicken Enchiladas 58
Chicken Gruyere 60
Chicken Nuggets 58
Chicken Quarters With Broccoli And Rice 67
Chicken Sausage In Dijon Sauce 65
Chicken Wings With Alfredo Sauce 88
Chicken With Mushrooms 62
Chili And Paprika Chicken Wings 67
Chili Calamari Rings 32
Chili Chicken Cutlets 55
Chili Fried Okra 118
Chili Loin Medallions 50
Chili Pepper Kale Chips 20
Chili Squid Rings 78
Chili-espresso Marinated Steak 43
Chili-lime Shrimp 78
Chinese Chicken Wings 66
Chipotle Chickpea Tacos 109
Chipotle Jicama Hash 33
Chives Spinach Frittata 6
Choco-berry Fudge Sauce 131
Choco-coconut Puddin 130
Chocolate And Avocado Cream 127
Chocolate Apple Chips 131
Chocolate Bacon Bites 34
Chocolate Banana Pastries 122
Chocolate Banana Sandwiches 128
Chocolate Brownie 127
Chocolate Candies 126
Chocolate Cheesecake 130
Chocolate Chip Cookies 132
Chocolate Cookie Dough Balls 33
Chocolate Macaroons 135
Chocolate Mayonnaise Cake 134
Chocolate Molten Lava Cake 119
Chocolate Mug Cake 128
Chocolate Peanut Butter Cups 122
Chocolate Pudding 132

Chocolate Raspberry Wontons 123
Chocolate Soufflé 123
Chocolate-covered Maple Bacon 130
Chocolate-hazelnut Bear Claws 8
Cilantro Cod Mix 77
Cilantro Drumsticks 59
Cinnamon Apple Chips 122
Cinnamon Apple Crisps 23
Cinnamon Balsamic Duck 59
Cinnamon Flavored Grilled Pineapples 8
Cinnamon Fried Plums 121
Cinnamon Pear Chips 115
Cinnamon Sugar Tortilla Chips 102
Citrusy Branzini On The Grill 82
Clams And Sauce 86
Classic Baked Banana 104
Classic Deviled Eggs 36
Classic French Fries 96
Cocktail Flanks 36
Cocoa Spread 121
Coconut Berries Bowls 11
Coconut Berry Pudding 130
Coconut Calamari 75
Coconut Cheese Sticks 32
Coconut Chives Sprouts 98
Coconut Cupcakes 125
Coconut Jerk Shrimp 70
Coconut Mushrooms Mix 89
Coconut Pillow 127
Coconut Pork And Green Beans 43
Coconut Sunflower Cookies 123
Cod And Sauce 71
Collard Greens And Bacon Recipe 99
Collard Greens Sauté 88
Cool Mini Zucchini's 105
Coriander Cod And Green Beans 83
Corn Cakes 105
Corn Dog Bites 24
Corn Muffins 90
Corn-crusted Chicken Tenders 97
Corned Beef 38
Cottage And Mayonnaise Stuffed Peppers 107
Cottage Cheese And Potatoes 103
Country Style Chard 21
Crab Legs 85
Crab Rangoon 72
Cranberry Cream Surprise 127
Cranberry Jam 131

Craving Cinnamon Toast 18
Cream Cheese Muffins 122
Cream Cheese Pork 49
Cream Cheese Pound Cake 131
Cream Cups 122
Creamy Cheddar Eggs 27
Creamy Chicken Breasts With Crumbled Bacon 62
Creamy Duck Strips 63
Creamy Onion Chicken 56
Creamy Parsley Soufflé 17
Creamy Pudding 123
Creamy Salmon 85
Crème Brulee 123
Crispy 'n Healthy Avocado Fingers 113
Crispy Air-fried Tofu 113
Crispy Bacon 16
Crispy Bacon With Butterbean Dip 95
Crispy Brussels Sprout Chips 111
Crispy Cajun Fried Chicken 60
Crispy Calamari 77
Crispy Cauliflower Bites 97
Crispy Chicken Nuggets 95
Crispy Chicken Thighs 65
Crispy Fish Fingers 78
Crispy Five-spice Pork Belly 40
Crispy Fruit Tacos 127
Crispy Ham Rolls 114
Crispy Kale Chips 25
Crispy Marinated Tofu 106
Crispy Pierogi With Kielbasa And Onions 37
Crispy Prawn In Bacon Wraps 80
Crispy Shawarma Broccoli 115
Crispy Shrimps 30
Crispy Smelts 83
Crispy Wings With Lemony Old Bay Spice 115
Croissant Rolls 106
Crouton-breaded Pork Chops 48
Croutons 22
Crumbed Sage Chicken Scallopini4 68
Crunchy Bacon Bites 25
Crunchy Fried Pork Loin Chops 46
Crunchy Parmesan Zucchini 116
Crust-less Meaty Pizza 32
Crust-less Quiche 9
Crusty 129
Crusty Pesto Salmon 71
Cumin Artichokes 87
Cumin Pork Steak 49

Curly's Cauliflower 28
Currant Cream Ramekins 121
Curried Cauliflower Florets 102
Curried Eggplant 109
Curried Sweet Potato Fries 30
Curried Sweet-and-spicy Scallops 73
Curry Cabbage Sauté 95

D
Dark Chocolate Cake 131
Dark Chocolate Peanut Butter S'mores 119
Delicious Apple Pie 121
Delicious Chicken Taquitos 97
Delicious Spiced Apples 134
Delicious Vanilla Custard 130
Delightful Mushrooms 107
Dill Tomato 96
Duck Fat Roasted Red Potatoes 92

E
Easy & Crispy Chicken Wings 66
Easy & Tasty Salsa Chicken 5
Easy & The Traditional Beef Roast Recipe 46
Easy Carrot Dip 28
Easy Celery Root Mix 91
Easy Corn Dog Bites 48
Easy Crispy Prawns 31
Easy Crispy Shawarma Chickpeas 104
Easy Egg Bites 11
Easy Fried Tomatoes 108
Easy Fry Portobello Mushroom 109
Easy Glazed Carrots 111
Easy Grilled Pesto Scallops 78
Easy Rib Eye Steak 50
Easy Roast Winter Vegetable Delight 103
Egg & Mushroom Scramble 13
Egg Baked Omelet 13
Egg Frittata With Smoked Trout 72
Egg Muffin Sandwich 14
Egg Muffins 5
Egg Porridge 10
Eggplant Caviar 109
Eggplant Fries 21
Eggplant Spread 5
Eggs & Tomatoes Scramble 6
Eggs Ramekins 17
Eggs Salad 12
Eggs, Mushrooms And Tomatoes Scramble 13

Elegant Carrot Cookies 91
Empanadas 38
English Lemon Tarts 135
Exquisite German Pancake 16
Extra Crispy Country-style Pork Riblets 52
Extreme Zucchini Fries 116

F
Fajita Style Chicken Breast 66
Family Farm's Chicken Wings 66
Family Favorite Potatoes 105
Fantastic Leg Of Lamb 50
Fat Burger Bombs 45
Feisty Baby Carrots 114
Feta Cheese Triangles 108
Fiesta Pastries 134
Fish Fillet Sandwich 74
Fish Fillets 74
Fish Sticks 78
Fish Sticks For Kids 72
Fish Taco Bowl 74
Fish-in-chips 77
Five Spice Duck Legs 69
Flatbread 100
Flavorful Cornish Hen 62
Flax Cheese Chips 22
Flaxseed Porridge 16
Foil Packet Lobster Tail 80
French Clams 80
French Toast Sticks 17
Friday's Fries 23
Fried Agnolotti 93
Fried Banana S'mores 129
Fried Catfish Fillets 79
Fried Chicken Halves 62
Fried Chicken Legs 56
Fried Chicken Thighs 69
Fried Goat Cheese 22
Fried Green Tomatoes 20
Fried Kale Chips 34
Fried Mashed Potato Balls 96
Fried Mozzarella Sticks 26
Fried Mushrooms 24
Fried Olives 23
Fried Pickles 30
Fried Shrimps With Sweet Chili Sauce 81
Fried Tilapia Bites 81
Fried Twinkies 122

Fruit Pastries 31
Fruity Tacos 123

G

Garden Fresh Green Beans 118
Garlic Asparagus 95
Garlic Butter Pork Chops 42
Garlic Chicken Wings 64
Garlic Dill Leg Of Lamb 46
Garlic Eggplant Chips 34
Garlic Fillets 47
Garlic Lamb Roast 51
Garlic Mushrooms 98
Garlic Pork And Ginger Sauce 47
Garlic Radishes 91
Garlic Tomatoes Recipe 92
Garlic-cheese Biscuits 7
Garlicky Chips With Herbs 98
Garlicky Lamb Chops 43
Garlicky Meatballs 61
Garlic-parmesan French Fries 92
Garlic-roasted Brussels Sprouts With Mustard 102
Garlic-rosemary Lamb Bbq 45
Ghee Lemony Endives 99
Ghee Savoy Cabbage 92
Ghee Shrimp And Green Beans 83
Glazed Chocolate Doughnut Holes 134
Glazed Ham 39
Glazed Pork Shoulder 39
Goulash 60
Gourmet Wasabi Popcorn 111
Grape Stew 125
Greek Chicken Meatballs 62
Greek Street Tacos 31
Greek Turkey Meatballs 27
Greek-style Grilled Scallops 83
Green Bean Casserole 114
Green Bean Crisps 90
Green Beans 98
Green Beans & S 25
Green Beans And Eggs 19
Green Beans And Tomatoes Recipe 101
Green Beans Bowls 15
Green Beans Salad 11
Green Olive And Mushroom Tapenade 29
Green Peas With Mint 101
Green Scramble 17
Grilled 'n Glazed Strawberries 115

Grilled Banana Boats 119
Grilled Cheese Sandwich 32
Grilled Cheese Sandwich Deluxe 31
Grilled Cheese Sandwiches 32
Grilled Chicken Pesto 69
Grilled Chicken Recipe From Jamaica 69
Grilled Chicken Wings With Curry-yogurt Sauce 67
Grilled Prosciutto Wrapped Fig 47
Grilled Sausages With Bbq Sauce 53
Grilled Scallops With Pesto 71
Grilled Tofu Sandwich 9
Ground Beef 40

H

Ham & Cheese Rolls 30
Ham And Egg Toast Cups 8
Ham Pinwheels 50
Ham Tilapia 84
Hard-boiled Eggs 18
Hash Brown 8
Hash Browns 12
Hashbrown Potatoes Lyonnaise 15
Hasselback Potatoes 110
Healthy And Easy To Make Salmon 82
Healthy Apple-licious Chips 111
Healthy Avocado Fries 105
Healthy Vegetable Kabobs 22
Hearty Apple Chips 116
Hearty Banana Pastry 133
Hearty Carrots 102
Herb Carrots 6
Herb Seasoned Turkey Breast 68
Herbed Beef Roast 38
Herbed Croutons With Brie Cheese 93
Herbed Duck Legs 55
Herbed Eggplant 117
Herbed Garlic Lobster 70
Herbed Garlic Radishes 87
Herbed Potatoes 108
Hillbilly Cheese Surprise 22
Hole In One 17
Homemade Mayonnaise 25
Homemade Potato Puffs 87
Honey & Garlic Chicken Breasts 56
Honey & Garlic Chicken Wings 60
Honey Chicken Drumsticks 57
Honey Mesquite Pork Chops 42
Honey-glazed Salmon 78

Honey-sriracha Pork Ribs 41
Horseradish-crusted Salmon Fillets 80
Hot Cheesy Dip 33
Hot Chicken Wingettes 94
Hot Coconut 'n Cocoa Buns 119
Hot Dogs 41
Hot Prawns 82

I
Indian Plantain Chips 113
Italian Chicken 15
Italian Chicken Thighs 68
Italian Mackerel 86
Italian Meatballs 43
Italian Pork 44
Italian Seasoned Easy Pasta Chips 111
Italian-style Tomato-parmesan Crisps 34

J
Jalapeno Chicken Breasts 56
Jalapeño Guacamole 35
Jalapeno Stuffed With Bacon 'n Cheeses 114
Japanese Citrus Soy Squid 79
Japanese Miso Steak 53
Jicama Fries 89
Juicy & Spicy Chicken Wings 64
Juicy Salmon And Asparagus Parcels 75
Juicy Turkey Breast Tenderloin 57
Jumbo Italian Meatballs 40

K
Keto Butter Balls 121
Kielbasa Chunks With Pineapple & Peppers 49
Kohlrabi Chips 34
Korean-style Wings 29
Kurkuri Bhindi (indian Fried Okra) 111

L
Lamb Burgers 41
Lamb Chops And Lemon Yogurt Sauce 42
Lamb Loin Chops With Lemon 49
Lamb With Paprika Cilantro Sauce 45
Layered Ravioli Bake 105
Leeks Dip 27
Lemon & Garlic Chicken 67
Lemon And Butter Artichokes 94
Lemon Bars 133
Lemon Bars Recipe 124

Lemon Berries Stew 124
Lemon Berry Jam 135
Lemon Butter Artichokes 6
Lemon Butter Scallops 81
Lemon Cookies 120
Lemon Curd 124
Lemon Dill Scallops 9
Lemon Garlic Shrimp 75
Lemon Green Beans 20
Lemon Grilled Chicken Breasts 63
Lemon Kale 91
Lemon Mousse 123
Lemon Pepper Chicken Legs 61
Lemon Shrimp And Zucchinis 73
Lemon Tempeh 89
Lemon-butter Veal Cutlets 45
Lemon-roasted Salmon Fillets 79
Lemony Green Beans 110
Lime 'n Chat Masala Rubbed Snapper 72
Lime And Mustard Marinated Chicken 64
Lime And Thyme Duck 63
Lime Cod 80
Lime, Oil 'n Leeks On Grilled Swordfish 75
Low-carb Pita Chips 96

M
Macaroni And Cheese 98
Macaroon Bites 126
Mahi-mahi "burrito" Fillets 81
Mango Shrimp Skewers 70
Maple Glazed Corn 89
Maple Glazed Salmon 82
Maple-bacon Doughnuts 8
Maple'n Soy Marinated Beef 48
Marinated Beef 44
Marinated Chicken 68
Marinated Flank Steak 46
Marinated Scallops With Butter And Beer 72
Marjoram Chicken 55
Marshmallow Pastries 127
Meatloaf 43
Mediterranean Bruschetta 95
Mediterranean Egg Sandwich 12
Medium Rare Simple Salt And Pepper Steak 10
Melted Cheese 'n Almonds On Tomato 117
Mesmerizing Honey Chicken Drumsticks 65
Midnight Nutella® Banana Sandwich 127
Milky Scrambled Eggs 16

Mini Pepper Poppers 21
Mini Tomato Quiche 14
Miso Fish 71
Miso-rubbed Salmon Fillets 81
Molten Lava Cake 132
Molten Lava Cakes 122
Monkey Bread 129
Moon Pie 121
Mouth-watering Salami Sticks 99
Mozzarella Asparagus Mix 89
Mozzarella Cups 12
Mozzarella Green Beans 88
Mozzarella Rolls 8
Mozzarella Sticks 32
Mozzarella Turkey Rolls 54
Mushroom 'n Bell Pepper Pizza 114
Mushroom Frittata 10
Mushroom Leek Frittata 9
Mushrooms Spread 16
Mushrooms, Sautéed 93
Mustard Beef Mix 45
Mustard Endives 96
Mustard Greens Mix 89
Mustard Lamb Loin Chops 38
Mustard Pork 44
Mustard'n Italian Dressing On Flank Steak 45

N
Nacho Chips Crusted Prawns 84
Naked Cheese, Chicken Stuffing 'n Green Beans 54
No Flour Lime Muffins 131
Not-so-english Muffins 18
Nutella And Banana Pastries 119
Nutritious Salmon 75
Nutty Fudge Muffins 131

O
Okra Chips 20
Okra Hash 17
Okra With Green Beans 111
Olives Eggs 13
One-tray Parmesan Wings 68
Onion And Cheese Omelet 17
Onion Dip 30
Onion Rings 34
Orange And Brown Sugar–glazed Ham 38
Orange Marmalade 129
Oregano And Coconut Scramble 14

Oregano Duck Spread 54
Oreo-coated Peanut Butter Cups 126
Outrageous Crispy Fried Salmon Skin 75

P
Pancakes 13
Paprika Asparagus 96
Paprika Beef And Spinach 39
Paprika Cauliflower Bake 9
Paprika Chicken Legs With Turnip 55
Paprika Chips 32
Paprika Duck 58
Paprika Green Beans 93
Paprika Jicama 90
Paprika Liver Spread 59
Paprika Zucchini Spread 9
Parmesan & Garlic Cauliflower 21
Parmesan Artichoke Hearts 98
Parmesan Asparagus 117
Parmesan Breakfast Casserole 7
Parmesan Chicken Tenders 59
Parmesan Crusted Pickles 99
Parmesan Green Beans Sticks 28
Parmesan Veggie Mix 97
Parmesan Walnut Salmon 77
Parmesan Zucchini Chips 27
Parsley Duck 64
Parsley Omelet 5
Parsley Savoy Cabbage Mix 92
Parsley-loaded Mushrooms 103
Peanut Butter Cookies 126
Peanut Cookies 126
Pepper Pork Chops 47
Pepper Turkey Bacon 55
Peppered Maple Bacon Knots 18
Peppers Bowls 16
Peppers Cups 7
Peppers Dip 27
Perfect Broccolini 92
Perfect Crispy Tofu 91
Perfect French Fries 95
Perfect Soft-shelled Crabs 85
Perfectly Roasted Mushrooms 117
Pesto Coated Rack Of Lamb 52
Pesto Vegetable Kebabs 113
Pesto-rubbed Veal Chops 41
Pickled Bacon Bowls 25
Pickled Fries 28

Pineapple Appetizer Ribs 103
Pineapple Cornbread 13
Pineapple Sticks 128
Poblano & Tomato Stuffed Squash 112
Pop Corn Broccoli 94
Popcorn Chicken 64
Poppin' Pop Corn Chicken 54
Pork And Garlic Sauce 46
Pork Belly Marinated In Onion-coconut Cream 43
Pork Chops 48
Pork Chops Marinate In Honey-mustard 50
Pork Chops On The Grill Simple Recipe 39
Pork Egg Rolls 29
Pork Rinds 27
Pork Tenderloin With Bacon & Veggies 37
Pork Tenderloin With Bacon And Veggies 53
Portobello Mini Pizzas 110
Potato Chips 31
Potato, Eggplant, And Zucchini Chips 102
Potato-wrapped Salmon Fillets 70
Prawns 82
Pretzel-coated Pork Tenderloin 52
Pretzel-crusted Chicken 62
Puerto Rican Tostones 31
Puffed Egg Tarts 12
Pumpkin Pie 135

Q
Quick & Easy Air Fried Salmon 79
Quick 'n Easy Brekky Eggs 'n Cream 59
Quick 'n Easy Tuna-mac Casserole 70
Quick And Crispy Chicken 55
Quick And Easy Popcorn 35
Quick And Easy Shrimp 72
Quick Chicken For Filling 55

R
Radish And Mozzarella Salad With Balsamic Vinaigrette 106
Radish Chips 26
Raspberry Pudding Surprise 128
Red Wine Infused Mushrooms 108
Restaurant-style Flounder Cutlets 76
Rib Eye Steak Seasoned With Italian Herb 51
Ribs And Chimichuri Mix 48
Rice Flour Coated Shrimp 76
Rice Flour Crusted Tofu 116
Rice Paper Bacon 10
Ricotta And Lemon Cake Recipe 132

Ricotta And Thyme Chicken 57
Ricotta Lemon Cake 128
Roasted Acorn Squash 92
Roasted Almond Delight 100
Roasted Almonds 31
Roasted Asparagus With Serrano & Parmesan 15
Roasted Belgian Endive With Pistachios And Lemon 100
Roasted Broccoli 93
Roasted Brussels Sprouts 111
Roasted Brussels Sprouts & Pine Nuts 109
Roasted Brussels Sprouts With Bacon 89
Roasted Carrots 25
Roasted Cauliflower 103
Roasted Chicken 58
Roasted Chicken With Potatoes 64
Roasted Coconut Carrots 97
Roasted Golden Mini Potatoes 18
Roasted Lamb 46
Roasted Mushrooms 93
Roasted Mushrooms In Herb-garlic Oil 112
Roasted Peanuts 34
Roasted Peppers 20
Roasted Potatoes & Cheese 89
Roasted Pumpkin Seeds & Cinnamon 125
Roasted Ribeye Steak With Rum 49
Roasted Spicy Hot Dogs 21
Roasted Vegetable Grilled Cheese 115
Rosemary Garlic Prawns 85
Rosemary Lamb Steak 53
Rosemary Olive-oil Over Shrooms N Asparagus 106
Rosemary Partridge 67
Rosemary Roasted Potatoes With Lemon 99
Rosemary-infused Butter Scallops 72
Rumaki 35
Rutabaga Fries 33

S
S'mores Pockets 133
Sage And Chicken Escallops 65
Sage Cream 121
Salmon And Blackberry Sauce 75
Salmon And Olives 85
Salmon Cakes 83
Salmon Croquettes 85
Salmon Patties 74
Salmon Topped With Creamy Avocado-cashew Sauce 76
Salted Beet Chips 105
Salted Garlic Zucchini Fries 117

Salted Porterhouse With Sage 'n Thyme Medley 37
Salted Steak Pan Fried Steak 39
Salty Lamb Chops 45
Sausage And Cheese Rolls 29
Sausage Bacon Fandango 17
Sausage Egg Muffins 19
Sausage Meatballs 50
Sausage Quiche 5
Sausage Solo 10
Sausage Stuffed Chicken 60
Sautéed Green Beans 115
Sautéed Spinach 112
Scotch Eggs 6
Scrambled Mug Eggs 15
Scrumptiously Healthy Chips 107
Seasoned Herbed Sourdough Croutons 19
Sesame Chicken Wings 69
Sesame Seeds Bok Choy(1) 108
Sesame Seeds Coated Tuna 75
Sesame Tortilla Chips 30
Sesame Tuna Steak 76
Shaking Tarragon Chicken Tenders 66
Shortbread Fingers 125
Shrimp And Parsley Olives 79
Shrimp Skewers 85
Simple Banana Chips 35
Simple Cheese Sandwich 94
Simple Chicken Wings 62
Simple Egg Soufflé 7
Simple Garlic 'n Herb Meatballs 43
Simple Herbs De Provence Pork Loin Roast 49
Simple Lamb Bbq With Herbed Salt 47
Simple Lamb Chops 39
Simple New York Strip Steak 49
Simple Paprika Duck 65
Simple Salmon Patties 74
Simple Stuffed Bell Peppers 88
Simple Taro Fries 96
Simple Turkey Breast 64
Skinny Fries 23
Skinny Pumpkin Chips 94
Smoked Brisket With Dill Pickles 44
Smoked Chili Lamb Chops 46
Smoked Fried Tofu 9
Smoked Halibut And Eggs In Brioche 71
Smoked Sausage And Bacon Shashlik 46
Snow Crab Legs 84
Soppressata Pizza 6

Southern Fried Chicken 60
Spaghetti Squash 114
Spanish Chorizo With Brussels Sprouts 90
Spanish Omelet 10
Spiced Up Potato Wedges 106
Spicy Celery Sticks 104
Spicy Cheese Lings 96
Spicy Chicken 60
Spicy Chicken Wings 56
Spicy Corn Fritters 110
Spicy Dip 28
Spicy Egg And Bacon Wraps 14
Spicy Mackerel 73
Spicy Potatoes 117
Spinach & Feta Crescent Triangles 104
Spinach 'n Bacon Egg Cups 66
Spinach And Feta Pinwheels 104
Spinach Dip 35
Spinach Egg Breakfast 16
Spinach Eggs And Cheese 18
Spinach Spread 12
Squash Fries 33
Sriracha Chili Chicken Wings 93
Steak Bites And Spicy Dipping Sauce 40
Steak Fingers 40
Steak Fries 87
Steak Kebabs 50
Steak Total 48
Strawberry Cups 132
Strawberry Frozen Dessert 120
Strawberry Oatmeal 15
Strawberry Pastry 6
Strawberry Pork Ribs 42
Strawberry Rhubarb Parfait 6
Strawberry Toast 7
Strawberry Turkey 59
Stuffed Chicken 57
Stuffed Mushrooms With Bacon & Cheese 106
Sugar Pork Rinds 123
Super Cabbage Canapes 100
Super Simple Steaks 51
Super-crispy Asparagus Fries 101
Super-simple Scallops 76
Surprisingly Tasty Chicken 56
Swedish Chocolate Mug Cake 121
Sweet & Sour Glazed Salmon 73
Sweet And Sour Brussel Sprouts 111
Sweet And Sour Glazed Cod 83

Sweet And Spicy Barbecue Tofu 102
Sweet And Spicy Breakfast Sausage 12
Sweet And Spicy Carrot Sticks 24
Sweet And Spicy Parsnips 107
Sweet Apple Fries 21
Sweet Butternut Squash 95
Sweet Chicken Breasts 65
Sweet Pork Belly 44
Sweet Potato Chips 32
Sweet Potato French Fries 112
Sweet Potato Pie Rolls 124
Sweet Potato Tots 20
Sweet Potato-cinnamon Toast 16
Sweet-mustardy Thighs 61
Swiss Cheese And Eggplant Crisps 105
Swordfish With Capers And Tomatoes 80

T

Taco Okra 96
Tacos 112
Taj Tofu 11
Tandoori Cauliflower 97
Tangy Asparagus And Broccoli 118
Tangy Chicken With Parsley And Lime 67
Tarragon & Garlic Roasted Chicken 58
Tasty Herb Tomatoes 90
Tender Butternut Squash Fry 108
Tender Eggplant Fries 99
Teriyaki Chicken Kebabs 61
Teriyaki Chicken Legs 65
Teriyaki Salmon 76
Texas Bbq Chicken Thighs 54
The Best Party Mix Ever 26
Thyme Butter Turkey Breast 56
Thyme Scallops 84
Thyme Turkey Nuggets 69
Tilapia Fish Fillets 82
Tilapia Teriyaki 71
Toasted Ravioli 114
Tofu 28
Tomato Candy 94
Tomato Chicken Mix 67
Tomato Salsa Topped Grilled Flank Steak 45
Tomatoes & Herbs 26
Tonkatsu 53
Top Loin Beef Strips With Blue Cheese 52
Tortilla Chips 35

Tortilla Fried Pies 132
Traditional Jacket Potatoes 102
Tuna And Arugula Salad 7
Turkey Bacon Dates 34
Turkey Scotch Eggs 62
Turkey Wings 63
Turkey-hummus Wraps 69
Turmeric Cauliflower Rice 90
Turmeric Crispy Chickpeas 107
Turmeric Kale Mix 99
Twice-baked Broccoli-cheddar Potatoes 109

V

Vanilla Bean Dream 135
Vanilla Toast 17
Veal Rolls 51
Vegetable Nuggets 116
Veggie Stuffed Beef Rolls 47
Vinegar Chicken 59

W

Warm And Salty Edamame 26
Wasabi-coated Pork Loin Chops 44
White Chocolate Berry Cheesecake 133
White Chocolate Chip Cookies 124
Whole Chicken 63

Y

Yeast Rolls 94
Yellow Squash And Zucchinis Dish 88
Yummy Banana Cookies 130
Yummy Ham Rolls 11
Yummy Shredded Chicken 63

Z

Za'atar Garbanzo Beans 31
Za'atar Lamb Loin Chops 38
Zesty Mahi Mahi 72
Zesty Ranch Chicken Drumsticks 57
Zesty Salmon Jerky 100
Zucchini And Tomato Salsa 24
Zucchini Garlic-sour Cream Bake 110
Zucchini Gratin 105
Zucchini Squash Mix 14
Zucchini Topped With Coconut Cream 'n Bacon 110
Zucchinis And Arugula Mix 88

Made in the USA
Monee, IL
25 June 2025